KRAUS' RECREATION AND LEISURE IN MODERN SOCIETY

Eighth Edition

Daniel D. McLean, PhD
Department of Recreation and Sports Management
University of Nevada, Las Vegas

Amy R. Hurd, PhD
School of Kinesiology and Recreation
Illinois State University

Nancy Brattain Rogers, PhD
Department of Recreation and Sport Management
Indiana State University

JONES AND BARTLETT PUBLISHERS
Sudbury, Massachusetts
BOSTON   TORONTO   LONDON   SINGAPORE

World Headquarters

Jones and Bartlett Publishers
40 Tall Pine Drive
Sudbury, MA 01776
978-443-5000
info@jbpub.com
www.jbpub.com

Jones and Bartlett Publishers
Canada
6339 Ormindale Road
Mississauga, ON L5V 1J2
CANADA

Jones and Bartlett Publishers
International
Barb House, Barb Mews
London W6 7PA
UK

Jones and Bartlett's books and products are available through most bookstores and online booksellers. To contact Jones and Bartlett Publishers directly, call 800-832-0034, fax 978-443-8000, or visit our website, www.jbpub.com.

Substantial discounts on bulk quantities of Jones and Bartlett's publications are available to corporations, professional associations, and other qualified organizations. For details and specific discount information, contact the special sales department at Jones and Bartlett via the above contact information or send an email to specialsales@jbpub.com.

Production Credits

Chief Executive Officer: Clayton Jones
Chief Operating Officer: Don W. Jones, Jr.
President, Higher Education and Professional Publishing: Robert W. Holland, Jr.
V.P., Design and Production: Anne Spencer
V.P., Manufacturing and Inventory Control: Therese Connell
V.P., Sales and Marketing: William J. Kane
Acquisitions Editor: Jacqueline Geraci
Associate Editor: Amy L. Flagg
Associate Production Editor: Jennifer M. Ryan
Marketing Manager: Wendy Thayer
Senior Photo Researcher and Photographer: Kimberly Potvin
Photo Research Assistant: Lee Michelsen
Cover Design: Kristin E. Ohlin
Cover Images: (Top) © Simon Krzic/Shutterstock, Inc. (Bottom) © Marlene DeGrood/Shutterstock, Inc.
Composition: Appingo
Printing and Binding: Malloy, Inc.
Cover Printing: LeHigh Press

Library of Congress Cataloging-in-Publication Data

McLean, Daniel D.
  Kraus' recreation and leisure in modern society / Daniel McLean, Amy Hurd, Nancy Rogers.–8th ed.
     p. cm.
  ISBN-13: 978-0-7637-4959-0 (alk. paper)
  1. Recreation–North America. 2. Recreation–North America–History. 3. Leisure–Social aspects–North America. 4. Play–North America–Psychological aspects. 5. Recreation–Vocational guidance–North America. I. Hurd, Amy R. II. Rogers, Nancy Brattain. III. Title. IV. Title: Recreation and leisure in modern society.
  GV51.K7 2007
  790'.097--dc22

6048

Printed in the United States of America
11 10 09 08   10 9 8 7 6 5 4 3 2

KRAUS'
RECREATION AND LEISURE IN MODERN SOCIETY

CONTENTS

4   Recreation and Leisure in the Modern Era   93

5   Personal Leisure Perspectives: Motivations and Age Group Factors   117

9   Specialized Leisure-Service Areas   237

10   Travel and Tourism   273

11   Sport as Leisure   293

12   Career Opportunities and Professionalism 317

PREFACE

Recreation and leisure touch the lives of all people in one way or another, whether through participation in sports and games, attending a theater production, visiting an art museum, traveling to another country, or simply enjoying your local park. A world without recreation and leisure is unfathomable—no parks, open space, swimming, lounging on beaches, or seeing other parts of the world just for fun. We often take these things for granted. The purpose of this text is for students to gain an understanding and appreciation of the value of the leisure-service industry from many perspectives. This text examines the profession from where it has been and where it is going. It is viewed from the standpoints of age, race, gender, and ethnicity, as well as societal and personal benefits. Furthermore, recreation and leisure is a viable career that employs hundreds of thousands of people in North America. A career overview includes the latest information in sport, tourism, nonprofits, therapeutic recreation, and more.

Recreation and Leisure in Modern Society is the eighth edition of a text that has been used by hundreds of college and university departments of recreation, parks, and leisure studies throughout the United States. It is designed for use in courses dealing with the history and philosophy of recreation and leisure on the world scene and, more specifically, with the role of organized leisure services today in American communities.

The book has been revised to reflect recent societal changes and the challenges that face leisure-service managers in the twenty-first century. It provides an in-depth analysis of the basic concepts of recreation and leisure, the motivations and values of participants, and trends in the overall field of organized community services.

Throughout the text, several important themes and emerging issues are emphasized, including:

- The changing nature of the political, economic, and social environment has forced park and recreation agencies to reevaluate traditional approaches to delivering public parks and recreation. Many communities are utilizing the human services approach by serving all segments of the populations. Many of these same communities and others, are also building super-sized recreation centers with membership fees and programs catering to upscale populations.

- Recreation and leisure increasingly are tied to the maturing fields of tourism and sport. Understanding these relationships is important for the success of leisure-service managers.

- Wellness will continue to be a major issue in the field, but obesity is the most immediate issue facing public parks and recreation agencies. Major efforts are being made to provide health and wellness opportunities, control obesity, and preserve cardiovascular health through parks and recreation.

- Tourism is the world's largest economy. Many communities are presenting themselves as a tourist destination in order to increase resources available to community members through jobs, attractions, and revenue generation.

- The baby boomers are beginning to retire and have a major impact on the parks and recreation profession. They have more discretionary income than ever before and are willing to spend it on experiences through travel and tourism, participation in programs, health and fitness, and adventure recreation.
- Sport is increasing its influence and importance in the local, national, and international arena. Youth sport are taking on the forms and actions of professional sport, frequently to the detriment of the participants. The Fan Cost Index depicts the actual cost of attending a professional sporting event. Sport and tourism have become major community partners emphasizing economic community development.
- There is a loss of an environmental ethic in the United States. Open space is shrinking due to community development of subdivisions, business, and more. Americans are using more than their share of natural resources: they comprise only 5% of the world's population, but use 25% of all natural resources.
- Globalization has impacted leisure through the ability to share models, lessons learned, adaptation to local settings, and the greater awareness a global perspective brings to the profession.
- Children are playing outdoors less despite the positive effects of being exposed to the natural environment.
- Socioeconomic status impacts leisure through available opportunities, activity choices, and ways in which leisure is experienced. Often urban communities provide expanding services at increasing consumer costs while inner-city urban areas continue to struggle to provide basic leisure services to residents.

The eighth edition represents the first major update of the twenty-first century. Society is changing so rapidly it is a challenge to capture the diversity and depth of change. The latest research, trends, and issues in the field are included in this new edition.

No discourse of change is complete without an intensified treatment of the impact of technology in our lives. There is an enhanced focus on social capital. As we find more competition for our time, the pace of American life in contemporary times and the impact on our definition of leisure is reviewed. The Hull House and its women have been revisited and expanded. The dramatic changes and historical accounts of leisure and recreation in the 1990s and early twenty-first century are strengthened.

Recreation therapy, as well as recreation's role in health and wellness, has taken on a great importance in the text and in daily life. As the Boomers move through the early stages of retirement, or what is called the "new retirement," the impact on generations, meanings of leisure, wealth, and the future are addressed.

The nature of work in the leisure profession has changed and it is acknowledged and shared. Leisure originally focused on public agencies. This is no longer the case. Leisure involves nonprofits, sport, and tourism agencies. This discussion has been expanded throughout the book, and sport and tourism are now separate chapters.

There are new real-world examples and updated research throughout. This text concludes with a discussion of the state of the profession and jobs in the field.

This text is meant to make readers think about the field and how it impacts their lives on a daily basis. Its aim is to make the reader appreciate the recreational opportunities that are available in North America. Lastly, it is meant to educate each reader on what it means to be a parks and recreation professional.

ACKNOWLEDGMENTS

There is little that is more valuable to the completion of this book than the stories, examples, brochures, reports, pictures, and information provided by the numerous public, private, nonprofit, commercial, and other organizations that have given material to us. Although it is difficult to thank everyone who has supported this edition, we truly appreciate the support of Indiana State University and Illinois State University, and our families who understand the sacrifices needed to complete this project. In addition thank you to: the Discovery Museum of McLean County, the YMCA of Greater Des Moines (IA), the National Recreation and Park Association, the National Institute for Child Centered Coaching, Carmel Clay Parks and Recreation Department, and the American Alliance for Health, Physical Education, Recreation and Dance for providing examples of their services.

In addition to these sources, the authors wish to acknowledge the important contributions made by a number of leading recreation and leisure-studies educators whose writings—both in textbooks and in scholarly articles—influenced their thinking. While it is not possible to name all of these individuals, they include the following: Lawrence Allen, Maria Allison, John Crompton, Dan Dustin, Geoffrey Godbey, Tom Goodall, Karla Henderson, Debra Jordan, John Kelly, Leo McAvoy, James Murphy, Ruth Russell, Wayne Stormann, and Charles Sylvester.

The authors would like to thank the reviewers of the eighth edition, whose comments and suggestions have truly made this a better text: David A. Brown, PhD, Scottsdale Community College; Dr. Robert E. Cipriano, Southern Connecticut State University; Dr. Tom Coates, East Tennessee State University; Julie Ernst, PhD, University of Minnesota Duluth; Diane B. Gaede, PhD, University of Northern Colorado; Barbara A. Hawkins, ReD, Indiana University; Barbi T. Honeycutt, PhD, North Carolina State University; Karen Paisley, PhD, University of Utah; and Jan H. van Harssel, EdD, Niagara University.

This book could not have been published without the efforts of the staff at Jones and Bartlett Publishers: Jacqueline Ann Geraci, Acquisitions Editor; Amy L. Flagg, Associate Editor; Julie Bolduc, Senior Production Editor; Jennifer Ryan, Associate Production Editor; and Wendy Thayer, Marketing Manager.

The authors particularly are indebted to the late Dr. Richard Kraus, who has left a tremendous gap in the parks and recreation field. To carry on his work is both important and critical. His efforts for more than 40 years as a writer, practitioner, and educator helped to shape this profession. This textbook has become a standard, and as future editions are prepared we hope to stay close to the roots that Dr. Kraus nurtured, while remaining current with the changes in the profession.

CHAPTER 1

RECREATION AND LEISURE
The Current Scene

• • •

A phone call is how the excitement all started. We made the decision to attend the NASCAR race in Las Vegas for the sixth year in a row. What is it that keeps drawing us back to this fun-packed weekend? Maybe it is the thrill of being involved in such an awesome event that truly puts the pedal to the metal. Preparing to get to a NASCAR race is just as exciting as being at the race. We go to dinner with the friends who are going with us at least once a month prior to the weekend of the race. The discussions we have about what we are going to do and how we are going to get there keeps the excitement alive. As the weekend gets closer and closer, our anticipation grows. The weekend before the race, we go to dinner one more time and finalize all of the weekend's plans. When we get to the race weekend, our anticipation is overwhelming. The behind-the-scenes action at the race is incredible. There is a carnival atmosphere behind the scenes that fans get to experience only when attending a race. You walk through the souvenir area and see all sorts of crazy items. In addition, there are over 20 NASCAR sponsors promoting their products from oil, to power tools, to home improvement stores. You walk through this carnival-like atmosphere and get caught up in the excitement because there are so many promotions and free goodies to take home. If you are lucky enough to get into the pits, this brings a whole different level of understanding and emotions. Going through the pits gets you close to the action of the race. It's amazing to see these pit crews make a simple adjustment on the race car simply to get it to go 1/10 of a second faster. You get caught up in their excitement and determination to win the race. In this sport, the drivers are incredible people; they truly believe that the fans are important to their success. When you walk through the pits and see your favorite driver, your emotions run high and you are on a natural high.

When you attend a NASCAR race and you have never been to one before, you get the real sense of the camaraderie among the fans. People from all walks of life are there, and have come together to watch this great sport. Your driver may not win the race, but the competition among the fans during the race keeps your level of adrenaline high. (One year we sat by a Jeff Gordon fan at a race. This fan was hilarious to watch as he showed so much emotion in his body language as Gordon was doing well—and then crashed.) It's fun to watch people interact as they talk about their favorite drivers. A local race track does not have the level of excitement as a NASCAR race does. It's exciting to meet people from all over the world. We are all there for one reason: to see a great race and experience the fun.

◆ ◆ ◆

INTRODUCTION

Recreation and leisure have multiple meanings based on individual perceptions. Recreation, from an individual perspective, involves, as an example, watching television, attending an opera, base jumping, mowing the lawn, taking your children to the zoo, playing checkers, downloading music, writing a book, an evening on the town, or whatever one chooses to make it. Theorists even struggle to agree on what to call these types of experiences. Is it recreation, leisure, free time, available time, creativity, selfishness, or hedonism? One's own perceptions are so important in the defining of leisure and recreation that researchers continue to argue its meaning to society, individuals, and culture. However, as this book will show, recreation, parks, and leisure services have become an important part of government operations and a vital program element of nonprofit, commercial, private-membership, therapeutic, and other types of agencies. Today, recreation constitutes a major force in our national and local economies and is responsible for millions of jobs in such varied fields as government, travel and tourism, popular entertainment and the arts, health and fitness programs, hobbies, and participatory and spectator sports. Beyond its value as a form of sociability, recreation also provides major personal benefits in terms of meeting physical, emotional, philosophical, and other important health-related needs of participants. In a broad sense, the leisure life of a nation reflects its fundamental values and character. The very games and sports, entertainment media, and group affiliations that people enjoy in their leisure help to shape the character and well-being of families, communities, and society at large.

For these reasons, it is the purpose of this text to present a comprehensive picture of the role of recreation and leisure in modern society, including (1) the field's conceptual base, (2) the varied leisure pursuits people engage in, (3) their social and psychological implications, (4) both positive and negative outcomes of play, (5) the network of community organizations that provide recreational programs and related social services, and (6) the development of recreation as a rich, diversified field of professional practice.

VARIED VIEWS OF RECREATION AND LEISURE

For some, recreation means the network of public agencies that provide such facilities as parks, playgrounds, aquatic centers, sports fields, and community centers in thousands of cities, towns, counties, and park districts today. They may view these facilities as an outlet for the young or a means of achieving family togetherness or pursuing interesting hobbies, sports, or social activities or as a place for growth and development for all ages.

Families enjoy recreation activities in community settings.

For others, recreation may be found in a senior center or golden age club, a sheltered workshop for people with mental retardation, or a treatment center for physical rehabilitation.

For others, traveling, whether it be by trailer, motorcoach, airplane, train, or cruise ship, is the preferred mode of recreation. The expansion of the travel and tourism industry has been staggering. Travel clubs have become increasingly popular, with several airlines built around short trips through extended travel. Disney has initiated a line of cruise ships that focuses on family and has extended the idea of travel and tourism yet again.

For a growing generation of young people, recreation and leisure have taken on new meanings of adventure, risk, excitement, and fulfillment as they seek to meld technology and recreation. The idea of recreation participation may not include any physical activity but focus instead on Internet games, downloading or sharing music, instant messaging, and new ventures we have yet to see or understand. The activity may be as dissimilar as sitting in front of a computer screen to being involved in extreme activities such as skateboarding on a Bob Burnquist–designed and built 360-foot skateboard ramp with a 70-foot gap that must be negotiated to safely complete the experience. It may involve participation in ESPNs X-Games. ESPN has defined extreme sports through sponsorship and promotion and includes activities such as in-line skating, BMX racing, snow sports including snowboards and skiing, surfing, streetball, and motorcycles.

Environmentalists may be chiefly concerned about the impact of outdoor forms of traditional and emerging play on our natural surroundings—the forests, mountains, rivers, and lakes that are the national heritage of all Americans.

Without question, recreation and leisure are all of these things. They represent a potentially rewarding and important form of human experience and constitute a major aspect of economic development and government responsibility today. It is important to recognize that this is not a new development. Recreation and leisure are concepts

Participants in extreme sport often take what many would call unnecessary risks.

that have fascinated humankind since the golden age of ancient Athens. Varied forms of play have been condemned and suppressed in some societies and highly valued and encouraged in others.

Today, for the first time, there is almost universal acceptance of the value of recreation and leisure. As a consequence, government at every level in the United States has accepted responsibility for providing or assisting leisure opportunities through extensive recreation and park systems, tourism support systems, and sport facilities and complexes.

Diversity in Participation

Often we tend to think of recreation primarily as participation in sports and games or in social activities and to ignore other forms of play. However, recreation includes an extremely broad range of leisure pursuits, including travel and tourism, cultural entertainment or participation in the arts, hobbies, membership in social clubs or interest groups, nature-related activities such as camping or hunting and fishing, attendance at parties or other special events, and fitness activities.

Recreation may be enjoyed along with thousands of other participants or spectators or may be an intensely solitary experience. It may be highly strenuous and physically demanding or may be primarily a cerebral activity. It may represent a lifetime of interest and involvement or may consist of a single, isolated experience.

Motivations for Recreational Participation

In addition to the varied forms that recreation may take, it also meets a wide range of individual needs and interests. Although later chapters in this text will describe play motivations and outcomes in fuller detail, they can be summarized as follows. Many participants take part in recreation as a form of relaxation and release from work pressures or other tensions. Often they may be passive spectators of entertainment provided by television, movies, or other forms of electronic amusement. However, other significant play motivations are based on the need to express creativity, vent hidden talents, or pursue excellence in varied forms of personal expression.

For some participants, active, competitive recreation may offer a channel for releasing hostility and aggression or for struggling against others or the environment in adventurous, high-risk pursuits. Others enjoy recreation that is highly social and provides the opportunity for making new friends or cooperating with others in group settings.

Other individuals take part in leisure activities that involve community service or that permit them to provide leadership in fraternal or religious organizations. Still others take part in activities that promote health and physical fitness as a primary goal. A steadily growing number of participants enjoy participation in the expanding world of computer-based entertainment and communication, including CD-ROMs, Internet games, video games, and personal digital assistants with games, iPods, the Internet, and much more. Others are deeply involved in forms of culture such as music, drama, dance, literature, and the fine arts. Exploring new environments through travel and tourism or seeking self-discovery or personality enrichment through continuing education or religious activity represent other important leisure drives.

SOCIAL FACTORS PROMOTING THE RECREATION AND PARK MOVEMENT

The social factors that helped bring about the growth of recreation and leisure programs and services in the United States stemmed from a variety of causes. Some of these involved changes in the economic structure of society or in dramatically shifting gender values and family relationships. Others were rooted in the kinds of social expectations that emerged as we moved from an essentially rural, agrarian society— where government played a limited role—to a complex industrial, urban culture where government assumed increasingly broad functions. As society moved out of the industrial age and into and through the information age, traditional forms of government support for public parks and recreation, participation patterns in recreation, and types of recreation activities have altered, contracted, and expanded. Ten of these important social trends are described briefly in the following section of this chapter and in fuller detail in later sections.

1. Increase in Discretionary Time   The growth of individual discretionary time has long been considered a major influence in the increased participation in recreation activities. Between 1900 and 1990, the growth in leisure time was steady if not spectacular. Freedom from an agrarian economy, increased holidays, paid vacations, and shorter work weeks combined to give people more opportunities for participation in recreation than at any time in history. A debate about the actual availability of free time began in the early 1980s and still continues. As Chapter 4 shows, the availability of free time is changing and may be based on the career, income, family status, or other factors. We do know the 40-hour work week is nonexistent for many. Manufacturing firms frequently mandate 20 or more hours of overtime for their employees. Corporate executives, mid-level managers, supervisors, and service employees experience a 24-7 (24 hours a day, 7 days a week) work life. The advent of the digital age has made everyone more available. The introduction of digital devices such as the Blackberry has made e-mail available anywhere, any time. Cellular telephones now are total communication devices with the availability of voice communication, video, Internet access, calendaring, text messaging, and more. Business travelers use their telephones or Blackberry devices until the flight attendants ask everyone to turn off their electronic devices. Vacations no longer provide time away from work, just time away from the office.

The availability of discretionary time is based on age, education, gender, and the presence or absence of a disability. Children and seniors have significantly more discretionary time than do individuals who are in the workforce. Children have less discretion about what they might participate in and seniors' physical, mental or economic condition may limit their ability to participate in recreation activities. Professionals and those with a college education typically work fewer hours than those in nonprofessional jobs, such as the service industry, manufacturing, construction, and the like. Many individuals with severe disabilities have limited opportunities to explore a range of recreation activities, but have long enforced hours of free time.

2. National Affluence—or Not!   A second critical factor stemmed from the dramatic growth of the gross national product (GNP) and personal income. Between 1990 and 2004, the GNP more than doubled; personal consumption expenditures almost tripled. During this same period poverty fluctuated between 12.1 and 15 percent of the total U.S. population. There is a growing debate in the country about the presence of poverty in a society that is so blatantly affluent.

Recreation expenditures as shown in Table 1.1 have continued to grow. Three areas have shown strong growth and are related to technology (computers, music, video devices), spectator experiences, and amusement parks or other commercial amusement experiences. Expenditures as a part of total personal consumption (all dollars spent for personal use) represented 6.6 percent of all expenditures in 1985 and in 2003 grew to 8.5 percent. When one recognizes that the Commerce Department's figures do not include hundreds of billions of dollars spent on travel and tourism, gambling, liquor, and less-easily measured forms of amusement or the operational expenses of thousands of public, nonprofit, and private leisure-service agencies, it is apparent that total leisure spending is substantially higher than the amounts shown in the table. The figure below shows the distribution of expenditures for personal consumption in 2003. Recreation represents the largest expenditure of the perceived disposable income and reflects a continuing growth over a 20-year period.

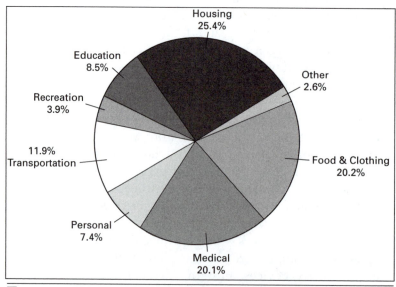

■ *Personal consumption expenditures by category, 2003.*
Source: *Statistical Abstract of the United States, 2005—Table 658,* (U.S. Department of Commerce, 2005).

In modern, postindustrial society, nonwork time has grown markedly for many individuals. Thanks to advanced mechanical equipment and automated processes in factories, agriculture, and the service fields, productive capacity increased dramatically during the second half of the nineteenth century and the first half of the twentieth. In effect, the workweek has been cut in half since the early days of the industrial revolution. In addition, more holidays and longer vacations are now taken for granted by most American employees. With improved Social Security benefits and pension plans, as well as medical advances leading to a longer life, many employees today are assured 15 or more years of full-time leisure after retiring from work. Finally, laborsaving devices in and around the home, such as dishwashers, snowblowers and lawnmowers, microwave ovens, and frozen foods, have simplified life's demands considerably. In fact, the term *throwaway society* has become more prevalent in describing the excesses of affluence.

TABLE 1.1

ANNUAL PERSONAL SPENDING ON RECREATION, 1985–2003

Type of Product or Service	1985	1990	1995	2000	2003
Total Recreation Expenditures (billions of dollars)	116.3	290.2	418.1	585.7	660.7
Pecentage of total personal consumption	6.6%	7.6%	8.4%	8.7%	8.5%
Books and maps	6.5	16.2	23.2	33.7	38.5
Magazines, newspapers, and sheet music	12	21.6	27.5	35	36.6
Nondurable toys and sport supplies	14.6	32.8	44.4	56.6	60.2
Wheel goods, sports, and photographic equipment	15.6	29.7	39.7	57.6	68
Video and audio products, computer equipment, and musical instruments	19.9	53	81.5	116.6	121.3
Video and audio goods, including musical instruments	n/a	44.1	57.2	72.8	75.2
Computers, peripherals, and software	n/a	8.9	24.3	43.8	46.1
Flowers, seeds, and potted plants	4.7	10.9	14	18	18.8
Admissions to specified spectator amusements	6.7	14.8	19.2	27.3	35.6
Motion picture theaters	2.6	5.1	5.5	8.1	9.9
Legitimate theater and opera and entertainments of nonprofit institutions	1.8	5.2	7.6	9.8	11.6
Spectator sports	2.3	4.5	6.1	9.3	14.1
Clubs and fraternal organizations, except insurance	3.1	13.5	17.4	19	22.1
Commercial participant amusements	9.1	25.2	48.8	75.8	89.2
Parimutuel net receipts	2.3	3.5	3.7	5	5.3
Other (includes lottery receipts, pets, cable TV, film processing, sports camps, video rentals, etc.)	19.4	65.4	93.4	133.9	160.9

Source: *Statistical Abstract of the United States, 2005—Table 1223* (revised 5 Aug 2004) (U.S. Department of Commerce, 2005).
See this source for a fuller explanation of product and service categories.
All numbers, except for the second row (in percent), are in billions of dollars. Hence, 116.3 represents $116,300,000,000.

Growing Gap Between Rich and Poor   At the same time that millions of newly rich families are enjoying what one economist has described as "luxury fever," there is strong evidence that the middle and lower socioeconomic classes have been left behind. A 2003 report by the Center on Budget and Policy Priorities found that between 2000 and 2002 the number of poor people rose to 34.6 million (12.7 percent of the U.S. population) and that those who were poor became poorer. The number of people who had incomes below the poverty line was greater in 2002 than at any time in history.[1]

As a result, economists have concluded that the United States is the most economically stratified of nations. While a growing class of millionaires is able to enjoy a host of expensive forms of recreation, those in the nation's urban ghettos and rural slums lack even minimal resources for needed recreation; a contrast that has been described as "recreation apartheid."

3. Commodification of Leisure   This contrast is heightened by what has been termed the "commodification" of leisure. Increasingly, varied forms of play today are developed in complex, expensive forms by profit-seeking businesses. More and more, giant conglomerates such as Time Warner, Disney, and Viacom have taken over control of huge corporations that run music, television, and movie businesses. These conglomerates also own sports stadiums and professional teams, cruise ships, theme parks, and other leisure operations.

Many elaborate new facilities offering varied forms of recreation are being developed as part of this trend toward commodification. In cities throughout the United States, huge public fitness centers that include aquatic areas, aerobics and dance rooms, and facilities for family play and a host of other activities are being built—often with charges for membership that cost several hundred dollars a year. Glenview, Illinois, operates a 100,000-square-foot community recreation center. The Plainfield, Indiana, Parks and Recreation Department constructed a $25 million indoor community center with fitness area, family aquatic center (indoor and outdoor), meeting rooms, and much more. Many other recreation centers or programs operated by public recreation and park agencies today require the payment of substantial fees that exclude the poor.

Lippke shared concerns about the commercialization of leisure upon individuals and society.[2] Citing the concern of commercialization, he suggests individuals "are subtly and not so subtly encouraged to indulge themselves in a consumption binge that, temporarily at least, distracts them from the cares and concerns of everyday life." The problem lies not with the distraction, but with the use of such leisure-time activities to replace what leisure theorists have called personal development, creativity, and flow. Lippke suggests that the commercialization of leisure promotes a lack of self-development, an increase in the inability of persons to direct their own lives as they become dependent on external stimulators. Third, the effects on social life focus on shallow relationships such as are promoted on today's reality-based television shows such as *American Idol, Fear Factor,* and *Survivor.* The Harris Interactive Poll reports that teens particularly find reality television a common ground for discussions with other teens. In 2006, 70 percent of surveyed teens watched *Fear Factor,* 67 percent watched *American Idol,* and other reality shows fared well.[3] Commercialization of recreation has created a competition for everyone to have the same things, or what one author called, "sneer group pressure." Look at the cell phone marketplace as an example. The ever-increasing "all-in-one" cell phone has captured the market as youth in particular desire the newest and coolest. Finally, there is a confusion about values and what is important. Advertisers and sellers of commercialization create expectations among potential buyers about believing life should be "filled with glamorous, exciting, or dramatic moments."[4]

4. *Population Trends*   In October 2006, the U.S. population passed the 300-million mark, making the United States the third most populous nation in the world behind China and India. The steady growth in the population and diversity has increasing impacts on recreation demand and participation.

Another marked influence on leisure programs has been the dramatic diversification, in racial and ethnic terms, that has taken place in the United States. A result of growing waves of immigrants from Asia, Latin America, and some third-world regions, often with markedly higher birth rates, the nation's identity as a primarily white society based heavily on northern European and English traditions is rapidly shifting. Hispanics are now the largest minority in the United States, surpassing African Americans in the 2000 census. The two largest growth minorities in terms of percentage of growth between 1990 and 2000 were Hispanics and Asians.

The aging of Americans has significant implications for recreation participation and delivery. By 2011, the first baby-boomers will be ready for retirement and by 2025, there will be twice as many people over 65 as there will be teenagers. By one estimate, the United States will need 31,000 geriatricians, compared to the 1,000 present in 2004.[5] This population represents the most financially independent aging group in history. The 55-plus age group controls more than 75 percent of the country's wealth. This group utilizes their financial resources to remain involved; to engage in travel, sport, and active leisure; and to continue their involvement in family and society. The

■ *Children playing in the urban core frequently have less opportunity for varied recreation experiences.*

new aging population cannot be considered "seniors." Programs of previous generations of seniors will not work with the new generation. They are already more active, have a more mobile lifestyle, are healthier, have a longer life expectancy, and use technology as a compensation for particular deficiencies, and will do so even more in the future. They are as diverse as any group in society and are changing the way recreation is considered for an aging population.

As later chapters will show, the emphasis in popular culture, sports, and other leisure-related areas reflects these population changes, with African Americans, Hispanics, and, to a lesser degree, Asian Americans playing a far more visible role.

Both in public recreation and park agencies and in major youth-serving organizations such as the Boy Scouts, Girl Scouts, Boys and Girls Clubs, and YMCA and YWCA, recreation programming and staffing practices today reflect a strong multicultural emphasis.

5. *Where People Live: Urban, Suburb, Exurb*   History has recorded the decline of rural populations, the growth of cities and industrialization, the growth of suburbs and exurbs, the decline of the inner city, and the simultaneous revitalization of cities and urban areas. In the 1950s, people began to commute into the city. In the 2000s, commuting has become even more of a way of life, but urban residents are as likely to commute to the suburbs to work as suburbanites are to commute to cities' business centers. Beyond the suburbs are the exurbs, a difficult to define, but easy to describe area. They exist beyond the suburbs in traditionally rural areas, that are now dotted with individual homes on acreage, subdivisions, and may include cities of 50,000 or more people. They are adjacent to large metropolitan areas and their distinctive feature is the residents' choice of place over people where the primary commonality is the need to commute to work. The exurbs are growing population areas as individuals are more willing to increase travel time for a perceived improved quality of life.

Recreation and park development has been seen as a key factor in promoting the revival of many larger cities, as the wealthy and young professionals have moved into newly rehabilitated or developed residential areas (the process has become known as gentrification). Rundown waterfront or factory areas have been transformed into attractive sites for shopping, sightseeing, cultural activities, and entertainment. Recreation has been stressed as critical to making cities more livable, attracting tourists, and retaining middle-class and wealthy residents. In numerous other communities, public recreation and park departments have constructed new water-play parks, tennis complexes, creative arts centers, marinas, and other recreational facilities. At the same time, there has been a pronounced shift of millions of residents from the older cities of northern and midwestern states to such sunbelt states as Florida, Arizona, and southern California. Millions of older men and women have retired to communities in these states, and many others have moved to them to find jobs in their flourishing economies.

Within each of these population shifts, recreation and leisure play an important role. Many individuals and families place high value on the recreational and cultural opportunities that are available in communities that they are considering moving to, and large corporations regard this factor as an important element with respect to staff recruitment and retention.

Parks and recreation areas and programs are increasingly important to urban, suburban, and rural residents. Increasing attention is being given to urban recreation and parks as reported by the Urban Institute and the Wallace Foundation.[6]

The "new view" of urban parks calls attention to the broader contributions they can make to the vitality of communities and their residents. These contributions include

- helping youth choose rewarding paths to adulthood by providing programs and opportunities to build physical, intellectual, emotional, and social strength;
- helping new entrants to the workforce find productive jobs by offering decent, entry-level employment opportunities in the community;
- helping community residents improve their health by providing a place to enjoy fresh air and exercise; and
- helping citizens join together to make their communities better, by encouraging them to participate in park planning and management.

6. *Influence of Technology*   Over the past several decades, sophisticated technology has played a key role in providing new forms of play for the American population. Outdoor recreation, for example, makes use of increasingly complex and expensive devices in such activities as skydiving, hang gliding, scuba diving, boating, hunting, fishing, rollerblading, skiing, and snowboarding. Computer dating provides a new form of social contact for single adults, and video games offer interactive competition or exposure to new varieties of play settings and virtual realities.

In 1995, 15 percent of U.S. adults were online. In April 2006, it was over 70 percent and growing at a slow, but steady rate.[7] The Internet may reflect the most dynamic change in American society in 50 years. The percentage of adults on the Internet has grown dramatically over an 11-year period (Figure 1.2) and is reflective of the influences of technology on daily life. It is the television of the late twentieth and early twenty-first century. Teens outpace adults as Internet adopters and users. In 2005, 87 percent of 12- to 17-year-olds used the Internet. Eighty-four percent own a computer, cell phone, or personal digital assistant.[8] The iPod has had a tremendous influence in teens. By 2005, 20 percent of the under-30 population had MP3 players and 11 percent of the over-18

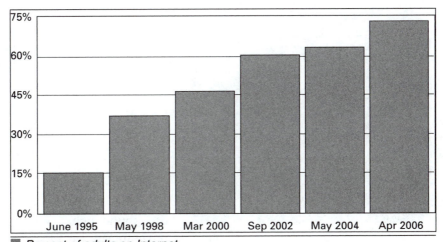

■ *Percent of adults on Internet.*
Source: Pew Internet & American Life Project. *www.pewinternet.org.*

population had MP3 players. Americans are changing the way they work, play, communicate, and think. The most popular television program in 2006 would not make the top 10 in 1975. It is not because television is less popular in 2006, but because of the availability of choice. In 1975, there were four networks, including public television. Today, there are over 200 networks. Technology mixed with affluence has allowed people to have greater choice than at any time in history.

The use of computers and technology, the growth of the Internet, and the availability of instant voice and data communications have become an integral part of travel and tourism, with airlines, cruise ships, resorts, and major parks maintaining Web pages that provide information and expand reservations and vacation choices.

Within every aspect of professional recreation, park, and leisure-service management, computer software has become indispensable in program planning, scheduling, public relations, fiscal and personnel management, and maintaining agency information systems. Home-based recreation has become increasingly dependent on varied forms of electronic entertainment, with television, interactive video games, CD-ROMs, cassette players, and similar devices. Some have speculated that reliance on such gadgetry has become an obsession for many individuals, with retreat into a virtual reality, "cyberworld" environment taking the place of face-to-face social contact with other humans.

■ *Digital music devices, or MP3s, are becoming common among pre-teens, teens, and young adults.*

The idea of the economy of abundance is an example of the influence of the Internet society. In today's technology-based society, Chris Anderson has suggested an economy based on scarcity is in decline. In his book, *The Long Tail*, he shows how the Internet and technology allow business owners to enter marketplaces that were heretofore unavailable or unprofitable. In a society where affluence continues to grow and personal expenditures are growing, consumers are no longer constrained to shopping at the local music store. Instead, they can download millions of songs from Amazon.com, iTunes, Napster, and other Internet music sites. The economy of abundance has grown out of the idea of gathering information across the Internet. It reflects not just the acquistion of goods, but also the acquisition of information. David Hornik states on his blog, "The Economy of Abundance allows business owners to defer choices to the end users. What better way to find out what consumers want than to give them everything and see what they actually buy. That is the paradigm of abundance. Why get your news programmed by CNN.com when you can have your news bubble up from the collective wisdom of end users at *Newsvine* or *Reddit*? Why get your television programmed by CBS when you can leverage the collective wisdom of the Web to find great shows like *Lonelygirl15* or *Ask a Ninja*? No longer will the success or failure of content be dictated solely by the Economy of Scarcity (e.g., Walmart). Rather, it will be dictated by the will of the consumers, as empowered by the Economy of Abundance."[9]

7. *Recreation's Contribution to Health and Fitness*   A key trend continuing in our society is public interest in exercise and physical fitness programs. Realizing that modern life is frequently inactive, sedentary, beset by tensions, and subject to a host of unhealthy habits such as overeating, smoking, and drinking, popular concern developed about improving one's health, vitality, and appearance through diet and exercise.

Participation in such activities as walking, aerobics, swimming, running and jogging, racquet sports, and similar vigorous pursuits has more than physiological effects. It also has psychological value; those who exercise regularly look and feel better. Experts have concluded that fitness is not a passing phase; the public's desire to be healthy and physically attractive is supported by continuing publicity, social values, personal vanity, and solid business sense.

Research showed that the most successful fitness programs were likely to be those that provided an ingredient of recreational interest and satisfaction. The National Recreation and Park Association (NRPA) recognizes the value of fitness and health and sponsors local involvement in "Step Up to Health: Start in the Parks," a nationwide fitness program delivered by local park and recreation agencies. Each agency is encouraged to develop fitness programs that encourage employee and community participation. Sandy, Utah, held a sprint triathlon composed of a 400-yard swim, a 9-mile bike ride, and a 5-kilometer run. Columbus, Georgia, sponsors two annual festivals, one in the spring and one in the fall, to encourage fitness in the parks. The Decatur, Illinois, Park District hosted a teen fitness summit. NRPA provides over 60 examples of programs on their website.

Parks provide an excellent location for individuals to improve personal fitness. *Healthy People 2010*, published by the U.S. Department of Health and Human Services, suggests that community parks, greenbelts, walking, bridle, and bicycle paths are key components in improving individual health. Cities can improve the utilization of these areas by locating them close to residential areas, maintaining safe, attractive, and accessible areas, and where they are perceived as part of the community. Building partnerships with other community groups, health care providers, and youth and senior groups all adds to the success of parks and health.

Certain recreational sports, such as youth soccer, volleyball, and ice hockey, have grown in popularity. Among high school boys, football remains the most popular sport, with over one million participants in over 13,000 high schools. Among girls, basketball is the most popular sport, with over 450,000 participants in over 17,000 schools. Sports participation in organized high school athletic programs is at an all-time high for girls and boys. Participation levels have grown at a steady rate for over 30 years. At the same time, a growing number of state school systems have reduced or eliminated physical education requirements, which means that organized recreation programs represent an even more important means of promoting physical fitness for children and youth.

8. *Environmental Concerns* As later chapters on the historical development of recreation and leisure will show, the establishment of public recreation programs in the United States was closely linked to the growing number of national, state, and local park systems. National park creation was an outgrowth of the preservation movement and occurred independent of the city parks movement. The recreation movement, while occurring about the same time as the public parks movement, was also independent. The first large city park was New York City's Central Park in the 1850s followed by Yellowstone National Park in 1872. Boston lays claim to the founding of the recreation movement. It has been the systematic and sometimes political additions to the public park and recreation estate at all levels of government that have positively influenced American's environment ethic.

Outdoor recreational activities such as camping, biking, backpacking, boating, hunting, fishing, skiing, and mountain climbing depend heavily on parks, forests, and water areas operated chiefly by public recreation and park agencies. However, the concern of many people regarding the health of the nation's outdoor resources stems from more than the need for outdoor recreation spaces. LaPage and Ranney point out that one of the most powerful sources of America's essential cultural fiber and spirit is the land itself:

> The roots of this new nation and its people became the forests and rivers, the deserts and mountains, and the challenges and inspirations they presented, not the ruins of ancient civilizations most other cultures look to for ancestral continuity. Thus, America developed a different attitude and identity.[10]

Natural, scenic, and historic areas are part of the recreation estate available to all Americans.

For such reasons, the environmental movement receives strong support from many recreation advocates and organizations. At the same time, it is recognized that such activities as fishing and hunting are just part of a bigger scene that requires clean—and safe—air and water and wise use of the land.

Growing national concern about the need to protect the environment was buttressed by the 1962 report of the Outdoor Recreation Resources Review Commission. During the following two decades, there was a wave of federal and state legislative action and funding support in the United States that was designed to acquire open space; to protect imperiled forests, wetlands, and scenic areas; to help endangered species flourish; and to reclaim the nation's wild rivers and trails. This movement was threatened during the early 1980s, when a new administration sought to reduce park and open space funding, eliminate conservation programs and environmental regulations, and subject the outdoors to renewed economic exploitation. In the mid-1990s, and again under the second Bush administration in the early- and mid-2000s, the effort to open protected wilderness areas to increased oil drilling, cattle grazing, lumbering, and other commercial uses gained strong political support.

Organizations such as the nonpartisan League of Conservation Voters, National Audubon Society, National Wildlife Federation, Wilderness Society, Sierra Club, and Nature Conservancy have been in the forefront of the continuing battle to protect the nation's natural resources. Numerous outdoor recreation organizations have joined with such groups, and the struggle will clearly continue as an important political issue in the years ahead.

As the world celebrated Earth Day 2000, 30 years after the first Earth Day in 1970, it was clear that North American air was cleaner and its water purer than for many past decades. There was more protected open space in national parks, wildlife refuges, and wilderness areas yet there is still cause for concern. Americans are purchasing large inefficient vehicles at a faster rate than ever before. Even as gasoline has hovered around or exceeded $3.00 per gallon, it does not seem to stem the tide of large auto purchases. While the world is struggling to come to grips with global warming and the potential impacts on the environment, there remain politicians who deny its reality. Americans, in the meantime, are growing away from their traditional environment ethic. Attendance is down at state and national parks, children are not exposed to the natural environment, and campers stay in the parks in their motorhomes and demand electricity, water, sewer, and cable and broadband hookups. Going outdoors is no longer fashionable. America's appreciation of the outdoors and the environment is clearly in jeopardy.

The emergence of managed-care systems with third-party payment by insurance companies that dominate the provision of medical care and rehabilitation has meant that socially oriented services such as therapeutic recreation often receive little support. Too often, hospitals have been forced to cut back their programs sharply or have been overwhelmed by excessive patient loads and limited budgetary support. At some levels, the development of independent intermediate care centers and out-patient rehabilitation centers has met some of these needs.

9. *The Changing Family*   Over the last 30 years, families have changed more than in the previous 200 years. The era of the stay-at-home mother, the single-income source, three or more children, family dinners, church on Sunday, and marriage as a lifetime commitment is disappearing. The nuclear family is as out of date in today's society as the transistor radio. World War II changed the United States as a society. Women experienced a freedom; soldiers coming home from the war had the GI Bill and gained

Although public interest in women's sports continues to be considerably lower than support for boys' and men's sports, there is growing interest in women's tennis, golf, gymnastics, track and field, and similar events on every level of competition. The U.S. women's soccer team won the World Cup in 1999 and fueled girls' participation in the sport. At the college level, Title IX has changed the face of women's sport. More women are participating in sport activities now than at any time in history. For many, increased participation in vigorous athletics and outdoor pastimes is symbolic of the need to overcome the past view of women as fragile, overemotional, or lacking in courage and drive. Outstanding women athletes in particular have helped to create a new image of feminine strength, determination, and self-confidence, which is closely linked to women achieving a higher degree of acceptance in formerly male-restricted fields such as the military, aviation, police and fire departments, law, and medicine.

more education than any generation before them. The 1960s and 1970s saw a change in societal mores, traditional family values, and perceptions. The notion of a traditional family changed with society. Politicians and the conservative religious movements have focused on the decay of the nuclear family, yet the facts show the nuclear family has been in decline for over 40 years. As early as 1960, the traditional nuclear family only comprised 45 percent of American households. The 2000 U.S. Census reported for the first time that less than one-quarter (23.5%) of American households consisted of a married man and woman and one or more of their children.[11]

Today's families are characterized as traditional nuclear, adoption with no marriage, wedding after the baby, single moms, two dads, two moms, and single dads. David Elkind calls these permeable families: "The permeable family is more fluid, more flexible, and more obviously vulnerable to pressures from outside itself."[12]

Today, less than 25 percent of American households are comprised of a single-wage earner; that means 75 percent of households are dependent on two or more wage earners. This places greater stresses on families, parents, and children. Many fathers are becoming more involved in the lives of their children—from changing diapers to taking time off for sick children. The roles of fathers are in transition because larger numbers of men are indicating a desire to be more nurturing with their children. Mothers always assumed the extra burden of the home, work, and child rearing and are more frequently sharing these duties. Contemporary research suggests effective strategies and positive outcomes for working mothers that strengthen families.

The challenge for recreation and family service agencies is to determine how to serve the new permeable family. Traditional after-school programs may no longer work when mothers expect to pick children up later in the day. Many agencies have gone to extended after-school programs, frequently partnering with schools to mix tutoring and leisure.

10. *Maturation of Organized Leisure-Service Field* The nature of municipal, state, and federal governments has changed dramatically in the almost 140 years of organized recreation in the United States. Today's city government is markedly different from that of our grandfathers and fathers. Government is more dependent on alternative

■ *Recreation centers are community gathering places for recreation, social activities, health-related opportunities, libraries, and other social services.*

income sources and less reliant on taxes. Public park and recreation agencies have, of necessity, become entrepreneurial. Where few fees once existed, now public agencies are dependent on fees and charges to make up as much as 90 percent of their operating budget. Parks and recreation agencies are hard pressed to serve all of those who either desire or have a need for services. Nonprofit and commercial agencies fill the gap in many instances. In today's rapidly changing demand for different types of leisure activities, public, commercial, and nonprofit organizations strive to respond, but often public and nonprofits do not have the resources, financial capital, or ability to respond. Commercial enterprises typically respond more quickly to what initially may appear as fringe activities such as paintball, skateboarding, laser tag, and the like.

Maturation does not suggest the organized leisure-services field is not changing, but rather that growth in the public and nonprofit sector is constrained by available funds, politics, public interest, and the perceived opportunity for growth. Public and nonprofit agencies have developed an infrastructure of parks, recreation centers, sports fields, cultural centers, and others that become a burden to the agencies to rapidly change. The traditional programming of public and nonprofit agencies remains in place, although there is less of it, and more of the emerging programs, but change is coming slowly. Where communities once built a 50-meter swimming pool, today they build a small to medium waterpark, except when politicians or other influential groups intervene and demand a traditional or old-fashioned approach. The leadership is changing and new, younger leaders are emerging. Values are being reassessed, commitments rethought, demands evaluated, and expectations challenged. Ten major categories of service providers make up the mature leisure-service delivery system:

1. *Public agencies*—federal, state, and local departments of recreation and parks that provide leisure services as a primary function, as well as hundreds of other agencies (such as those concerned with social service, education, special populations, and the armed forces) that offer or assist recreation programs as a secondary responsibility.

2. *Nonprofit organizations,* which are nongovernmental, nonprofit agencies, both sectarian and nonsectarian, serving the public at large or selected elements of it with multiservice programs that often include a substantial element of recreational opportunity. Such organizations include national youth programs such as the Boy Scouts and Girl Scouts and the YMCA, YWCA, and YM-YWHA (Young Men's–Young Women's Hebrew Association).

3. *Private-membership organizations,* such as golf, tennis, yacht, athletic, and country clubs, along with a wide range of service clubs and fraternal bodies, that provide recreational and social activities for their own members and in some cases assist community recreation needs as well. Under this heading are the recreation sponsors connected to residence, as in the case of swimming pools, sports or fitness complexes, or clubs attached to leisure villages, apartment or condominium units, or retirement communities.

4. *Commercial recreation enterprises,* including a great variety of privately owned, for-profit businesses, such as ski centers, bowling alleys, laser tag centers, Internet cafes, nightclubs, movie houses or theaters, health spas or fitness centers, dance schools, amusement or theme parks, and other enterprises that provide leisure services.

5. *Employee recreation programs,* which serve those who work for given companies or other employers by providing recreation, often as part of a total personnel benefits package linked to other services concerned with employee health and fitness.

6. *Armed forces recreation,* which, although it is obviously a form of government-sponsored activity, is unique in its setting and purpose. Each of the major branches of the armed forces tends to operate an extensive network of recreation facilities and programs worldwide. In times of national emergency, the demand for these services is even greater.

7. *Campus recreation,* which includes intramural athletics or sports clubs, social activities, trip-and-travel programs, performing arts groups, entertainment, lounges, film series, and numerous other forms of recreation on college and university campuses.

8. *Therapeutic recreation services,* including any type of program or service designed to meet the needs of persons with physical or mental disabilities, individuals with poor health, dependent aging persons, socially deviant persons in correctional facilities or other treatment settings, and similar special groups.

9. *Sports management,* including professional sports, collegiate sports, public parks and recreation, private sport enterprises, youth sports, sports for individuals with disabilities, and the many other forms of sport.

10. *Tourism, and hospitality management,* which involves all of the travel and tourism industry, such as airlines, cruise ships, destination resorts, conference and resort centers, amusement parks, festivals, and the like.

■ *Park employees and rangers are symbols of authority, stability, and safety.*

Need for Professional Leadership

Within each of these fields of specialization, there is a continuing need for qualified professional leadership. Too often, people assume that the task of organizing and conducting recreation programs is a relatively simple one and that "anyone" can do it without specialized training. They do so because they see that many youths and adults in society provide recreational leadership without such training. Volunteer leaders or coaches in the scouting movements, Little League, hospitals, and similar organizations often help run excellent programs.

However, the professional's assignment within the organized recreation field tends to be far more complex and difficult than that of the typical volunteer leader or coach. It must involve carefully thought-out goals and objectives and often requires sophisticated planning techniques. Reflecting on community needs, wants, and capabilities while balancing demands and resources requires a trained recreation and park professional. Today's training looks more and more like a business model and less and less like a social justice model.

To pick a dramatic example, in the large-scale commercial recreation enterprises, consider the far-flung Disney theme park operations, including Disneyland in California; Disney World, including Epcot and other attractions in Florida; and other parks in Japan and France. The immense investment that is at stake requires shrewd marketing, management, and creative design approaches. Literally hundreds of millions of dollars are involved in such ventures.

Even when the scope of the program is on a lesser scale, professional management involves such varied tasks as planning and building recreation facilities that may range from golf courses to swimming complexes, supervising leadership and maintenance

■ *Playground equipment in some park settings is in a serious state of disrepair. An example of the challenges of sufficient funding for parks and recreation.*

personnel, carrying out effective public relations campaigns, and assessing public needs and demands. Often it will require working closely with boards or commissions, advisory groups, or civic officials; it may also involve effective liaison with other levels of government.

In the case of therapeutic programs that serve persons with disabilities, the recreation specialist may need an intensive knowledge of illness and its effects, medical terminology, anatomy, kinesiology, and psychopathology. Those working with the aging must have a solid understanding of geriatrics and gerontology and should be aware of the varied roles played by other community agencies that work with older populations.

On all levels, recreation professionals should be familiar with a wide range of activities and their potential values and outcomes. They should possess the skills needed for direct leadership and supervision, understanding and controlling group dynamics, assessing patients or clients, and have the ability to carry out basic evaluation or research and write literate and meaningful reports. Underlying each of these areas of competence is a need for recreation professionals to be fully aware of the meaning of recreation and leisure in human society and of the history and traditions of this field.

Professional Identity

As employment in recreation, park, and leisure-service agencies and programs grew over the past several decades, it gained public recognition as a flourishing career field. Millions of men and women became employed in various specialized sectors of leisure service, with hundreds of thousands holding professional-level jobs as recreation leaders, supervisors, planners, managers, and resource specialists.

Emerging professionalism had a number of important aspects: the identification of recreation as a specialized field of service, making significant contributions to society and requiring unique competencies and skills; heightened visibility for the field itself and the development of means for influencing public policy in matters related to recreation and leisure; and a higher level of status for those working in the field, accompanied by the widespread acceptance of recreation as a legitimate field of social responsibility. Particularly through the efforts of national and state societies, higher standards for practice were developed and professional certification and academic and public agency accreditation were established.

Influence of Professional Specialization

As the overall leisure-service field expanded, each of its specialized disciplines also gained strength and a sense of unique identity. Specialists began to form their own professional societies in such areas as armed forces recreation, therapeutic recreation, campus recreation, and employee services. In some cases, they established their own certification processes and set up linkages to other professional disciplines functioning in areas related to their specializations.

It must be understood that recreation leadership and management does not represent a single, unified field of professional practice today. Its practitioners have varying areas of responsibility and have developed specialized missions and operational strategies suited to their unique service areas.

However, representatives of each of the 10 types of program sponsors within the overall leisure-service field have a common concern with the provision of constructive recreation programs that meet societal needs and contribute to individual physical and mental health and positive community relationships. Increasingly, they are joining in partnerships that share human, fiscal, and other agency resources to achieve such goals. It is essential that all leisure-service practitioners seeking to be regarded as professionals recognize that they must have more than nuts-and-bolts competence in conducting program activities.

In addition to such competence, recreation professionals must meet high standards of specialized training, be affiliated with appropriate professional societies, and have a rich understanding of the full range of public leisure needs and of the social challenges that face this field.

CHALLENGES FACING THE LEISURE-SERVICE FIELD

This chapter outlines a number of the critical social trends that were responsible for the growth of recreation's popularity in modern society—and that also pose a number of serious challenges to its practitioners and planners. Leisure-service professionals therefore must be able to deal creatively with the following kinds of questions.

- How can the organized recreation movement contribute to a public understanding of leisure's role in daily life and to upgrading the level of the public's choices of leisure pursuits?
- What role can public, voluntary, therapeutic, and other community-based agencies play in helping to improve family life and to reduce crime, violence, substance abuse, and other serious societal problems?
- How can recreation contribute to promoting positive intercultural understanding and relationships and to enriching the lives of persons with disabilities?
- How can the organized recreation movement play a meaningful role in a society that has increasingly become dominated by commercial interests—particularly conglomerates in the mass media of communication and entertainment—that place dollar profits at a higher priority than important human values?

- How can recreation, park, and sport organizations help build communities that create a quality of life that positively affects all community members?
- In an era marked by striking economic prosperity, how can recreation and leisure-service professionals develop programs designed to serve the less fortunate in society?
- Particularly for practitioners in park agencies that sponsor outdoor recreation services or manage extensive natural resources, what policies will serve important ecological needs in the years ahead?

PURPOSES OF THIS TEXT

This text is intended to provide comprehensive information that will be helpful to its readers in developing sound personal philosophies and gaining a broad awareness of the leisure-service field and in answering questions not with learned-by-rote solutions, but rather through intelligent analysis, critical thinking, and problem solving.

Leisure-service professionals should have in-depth understanding of the full range of recreational needs and motivations and agency programs and outcomes. This understanding should be based on a solid foundation with respect to the behavioral and social principles underlying recreation and leisure in contemporary society.

To have a sound philosophy of the goals and values of recreation and leisure in modern life, it is essential to understand recreation's history and to be aware of its social, economic, and psychological characteristics in today's society. Should recreation be regarded chiefly as an amenity or should it be supported as a form of social therapy? What are the recreation needs of such populations as girls and women, the aging, the disadvantaged, racial minorities, persons with disabilities, or others who have not been served fully in the past?

What environmental priorities should recreation and park professionals fight to support, and how can outdoor forms of play be designed to avoid destructive ecological outcomes? How can leisure-service practitioners strike a balance between entrepreneurial management approaches, which emphasize fiscal self-sufficiency, and human service programming that responds to the issues raised in this chapter?

Throughout this text, contemporary issues are discussed in detail. Through a vivid depiction of the field's conceptual base, history, and current status; through an examination of existing agencies and programs; and through a comprehensive summary of research studies and recent reports, the reader should gain a full, in-depth understanding of the role of recreation and leisure in modern society.

Although this text promotes no single philosophical position, its purpose is to clarify the values promoted by recreation and leisure in modern society. Ultimately, these values will be responsible for the field's ability to flourish as a significant form of governmental or voluntary-agency service or as a commercial enterprise.

SUMMARY

This chapter provides an introduction to the study of recreation, park, and leisure services, seen as vital ingredients in the lives of Americans and as growing areas of career opportunity and professional responsibility. It outlines several of the unique characteristics of leisure involvement, such as the diverse forms of recreational involvement and play motivations shared by persons of all ages and backgrounds. It then presents several important factors or social trends that have promoted the growth of the recreation and park movement. These trends range from the increase of discretionary time and growing affluence to expanded interest in health and fitness and concern about the natural environment. Emphasis is placed on the development of the organized recreation system over the past several decades, with a discussion of different types of leisure-service agencies that are responsible for facility development and activity program management.

The chapter ends by briefly describing the recreation, park, and leisure-service profession and emphasizing the need for specialized educational preparation for those holding responsible positions in this field. It also suggests a number of critical social challenges that will face leisure-service practitioners in the years ahead; these will be discussed more fully in the chapters that follow.

QUESTIONS FOR CLASS DISCUSSION OR ESSAY EXAMINATION

1. Identify and discuss at least three important social factors (example: increased affluence) that have contributed to the growth of recreation and leisure concerns over the past several decades.
2. What are the special meanings and values of recreation and leisure for different population groups in modern society, based on socioeconomic, age, gender, or ability/disability factors?
3. This chapter briefly summarizes the growth of professional leadership in recreation and parks management roles. Why should leisure-service professionals be expected to have an understanding of the history, psychology, and sociology of recreation and leisure?
4. What do you regard as some of the most critical challenges facing recreation leisure-service agencies and practitioners in the years that lie ahead? Justify your response.

ENDNOTES

1. Center for Budget and Policy Priorities, "Poverty Increase and Median Income Declines for the Second Consecutive Year" (29 September 2003).
2. Richard L. Lippke, "Five Concerns Regarding the Commercialization of Leisure," *Business and Society Review* (Vol. 106, No. 2, 2001): 107–126.
3. Suzanne Martin and Dana Markow (eds), "Youth and Reality TV." www.HarrisInteractive.com, 2006.
4. Lippke, *Business and Society Review*: 120.
5. R. Kennedy, "Aging in America." www.medical-library.net/sites/framer.html?/sites/_aging_in _america.html, 2004.
6. C. Walker, *The Public Value of Urban Parks* (The Urban Institute, 2004).
7. www.pewinternet.org/trends/User_Demo_4.26.06.htm.
8. A. Lenhart, M. Madden, and P. Hitlin, "Teens and Technology: Youth Are Leading the Transition to a Fully Wired and Mobile Nation" (Pew Internet and American Life Project. 27 July 2005).
9. D. Hornick, "The Softwareless Software Company." http://p6.hostingprod.com/@www.ventureblog.com/, 31 Oct 2006.

10. W. F. LaPage and S. R. Ranney, "America's Wilderness: The Heart and Soul of Culture," *Parks and Recreation* (July 1988): 24.

11. Population Resource Center. "Executive Summary: The Changing American Family." www.prcdc.org/summaries/family/family.html, June 2001.

12. M. Sherer, "On Our Changing Family Values: A Conversation with David Elkind," *Educational Leadership* (Vol. 53, No.7, 1996): 4–9.

CHAPTER 2

BASIC CONCEPTS
Philosophical Analysis of Play, Recreation, and Leisure

◆ ◆ ◆

What would life be without play? Play is fun, freedom, a way to socialize, our reward after hard work. When we play at something, we enjoy it for its own sake. It's a refuge from ordinary life where one is exempt from the usual obligations, customs, and rules. Play is our brain's favorite way of learning. . . . We evolved through play. Our culture thrives on play.[1]

◆ ◆ ◆

INTRODUCTION

Any consideration of the broad field of recreation and leisure should include a clarification of terms and concepts. The words *play*, *leisure*, and *recreation* are frequently used interchangeably, as if they meant the same thing. However, although related, they have distinctly different meanings and it is important for both students and practitioners in this field to understand their varied implications and the differences among them.

The rationale for stressing such conceptual understanding is clear. Just as a doctor must know chemistry, anatomy, kinesiology, and other underlying sciences in order to practice medicine effectively, so too the recreation and park professional must understand the meaning of leisure and its motivations and satisfactions if he or she is to provide effective recreation programs and services. Similarly, the leisure scholar should not withdraw from the real world of leisure programming and participation by focusing only on abstract or theoretical models of free-time behavior. Instead, the scholar should become familiar with the profession of recreation service and should contribute to its effective performance. Such conceptual understandings are critical to the development of a sound philosophy of recreation service and to interpreting leisure-service goals and outcomes to the public at large.

THE MEANING OF PLAY

The word *play* is derived from the Anglo-Saxon *plega,* meaning a game or sport, skirmish, fight, or battle. This is related to the Latin *plaga,* meaning a blow, stroke, or thrust. It is illustrated in the idea of striking or stroking an instrument or playing a game by striking a ball. Other languages have words derived from a common root (such as the German *spielen* and the Dutch *spelen*) whose meanings include the playing of games, sports, and musical instruments. Play is traditionally considered a child's activity, in contrast to recreation, which is usually described as an adult activity. Today, however, it is recognized that people of all ages take part in play.

Historical Perspectives

In ancient Greece, play was assigned a valuable role in the lives of children, based on the writings of Plato and Aristotle. The Athenians placed great value on developing qualities of honor, loyalty, and beauty and other elements of productive citizenship in children. For them, play was an integral element of education and was considered a means of positive character development and teaching the values of Greek society.

Later, as the Catholic Church gained dominance among the developing nations of western Europe, play came to be regarded as a social threat. The body was thought to detract from more spiritual or work-oriented values, and every effort was made to curb the pleasurable forms of play that had been popular in the Greek and Roman eras.

Gradually, however, educators and philosophers such as Froebel, Rousseau, and Schiller came to the defense of play as an important aspect of childhood education. For example, Froebel wrote of play as the highest expression of human development in childhood:

Play is the purest, most spiritual activity of man at this stage. . . . A child that plays thoroughly with self-active determination, perseveringly until physical fatigue forbids, will surely be a thorough, determined man, capable of self-sacrifice for the promotion of the welfare of himself and others.[2]

EARLY THEORIES OF PLAY

In the nineteenth and early twentieth centuries, a number of influential scholars evolved comprehensive theories of play that explained its development and its role in human society and personal development.

Surplus-Energy Theory

The English philosopher Herbert Spencer, in his mid-nineteenth–century work *Principles of Psychology,* advanced the view that play was primarily motivated by the need to burn excess energy. He was influenced by the earlier writings of Friedrich von Schiller, who suggested that when animals or birds were fully fed and had no other survival needs, they vented their exuberant energy in a variety of aimless and pleasurable forms of play. Spencer saw play among children as an imitation of adult activities; the sport of boys, such as chasing, wrestling, and taking one another prisoner, involved "predatory instincts."

Recreation Theory

An early explanation of play that was regarded as the converse of the Schiller-Spencer view was developed by Moritz Lazarus, a German philosopher, who argued that rather than serving to burn excess energy, the purpose of play was to conserve or restore it. In other words, when one is exhausted through toil, play recharges one's energy for renewed work. Lazarus distinguished between physical and mental energy, pointing out that when the brain is "tired" (provided that it is not overtired), a change of activity, particularly in the form of physical exercise, will restore one's nervous energy. To illustrate, the desk worker who plays tennis after a long day's work simultaneously discharges surplus physical energy and restores mental energy.

Instinct-Practice Theory

A more elaborate explanation of play was put forward by Karl Groos, a professor of philosophy at Basel, who wrote two major texts: one in 1896 on the play of animals and another in 1899 on the play of humans. Groos argued that play helped animals survive by enabling them to practice and perfect the skills they would need in adult life. He concluded that the more adaptable and intelligent a species was, the more it needed a period of protected infancy and childhood for essential learning to take place. Thus, among humans, there was a lengthy early period during which children engaged in varied activities to perfect skills before they really needed them.

Catharsis Theory

The catharsis theory is based on the view that play—particularly competitive, active play—serves as a safety valve for the expression of bottled-up emotions. Among the ancient Greeks, Aristotle saw drama as a means of purging oneself of hostile or aggressive emotions; by vicarious sharing in the staged experience, onlookers purified

Modern ethologists who have systematically studied the behavior of animals and birds in interaction with each other and with their environment have identified varied forms of play that appear to illustrate the instinct-practice theory. For example, much play among young animals, particularly primates, involves aggressive teasing and mock battles. Such play represents a ritualized form of combat, in which the combatants practice their fighting skills and learn to interact with each other in establishing a "pecking order."

Anthropologists who have observed preindustrial tribal societies point out that "playing house" is often a form of rehearsal for adult roles. In some African rural villages, it may involve both technical and social skills, as boys and girls build and thatch small houses and make various tools and utensils. Often the play forms are gender related: Boys typically make axes, spears, shields, slings, bows, and arrows or build miniature cattle kraals, whereas girls make pottery for cooking real or imaginary food or perhaps weave mats or baskets of plaited grass.

themselves of harmful feelings. A number of early twentieth-century writers expanded this theory. Harvey Carr, an American psychologist, wrote:

> Catharsis . . . implies the idea of purging or draining of that energy which has antisocial possibilities. . . . The value of football, boxing, and other physical contests in relieving the pugnacious tendencies of boys is readily apparent as examples. Without the numberless well-organized set forms of play possessed by society which give a harmless outlet to the mischievous and unapplied energy of the young, the task of the teacher and parent would be appalling.[3]

Coupled with the surplus-energy theory, the catharsis theory suggested a vital necessity for active play to help children and youth burn excess energy and provide a socially acceptable channel for aggressive or hostile emotions and drives.

TWENTIETH-CENTURY CONCEPTS OF PLAY

During the first three decades of the twentieth century, a number of psychologists and educators examined play, particularly as a developmental and learning experience for children.

Self-Expression Theory

Two leading physical educators, Elmer Mitchell and Bernard Mason, saw play primarily as a result of the need for self-expression. Humans were regarded as active, dynamic beings with the need to find outlets for their energies, use their abilities, and express their personalities. The specific types of activity that an individual engaged in were, according to Mitchell and Mason, influenced by such factors as physiological and anatomical structure, physical fitness level, environment, and family and social background.[4]

Play as a Social Necessity

During the late nineteenth century, leaders of the public recreation movement called for the provision of organized recreation for all children. Joseph Lee, who is widely regarded as the father of the play movement in America and who promoted the establishment of numerous playgrounds and recreation centers, was instrumental in the public acceptance of play as an important force in child development and community life. Jane Addams, founder of the Hull House Settlement in Chicago and a Nobel Peace Prize winner, advocated the need for organized play opportunities that served as an alternative to the difficult life children living in poverty faced on the streets. These values continue to be embraced by contemporary communities, as is evidenced by public and private support of parks and recreation departments, community recreation programs, after-school programs, and other play-based activities.

Typologies of Play Activity

In the twentieth century, more and more social and behavioral scientists began to examine play empirically. One such investigator, the French sociologist Roger Caillois, examined the play experience itself by classifying the games and play activities that

Joseph Lee believed that play contributed to the wholesome development of personal character because it involved lessons of discipline, sacrifice, and morality. He saw it as more than a mere pleasurable pastime, but rather as a serious element in the lives of children and—along with his contemporary pioneer, Luther Halsey Gulick—as a vital element in community life. This view extended itself to a literal application of play as a means of preparing children for the adult work world. Wayne Stormann points out that play was considered a useful form of manual training because it coordinated bodily functions, promoted health, and prepared children for the "indoor confinement," first of schools and then of factory life.[5]

were characteristic of various cultures and identifying their apparent functions and values. Caillois established four major types of play and game activity: agon, alea, mimicry, and ilinx.

Agon refers to activities that are competitive and in which the equality of the participants' chances of winning is artificially created. Winners are determined through such qualities as speed, endurance, strength, memory, skills, and ingenuity. Agonistic games may be played by individuals or teams; they presuppose sustained attention, training and discipline, perseverance, limits, and rules. Clearly, most modern games and sports, including many card and table games involving skill, are examples of agon.

Alea includes games of chance—those games or contests over whose outcome the contestant has no control; winning is the result of fate rather than the skill of the player. Games of dice, roulette, and baccarat, as well as lotteries, are examples of alea.

Mimicry is based on the acceptance of illusions or imaginary universes. Children engage in mimicry through pretend play. This category includes games in which players make believe, or make others believe, that they are other than themselves. For children, Caillois writes:

> The aim is to imitate adults. . . . This explains the success of the toy weapons and miniatures which copy the tools, engines, arms and machines used by adults. The little girl plays her mother's role as cook, laundress and ironer. The boy makes believe he is a soldier, musketeer, policeman, pirate, cowboy, Martian, etc.[6]

Ilinx consists of play activities based on the pursuit of vertigo or dizziness. Historically, ilinx was found in primitive religious dances or other rituals that induced the trancelike state necessary for worship. Today it may be seen in children's games that lead to dizziness by whirling rapidly, and in the use of swings and seesaws. Among adults, ilinx may be achieved through certain dances involving rapid turns, such amusement park rides as roller coasters, and a variety of adventure activities, including skydiving and bungee jumping.

Contrasting Styles of Play

Caillois also suggested two extremes of play behavior. The first of these, *paidia*, involves exuberance, freedom, and uncontrolled and spontaneous gaiety. The second, *ludus*, is characterized by rules and conventions and represents calculated and contrived activity. Each of the four forms of play may be conducted at either extreme of paidia or ludus or at some point on a continuum between the two.

The Play Element in Culture

Probably the most far-reaching and influential theory of play as a cultural phenomenon was advanced by the Dutch social historian Johan Huizinga in his provocative work *Homo Ludens* (*Man the Player*). Huizinga presented the thesis that play pervades all of life. He saw it as having certain characteristics: It is a voluntary activity, marked by freedom and never imposed by physical necessity or moral duty. It stands outside the realm of satisfying physiological needs and appetites. It is separate from ordinary life both in its location and its duration, being "played out" within special time periods and in such special places as the arena, the card table, the stage, and the tennis court. Play is controlled, said Huizinga, by special sets of rules, and it demands absolute order. It is also marked by uncertainty and tension. Finally, it is not concerned with good or evil, although it has its own ethical value in that its rules must be obeyed.

In Huizinga's view, play reveals itself chiefly in two kinds of activity: contests for something and representations of something. He regarded it as an important civilizing influence in human society and cited as an example the society of ancient Greece, which was permeated with play forms. He traced historically the origins of many social institutions as ritualized forms of play activity. For example, the element of play was initially dominant in the evolution of judicial processes. Law consisted of a pure contest between competing individuals or groups. It was not a matter of being right or wrong; instead, trials were conducted through the use of oracles, contests of chance that determined one's fate, trials of strength or resistance to torture, and verbal contests. Huizinga suggested that the same principle applied to many other cultural institutions:

> In myth and ritual the great instinctive forces of civilized life have their origin: law and order, commerce and profit, craft and art, poetry, wisdom, and science. All are rooted in the primeval soil of play.[7]

PSYCHOLOGICAL ANALYSIS OF PLAY

Over the past several decades, numerous authorities in the fields of psychology and psychoanalysis have examined play and its role in personality development, learning theory, mental health, and related areas.

Play in Personality Development

A respected child psychologist, Lawrence K. Frank, points out that play is important to the psychological and emotional development of children:

> Play, as we are beginning to understand, is the way the child learns what no one can teach him. It is the way he explores and orients himself to the actual world of space and time, of things, animals, structures, and people. Through play he learns to live in our symbolic world of meaning and values, of progressive striving for deferred goals, at

■ *Play can be viewed from developmental, psychological, anthropological, creative, and cultural perspectives.*

the same time exploring and experimenting and learning in his own individual way. Through play the child practices and rehearses endlessly the complicated and subtle patterns of human living and communication which he must master if he is to become a participating adult in our social life.[8]

Psychoanalytical Perspectives on Play

Sigmund Freud, the father of modern psychoanalysis, had a number of distinctive views regarding the meaning and purpose of play. Freud saw play as a medium through which children are able to gain control and competence and to resolve conflicts that occur in their lives. He felt that children are frequently overwhelmed by their life circumstances, which may be confusing, complex, and unpleasant. Through play, they are able to reexperience threatening events and thus to control and master them. In this sense, play and dreams serve a therapeutic function for children. In general, Freud felt that play represented the child's way of dealing with reality—in effect, by playing with it, making it more acceptable, and exerting mastery over it.

> Might we not say that every child at play behaves like a creative writer, in that he creates a world of his own, or, rather, rearranges the things of his world in a new way which pleases him? It would be wrong to think he does not take his play seriously; on the contrary he takes his play very seriously and he expends large amounts of emotion on it. The opposite of play is not what is serious but what is real.[9]

A number of Freud's other theories, such as the "pleasure principle" and the "death wish," have also been seen as having strong implications for the analysis of play. The Freudian view of play influenced many psychotherapists and educators in their approach to childhood education and treatment programs. Bruno Bettelheim, Erik

Erikson, and Anna Freud, Freud's daughter, all experimented with the use of play in treating disturbed children.

Play as Creative Exploration

Other contemporary theories of play emphasize its role in creative exploration and problem solving. Studies of arousal, excitement, and curiosity led to two related theories of play: the stimulus-arousal and competence-effectance theories.

Stimulus-Arousal Theory   This approach is based on the observation that both humans and animals constantly seek stimuli of various kinds, both to gain knowledge and to satisfy a need for excitement, risk, surprise, and pleasure. Often this is connected with the idea of fun, expressed as light amusement, joking, and laughter.

However, the expectation that play is always light, enjoyable, pleasant, or humorous can be misleading. Often, play activities can be frustrating, boring, unpleasant, or even physically painful—particularly when they lead to addiction (as in the case of drug, alcohol, or gambling abuse) and subsequent ill health or economic losses.

Competence-Effectance Theory   A closely related theory holds that much play is motivated by the need of the player to test the environment, solve problems, and gain a sense of mastery and accomplishment. Typically, it involves experimentation or information-seeking behavior, in which the player—whether human or animal—observes the environment, tests or manipulates it, and observes the outcome. Beyond this, the player seeks to develop competence, defined as the ability to interact effectively with the environment. Often this is achieved through repetition of the same action even when it has been mastered. The term *effectance* refers to the player's need to be able to master the environment and, even when uncertainty about it has been resolved, to produce desired effects in it.

Cziksentmihalyi's "Flow" Principle   Related to the competence-effectance theory is Mihaly Cziksentmihalyi's view of play as a process in which ideally the player's skills are pitched at the challenge level of the tasks. If the task is too simple, it may become boring and lacking in appeal. If it is too difficult, it may produce anxiety and frustration, and the player may discontinue the activity or change the approach to it so it becomes more satisfying. Beyond this idea, Cziksentmihalyi suggests that there is a unique element in true play, which he identifies as a sense of flow. This is the sensation players feel when they are totally involved with the activity. It involves a feeling of harmony and full immersion in play; at a peak level, players might tend to lose their sense of time and their surroundings and experience an altered state of being. Such flow, he argues, could be found in some work situations, but it is much more commonly experienced in play such as games or sport.[10]

Play Defined

It is difficult to arrive at a single definition of play because it takes so many forms and appears in so many contexts. However, a general definition would describe it as a form of human or animal activity or behavioral style that is self-motivated and carried on for

■ *If the slopes match the skiers ability, downhill skiing is an optimal activity in which an individual might experience flow.*

intrinsic, rather than external, purposes. It is generally pleasurable and is often marked by elements of competition, humor, creative exploration and problem solving, and mimicry or role playing. It appears most frequently in leisure activities, but may be part of work. It is typically marked by freedom and lack of structure, but may involve rules and prescribed actions, as in sport and games.

THE MEANING OF LEISURE: SIX VIEWS

What exactly is leisure? The concept of leisure as a unique, desirable component of the human experience was first articulated by ancient Greeks. In more recent centuries, scholars attempted to define leisure in terms of both its role in society and impact on the individual. For the Athenians particularly, leisure was the highest value of life, and work the lowest. Since the upper classes were not required to work, they were free to engage in intellectual, cultural, and artistic activity. Leisure represented an ideal state of freedom and the opportunity for spiritual and intellectual enlightenment. Within modern philosophies of leisure that have descended from this classical Athenian view, leisure is still seen as occurring mostly in time that is not devoted to work. However, it is considered far more than just a temporary release from work used to restore one for more work. Etymologically, the English word *leisure* seems to be derived from the Latin *licere*, meaning "to be permitted" or "to be free." From *licere* came the French *loisir*, meaning "free time," and such English words as *license* (originally meaning immunity from public obligation) and *liberty*. These words are all related; they suggest free choice and the absence of compulsion.

The early Greek word *scole* or *skole* meant "leisure." It led to the Latin *scola* and the English *school* or *scholar*—thus implying a close connection between leisure and education. The word *scole* also referred to places where scholarly discussions were held. One such place was a grove next to the temple of Apollo Lykos, which became known as the *lyceum*. From this came the French *lycée*, meaning "school"—again implying a bond between leisure and education.

The Classical View of Leisure

Aristotle regarded leisure as "a state of being in which activity is performed for its own sake." It was sharply contrasted with work or purposeful action, involving instead such pursuits as art, political debate, philosophical discussion, and learning in general. The Athenians saw work as ignoble; to them it was boring and monotonous. A common Greek word for work is *ascholia*, meaning the absence of leisure—whereas we do the opposite, defining leisure as the absence of work.

How meaningful is this classical view of leisure today? Although the Greek view of leisure as a necessary and integral piece of a holistic life has merit, this view has two flaws. First, it is linked to the idea of an aristocratic class structure based on the availability of a substantial underclass and slave labor. When Aristotle wrote in his *Treatise on Politics* that "it is of course generally understood that in a well-ordered state, the citizens should have leisure and not have to provide for their daily needs," he meant that leisure was given to a comparatively few patricians and made possible through the strenuous labor of the many.

In modern society, leisure cannot be a privilege reserved for the few; instead, it must be widely available to all. It must exist side by side with work that is respected in our society, and it should have a meaningful relationship to work. The implication is that leisure should be calm, quiet, contemplative, and unhurried, as implied by the word *leisurely*. Obviously, this concept would not apply to those uses of leisure today that are dynamic, active, and demanding or that may have a degree of extrinsic purpose about them.

Leisure as a Symbol of Social Class

The view of leisure as closely related to social class stemmed from the work of Thorstein Veblen, a leading American sociologist of the late nineteenth century. Veblen showed how, throughout history, ruling classes emerged that identified themselves sharply through the possession and use of leisure. In his major work, *The Theory of the Leisure Class*, he pointed out that in Europe during the feudal and Renaissance periods and finally during the industrial age, the possession and visible use of leisure became the hallmark of the upper class. Veblen attacked the "idle rich"; he saw leisure as a complete way of life for the privileged class, regarding them as exploiters who lived on the toil of others. He coined the phrase "conspicuous consumption" to describe their way of life throughout history. This theory is dated because of the rise of greater working class leisure, and because many members of extremely wealthy families work actively in business, politics, or other demanding professions.

To some degree, however, Veblen's analysis is still relevant. The wealthy or privileged class in modern society continues to engage in a wide variety of expensive, prestigious, and sometimes decadent leisure activities even though its members may not have an immense amount of free time. They tend to travel widely, entertain, patronize the arts, and engage in exclusive and high-status pastimes. Recent scholars have characterized contemporary leisure in Western cultures as consumerist and motivated by the pursuit of diversionary experiences that can be purchased. Ramsey expressed the following critique of consumerist leisure:

> So the nasty face of consumerist leisure expresses acquisitiveness, possessiveness, what the ancient Greeks called *plenoxia*: the desire for more than one's appropriate share. . . . The paradox around obligation-free leisure time is the drive quality, the compulsions and obsessions around purchase and use, to which many people are vulnerable due to the sheer vastness and success and ease of consumerism.[11]

Leisure as Unobligated Time

The most common approach to leisure is to regard it as unobligated or discretionary time. In a number of sociological references, this concept of leisure is clearly stated. The *Dictionary of Sociology* offers the following definition:

> Leisure is the free time after the practical necessities of life have been attended to. . . . Conceptions of leisure vary from the arithmetic one of time devoted to work, sleep, and other necessities, subtracted from 24 hours—which gives the surplus time— to the general notion of leisure as the time which one uses as he pleases.[12]

This view of leisure sees it essentially as time that is free from work or from such work-related responsibilities as travel, study, or social involvements based on work. It also

Time-Strapped Americans?

In 1992, Juliet Schor published her seminal text, *The Overworked American: The Unexpected Decline of Leisure*. Her primary thesis was that during the latter part of the twentieth century the American workweek started to increase after almost 100 years of decline; this due to the work and spend lifestyles of most Americans and increasing pressure from employers to work longer hours.[13]

In response to Dr. Schor's research, many other scholars utilized time-diary studies to better understand the nature and pace of American life. Some of the most notable research in this area by Geoffrey Godbey and John Robinson contradicted the findings of Schor. They found that paid work and housework hours actually declined from the 1960s to the 1990s. During this time period, they found a slight increase in free time and television viewing time. Godbey and Robinson concurred with other scholars that a growing number of Americans felt time pressure. This sense could be driven by a number of factors, including the increase of two-income households and growing materialism.

excludes time devoted to essential life-maintenance activities, such as sleep, eating, or personal care. Its most important characteristic is that it lacks a sense of obligation or compulsion. This approach to defining leisure is most popular among economists or sociologists who are particularly concerned with trends in the economic and industrial life of the nation. Other scholars, including feminists, have found this definition useful in the study of time constraints faced by working adults in contemporary society.

Although this definition appears to be convenient and largely a matter of arithmetic (subtracting work and other obligated tasks from the 24 hours that are available each day and coming out with a block of time that can be called leisure), it has some built-in complexities. For example, is it possible to say that any time is totally free of obligation or compulsion or that any form of leisure activity is totally without some extrinsic purpose? Is it also possible to say that all unobligated time is intrinsically rewarding and possesses the positive qualities typically associated with leisure? For example, some uses of free time that are not clearly work or paid for as work may contribute to success at work. A person may read books or articles related to work, attend evening classes that contribute to work competence, invite guests to a party because of work associations, or join a country club because of its value in establishing business contacts or promoting sales. Within community life, those nonwork occupations that have a degree of obligation about them—such as serving on a school board or as an unpaid member of a town council—may also be viewed as part of a person's civic responsibility.

The strict view of leisure as time that lacks any obligation or compulsion is suspect. If one chooses to raise dogs as a hobby or to play an instrument in an orchestra, one begins to assume a system of routines, schedules, and commitments to others. Stebbins discusses the concept of obligation as an aspect of leisure experience, pointing out that so-called "semi-leisure" may degenerate into "anti-leisure," defined by Godbey as

> activity which is undertaken compulsively, as a means to an end, for a perception of necessity, with a high degree of externally imposed constraints, with considerable anxiety, and with a minimum of personal autonomy.[14]

Leisure as Activity

A fourth common understanding of leisure is that it is activity in which people engage during their free time. For example, the International Study Group on Leisure and Social Science defines it thus:

> Leisure consists of a number of occupations in which the individual may indulge of his own free will—either to rest, to amuse himself, to add to his knowledge and improve his skills disinterestedly and to increase his voluntary participation in the life of the community after discharging his professional, family, and social duties.[15]

American sociologist Bennett Berger echoes this concept by pointing out that the sociology of leisure during the 1950s and 1960s consisted of "little more than a reporting of survey data on what selected samples of individuals do with the time in which they are not working, and the correlation of these data with conventional demographic variables." Obviously, this concept of leisure is closely linked to the idea of recreation, because it involves the way in which free time is used. Early writers on recreation stressed the importance of activity; for example, Jay B. Nash urged that the procreative act be thought of as an active, "doing" experience. Recuperation through play, he wrote, isn't wholly relegated to inertia—doing nothing—but is gained through action.

For many individuals, Nash's view of leisure would be too confining. They would view relatively passive activities, such as reading a book, going to a museum, watching a film, or even dozing in a hammock or daydreaming, to be appropriate leisure pursuits, along with forms of active play.

Feminist scholars have criticized conceptualizations of leisure as activity as irrelevant for many women whose everyday life experiences cannot be easily categorized into a work/leisure dichotomy. Furthermore, definitions of leisure as activity do not accommodate individual perceptions about particular activities. Some individuals may view preparing a meal as a pleasurable activity of self-expression, whereas others view the activity as a monotonous, domestic obligation. In response to this criticism, contemporary scholars who study leisure as activity are primarily concerned with the outcomes of a particular activity rather than the activity itself. Therapeutic recreation scholar David Austin offers this definition of leisure:[16]

> Intrinsic motivation is also a central defining property of leisure. It is the intrinsically motivated, self-determined nature of participation, coupled with the match between abilities and challenges, which defines leisure and makes it so involving. Leisure allows people self-determined opportunities to stretch themselves by successfully applying their abilities in order to meet challenges. Such experiences are growth producing, leaving participants with feelings of accomplishment, confidence, and pleasure (Austin & Crawford, 1996).

Leisure as a State of Being Marked by Freedom

The fifth concept of leisure places the emphasis on the perceived freedom of the activity and on the role of leisure involvement in helping the individual achieve personal fulfillment and self-enrichment. Neulinger writes:

> To leisure means to be engaged in an activity performed for its own sake, to do something which gives one pleasure and satisfaction, which involves one to the very core of one's being. To leisure means to be oneself, to express one's talents, one's capacities, one's potentials.[17]

This concept of leisure implies a lifestyle that is holistic, in the sense that one's view of life is not sharply fragmented into a number of spheres such as family activities, religion, work, and free time. Instead, all such involvements are seen as part of a whole in which the individual explores his or her capabilities, develops enriching experiences with others, and seeks "self-actualization" in the sense of being creative, involved, expressive, and fully alive. The idea of leisure as a state of being places great emphasis on the need for perceived freedom. Recognizing the fact that some constraints always exist, Godbey defines leisure in the following way:

> Leisure is living in relative freedom from the external compulsive forces of one's culture and physical environment so as to be able to act from internal compulsion in ways which are personally pleasing and intuitively worthwhile.[18]

Such contemporary leisure theorists stress the need for the true leisure experience to yield a sense of total freedom and absence from compulsion of any kind. Realistically, however, there are many situations in which individuals are pressured to participate or in which the activity's structure diminishes his or her sense of freedom and intrinsic motivation.

Leisure as Spiritual Expression

A sixth way of conceptualizing leisure today sees it in terms of its contribution to spiritual expression or religious values. Newly founded faith-based social welfare organizations in the late nineteenth century were a driving force behind the growth of public and philanthropic leisure services during that time. During the early decades of the twentieth century, play and recreation were often referred to as uplifting or holy kinds of human experiences. In a systematic study of the professional literature of this period, Charles Sylvester found numerous references to God, Christ, divine ends, or other terms that suggested a clear linkage between leisure and religion.[19]

Philosopher and scholar Hayden Ramsay suggested that contemporary leisure often is self-indulgent and egotistic, rather than reflective. As a result, life is more stressful and happiness is less likely. Ramsay writes of his ideal leisure:

. . . why should physical exercise, games, reading, dancing, and butterfly-spotting not assist reflection on life, ourselves, our relationships, God, truth, justice, meaning, and so on? Leisure activities involve removing ourselves from the pursuit or external purposes and simply enjoying locating ourselves within freely chosen activities. The freedom of mind this brings is playful, and the relaxation of spirit it offers suitable for the deeper thinking we find it difficult to engage in at other, busier times—difficult today even in study and religion.[20]

■ *Volunteering is an excellent leisure activity that promotes the public good and builds social capital.*

Leisure and Social Capital

Social capital is a concept related to the success people experience in various settings due to their connections with other people. As early as the nineteenth century, authors described the individual and communal benefits of the propensity of Americans to associate with one another.

> Americans of all ages, all conditions, all minds constantly unite. Not only do they have commercial and industrial associations in which all take part, but they also have a thousand other kinds: religious, moral, grave, futile, very general and very particular, immense and small; Americans use associations to give fetes, to found seminaries, to build inns, to raise churches, to distribute books, to send missionaries to the antipodes in this manner they create hospitals, prisons, schools. Finally if it is a question of bringing to light a truth or developing a sentiment with the support of a great example, the associate. Everywhere that, at the head of a new undertaking, you see the government of France and a great lord in England, count on it that you will perceive an association in the United States. [21]

In 2000, Harvard University Professor, Robert Putnam, brought the concept of social capital to the attention of the private and public sectors through his book, *Bowling Alone*. According to Putnam, people in the United States have become less connected to each other. Over the past 30 years, Americans' participation in clubs and associations has decreased, neighbors have become less likely to know each other, and time spent socializing with friends and families has declined. We are even less likely to participate in bowling leagues—even through more of us bowl than ever before. The impact of this decline in social capital includes increased distrust in government, decreased participation in voting, decreased public safety, and a decline in child welfare.[22]

In the twenty-first century, civic leaders have expressed the need for communities to increase social capital. One of the primary means of achieving this increase is through communitarian leisure that reinforces social connectedness and promotes collective endeavor. This view of leisure requires a philosophical shift away from viewing leisure as an exercise of personal freedom with principle outcomes related to individual interests.

Leisure Defined

Recognizing that each of the six concepts of leisure just presented stems from a different perspective, a general definition that embraces several of the key points follows.

Leisure is that portion of an individual's time that is not directly devoted to work or work-connected responsibilities or to other obligated forms of maintenance or self-care. Leisure implies freedom and choice and is customarily used in a variety of ways, including to meet one's personal needs for reflection, self-enrichment, relaxation, pleasure, and affiliation. Although it usually involves some form of participation in a voluntarily chosen activity, it may also be regarded as a holistic state of being or even a spiritual experience.

THE MEANING OF RECREATION

In a sense, recreation represents a fusion between play and leisure and is therefore presented as the third of the important concepts that provide the framework for this overall field of study. The term itself stems from the Latin word *recreatio*, meaning that which refreshes or restores. Historically, recreation was often regarded as a period of light and restful activity, voluntarily chosen, that permits one to regain energy after heavy work and to return to work renewed.

This point of view lacks acceptability today for two reasons. First, as most work in modern society becomes less physically demanding, many people are becoming more fully engaged, both physically and mentally, in their recreation than in their work. Thus, the notion that recreation should be light and relaxing is far too limiting. Second, the definition of recreation as primarily intended to restore one for work does not cover the case of persons who have no work including the growing retiree population, but who certainly need recreation to make their lives meaningful.

In contrast to work, which is often thought of as tedious, unpleasant, and obligatory, recreation has traditionally been thought of as light, pleasant, and revitalizing. However, this contrast too should be reconsidered. A modern, holistic view of work and recreation would be that both have the potential for being pleasant, rewarding, and creative and that both may represent serious forms of personal involvement and deep commitment.

CONTEMPORARY DEFINITIONS OF RECREATION

Most modern definitions of recreation fit into one of three categories: (1) Recreation has been seen as an activity carried on under certain conditions or with certain motivations; (2) recreation has been viewed as a process or state of being—something that happens within the person while engaging in certain kinds of activity, with a given set of expectations; and (3) recreation has been perceived as a social institution, a body of knowledge, or a professional field.

Typically, definitions of recreation found in the professional literature have included the following elements:

1. Recreation is widely regarded as activity (including physical, mental, social, or emotional involvement), as contrasted with sheer idleness or complete rest.
2. Recreation may include an extremely wide range of activities, such as sport, games, crafts, performing arts, fine arts, music, dramatics, travel, hobbies, and social activities. These activities may be engaged in by individuals or by groups and may involve single or episodic participation or sustained and frequent involvement throughout one's lifetime.
3. The choice of activity or involvement is voluntary, free of compulsion or obligation.
4. Recreation is prompted by internal motivation and the desire to achieve personal satisfaction, rather than by extrinsic goals or rewards.
5. Recreation is dependent on a state of mind or attitude; it is not so much what one does as the reason for doing it, and the way the individual feels about the activity, that makes it recreation.

6. Although the primary motivation for taking part in recreation is usually pleasure seeking, it may also be meeting intellectual, physical, or social needs. In some cases, rather than providing "fun" of a light or trivial nature, recreation may involve a serious degree of commitment and self-discipline and may yield frustration or even pain.

Within this framework, many kinds of leisure experiences may be viewed as recreation. They may range from the most physically challenging pursuits to those with much milder demands. Watching television, listening to a symphony orchestra, reading a book, or playing chess are all forms of recreation.

Voluntary Participation

Although it is generally accepted that recreation participation should be voluntary and carried out without any degree of pressure or compulsion, often this is not the case. We tend to be influenced by others, as in the case of the child whose parents urge him to join a Little League team, or the gymnast or figure skater who is encouraged in the thought that he or she might become a professional performer. Although ideally recreation is thought of as being free of compulsion or obligation, once one has entered into an activity—such as joining a company bowling league or playing with a chamber music group—one accepts a set of obligations to the other members of the team or group. Thus, recreation cannot be entirely free and spontaneous and, in fact, assumes some of the characteristics of work in the sense of having schedules, commitments, and responsibilities.

Motives for Participation

Definitions of recreation generally have stressed that it should be conducted for personal enjoyment or pleasure—ideally of an immediate nature. However, many worthwhile activities take time to master before they yield the fullest degree of satisfaction. Some complex activities may cause frustration and even mental anguish—as in the case of the golf addict who is desperately unhappy because of poor putting or driving. In such cases it is not so much that the participant receives immediate pleasure as that he or she is absorbed and challenged by the activity; pleasure will probably grow as the individual's skill improves.

What of the view that recreation must be carried on for its own sake and without extrinsic goals or purposes? It is essential to recognize that human beings are usually goal-oriented, purposeful creatures. James Murphy and his coauthors have identified different recreational behaviors that suggest the kinds of motives people may have when they engage in activity:

- *Socializing behaviors:* Activities such as dancing, dating, going to parties, or visiting friends, in which people relate to one another in informal and unstereotyped ways.
- *Associative behaviors:* Activities in which people group together because of common interests, such as car clubs; stamp-, coin-, or gem-collecting groups; or similar hobbies.

- *Competitive behaviors:* Activities including all of the popular sport and games, but also competition in the performing arts or in outdoor activities in which individuals compete against the environment or even against their own limitations.
- *Risk-taking behaviors:* An increasingly popular form of participation in which the stakes are often physical injury or possible death.
- *Exploratory behaviors:* In a sense, all recreation involves some degree of exploration; in this context, it refers to such activities as travel and sightseeing, hiking, scuba diving, spelunking, and other pursuits that open up new environments to the participant.[23]

To these may be added the following motives: *vicarious experience,* such as watching movies or sports events; *sensory stimulation,* which might include drug use, sexual involvement, or listening to rock music; and *physical involvement for its own sake,* as opposed to competitive games. Creative arts, intellectual pursuits, or community volunteerism might also be considered important categories of recreational experience.

Recreation as an Outcome

Recognizing that different people may have many different motives for taking part in recreation, Gray and Greben suggest that it should not be considered simply as a form of activity. Instead, they argue that recreation should be perceived as the outcome of participation—a "peak experience in self-satisfaction" that comes from successful participation in any sort of enterprise.

■ *Visitors get an up-close look at the animals at Kuranda Koala Gardens in Cairns, Australia.*

Recreation is an emotional condition within an individual human being that flows from a feeling of well-being and self-satisfaction. It is characterized by feelings of mastery, achievement, exhilaration, acceptance, success, personal worth, and pleasure. It reinforces a positive self-image. Recreation is a response to aesthetic experience, achievement of personal goals, or positive feedback from others. It is independent of activity, leisure, or social acceptance.[24]

Historically, leisure researchers have focused on the social-psychological outcomes of recreation. More recently, significant attention has been given to physical outcomes. Researchers and practitioners are particularly interested in the relationship between recreation participation and physical health outcomes, including reduction of obesity and other chronic health conditions.

The degree to which many individuals become deeply committed emotionally to their recreational interests may be illustrated within the realms of sports and popular entertainment. So fervently do many Americans root for popular sports teams and stars that sport has increasingly been referred to as a form of religion. The glorification of leading athletes as folk idols and the national preoccupation with such major events as the Stanley Cup, the World Series, or the Super Bowl demonstrate the degree to which sports—as a popular form of recreation—capture the emotional commitment of millions of Americans today.

Social Acceptability

Another question arises with respect to defining recreation. Should activity that is often widely disapproved, such as drug use or vandalism, be regarded as a form of recreation? One school of thought maintains that *any* form of voluntarily chosen, pleasurable, leisure-time activity should be regarded as recreation. This view is expressed in the commonly used terms, "recreational sex" or "recreational drug use."

Other writers take the opposite view—that recreation must be wholesome for the individual and for society and must serve to recreate the participant physically, psychologically, spiritually, or mentally. Some even argue that recreation should be clearly distinguished from mere amusement, time-filling, or negative forms of play. Rojek characterizes this approach to defining recreation and leisure as an element in "moral regulation" theory, in which different noneconomic societal institutions are used to control and "civilize" the behavior of the working classes.[25] Whether one accepts this position, it is important to recognize that all publicly and philanthropically financed programs must have significant goals and objectives in order to deserve and obtain support. It therefore becomes necessary to make an important distinction. Recreation, as such, may not imply social acceptability or a set of socially oriented goals or values. When, however, it is provided as a form of community-based service, supported by taxes or voluntary contributions, it must be attuned to prevailing social values and must be aimed at achieving desirable and constructive results.

The task of determining exactly what is socially acceptable or morally desirable is complex, particularly in a heterogeneous society with many different cultures and with laws that may vary greatly from state to state or even county to county. Society's attitudes toward varied leisure pursuits have been ambiguous from a moral perspective. Certain forms of gambling have traditionally been morally or legally disapproved. Compulsive gambling is seen as an illness, and the law prohibits private gambling games, the "numbers" game, and similar pastimes, yet gambling is legal in the majority of states, and many states depend heavily for income on licensed casinos or state lotteries. Similarly, many churches sponsor bingo games, a form of gambling. Is one form of gambling recreation because it is countenanced, and another not? Apart from the obvious point that it is difficult to make such distinctions, it should be stressed that recreation is carried on within a social context. It must respond to social needs and expectations, and it is influenced by prevailing social attitudes and values. Indeed, although we tend to think of recreation as a form of personal involvement or experience, it must also be defined as a social institution.

Recreation as a Social Institution

Recreation is identified as a significant institution in the modern community, involving a form of collective behavior carried on within specific social structures. It has numerous traditions, values, channels of communication, formal relationships, and other institutional aspects.

Once chiefly the responsibility of the family, the church, or other local social bodies, recreation in contemporary society is the responsibility of a number of major agencies in today's society. These may include public, voluntary, or commercial organizations that operate parks, beaches, zoos, aquariums, stadiums, or sports facilities. Recreational activities may also be provided by organizations such as hospitals, schools, correctional institutions, and branches of the armed forces. Clearly, recreation emerged in the twentieth century as a significant social institution, complete with its own national and international organizations and an extensive network of programs of professional preparation in colleges and universities.

Beyond this development, over the past century, there has been general acceptance of the view that community recreation, in which citizens take responsibility for planning and supporting organized leisure services to meet social needs, contributes significantly to democratic citizenship. Hemingway, for example, contrasts two opposing patterns—"participatory" and "representative" democracy—and discusses the role of leisure in contributing to "social capital."[26]

Stormann carries the point further by examining the role of recreation in contributing to community development. He describes the work of neighborhood groups in developing vest-pocket parks and community gardens in Loisaida, a primarily Puerto Rican section of New York City's Lower East Side. Men and women involved in transforming littered vacant lots into productive and pleasant environments gained a larger vision of what their community might become and

■ *Gardening for some is an example of a recreation activity that is freely chosen and has an element of intrinsic and extrinsic motivation.*

learned to work with other social activists on health care, education, housing, and job development. Stormann writes:

> Leisure is invested with communalism and divested of privatism. The empty and dangerous, garbage-infested, unused space became the impetus for an overpowering leisure time. Unused space became meaningful "urban space" [and led to positive] democratic human relations.[27]

Leisure Opportunity and "Social Justice" From a broader perspective, Allison makes the case that organized recreation—seen as a social institution intended to provide the "good life" for all citizens—often fails to meet the need of historically disenfranchised or marginalized groups, such as "women, people of color, individuals with disabilities, gays and lesbians, the poor, and the elderly." For example, she writes:

> Individuals with disabilities and the elderly suffer a host of injustices around issues of organizational exclusion, discrimination, and stigmatization [with] structural and institutional barriers that continue to diminish the rights and opportunities of these individuals in . . . recreation/travel environments (e.g., employment opportunities, program accessibility).[28]

Recreation Defined

Acknowledging these contrasting views of the meaning of recreation, the following definition of the term is offered. Recreation consists of human activities or experiences that occur in leisure time. Usually, they are voluntarily chosen for intrinsic purposes and are pleasurable, although they may involve a degree of compulsion, extrinsic purpose, and discomfort, or even pain or danger. Recreation may also be regarded as the emotional state resulting from participation or as a social institution, a professional career field, or a business. When provided as part of organized community or voluntary-agency programs, recreation should be socially constructive and morally acceptable in terms of prevailing community standards and values.

RELATIONSHIPS AMONG PLAY, LEISURE, AND RECREATION

Obviously, the three terms discussed in this chapter are closely interrelated. Leisure, for example, provides an opportunity to carry on both play and recreation. Much of our free time in modern society is taken up by recreation, although leisure may also include such activities as continuing education, religious practice, or community service, which are not usually thought of as forms of recreation. In turn, it should be understood that although play and recreation tend to overlap, they are not identical. Play is not so much an activity as a form of behavior, marked stylistically by teasing, competition, exploration, or make-believe. Play can occur during work or leisure, whereas recreation takes place only during leisure.

Recreation obviously includes many forms of play, but it also may involve distinctly nonplaylike activities such as traveling, reading, going to museums, and pursuing other cultural or intellectual activities. As a social institution, recreation has broader applications than play or leisure in two ways: Recreation is often provided by institutions that do not have leisure as a primary concern, such as the armed forces or business concerns; and recreation agencies often provide other social or environmental services and may in fact become an important linkage between municipal governments and the people they serve.

Leisure is a subject of scholarly study for many economists and sociologists; it also has come increasingly under the scrutiny of psychologists and social psychologists. However, to the public at large, leisure tends to be a somewhat abstract or remote concept. Although many academic departments and some community agencies use the term *leisure* in their titles, it lacks a sense of urgency or strong appeal as a public issue or focus of government action.

Of the three terms, *recreation* is at once the most understandable and significant for most persons. It is easily recognizable as an area of personal activity and social responsibility, and its values are readily apparent for all age groups and special populations as well. For these reasons, it will be given primary emphasis in the chapters that follow, particularly in terms of program sponsorship and professional identity.

Role of Recreation and Leisure in Professional Education Curricula

Both recreation and leisure are the focus of higher education curricula for individuals planning to enter the overall leisure-service field. Mannell and Kleiber point out that they demand different teaching emphases. Leisure studies scholars, they write, draw on the knowledge and approaches of both the social and management sciences, with their findings reported in varied national and international journals and conferences dealing with leisure studies. They continue:

> Most college and university recreation and leisure studies programs encourage their students to integrate and understand the interplay between "people," "resource" and "policy" issues.
>
> In other words, leisure studies curricula require students to study individual and group leisure behavior as a function of social and cultural factors, the planning and management of natural and built resources for free time use, and policy/management issues associated with the provision of public and private leisure services.[29]

The themes that have just been introduced will be explored more fully throughout this text, as the historical development of recreation and play and the evolution of the present-day leisure-service system are described. Throughout, issues related to the social implications of recreation and leisure and to the role of recreation and park professionals will be fully discussed, along with the challenges that face practitioners in this field in the twenty-first century.

SUMMARY

Play, recreation, and leisure represent important basic concepts that are essential aspects of the overall field of organized leisure services. They have been explored by philosophers, psychologists, historians, educators, and sociologists from ancient Greek civilizations to the present.

Play may best be understood as a form of activity or behavior that is generally nonpurposeful in terms of having serious intended outcomes, but that is an important element in the healthy growth of children and in other societal functions. The chapter presents various theories of play, ranging from the classical views of Herbert Spencer and Karl Groos to more contemporary concepts that link play to Freudian theory or to exploratory drives of human personality.

Six concepts of leisure are presented that depict it as the possession of the upper classes or aristocrats throughout history, as free time or activity, as a state of being, and as a form of spiritual expression. Recreation is also explored from different perspectives, with a key issue being whether it must be morally constructive or socially approved to be considered recreation. The role of recreation as an important contemporary social institution and force in economic life is also discussed.

QUESTIONS FOR CLASS DISCUSSION OR ESSAY EXAMINATION

1. This chapter presents several perspectives on play, including a review of traditional definitions of play, its role as a social ritual in community life, and its contribution to personality development. Which of these do you find most interesting and useful? Why?

2. Recreation has been simply defined as socially desirable activity carried on voluntarily in free time for purposes of fun or pleasure. Critically analyze this definition. For example, must activity always be considered socially desirable in order to be regarded as recreation? Is recreation always pleasurable? Is it always carried on voluntarily? What elements would you add to this definition to make it more meaningful?

3. The chapter presents two contrasting views of leisure—one as the slow-paced, relaxed, or contemplative use of free time and the other as active participation in a wide range of often challenging or demanding activities. Which of these do you believe is the more accurate picture of leisure today?

4. Discuss the contrasting meanings of *play*, *leisure*, and *recreation*, and show how they overlap and differ from each other in their separate meanings. Which of the three do you feel is the more useful term as far as public understanding of this field is concerned?

ENDNOTES

1. Diane Ackerman, "Why We Need to Play," *Parade* (25 April 1999): 12.

2. Friedrich Froebel, cited in George Torkildsen, *Leisure and Recreation Management* (London: E. and F. N. Spon, 1992): 48–49.

3. Harvey Carr, cited in H. C. Lehman and P. A. Witty, *The Psychology of Play Activities* (New York: A. S. Barnes, 1927): 19.

4. The original source of this theory was W. P. Bowen and Elmer D. Mitchell, *The Theory of Organized Play* (New York: A. S. Barnes, 1923).

5. Wayne Stormann, "The Recreation Profession, Capital and Democracy," *Leisure Sciences* (Vol. 15, No. 1, 1993): 51.

6. Roger Caillois, *Man, Play, and Games* (London: Thames and Hudson, 1961): 21.

7. Johan Huizinga, *Homo Ludens: A Study of the Play Element in Culture* (Boston: Beacon Press, 1944; 1960): 5.

8. Lawrence K. Frank, quoted in R. Hartley and R. Goldenson, *The Complete Book of Children's Play* (New York: Thomas Y. Crowell, 1963): 43.

9. Sigmund Freud, quoted in M. J. Ellis, *Why People Play* (Englewood Cliffs, NJ, 1973): 60.

10. Mihaly Cziksentmihalyi, *Beyond Boredom and Anxiety* (San Francisco: Jossey Bass, 1975).

11. Hayden Ramsey, *Reclaiming Leisure: Art, Sport and Philosophy* (New York: Palgrave Macmillan, 2005).

12. Cited in M. H. Neumeyer and E. Neumeyer, *Leisure and Recreation* (New York: Ronald Press, 1958): 19.

13. Juliet Schor, *The Overworked American: The Unexpected Decline of Leisure* (New York: Basic Books, 1991).

14. Robert Stebbins, "Obligation as an Aspect of Leisure Experience," *Journal of Leisure Research* (Vol. 32, No. 1, 2000): 153.

15. See I. Cosgrove and R. Jackson, *The Geography of Recreation and Leisure* (London: Hutchinson University Library, 1972): 13.

16. David Austin, *Therapeutic Recreation: Processes and Techniques*. 5th ed. (Champaign, IL: Sagamore Publishing, 2003): 181.

17. John Neulinger, *The Psychology of Leisure* (Springfield, IL: Charles C. Thomas, 1974): xi.

18. Geoffrey Godbey, *Leisure in Your Life: An Exploration* (Philadelphia: W. B. Saunders, 1981): 10.

19. Charles Sylvester, "The Ethics of Play, Leisure and Recreation in the Twentieth Century, 1900–1965," *Leisure Sciences* (Vol. 9, 1987): 173–188.

20. Hayden Ramsey, *Reclaiming Leisure: Art, Sport and Philosophy* (New York: Palgrave Macmillan, 2005): 202.

21. Alexis de Tocqueville, R. Heffner, ed. in, *Democracy in America* (New York: Signet Classics, 2001): 489.

22. Robert D. Putnam. *Bowling Alone: The Collapse and Revival of American Community* (New York: Simon & Schuster, 2000).

23. James Murphy et al., *Leisure Service Delivery Systems: A Modern Perspective* (Philadelphia: Lea and Febiger, 1973): 73–76.

24. David Gray and Seymour Greben, "Future Perspectives," *Parks and Recreation* (July 1974): 49.

25. Chris Rojek, *Capitalism and Leisure Theory* (London: Tavistock, 1985): 42.

26. J. L. Hemingway, "Leisure, Social Capital, and Democratic Citizenship," *Journal of Leisure Research* (Vol. 31, No. 2, 1999): 150–165.

27. Wayne Stormann, "Recreation's Role in Community Development: Community Re-creation," *Journal of Applied Recreation Research* (Vol. 21, No. 2, 1996): 161.

28. Maria Allison, "Leisure, Diversity, and Social Justice," *Journal of Leisure Research* (Vol. 32, No. 1, 2000): 4.

29. Roger Mannell and Douglas Kleiber, *A Social Psychology of Leisure* (State College, PA: Venture Publishing, 1997): 11.

CHAPTER 3

EARLY HISTORY OF RECREATION AND LEISURE

• • •

In the year A.D. 80, the Colosseum opened with what must stand as quite the longest and most disgusting mass binge in history. . . . Various sorts of large-scale slaughter, both of animals and men, were appreciatively watched by the Emperor Titus and a packed audience for 100 days. . . . Titus was quite happy footing the enormous bill just as he and his father, the imperial Vespasian, had already footed the bill for building this vast arena. Such payments were the privilege of power.[1]

In the long run, industrialization brought the reduction of work-time. The hours per year committed to work have declined in the industrial West in a range from 3,000–3,600 to 1,800–2,000 from 1840 to the present. . . . This redistribution of time has been accompanied by a drastic "repackaging" of leisure hours making possible new forms of leisure time, including the typically modern notions of free evenings, the weekend, paid summer vacations, as well as a lengthy childhood and retirement.[2]

• • •

INTRODUCTION

To provide a meaningful background for the study of recreation and leisure in modern society, it is helpful to have a clear understanding of its role in the past. We can trace the origins of many of our contemporary views of leisure and related cultural customs to the traditions and practices of ancient cultures. The history of recreation and leisure is a rich tapestry of people, places, events, and social forces, showing the role of religion, education, and government and the customs and values of different cultures, their arts, sport, and pastimes. By becoming familiar with the evolution of our recreation and leisure, we are better able to understand and deal effectively with the present.

Tribal people do not make the same sharp distinction between work and leisure that more technologically advanced societies do. Whereas the latter set aside different periods of time for work and relaxation, a tribal, pretechnological society has no such precise separations. Instead, work is customarily done when it is available or necessary, and it is often infused with rites and customs that lend it variety and pleasure. In such tribal societies, work tends to be varied and creative, rather than being a narrow, specialized task demanding a sharply defined skill, as in modern industry. Work is often accompanied by ritual that is regarded as essential to the success of the planting or harvesting or to the building or hunting expedition. The ritual may involve prayer, sacrifice, dance, or feasting, which thus become part of the world of work.

THE PLAY OF EARLY SOCIETIES

One would expect a chronological study to begin by examining the play of prehistoric peoples during the Paleolithic and Neolithic epochs. However, relatively little is known about the nature of leisure and play in these early periods. Archaeologists have uncovered artifacts that provide some first-hand evidence of the creative, athletic, and recreation activities of primitive peoples from around the world. We also have extrapolated from the accounts of "primitive" societies written by missionaries and anthropologists in the nineteenth and early twentieth centuries.

Origins of Games and Sport

In primitive societies, play may have had many sources. Popular games were often vestiges of warfare, practiced as a form of sport. Musical instruments were likely created for use in religious rituals. Pottery, painting, drawings, and other early art provided a record of both daily life and cultural mythology. Beads and other types of jewelry were created as external symbols of individual status and group affiliations. When an activity was no longer useful in its original form (such as archery for hunting or warfare), it became a form of sport offering individuals and groups the opportunity to prove physical skill and strategy. Often, the origin was a religious ritual, in which games were played to symbolize a continuing struggle between good and evil or life and death.

The game of *tlachtli*, widely practiced in Central America centuries ago, is an example of such a contest. Tlachtli courts were about 200 feet long and 30 feet wide and were situated near temples. A stone ring was fixed about halfway up a wall at either end. The players struck a rubber ball with their knees or hips, the purpose being to drive it through one of the hoops. Blank writes:

> The rubber ball used in the ancient game symbolized the sun, and by making it carom across the court, players hoped to perpetuate the daily arc of the heavenly sphere. . . . Mesoamerican ball was no schoolyard shoot-around: Win or lose, the athletes played for keeps. . . . [I]n pre-Columbian games, members of the losing team were commonly offered up for ritual sacrifice, their hearts cut out with blades of razor sharp obsidian. That's one way to shorten the post-game interviews.[3]

Other Play Functions

On the North American continent, play had similar functions among Native American tribes, helping to equip the young for adult life. Boys practiced warriors' skills and were taught to survive unarmed and unclothed in the wilderness. Girls were taught the household crafts expected of mature women. Through dancing, singing, and storytelling, both sexes learned the history and religion of their cultures. Among such southwestern Native American tribes as the Navajo, Zuni, or Hopi, shamans or medicine men practiced healing rites that made use of chanting, storytelling, dancing, sacred *kachina* dolls, and elaborate, multicolored sand paintings.

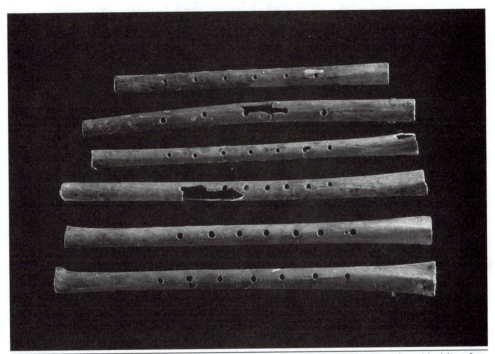

■ *Six flutes dating back from 7000 to 9000* B.C. *provide insight into the cultural habits of an ancient Chinese society.*

In a period ranging from May 1986 to June 1987, archaeologists at the early Neolithic site of Jiahu in Henan province, China, uncovered 25 flutes between 7,000 and 9,000 years old. Most of the flutes were found at grave sites. Six of the instruments were intact and are now believed to be the earliest, playable multinote instruments. The flutes, which were made of bone, contain seven holes that correspond to a scale similar to the Western eight-note scale. This tone scale indicates that musicians living in 7000 B.C. could compose and play music. Archaeologists cannot be certain of why so many flutes were located in this part of China. Some believe that the flutes were part of religious rituals; others believe that music was simply a part of community life. In any case, the discovery of these flutes helps us recognize the very old tradition of using music as a means of personal expression and cultural celebration.[4]

RECREATION AND LEISURE IN ANCIENT CIVILIZATIONS

As prehistoric societies advanced, they developed specialization of functions. Humans learned to domesticate plants and animals, which permitted them to shift from a nomadic existence based on hunting and food gathering to a largely stationary way of life based on grazing animals and planting crops. Ultimately, ruling classes developed, along with soldiers, craftsmen, peasants, and slaves. As villages and cities evolved and large estates were tilled (often with complex water storage and irrigation systems) and harvested by lower-class workers, upper-class societies gained power, wealth, and leisure. Thus, in the aristocracy of the first civilizations that developed in the Middle East during the five millennia before the Christian era, we find for the first time in history a leisure class.

Ancient Egypt

The Egyptian culture was a rich and diversified one; it achieved an advanced knowledge of astronomy, architecture, engineering, agriculture, and construction. The Egyptians had a varied class structure, with a powerful nobility, priesthood, and military class and lesser classes of workers, artisans, peasants, and slaves. This civilization, which lasted from about 5000 B.C. well into the Roman era, was richly recorded in paintings, statuary, and hieroglyphic records.

The ancient Egyptians led a colorful and pleasant life; it is said that their energies were directed to the arts of living and the arts of dying. They engaged in many sport as part of education and recreation, including wrestling, gymnastic exercises, lifting and swinging weights, and ball games. Bullfighting was a popular spectacle and, at least at its inception, was religiously motivated. Music, drama, and dance were forms of religious worship as well as social entertainment. The Egyptians had complex orchestras that included various stringed and percussive instruments. Groups of female performers were attached to temples, and the royal houses had troupes of entertainers who performed on sacred or social occasions.

Ancient Assyria and Babylonia

The land known as the "fertile crescent" between two great rivers, the Tigris and the Euphrates, was ruled by two powerful empires, Assyria in the north and Babylon in the south. These kingdoms were in power for approximately 26 centuries, from about 2900 B.C. until the invasion by Alexander the Great in 330 B.C. Like the ancient Egyptians, the Assyrians and Babylonians had many popular recreation activities, such as boxing, wrestling, archery, and a variety of table games.

In addition to watching dancing, listening to music, and giving banquets, Assyrians were also devoted to hunting; the nobles of Assyria went lion hunting in chariots and on foot, using spears. The chase was a daily occupation, recorded for history in numerous reliefs, sculptures, and inscriptions. As early as the ninth century B.C., parks were established as sites for royal hunting parties. They also provided settings for feasts, assemblies, and royal gatherings. On the estates of other monarchs during the ninth and tenth centuries B.C. were vineyards, fishponds, and the famed hanging gardens of Babylon.

Ancient Israel

Among the ancient Israelites, music and dancing were performed for ritual purposes as well as for social activities and celebrations. The early Hebrews distinguished dances of a sacred or holy character from those that resembled pagan ceremonies. Although there are no wall reliefs or paintings to tell of dance as performed by the ancient Hebrews, there are abundant references to this practice in the Old Testament. Dance was highly respected and was particularly used on occasions of celebration and triumph.

Like other ancient societies, the ancient Hebrews also engaged in hunting, fishing, wrestling, and the use of such weapons as the sword and javelin for both recreational and defensive purposes. As for leisure itself, their major contribution was to set aside the seventh day—the Sabbath—as a time for people to rest from work and to worship.

Ancient Greece

In the city-states of ancient Greece, particularly in Athens during the so-called Golden Age of Pericles from about 500 to 400 B.C., humankind reached a new peak of philosophical and cultural development. The Athenians took great interest in the arts, in learning, and in athletics. These pursuits were generally restricted to wellborn, aristocratic noblemen, who had full rights of citizenship, including voting and participation in affairs of state. Craftsmen, farmers, and tradespeople were also citizens, but had limited rights and less prestige. Labor was performed by slaves and foreigners, who outnumbered citizens by as much as two or three to one.

The amenities of life were generally restricted to the most wealthy and powerful citizens, who represented the Athenian ideal of the balanced man—a combined soldier, athlete, artist, statesman, and philosopher. This ideal was furthered through education and the various religious festivals, which occupied about 70 days of the year. The arts of music, poetry, theater, gymnastics, and athletic competition were combined in these sacred competitions.

Sport appears to have been part of daily life and to have occurred mainly when there were mass gatherings of people, such as the assembly of an army for war or the wedding or funeral of some great personage. There were also bardic or musical events, offering contests on the harp and flute, poetry, and theatrical presentations. Physical prowess was celebrated in sculpture and poetry, and strength and beauty were seen as gifts of the gods.

From earliest childhood, Athenian citizens engaged in varied athletic and cultural activities. Young children enjoyed toys, dolls, carts, skip ropes, kites, and seesaws. When boys reached the age of seven, they were enrolled in schools in which gymnastics and music were primary elements. They were intensively instructed in running and leaping, wrestling, throwing the javelin and discus, dancing (taught as a form of military drill), boxing, swimming, and ball games.

Greek Philosophy of Recreation and Leisure   The Athenian philosophers believed strongly in the unity of mind and body and in the strong relationship of all forms of human qualities and skills. They felt that play activity was essential to the healthy physical and social growth of children.

Plato believed that education should be compulsory and that it should provide natural modes of amusement for children:

Education should begin with the right direction of children's sports. The plays of childhood have a great deal to do with the maintenance or nonmaintenance of laws.[5]

Women did not enjoy the leisurely pursuits of men in ancient Greece, although there are some historical accounts of women receiving modest education, and young girls participated in some athletic competitions. Citizens were, by definition, men.

Changes in the Greek Approach to Leisure   The ancient Greeks developed the art of town planning and customarily made extensive provisions for parks and gardens, open-air theaters and gymnasiums, baths, exercise grounds, and stadiums. During the time of Plato, the gymnasium and the park were closely connected in beautiful natural settings, often including indoor halls, gardens, and buildings for musical performances. Early Athens had many public baths and some public parks, which later gave way to privately owned estates.

A gradual transition occurred in the Greek approach to leisure and play. At first, all citizens were expected to participate in sports and games, and the Olympic games were restricted to free-born Greeks only. Gradually, however, the religious and cultural functions of the Olympic games and other festivals were weakened by athletic specialization, corruption, and commercialism. In time, sport and other forms of activity such as drama, singing, and dance were performed only by highly skilled specialists (drawn from the lower classes or even slaves) who trained or perfected their skills throughout the year to appear before huge crowds of admiring spectators.

Ancient Rome

Like the Greek city-states, the Roman republic during its early development was a vigorous and nationalistic state. The Roman citizen, although he belonged to a privileged class, was required to defend his society and fight in its wars. Citizens participated in sport and gymnastics, intended to keep the body strong and spirit courageous. Numerous games held in connection with the worship of various Roman gods later developed into annual festivals. Such games were carefully supervised by the priesthood and were supported by public funds, frequently at great cost. The most important of the Roman games were those that celebrated military triumphs, which were usually held in honor of the god Jupiter, the head of the Roman pantheon.

Like the early Greeks, young Roman children had toy carts, houses, dolls, hobbyhorses, stilts, and tops and engaged in many sport and games. Young boys were taught various sport and exercises such as running and jumping, sword and spear play, wrestling, swimming, and horseback riding. The Romans, however, had a different concept of leisure than the Greeks. Although the Latin words for "leisure" and "business" are *otium* and *negotium*, suggesting the same view of leisure as a positive value (with work defined negatively as a lack of leisure), the Romans supported play for utilitarian rather than aesthetic or spiritual reasons. The Romans were much less

■ *The Roman Colosseum is perhaps the greatest architectural achievement of antiquity. Built over 1925 years ago, the Colosseum is a monument to the achievements of ancient Rome.*

interested than the Athenians in varied forms of cultural activity. Although they had many performing companies, usually composed of Greek and southern Italian slaves, the Romans themselves did not actively participate in the theater.

Even more than the Greeks, the Romans were systematic planners and builders. Their towns generally included provisions for baths, open-air theaters, amphitheaters, forums for public assemblies, stadiums, and sometimes parks and gardens. They developed buildings for gymnastic sport, modeled after the Greek *palaestra* and including wrestling rooms, conversation areas for philosophers, and colonnades where games might be held in winter despite bad weather. Wealthier Romans often had private villas, many with large gardens and hunting preserves.

As the empire grew more powerful, the simple agricultural democracy of the early years, in which all male Romans were citizens and free men, shifted to an urban life with sharply divided classes. There were four social levels: the *senators*, who were the richest, holding most of the land and power; the *curiae*, who owned more than 25 acres of land and were officeholders or tax collectors; the *plebs*, or free common people, who owned small properties or were tradesmen or artisans; and the *coloni*, who were lower-class tenants of the land.

The society became marked by the wealth and profiteering of businessmen and speculators, with the cooperation of the rulers and governing officials. In time, a huge urban population of plebs lived in semi-idleness, because most of the work was done by coloni and slaves brought to Rome. Gradually it became necessary for the Roman emperors and senate to amuse and entertain the plebs; they did so with doles of grain and with public games—in other words, "bread and circuses."

As early as the reign of the Emperor Claudius in the first century A.D., there were 159 public holidays during the year, 93 of which were devoted to games at public expense, including many new festivals in honor of national heroes and foreign victories. By A.D. 354, there were 200 public holidays each year, including 175 days of games. Even on working days, the labor began at daybreak and ended shortly after noon during much of the year.

As leisure increased and the necessity for military service and other forms of physical effort declined for the Roman citizen, entertainment became the central life activity of many citizens. The normal practice was for the citizen to be entertained or to follow a daily routine of exercise, bathing, and eating. Men were no longer as active in sport as they once had been. They now sought to be amused and to entertain their guests with paid acrobats, musicians, dancers, and other artists. Athletes now performed as members of a specialized profession with unions, coaches, and training schools and with conditions of service accepted and approved by the emperor himself.

Corruption of Entertainment Gradually, the focus on the traditional sports of running, throwing, and jumping gave way to an emphasis on human combat—first boxing and wrestling and then displays of cruelty in which gladiators fought to the death for the entertainment of mass audiences. By the time of Emperor Tiberius (A.D. 14–37), competitive sport in the Roman Empire had become completely commercialized. To maintain political popularity and placate the bored masses, the emperors and the senate provided great parades, circuses, and feasts.

The Roman games featured contests that were fought to the death between gladiators using various weapons, on foot, on horseback, or in chariots. Even sea battles were fought in artificially constructed lakes in the Roman arenas. Imported wild beasts, such as tigers and elephants, were pitted against each other or against human antagonists. Christians, in particular, were slaughtered in such games. Tacitus wrote that many

> were dressed in the skins of wild beasts, and exposed to be torn to pieces by dogs in the public games, were crucified, or condemned to be burnt; and at nightfall serve in place of lamps to light the darkness, Nero's own gardens being used for the purpose.[6]

Both animals and humans were maimed and butchered in cruel and horrible ways. Spectacles were often lewd and obscene, leading to mass debauchery, corruption, and perversion that profoundly weakened the Roman state.

EARLY CHRISTIAN ERA: DARK AND MIDDLE AGES

Under attack by successive waves of northern European tribes, the Roman Empire finally collapsed. For a period of several centuries, Europe was overrun with warring tribes and shifting alliances. The organized power of Rome, which had built roads, extended commerce, and provided civil order, was at an end. Gradually the Catholic Church emerged to provide a form of universal citizenship within Europe. Having suffered under the brutal persecutions of the Romans, the early Christians condemned all that their pagan oppressors had stood for—especially their hedonistic way of life. Indeed, the early church fathers believed in a fanatical asceticism, which in the Byzantine, or Eastern, Empire was marked by the Anchorite movement, with its idea of salvation through masochistic self-deprivation.

any aspects of Roman life were forbidden during the Dark and Middle Ages. The stadiums, amphitheaters, and baths that had characterized Roman life were destroyed. The Council of Elvira ruled that the rite of baptism could not be extended to those connected with the stage, and in A.D. 398 the Council of Carthage excommunicated those who attended the theater on holy days. The great spectacles and organized shows of imperial Rome were at an end. The Roman emphasis on leisure was replaced by a Christian emphasis on work. The influential Benedictine order in particular insisted on the dignity of labor. Their rule read, "Idleness is the great enemy of the soul. Therefore, monks should always be occupied either in manual labor or in sacred readings."

It would be a mistake, however, to assume that the Catholic Church eliminated all forms of play. Many early Catholic religious practices were based on the rituals of earlier faiths. Priests built churches on existing shrines or temple sites, set Christian holy days according to the dates of pagan festivals, and used such elements of pagan worship as bells, candles, incense, singing, and dancing.

Pastimes in the Middle Ages

Despite disapproval from the church, many forms of play continued during the Middle Ages: Medieval society was marked by rigid class stratification; below the nobility and clergy were the peasants, who were divided into such ranks as freemen, villeins, serfs, and slaves.

Life in the Middle Ages, even for the feudal nobility, was crude and harsh. Manors and castles were little more than stone fortresses—crowded, dark, and damp. Knights were responsible for fighting in the service of their rulers; between wars, their favorite pastimes were hunting and hawking. Hunting skill was considered a virtue of medieval rulers and noblemen. The sport was thought to be helpful in keeping hunters from the sin of idleness. (A vigorous and tiring sport, it was also believed to prevent sensual temptation.) Hunting also served as a useful preparation for war. In a later era, the Italian Machiavelli pointed out that since the main concern of the prince must be war, he must never cease thinking of it. In times of peace, thoughts of war should be directed to the sport of hunting.

Other pastimes during the Middle Ages were various types of games and gambling, music and dance, sport, and jousting. The games played in castles and medieval manors included early forms of chess, checkers, backgammon, and dice. Gambling was popular, although forbidden by both ecclesiastical and royal authority.

As the chaos of the Dark Ages yielded to greater order and regularity, life became more stable. Travel in reasonable safety became possible, and by the eleventh century, commerce was widespread. The custom of jousting emerged within the medieval courts, stemming from the tradition that only the nobility fought on horseback; common men fought on foot. Thus, the term *chivalry* (from the French *cheval*, meaning horse) came into being. By the dawn of the twelfth century, the code of chivalry was developed, having originated in the profession of arms among feudal courtiers. (The tournament was a contest between teams, and the joust was a trial of skill between two individual knights.) An elaborate code of laws and regulations was drawn up for the combat, and no one below the rank of esquire was permitted to engage in tournaments or jousting.

Games of the Common People   Meanwhile, what of the life of the peasantry during the Middle Ages? Edward Hulme suggests that life was not all work for the lower classes. There were village feasts and sport, practical joking, throwing weights, cockfighting, bull baiting, and other lively games. "Ball games and wrestling, in which men of one village were pitted against men of another, sometimes resulted in bloodshed."[7]

There was sometimes dancing on the green, and, on holidays, there were miracle and morality plays (forms of popular religious drama and pageantry). However, peasants usually went to bed at dark, reading was a rare accomplishment, and there was much drinking and crude brawling. For peasants, hunting was more a means of obtaining food than a sport. Although the nobility usually rode through the hedges and trampled the fields of the peasantry, peasants were not allowed to defend their crops against such forays or even against wild animals. If peasants were caught poaching, they were often maimed or hanged as punishment.

Typically, certain games were classified as rich men's sport and others as poor men's sport; sometimes a distinction was also made between urban and rural sport. As life in the Middle Ages became somewhat easier, a number of pastimes emerged. Many modern sport were developed at this time in rudimentary form.

The people of the Middle Ages had an insatiable love of sightseeing and would travel great distances to see entertainments. There was no religious event, parish fair, municipal feast, or military parade that did not bring great crowds of people. When the kings of France assembled their principal retainers once or twice a year, they distributed food and liquor among the common people and provided military displays, court ceremonies, and entertainment by jugglers, tumblers, and minstrels.

An illustration of the extent to which popular recreation expanded during the Middle Ages is found in the famous painting of children's games by the Flemish artist Pieter Breughel. This painting depicts more than 90 forms of children's play, including marbles, stilts, sledding, bowling, skating, blind man's bluff, piggyback, leapfrog, follow-the-leader, archery, tug-of-war, doll play, and dozens of others, many of which have lasted to the present day.

THE RENAISSANCE

Historians generally view the first half of the Middle Ages in Europe (roughly from A.D. 400 to 1000) as the Dark Ages, and the next 400 to 500 years as *le haut Moyen Age*, or High Middle Age. The Renaissance is said to have begun in Italy about A.D. 1350, in France about 1450, and in England about 1500. It marked a transition between the medieval world and the modern age. The term *renaissance* means rebirth and describes the revived interest in the scholarship, philosophy, and arts of ancient Greece and Rome that developed at this time. More broadly, it also represented a new freedom of thought and expression, a more rational and scientific view of life, and the expansion of commerce and travel in European life.

As the major European nations stabilized during this period under solidly established monarchies, power shifted from the church to the kings and their noblemen. In Italy and France, particularly, the nobility became patrons of great painters, sculptors, musicians, dancers, and dramatists. These artists were no longer dominated by the ideals and values of the Catholic Church, but were free to serve secular goals. A great wave of music and literature swept through the courts of Europe, aided by the development of printing. Dance and theater became more complex and elaborate, and increasingly lavish entertainments and spectacles were presented in the courts of Italy and France.

Play as Education

Varied forms of play became part of the education of the youth of the nobility at this time. The French essayist Michel de Montaigne, in discussing the education of children, wrote:

> Our very exercises and recreations, running, wrestling, music, dancing, hunting, riding, and fencing will prove to be a good part of our study. . . . It is not a soul, it is not a body, that we are training up; it is a man, and we ought not to divide him into two parts.[8]

The Athenian philosophy that had supported play as an important form of education was given fuller emphasis during the Renaissance by such educators and writers as François Rabelais, John Locke, and Jean Jacques Rousseau. In early sixteenth-century France, Rabelais advanced a number of revolutionary theories on education, emphasizing the need for physical exercises and games as well as singing, dancing, modeling and painting, nature study, and manual training. His account of the education of Gargantuan describes play as an exercise for mind and body. Locke, an Englishman who lived from 1632 to 1704, was also concerned with play as a medium of learning. He recommended that children make their own playthings and felt that games could contribute significantly to character development if they were properly supervised and directed. "All the plays and diversions of children," he wrote, "should be directed toward good and useful habits." Locke distinguished between the play of children and recreation for older youth and adults. "Recreation," he said, "is not being idle . . . but easing the wearied part by change of business."

INFLUENCE OF THE PROTESTANT REFORMATION

The Reformation was a religious movement of the 1500s that resulted in the establishment of a number of Protestant sects whose leaders broke away from Roman Catholicism. It was part of a broader stream that included economic, social, and political currents. In part it represented the influence of the growing middle classes, who allied with the nobility in the emerging nations of Europe to challenge the power of the church.

Throughout Europe, there was an aura of grim dedication to work and a determination to enforce old codes against play and idleness. The "Protestant work ethic" that emerged during the Reformation led to periods of strict limitations on leisure and recreation throughout the history of many Christian cultures, including societies in North America. This same ethic has heavily influenced our contemporary Western views of the relative value of work and leisure.

The new Protestant sects tended to be more solemn and austere than the Catholic Church. Calvin established an autocratic system of government in Geneva in 1541 that was directed by a group of Presbyters, morally upright men who controlled the social and cultural life of the community to the smallest detail. They ruthlessly suppressed heretics and burned dissenters at the stake. Miller and Robinson describe the unbending Puritanism in Geneva:

"Purity of conduct" was insisted upon, which meant the forbidding of gambling, card playing, dancing, wearing of finery, singing of gay songs, feasting, drinking and the like. There were to be no more festivals, no more theaters, no more ribaldry, no more light and disrespectful poetry or display. Works of art and musical instruments were removed from the churches.[9]

Puritanism in England

The English Puritans waged a constant battle to limit or condemn sport and other forms of entertainment during the period from the sixteenth to the eighteenth century. Maintaining strict observation of the Sabbath was a particular issue. Anglican clergy during the Elizabethan period bitterly attacked stage plays, church festival gatherings, dancing, gambling, bowling, and other "devilish pastimes" such as hawking and hunting, holding fairs and markets, and reading "lascivious and wanton books."

James I, however, recognized that the prohibition of harmless amusements such as dancing, archery, and the decorating of maypoles caused public anger. In 1618 he issued a Declaration on Lawful Sports, in which he asked, "When shall the common people have leave to exercise, if not upon the Sundayes and holy daies, seeing they must apply their labour and win their living in all working daies?" James stressed the military value of sport and the danger of an increase in drinking and other vices as substitute activities if sport were denied to people.

DEVELOPMENT OF PARKS AND RECREATION AREAS

During the Middle Ages, the need to enclose cities within protective walls necessitated building within a compact area that left little space for public gardens or sports areas. As the walled city became more difficult to defend after the invention of gunpowder and cannon, residents began to move out of the central city. Satellite communities developed around the city, but usually with little definite planning.

As the Renaissance period began, European town planning was characterized by wide avenues, long approaches, handsome buildings, and similar monumental features. The nobility decorated their estates with elaborate gardens, some of which were open to public use, as in Italy at the end of the thirteenth century. There were walks and public squares, often decorated with statuary. In some cases, religious brotherhoods built clubhouses, gardens, and shooting stands for archery practice that were used by townspeople for recreation and amusement.

hree major types of large parks came into existence during the late Renaissance. The first were royal hunting preserves or parks, some of which have become famous public parks today, such as the 4,000-acre Prater in Vienna and the Tiergarten in Berlin. Second were the ornate and formal garden parks designed according to the so-called French style of landscape architecture. Third were the English garden parks, which strove to produce naturalistic landscape effects. This became the prevailing style in most European cities.

In England, efforts at city planning began during the eighteenth century. Business and residential streets were paved and street names posted. Because it was believed that overcrowding led to disease (in the seventeenth century, London had suffered from recurrent attacks of the plague), an effort was made to convert open squares into gardens and to create more small parks. Deaths from contagious disease declined during each successive decade of the eighteenth century, and this improvement was believed to have been due to increased cleanliness and ventilation within the city.

Use of Private Estates

From 1500 to the latter part of the eighteenth century, the European nobility developed increasingly lavish private grounds. These often included topiary work (trees and shrubbery clipped in fantastic shapes), aviaries, fishponds, summer houses, water displays, outdoor theaters, hunting grounds and menageries, and facilities for outdoor games. During this period, such famed gardens as the Tuileries and the Luxembourg in Paris, as well as the estate of Versailles, were established by the French royalty; similar gardens and private estates were found all over Europe. Following the early Italian example, it became the custom to open these private parks and gardens to the public— at first occasionally and then as a regular practice.

Popular Diversions in England

Great outdoor gardens were established in England to provide entertainment and relaxation. Vauxhall, a pleasure resort founded during the reign of Charles II, was a densely wooded area with walks and bowers, lighting displays, water mills, fireworks, artificial caves and grottoes, entertainment, eating places, and tea gardens. The park was supported by the growing class of merchants and tradesmen, and its admission charge and distance from London helped to "exclude the rabble."

Following the Restoration period in England, Hyde Park and St. James Park became fashionable centers for promenading by the upper classes during the early afternoon. Varied amusements were provided in the parks: wrestling matches, races, military displays, fireworks, and illuminations on special occasions. Aristocrats, merchants, and tradesmen all rode, drove carriages, and strolled in the parks. Horse racing, lotteries, and other forms of gambling became the vogue.

Among the lower classes, tastes in entertainment varied according to whether one lived in the country or city. Countrymen continued to engage vigorously in such sport as football, cricket, wrestling, or "cudgel playing," and to enjoy traditional country or Morris dancing and the singing of old folk songs.

Concerns About Leisure: Class Differences

Gradually, concerns about the growing number of holidays and the effect of leisure activities on the working classes began to be voiced. In France, for example, in the eighteenth century, wealthy individuals had the opportunity for amusement all week long—paying social visits, dining, and passing evenings at gaming, at the theater, ballet, or opera, or at clubs. In contrast, the working classes had only Sundays and fête days, or holidays, for their amusements. La Croix points out, however, that these represented a third of the whole year. In addition to those holidays decreed by the state, many other special celebrations had been either authorized or tolerated by the Catholic Church. Many economists and men of affairs argued that the ecclesiastic authorities should be called upon to reduce the number. Voltaire wrote in 1756:

> Twenty fête days too many in the country condemn to inactivity and expose to dissipation twenty times a year ten millions of workingmen, each of whom would earn five pence a day, and this gives a total of 180 million livres . . . lost to the state in the course of a twelve-month. This painful fact is beyond all doubt.[10]

In the larger cities in France, many places of commercial amusement sprang up. Cafés provided meeting places to chat, read newspapers, and play dominoes, chess, checkers, or billiards.

RECREATION IN AMERICA: THE COLONIAL PERIOD

We now cross the Atlantic to examine the development of recreation and leisure in the early American colonies. First, it needs to be recognized that when English and other European settlers came to the New World, they did not entirely divorce themselves from the customs and values of the countries they had left. Commerce was ongoing; governors and military personnel traveled back and forth; and newspapers, magazines, and books were exchanged regularly. Thus, there was a constant interchange of ideas and social trends; one historian has summed it up by saying that an Atlantic civilization existed that embraced both sides of the great ocean. Michael Kraus writes:

> What came from the New World . . . was embedded . . . in the pattern of European life. The revolutions of the sixteenth and seventeenth centuries—political, scientific, religious, and commercial—make for a remarkable fertility of speculation and social reorientation. . . . The era of democratization was thus well begun, and this, truly, was in large measure the creation of the Atlantic civilization.[11]

Despite this linkage, the North American settlements represented a unique and harsh environment for most Europeans who arrived during the period of early colonization. The first need of seventeenth-century colonists was for survival. They had to plant crops, clear forests, build shelters, and in some cases defend themselves against attack by hostile Native American tribes. More than half of the colonists who arrived on the *Mayflower* did not survive the first harsh winter near Plymouth. In such a setting, work was all-important; there was little time, money, or energy to support amusements or public entertainment. Without a nobility possessing the wealth, leisure, and inclination to patronize the arts, there was little opportunity for music, theater, or dance to flourish—but the most important hindrance to the development of recreation was the religious attitude.

Restrictions in New England

The Puritan settlers of New England came to the New World to establish a society based on a strict Calvinist interpretation of the Bible. Although the work ethic had not originated with the Puritans, they adopted it enthusiastically. Idleness was detested as the "devil's workshop," and a number of colonies passed laws binding "any rougs, vagabonds, sturdy beggars, masterless men or other notorious offenders" over to compulsory work or imprisonment.

Puritan magistrates attempted to maintain curbs on amusements long after the practical reasons for such prohibitions had disappeared. Early court records show many cases of young people being fined, confined to the stocks, or publicly whipped for such "violations" as drunkenness, idleness, gambling, dancing, or participating in other forms of "lascivious" behavior. However, despite these restrictions, many forms of play continued. Football was played by boys in Boston's streets and lanes, and although playing cards (the "devil's picture-books") were hated by the Puritans, they were freely imported from England and openly on sale.

Other ordinances banned gambling, drama, and nonreligious music, with dancing—particularly between men and women—also condemned. There was vigorous enforcement of the Sabbath laws: Sunday work, travel, and recreation, even "unnecessary and unseasonable walking in the streets and fields," were prohibited. Merrymaking on religious holidays such as Christmas or Easter was banned.

Leisure in the Southern Colonies

A number of the southern colonies had similar restrictions during the early years of settlement. The laws of Virginia, for example, forbade Sunday amusements and made imprisonment the penalty for failure to attend church services. Sabbath-day dancing, fiddling, hunting, fishing, and card playing were strictly banned. Gradually, however, these stern restrictions declined in the southern colonies. There, the upper classes had both wealth and leisure from their large estates and plantations, on which the labor was performed by indentured servants and slaves. Many of them had ties with the landed gentry in England and shared their tastes for aristocratic amusements. As southern settlers of this social class became established, plantation life for the upper class became marked by lavish entertainment and hospitality.

The lifestyles of slaves in the colonies were a stark contrast to the lavish lifestyles of their owners. The majority of slaves in the colonies were of West African ancestry. They were able to bring nothing with them to the colonies other than language and customs, both of which they were compelled to disregard upon arrival. The customs that thrived in the harsh life of the colonies included music, folktales and storytelling, and dance. Music and dance were an integral piece of the culture of most West African societies. Dance was associated with religious and cultural celebrations, as well as secular recreation. Storytelling was an important instrument for passing history from one generation to the next. In the colonies, and later in the southern states, slaves had very few opportunities for leisure. Most worked 14 hours a day or more, six days a week. Free time that was available was highly cherished and spent in the company of fellow slaves. Slave masters used free time as a "reward" to improve morale and often enforced strict rules about what could happen during that free time. Owners were especially interested in assimilating slaves into Western culture and, as a consequence, limited expression of African culture through music and dance and required practice of European customs, including Christian worship.[12]

Decline of Religious Controls

Despite the stern sermons of New England ministers and the severe penalties for infractions of the established moral code, it was clear that play became gradually tolerated in the colonies. The lottery was introduced during the early 1700s and quickly gained the sanction and participation of the most esteemed citizens. Towns and states used lotteries to increase their revenues and to build canals, turnpikes, and bridges. This "acceptable" form of gambling helped to endow leading colleges and academies, and even Congregational, Baptist, and Episcopal churches had lotteries "for promoting public worship and the advancement of religion."

Even in the area of drinking, the climate began to change despite the very strong opposition of the Puritan magistrates in New England. Under Puritan law, drunkards were subject to fines and imprisonment in the stocks, and sellers were forbidden to provide them with any liquor thereafter. A frequent drunkard was punished by having a large *D* made of "Redd Cloth" hung around his neck or sewn on his clothing, and he lost the right to vote. Yet, by the early part of the eighteenth century, taverns were widely established throughout New England, providing places where gentlemen might "enjoy

Gradually, restrictions against play were relaxed in New England and elsewhere. Recreation became more acceptable when amusements could be attached to work, and thus country fairs and market days became occasions for merrymaking. Social gatherings with music, games, and dancing were held in conjunction with such work projects as house raisings, sheep shearing, logrolling, or cornhusking bees. Many social pastimes were linked to other civic occasions such as elections or training days for local militia. On training days in Boston, over a thousand men would gather on the Boston Common to drill and practice marksmanship, after which they celebrated at nearby taverns.

their bowl and bottle with satisfaction" and engage in billiards, cards, skittles, and other games.

By the mid-1700s, the stern necessity of hard work for survival had lessened, and religious antagonism toward amusements had also declined. However, the Sunday laws continued in many settlements, and there was still a strong undercurrent of disapproval of play.

Parks and Conservation in the Colonial Era

Compared with the nations of Europe, the early American colonies showed little concern for developing parks in cities and towns. With land so plentiful around the isolated settlements along the eastern seaboard, there seemed to be little need for such planning. The earliest planned outdoor spaces were "commons" or "greens," found in many New England communities and used chiefly for pasturing cattle and sheep but also for military drills, market days, and fairs. Similar open areas were established in towns settled by the Spanish in the South and Southwest, in the form of plazas and large squares in the center of towns or adjacent to principal churches.

Beautiful village greens established during the colonial period still exist throughout Massachusetts, Connecticut, Vermont, and New Hampshire. In the design of new cities, the colonists began to give attention to the need for preserving or establishing parks and open spaces. Among the first cities in which such plans were made were Philadelphia, Savannah, and Washington, D.C.

Early Conservation Efforts

Almost from the earliest days of settlement, there was concern for the conservation of forests and open land in the New England countryside. As early as 1626 in the Plymouth Colony, the cutting of trees without official consent was prohibited by law. The Massachusetts Bay Colony passed the Great Ponds Act in 1641, which set aside 2,000 bodies of water, each over 10 acres in size, for such public uses as "fishing and fowling." The courts supported this conservation of land for recreational use. Pennsylvania law in 1681 required that for every five acres of forest land that were cleared, one was to be left untouched. Other laws prohibiting setting woods on fire or cutting certain types of trees were enacted long before the Revolution.

As early as the late seventeenth century, Massachusetts and Connecticut defined hunting seasons and established rules for hunting certain types of game. Although originally a means of obtaining food, hunting rapidly became a sport in the colonies. What appeared to be an inexhaustible supply of wildlife began to disappear with the advance of settlements and the destruction of the forests. Wildfowl in particular were ruthlessly hunted, especially in New England, and so unlicensed had the destruction of the heath hen become in New York that in 1708 the province determined to protect its game by providing for a closed season. Thus, before the Revolution, the colonists had shown a concern for the establishment of parks and urban open spaces and for the conservation of forests and wildlife.

NINETEENTH-CENTURY CHANGES: IMPACT OF THE INDUSTRIAL REVOLUTION

During the nineteenth century, great changes took place in both Europe and the United States. It was a time of growing democratization, advancement of scientific knowledge and technology, and huge waves of immigration from Europe to the New World. More than any other factor, the Industrial Revolution changed the way people lived, and it also had a major effect on popular patterns of recreation and leisure. By the early decades of the twentieth century, leisure was more freely available to all, and a widespread recreation movement had begun in the United States.

The Industrial Revolution extended from the late eighteenth through the twentieth century. Science and capital combined to increase production, as businessmen invested in the industrial expansion made possible by newly invented machines. Industry moved from homes and small workshops to new mills and factories with mechanical power. The invention of such devices as the spinning jenny, the water frame, the weaving machine, and the steam engine (all during the 1760s) drastically altered production methods and increased output.

Urbanization

Throughout the Western world, there was a steady shift of the population from rural areas to urban centers. Because factory wages were usually higher than those in domestic industry or agriculture, great numbers of people moved from rural areas to the cities to work. Millions of European peasant families immigrated because of crop failures, expulsion from their land, religious or social discrimination, or political unrest. During the latter part of the nineteenth century, tens of thousands of African Americans, disillusioned by the failed reconstruction, emigrated to northern cities in search of a better quality of life.

The American population increased rapidly during this period. When Andrew Jackson became president in 1829, about 12.5 million people lived in the United States. By 1850 the total had reached 23 million, and a decade later America's population was 31 million. In the large cities, the proportion of foreign-born inhabitants was quite high: 45 percent of New York City's population in 1850 was foreign born, mostly Irish and German. About 85 percent of the population in 1850 was still rural, living in areas with populations of less than 2,500. However, as more and more people moved into factory towns and large cities along the eastern seaboard or around the Great Lakes, the United States became an urban civilization.

Rural townspeople and foreign immigrants moved into the congested tenement areas of growing cities, living in quarters that were inadequate for decent family life. Often a family lived crowded in a single room under unsanitary and unsafe conditions. The new urban slums were marked by congestion and disease. Their residents were oppressed by low wages and recurrent unemployment and by monotonous and prolonged labor, including the use of young children in mills, mines, and factories and at piecework tasks at home.

Reduction in Work Hours

Throughout this period, there was steady pressure to reduce the workweek, both through industry-labor negotiation and legislation. Benjamin Hunnicutt points out that the effort to obtain shorter work hours was a critical issue in reform politics in the United States throughout the nineteenth century and up until the period of the Great Depression:

> It was an issue for the idealistic antebellum [pre–Civil War] reformers. It had a prominent place in the Populists' Omaha platform and the Bull Moose platform, and appeared in both the Democratic and Republican platforms as late as 1932.[13]

The eight-hour day had been a union objective for many years in the United States, paralleling efforts to reduce the workweek in other countries. In 1868, Congress established the eight-hour day by law for mechanics and laborers employed by or under contracts with the federal government. Following the 1868 law, labor unions made a concerted effort to obtain the eight-hour day in other areas, and in 1890 began to achieve success.

Overall, the average workweek declined from 69.7 hours per week for all industries (including agriculture) in 1860 to 61.7 hours in 1890, and to 54.9 hours in 1910. As a consequence, during the last half of the nineteenth century, concerns about increases in free time began to appear—including fears about the dangers of certain forms of play and the broader question of what the potential role of leisure might be in the coming century.

Religious Revivalism and Recreation

Fueled by a religious revival before the Civil War, there was a strong emphasis on the importance of "honest toil," during the middle and latter parts of the nineteenth century. Many Americans believed, and continue to believe, that hard work alone is sufficient for an individual to improve his or her social and economic status. Clergy, policymakers, civic leaders, and scholars were particularly concerned that new immigrants and the urban poor develop appropriate social values through hard work and appropriate, disciplined use of leisure time.

Work was considered the source of social and moral values, and therefore the proper concern of churches, which renewed their attack upon most forms of play. The churches condemned many commercial amusements as "the door to all the sins of iniquity." As late as 1844, Henry Ward Beecher, a leading minister, savagely attacked the stage, the concert hall, and the circus, charging that anyone who pandered to the public taste for commercial entertainment was a moral assassin.

GROWTH OF POPULAR PARTICIPATION IN AMERICA

Despite such antiamusement efforts, the first half of the nineteenth century saw a gradual expansion of popular amusements in the United States. The theater, which had been banned during the American Revolution, gradually gained popularity in cities along the eastern seaboard and in the South. Large theaters were built to accommodate audiences of as many as 4,000 people. Performances were usually by touring players who joined local stock companies throughout the country in presenting serious drama as well as lighthearted entertainment, which later became burlesque and vaudeville. By the 1830s, about 30 traveling shows were regularly touring the country with menageries and bands of acrobats and jugglers. Ultimately, the latter added riding and tumbling acts and developed into circuses.

Drinking also remained a popular pastime. At this time, the majority of American men were taverngoers. Printed street directories of American cities listed tavern keepers in staggering numbers. J. Larkin writes that as the nation's most popular centers of male sociability,

> taverns were often the scene of excited gaming and vicious fights and always of hard drinking, heavy smoking, and an enormous amount of alcohol-stimulated talk. . . . Taverns accommodated women as travelers, but their barroom clienteles were almost exclusively male. Apart from the dockside dives frequented by prostitutes, or the liquor-selling groceries of poor city neighborhoods, women rarely drank in public.[14]

Growing Interest in Sport

A number of sport gained their first strong impetus during the early nineteenth century. Americans enjoyed watching amateur wrestling matches, foot races, shooting events, and horse races during colonial days and along the frontier. In the early 1800s, professional promotion of sport events began as well.

Professionalism in Sport   Crowds as large as 50,000 drawn from all ranks of society attended highly publicized boating regattas, and 5- and 10-mile races of professional runners during the 1820s. The first sport promoters were owners of resorts or of commercial transportation facilities such as stagecoach lines, ferries, and, later, trolleys

Social class differences had a strong influence on sport involvement and attendance. George Will points out that professional baseball initially appealed to the brawling urban working classes:

> The sport was so tangled up with gambling and drinking that its first task was to attract a better class of fans. This it did by raising ticket prices, banning beer, not playing on Sundays, and giving free tickets to the clergy. Most important, baseball replaced wooden ball parks with permanent structures of concrete and steel [with impressive lobbies and other architectural features].[15]

and railroads. These new sport impresarios initially made their profits from transportation fares and accommodations for spectators; later, they erected grandstands and charged admission.

Horse racing flourished; both running and trotting races attracted crowds as large as 100,000 spectators. Prize fighting also gained popularity as a professional contest. It began as a brutal, bare-knuckled sport that was often prohibited by legal authorities; by the time of the Civil War, however, gloves were used and rules established, and boxing exhibitions were becoming accepted. Baseball was enjoyed as a casual diversion in the towns of New England through the early decades of the nineteenth century (in the form of "rounders" or "townball"), and amateur teams, often organized by occupation (merchants and clerks or shipwrights and mechanics), were playing on the commons of large eastern cities by the mid-1850s.

CHANGING ATTITUDES TOWARD PLAY

During the last half of the nineteenth century, the Industrial Revolution was flourishing, with factories, expansion of urban areas, and railroads criss-crossing the country. Free public education had become a reality in most regions of the country, and health care and life expectancy were improving. As the industrial labor force began to organize into craft unions, working conditions improved, levels of pay increased, and the hours of work were cut back. Children, who had worked long, hard hours in factories, mines, and big-city sweatshops, were freed of this burden through child labor legislation.

Gradually, the climate grew more receptive toward play and leisure. Although the work ethic was still widely accepted and there was almost no public provision for recreation, leisure was about to expand sharply. The strong disapproval of play that had characterized the colonial period began to disappear.

By the 1880s and 1890s, church leaders recognized that religion could no longer arbitrarily condemn all play and offered "sanctified amusement and recreation" as alternatives to undesirable play. Many churches made provisions for libraries, gymnasiums, and assembly rooms.

The growth of popular amusements, such as music, vaudeville, theater, and dance, that characterized the first half of the century became even more pronounced. Popular hobbies such as photography caught on and were frequently linked to new outdoor recreation pursuits. Sport was probably the largest single area of expanded leisure participation, with increasing interest being shown in tennis, archery, bowling, skating, bicycling, and team games such as baseball, basketball, and football.

Athletic and outdoor pastimes steadily became more socially acceptable. Skating became a vogue in the 1850s, and rowing and sailing also grew popular, especially for the upper social classes. The Muscular Christianity movement—so named because of the support given to it by leading church figures and because sport and physical activity were thought to build morality and good character—had its greatest influence in schools and colleges, which began to initiate programs of physical education and athletic competition. In addition, the newly founded Young Men's Christian Association (YMCA) based its program on active physical recreation.

College Sport

In the United States, colleges initiated their first competitive sports programs. In colonial New England, youthful students had engaged in many pastimes, with some tolerated by college authorities and others prohibited. The first college clubs had been founded as early as 1717, and social clubs were in full swing by the 1780s and 1790s. By the early nineteenth century, most U.S. colleges had more or less officially recognized clubs and their social activities. The founding of social fraternities in the 1840s and the building of college gymnasiums in the 1860s added to the social life and physical recreation of students.

Intercollegiate sport competition in rowing, baseball, track, and football was organized. The first known intercollegiate football game was between Princeton and Rutgers in 1869; interest spread rapidly, and by the late 1880s college football games were attracting as many as 40,000 spectators.

Amateur Sport

Track and field events were widely promoted by amateur athletic clubs, some of which, like the New York Athletic Club, had many influential members who formed the Amateur Athletic Union and developed rules to govern amateur sport competition. Gymnastic instruction and games were sponsored by the German *turnvereins*, the Czech *sokols*, and the YMCA, which had established some 260 large gymnasiums around the country by the 1880s and was a leader in sport activities.

Other Activities

Other popular pastimes included croquet, archery, lawn tennis, and roller-skating, which became so popular that skating rinks were built to accommodate thousands of skaters and spectators. Women began to participate in recreational pastimes, enjoying gymnastics, dance, and other athletics in school and college physical education programs. Bicycling was introduced in the 1870s, and within a few years hundreds of thousands of people had become enthusiasts. During the last decades of the nineteenth century, there was a growing vogue for outdoor activities. Americans began to enjoy hiking and mountain climbing, fishing and hunting, camping in national forests and state parks, and nature photography.

During the late 1800s, a number of economic factors also combined to promote sport interest. With rising wages and a shorter workweek, many workers began to take part in organized sport on newly developed sports fields in city parks. Cheap train service carried players and fans to games, and newspapers publicized major sporting events to build circulation.

GROWTH OF COMMERCIAL AMUSEMENTS

Particularly in larger cities, new forms of commercial amusement sprang up or expanded during the nineteenth century. The theater, in its various forms, was more popular than ever. Dime museums, dance halls, shooting galleries, bowling alleys, billiard parlors, beer gardens, and saloons provided a new world of entertainment for pay. In addition to these, many cities had "red light districts" where houses of prostitution flourished. Drinking, gambling, and commercial vice gradually became serious social problems, particularly when protected by a tacit alliance between criminal figures and big-city political machines.

Amusement parks grew on the outskirts of cities and towns, often established by new rapid transit companies offering reduced-fare rides to the parks in gaily decorated trolley cars. Amusement parks featured such varied attractions as parachute jumps, open-air theaters, band concerts, professional bicycle races, freak shows, games of chance, and shooting galleries. Roller coasters, fun houses, and midget-car tracks also became popular.

Concerns About Leisure

Intellectual and political leaders raised searching questions about the growing amusement industry. The English author Lord Lytton commented, "The social civilization of a people is always and infallibly indicated by the intellectual character of its amusements." In 1876, Horace Greeley, a leading American journalist, observed that although there were teachers for every art, science, and "elegy," there were no "professors of play." He asked, "Who will teach us incessant workers how to achieve leisure and enjoy it?" And, in 1880, President James Garfield declared in a speech at Lake Chautauqua, "We may divide the whole struggle of the human race into two chapters: first, the fight to get leisure; and then the second fight of civilization—what shall we do with our leisure when we get it."

This new concern was an inevitable consequence of the Industrial Revolution. Americans now lived in greater numbers in large cities, where the traditional social activities of the past and the opportunity for casual play were no longer available.

THE BEGINNING RECREATION MOVEMENT

The period extending from the mid-nineteenth through the early twentieth century is referred to by recreation scholars as the *public recreation movement*. The period was characterized by the widespread development of organized recreation activities and facilities by government and voluntary agencies with the intent of achieving desirable social outcomes. There were four major streams of development during the public recreation movement: the adult education movement; the development of national, state, and municipal parks; the establishment of voluntary organizations; and the playground movement.

The Adult Education Movement

During the early nineteenth century, there was considerable civic concern for improving intellectual cultivation and providing continuing education for adults. Again, this was found in other nations as well; in France, workers' societies were determined to gain shorter workdays and more leisure time for adult study and cultural activities, and they pressed vigorously for the development of popular lectures, adult education courses, and municipal libraries.

In the United States, there was a growing conviction that leisure, properly used, could contribute to the idealistic liberal values that were part of the American intellectual heritage. As early as the founding of the republic, such leaders as Thomas Jefferson and John Adams envisioned the growth of a rich democratic culture. Adams wrote of his children's and America's future as follows:

> I must study Politicks and War that my sons may have liberty to study Mathematicks and Philosophy. My sons ought to study Mathematicks and Philosophy, Geography, Natural History, Naval Architecture, Navigation, Commerce and Agriculture, in order to give their Children a right to study Painting, Poetry, Musick, Architecture, Statuary, Tapestry and Porcelaine.[16]

One of the means of achieving this dream took the form of the Lyceum movement, a national organization with more than 900 local chapters. Its program consisted chiefly of lectures, readings, and other educational events, reflecting the view that all citizens should be educated in order to participate knowledgeably in affairs of government.

The Lyceum movement was widely promoted by such organizations as Chautauqua, which sponsored both a lecture circuit and a leading summer camp program in upstate New York for adults and families, with varied cultural activities, sport, lectures, and other educational features. While the professed purpose of Chautauqua was education, it actually provided substantial entertainment and amusement to its audiences as well. By the twentieth century, circuit Chautauquas were formed, in a fusion of the Lyceum movement and independent Chautauquas, to provide educational programs, culture, and entertainment.

■ *Old Faithful and the geysers of Yellowstone have made this first national park a popular travel destination for over 130 years.*

A closely related development was the expansion of reading as a recreational experience, which was furthered by the widespread growth of free public libraries. This development was linked to the adoption of compulsory universal education and to the increasing need for better-educated workers in the nation's industrial system. As an example of the growing interest in cultural activity, the arts and crafts movement found its largest following in the United States in the beginning of the twentieth century. Between 1896 and 1915, thousands of organized groups were established throughout the country to bring artists and patrons together, sponsor exhibits and publications, and promote the teaching of art in the schools.

The Development of National, State, and Municipal Parks

Concern for preservation of the natural heritage of the United States in an era of increasing industrialization and despoilment of natural resources began in the nineteenth century. The first conservation action was in 1864, when Congress set aside an extensive area of wilderness primarily for public recreational use, consisting of the Yosemite Valley and the Mariposa Grove of Big Trees in California. This later became a national park. The first designated national park was Yellowstone, founded in 1872. In 1892, the Sierra Club was founded by John Muir, a leading Scottish-born conservationist who, along with Theodore Roosevelt, encouraged national interest in the outdoors and ultimately the establishment of the National Park Service.

All such developments did not lend themselves immediately to an emphasis on recreation. The primary purpose of the national parks at the outset was to preserve the nation's natural heritage and wildlife. This contrasted sharply with the Canadian approach to wilderness, which saw it as primitive and untamed. Parks, as in Great

Central Park remains one of the great urban parks in the world. Each year over 25 million people visit the park.

Britain and Europe, were seen as landscaped gardens, and intensive development for recreation and tourism guided early Canadian policy. Indeed, Banff National Park was initially a health spa, and early provincial parks were designed to be health resorts.[17]

State Parks   As federal park development gained momentum in the United States, state governments also became concerned with the preservation of their forest areas and wildlife. As early as 1867, Michigan and Wisconsin established fact-finding committees to explore the problem of forest conservation; their example was followed shortly by Maine and other eastern states. Within two decades, several states had established forestry commissions. Between 1864 and 1900, the first state parks were established, as were a number of state forest preserves and historic parks.

Municipal Parks   Until the nineteenth century, North America lagged far behind Europe in the development of municipal parks, partly because this continent had no aristocracy with large cultivated estates, hunting grounds, and elaborate gardens that could be turned over to the public. The first major park to be developed in an American city was Central Park in New York; its design and the philosophy on which it was based strongly influenced other large cities during the latter half of the nineteenth century.

There long had been a need for open space in New York City. During the first 30 years of the nineteenth century, plans were made for several open squares to total about 450 acres, but these were not carried out completely. By the early 1850s, the entire amount of public open space in Manhattan totaled only 117 acres. Pressure mounted among the citizens of the city for a major park that would provide relief from stone and concrete. The poet William Cullen Bryant wrote:

> Commerce is devouring inch by inch the coast of the island, and if we would rescue any part of it for health and recreation it must be done now. All large cities have their extensive public grounds and gardens, Madrid and Mexico [City] their Alamedas, London its Regent's Park, Paris its Champs Elysées, and Vienna its Prater.[18]

When the public will could no longer be denied, legislation was passed in 1856 to establish a park in New York City. Construction of the 843-acre site began in 1857. Central Park, designed by landscape architects Frederick Law Olmsted and Calvert Vaux, was completely man-made: "Every foot of the park's surface, every tree and bush, as well as every arch, roadway and walk has been fixed where it is with a purpose." The dominant need was to provide, within the densely populated heart of

There was concern about the reckless and haphazard course of urban growth in the nineteenth century, which had been guided almost exclusively by narrow commercial interests. Reformers were disturbed not only by the obvious "social failures"—the growing number of criminals, prostitutes, alcoholics, and insane—but also by the effects of the relentless commercial environment on the culture of cities. Large public parks came to be seen as "necessary institutions of democratic recreation and indispensable antidotes to urban anomie."

an immense metropolis, "refreshment of the mind and the nerves" for city dwellers through the provision of greenery and scenic vistas. The park was to be heavily wooded and to have the appearance of rural scenery, with roadways screened from the eyes of park users wherever possible. Recreational pursuits permitted in the park included walking, pleasure driving, ice skating in the winter, and boating—but not organized or structured sport. It also was designed to provide needed social controls to prevent misuse of the park environment or destructive behavior by the "lower" classes.

County Park Systems Planning for what was to become the nation's first county park system began in Essex County, New Jersey. Bordering the crowded industrial city of Newark, it was outlined in a comprehensive proposal in 1894 that promised that the entire cost of the park project would be realized through tax revenues from increased property values. Set in motion in the following year, the Essex County park system proved to be a great success and set a model to be followed by hundreds of other county and special district park agencies throughout the United States in the early 1900s.

Establishment of Voluntary Organizations

During the nineteenth century, a number of voluntary (privately sponsored, nonprofit) organizations were founded that played an important role in providing recreation services, chiefly for children and youth. In many cases, voluntary organizations were the outgrowth of their founders' desires to put religious principles into action through direct service to the unprivileged. The widespread establishment of voluntary organizations in the nineteenth and early twentieth centuries should be viewed as both a religious and a social movement. One such body was the Young Men's Christian Association, founded in Boston in 1851 and followed by the Young Women's Christian Association (YWCA) 15 years later. At first, the Y's provided fellowship between youth and adults for religious purposes. They gradually enlarged their programs, however, to include gymnastics, sport, and other recreational and social activities.

Another type of voluntary agency that offered significant leisure programs was the settlement house—neighborhood centers established in the slum sections of the East and Midwest. Among the first were University Settlement, founded in New York City in 1886, and Hull House, founded in Chicago in 1889. Their staffs sought to help poor people, particularly immigrants, adjust to modern urban life by providing services concerned with education, family life, and community improvement.

The Playground Movement

To understand the need for playgrounds in cities and towns, it is necessary to know the living conditions of poor people during the latter decades of the nineteenth century.

The wave of urbanization that had begun earlier now reached its peak. The urban population more than doubled—from 14 to 30 million—between 1880 and 1900 alone. By the century's end, there were 28 cities with over 100,000 residents because of the recent waves of migration. A leading example was New York, where nearly five of every six of the city's 1.5 million residents lived in tenements in 1891. Social reformers of the period described these buildings as crowded, with dark hallways, filthy cellars, and inadequate cooking and bathroom facilities. In neighborhoods populated by poor immigrants, there was a tremendous amount of crime, gambling, gang violence, and prostitution.

Boston Sand Garden: A Beginning   Within poor working class neighborhoods, there were few safe places where children might play. The first such facility—and the one that is generally regarded as a landmark in the development of the recreation movement in the United States—was the Boston Sand Garden. The city of Boston had been the arena for many important developments in the park and recreation movement in the United States. The Boston Common, established in 1634, generally has been regarded as the first municipal park; a 48-acre area of green, rolling hills and shade trees, it is located in the heart of the city. Boston was also the site of the first public garden with the establishment of an outstanding botanic garden in 1838.

The famous Boston Sand Garden was the first playground in the country designed specifically for children. A group of public-spirited citizens had a pile of sand placed behind the Parmenter Street Chapel in a working class district. Young children in the neighborhood came to play in the sand with wooden shovels. Supervision was voluntary at first, but by 1887 when 10 such centers were opened, women were employed to supervise the children. Two years later, the city of Boston began to contribute funds to support the sand gardens. So it was that citizens, on a voluntary basis, began to provide play opportunities for young children.

New York's First Playgrounds   In the nation's largest city, Walter Vrooman, founder of the New York Society for Parks and Playgrounds, directed the public's attention to the fact that in 1890 there were 350,000 children without a single public playground of their own. Although the city now had almost 6,000 acres of parkland, none of it was set aside specifically for children. Civic leaders pointed out that children of working parents lacked supervision and were permitted to grow up subject to various temptations. Vrooman wrote that such children

> are driven from their crowded homes in the morning . . . are chased from the streets by the police when they attempt to play, and beaten with the broom handle of the janitor's wife when found in the hallway, or on the stairs. No wonder they learn to chew and smoke tobacco before they can read, and take a fiendish delight in breaking windows, in petty thievery, and in gambling their pennies.[19]

Gradually, the pressure mounted. Two small model playgrounds were established in poor areas of the city in 1889 and 1891 by the newly formed New York Society for Parks and Playgrounds, with support from private donors. Gradually, the city assumed financial and legal responsibility as many additional playgrounds were built in the years that followed, often attached to schools.

The period between 1880 and 1900 was of critical importance to the development of urban recreation and park programs. More than 80 cities initiated park systems; a lesser number established "sand gardens," and, shortly after, playgrounds. Illinois passed a law permitting the establishment of local park districts in which two or more municipalities might join together to operate park systems.

EFFECTS OF RACIAL AND ETHNIC DISCRIMINATION

Throughout this period, public and nonprofit youth-serving organizations often discriminated against members of racial or ethnic minorities. As late as the 1930s and 1940s, prejudice against those perceived as lower-class "undesirables" or those from less-favored European nations was evidenced in many organizations. Such practices reflected widespread attitudes of snobbery, as well as the nativist political agitation of the nineteenth century that opposed the flow of immigration from Europe, preached hatred against Catholics and Jews, and barred citizens of color from mainstream American life.

Prejudice Against Minorities

Generally, the most severe discrimination was leveled against African Americans, who, though no longer slaves, were kept in a position of economic servitude through the practice of sharecropping and were without civil, political, or judicial rights in the southern and border states. However, there was an extreme degree of prejudice against Mexican Americans and other Hispanics of mixed racial origins. For example, Anglo settlers in Texas regarded Mexicans as savage "heathens" who historically practiced human sacrifice, and saw them as a decadent and inferior people. Most prejudice was expressed in racial terms.

A popular journal, the *Southern Review,* expressed the dominant feeling of many white Americans at this time with respect to *mongrelism,* the term often applied to mixing among different racial groups. In time, intermarriage between whites and blacks or Native Americans was defined as *miscegenation* and forbidden by law throughout much of the country.

There was also widespread prejudice expressed against Asian Americans, mostly Chinese nationals who began to arrive in California in the mid-1800s and who worked on the transcontinental railroad. As the number of Asians grew, so did xenophobia. Americans viewed them as heathens who could not readily be assimilated within the nation's essentially Anglo-Saxon framework, and condemned them as unsanitary, immoral, and criminal. Based on such prejudice, Chinese were often the victims of mob violence, particularly at times of national depression, and were barred from entry into the United States by the Oriental Exclusion Acts of 1882 and 1902.

Similar views were frequently expressed against Americans of African origin, who were increasingly barred from social contact, economic opportunity, or recreational involvement with whites by a wave of state legislation and local ordinances in the late nineteenth and early twentieth centuries.

RECREATION AND PARKS: EARLY TWENTIETH CENTURY

For the majority of Americans, however, the beginning of the twentieth century was an exciting period marked by growing economic and recreational opportunity. By 1900,

14 cities had made provisions for supervised play facilities. Among the leading cities were Boston, Providence, Philadelphia, Pittsburgh, Baltimore, Chicago, Milwaukee, Cleveland, Denver, and Minneapolis.

At the same time, municipal parks became well established throughout the United States. In addition to the urban parks mentioned earlier, the first metropolitan park system was established by Boston in 1892. In the West, San Francisco and Sacramento in California as well as Salt Lake City, Utah, were among the first to incorporate large open spaces in town planning before 1900. The New England Association of Park Superintendents, the predecessor of the American Institute of Park Executives, was established in 1898 to bring together park superintendents and promote their professional concerns.

Growth of Public Recreation and Park Agencies

Gradually, the concept that city governments should provide recreation facilities, programs, and services became widely accepted. By 1906, 41 cities were sponsoring public recreation programs, and by 1920, the number was 465. More and more states passed laws authorizing local governments to operate recreation programs, and between 1925 and 1935 the number of municipal recreation buildings quadrupled.

Municipalities were also discovering new ways to add parks. Many acquired areas outside their city limits, while others required that new real estate subdivision plans include the dedication of space for recreation. Some cities acquired major park properties through gifts. The pattern that began to develop was one of placing a network of small, intensively used playgrounds throughout the cities, particularly in neighborhoods of working-class families, and placing larger parks in outlying areas.

Federal Park Expansion

As president, Theodore Roosevelt, a dedicated outdoorsman, encouraged the acquisition of numerous new areas for the federal park system, including many new forest preserves, historic and scientific sites, and wildlife refuges. Thanks in part to his assistance and support, the Reclamation Act of 1902, which authorized reservoir-building irrigation systems in the West, was passed, along with the Antiquities Act of 1906, which designated the first national monuments. Establishment of the U.S. Forest Service in 1905 and of the National Park Service 11 years later helped place many of the scattered forests, parks, and other sites under more clearly defined policies for acquisition, development, and use.

EMERGENCE OF THE RECREATION MOVEMENT: THREE PIONEERS

As the recreation field developed during the first three decades of the twentieth century, several men and women emerged as influential advocates of play and recreation. Three of the most effective were Joseph Lee, Luther Halsey Gulick, and Jane Addams.

Joseph Lee

Regarded as the "father" of the playground movement, Joseph Lee was a lawyer and philanthropist who came from a wealthy New England family. Born in 1862, he took part in a survey of play opportunities conducted by the Family Welfare Society of Boston in 1882. Shocked to see boys arrested for playing in the streets, he organized a playground for them in an open lot, which he helped supervise. In 1898, Lee helped create a model playground on Columbus Avenue in Boston that included a play area for small children, a boys' section, a sport field, and individual gardens. Lee's influence soon expanded; he was in great demand as a speaker and writer on playgrounds and served as vice president for public recreation of the American Civic Association. President of the Playground Association of America for 27 years, he was also the president and leading lecturer of the National Recreation School, a one-year program for carefully selected college graduates.

Lee's view of play was idealistic and purposeful. In *Play in Education*, he outlined a set of major play instincts that he believed all children shared and that governed the specific nature of play activities. He believed that play forms had to be taught and that this process required capable leadership. Lee did not make a sharp distinction between work and play, but saw them as closely related expressions of the impulses to achieve, to explore, to excel, and to master.

Luther Halsey Gulick

Another leading figure in the early recreation movement was Luther Halsey Gulick. A physician by training, he developed a special interest in physical education and recreation. He also had a strong religious orientation, as did many of the early play leaders. Beginning in 1887, Dr. Gulick headed the first summer school of "special training for gymnasium instructors" at the School for Christian Workers (now Springfield College) in Massachusetts. He was active in the YMCAs in Canada and the United States, was the first president of the Camp Fire Girls, and was instrumental in the establishment of the Playground Association of America in 1906. Gulick lectured extensively on the significance of play and recreation and taught a course in the psychology of play as early as 1899. He also vigorously promoted expanded recreation programs for girls and women.

Gulick distinguished play from recreation. He defined play as "doing that which we want to do, without reference primarily to any ulterior end, but simply for the joy of the process." But, he went on to say, play is not less serious than work:

> The boy who is playing football with intensity needs recreation as much as does the inventor who is working intensely at his invention. Play can be more exhausting than work, because one can play much harder than one can work. No one would dream of pushing a boy in school as hard as he pushes himself in a football game. If there is any difference of intensity between play and work, the difference is in favor of play. Play is the result of desire; for that reason it is often carried on with more vigor than work.[20]

The Radical Women of Hull House

Jane Addams and Ellen Gates Starr were among the first college-educated women in the United States to dedicate their lives to public service. Addams and Starr opened the Hull House Settlement in 1889. Although Addams, Starr, and their colleagues were sometimes viewed as radical and dangerous, their work is a testament to the ability of women to collectively improve social conditions. The women of Hull House were directly involved in the establishment of the following social programs and movements of the Industrial Revolution:

- Immigrant aid and protection
- Public school nursing
- Labor reform
- Development of public playgrounds and kindergarten
- Industrial medicine
- Establishment of the juvenile court system
- Birth control
- Consumer advocacy
- Antialcohol and drug legislation
- Pure food and drug laws
- Public sanitation
- Elimination of child labor
- Infant and maternity health care
- Child day care
- Visiting nurses
- Public school lunches
- Industrial health and safety
- Peace initiatives
- Suffrage

Jane Addams

Jane Addams was a social work pioneer who established Hull House in Chicago. Her interest in the needs of children and youth, and in the lives of immigrant families and the poor in America's great cities, led her to develop outstanding programs of educational, social, and recreational activities. Beyond this, she was a leading feminist pioneer and so active a reformer that she was known as "the most dangerous woman in America."

Mary Duncan points out that Jane Addams, along with a number of other recreation and park leaders in the late nineteenth and early twentieth centuries, was part of a wider radical reform movement in America's cities. Joining with muckraking editors, writers, ministers, and other social activists, they continually fought city hall, organized labor strikes, marched in the street, gave public speeches, and wrote award-winning articles deploring the living conditions of the poor. The issues and problems they faced were well defined: slavery, the aftermath of the Civil War, thousands of new immigrants, slums, child labor, disease, the suffrage movement, World War I, and a rapidly industrializing nation.[21]

Contrasting Roles of Recreation Pioneers

Although Lee, Gulick, and Addams were described as muckraking radicals, it is clear that they also were individuals who worked through the major societal institutions of government and voluntary agencies. Addams, for example, helped to found the Playground Association of America, encouraged the Chicago School Board's involvement in playground and recreational sport programs, and supported the early development of the Chicago Park District. Indeed, these early recreation pioneers often walked a tightrope between their desire on the one hand to promote individuality, to give youth the opportunity for creative development, and to overcome old barriers of prejudice and class distinction and the need on the other hand to maintain order and control and to indoctrinate youth with traditional social goals.

While these three fought to help the downtrodden and illiterate immigrant families living in crowded urban slums, they were also using recreation to maintain the status quo and enforce traditional values. Play was seen as a means of "Americanizing" foreigners and perpetuating and protecting the traditional small-town, moralistic, white Anglo-Saxon heritage that had dominated national culture over the past century. Recreation would be used as a way of repressing the "overwhelming temptation of illicit and soul-destroying pleasures."

EMERGING NEW LIFESTYLES

Such views of recreation, play, and leisure were not shared by the entire population. The early twentieth century was a time when the traditional Victorian mentality that had been taught and enforced by the home, school, and church was being challenged. For the first time, many young women took jobs in business and industry in cities throughout the country. With relative freedom from disapproving, stern parental authority, and with money to spend, they frequented commercial dance halls, boat rides, drinking saloons, social clubs, and other sources of popular entertainment. Kathy Peiss describes the new freedom for working-class youth in general:

> They fled the tenements for the streets, dance halls, and theaters, generally bypassing their fathers' saloons and lodges. Adolescents formed social clubs, organized entertainments, and patronized new commercial amusements, shaping, in effect, a working-class youth culture expressed through leisure activity.[22]

Part of what appealed to young people were the playgrounds, parks, public beaches, and picnic grounds. However, often these were considered too tame and unexciting, and more and more young people became attracted to commercial forms of entertainment involving liquor, dancing, and sex that were viewed by the establishment as immoral and dangerous. Increasingly, organized recreation programs were promoted by churches, law enforcement agencies, and civic associations in an attempt to resist the new, hedonistic forms of play. They sought to promote traditional, idealistic activities, such as youth sport, music, games, crafts, and dramatic activities, as a way to repress the urge for more "sinful" behavior.

PUBLIC CONCERNS ABOUT THE USE OF LEISURE

To some degree, the support for public recreation was based on the fear that without public programs and facilities, adult leisure would be used unwisely. Many industrial leaders and civic officials believed that the growth of leisure for the working classes represented a dangerous trend; when unemployment increased, they expressed concern about what idle men would do with their time. Similarly, when the eight-hour workday laws first came under discussion, temperance societies prepared for increased drunkenness, and social reformers held international conferences on the worker's spare time and ways to use it constructively.

The major concern, however, was for children and youth in the large cities and their need for healthful and safe places to play. Indeed, much "juvenile delinquency" arose from children being arrested for playing on city streets. Authorities during this period reported reduced rates of juvenile delinquency in slum areas where playgrounds had been established. A probation officer of the juvenile court in Milwaukee described "a very noticeable dropping off of boys coming before the court" and a disappearance of "dangerous gangs," concluding that playgrounds and social centers were "saviors" for American youth. Typically, the judge of the juvenile department of the Orange County Court in Anaheim, California, noted that after the opening of supervised playgrounds in the public park in the summer of 1924, juvenile delinquency decreased. During the first six months of 1925, it was 70 percent less than for the same period in 1924.[23]

Concern About Commercial Amusements

At this time, there was also fear that unregulated and unsupervised places of commercial amusement posed a serious threat to children and youth. Commercially sponsored forms of entertainment and recreation had grown rapidly during the early twentieth century, with many new pool and billiard parlors, dance halls, vaudeville shows and burlesque, and other amusement attractions. In major cities such as Milwaukee, Detroit, Kansas City, and San Francisco, extensive recreation surveys scrutinized the nature of commercial amusements, the extent and kind of their patronage, and their character. There was much concern about movies and stage performances, with frequent charges that they were immoral and led to the sexual corruption of youth.

A high percentage of privately operated dance halls had attached saloons that were freely patronized by young girls. Dancing seemed to be only a secondary consideration. Pickups occurred regularly, often of young girls who had come to cities from the nation's farms and small towns with a presumed degree of innocence; so-called white slavers, who trapped or recruited girls and women into prostitution, appeared to ply their trade with little interference. Dance halls were often attached to disreputable rooming houses, and girls in their early and middle teens were easily recruited into prostitution.

The same studies that examined commercial amusements also surveyed the socially approved forms of recreation. They found that in many cities the schools were closed in the evening and throughout the summer, that libraries closed at night and on weekends, that churches closed for the summer, and that publicly provided forms of recreation were at a minimum. Jane Addams concluded that the city had "turned over the provision for public recreation to the most evil-minded and the most unscrupulous members of the community." Gradually, pressure mounted for more effective control of places of public amusement. In city after city, permits were required for operating dance halls, pool parlors, and bowling alleys, and for the sale of liquor.

There was also a fear that Americans were moving away from the traditional active ways of using their leisure to pursuits in which they were passive spectators. Some critics commented that instead of believing in the wholesome love of play, Americans now had a love of being "played upon." It had become wholly outdated to make one's own fun.

Emerging Mass Culture

Such complaints and fears were the inevitable reactions of civic leaders to what they perceived to be a threat to traditional morality and values. The reality is that the United States in the early decades of the twentieth century was undergoing massive changes in response to changing economic and social conditions. These included the emergence of new middle-class and working-class people who had the time and money to spend on leisure, as well as a steady infusion of varied ethnic peoples who contributed new ideas and values to American society. Part of the change involved a growing rejection of authoritarian family structures and church-dominated social values, as well as a readiness to accept new kinds of roles for young people and women. All of these influences resulted in a new mass culture that emerged during the new century. John Kasson writes:

> At the turn of the century this culture was still in the process of formation and not fully incorporated into the life of society as a whole. Its purest expression at this time lay in the realm of commercial amusements, which were creating symbols of the new cultural order.[24]

Kasson goes on to point out that nineteenth-century America was governed by a coherent set of values—highly Victorian in nature and directed by a self-conscious elite group of ministers, educators, and reformers drawn chiefly from the Protestant middle class of the urban Northeast. These apostles of culture preached the values of character, moral integrity, self-control, sobriety, and industriousness. They believed that leisure should be spent in ways that were edifying and that had moral and social utility. They founded museums, art galleries, libraries, and symphony orchestras, and they lent moral sanction to the recreation and park movement. However, they were unable to exert a significant influence on the growing masses of urban working classes and new immigrant groups.

MAJOR FORCES PROMOTING ORGANIZED RECREATION SERVICES

At the same time that mass culture was providing new kinds of pastimes that challenged traditional community values and standards, the forces that sought to guide the American public in what they regarded as constructive uses of leisure were becoming active.

As a single example of the new craze for excitement and freedom in leisure, a host of amusement parks were developed close to various cities around the country. Typically, they put together a mélange of popular attractions, including bathing facilities, band pavilions, dance halls, vaudeville theaters, sideshows, circus attractions, freak displays, food and drink counters, and daredevil rides of every description.

Growth of Voluntary Organizations

In the opening decades of the twentieth century, a number of important youth-serving, nonprofit organizations were formed, either on a local basis or through nationally organized movements or federations. The National Association of Boys' Clubs was founded in 1906, the Boy Scouts and the Camp Fire Girls in 1910, and the Girl Scouts in 1912. Major civic clubs and community service groups such as the Rotary Club, Kiwanis Club, and the Lions Club were also founded between 1910 and 1917.

By the end of the 1920s, these organizations had become widely established in American life and were serving substantial numbers of young people. One of every seven boys in the appropriate age group in the United States was a Scout. The YMCA and YWCA had more than 1.5 million members in 1926. In contemporary society, voluntary organizations are a significant provider of community recreation services that are utilized by tens of millions of children and adults.

Playground Association of America

In the early 1900s, leading recreation directors called for a conference to promote public awareness of and effective practices in the field of leisure services. Under the leadership of Luther Halsey Gulick, representatives of park, recreation, and school boards throughout the United States met in Washington, D.C., in April 1906. Unanimously agreeing upon the need for a national organization, the conference members drew up a constitution and selected Gulick as the first president of the Playground Association of America. The organization had President Theodore Roosevelt's strong support.

A basic purpose of the Playground Association was to develop informational and promotional services to assist people of all ages in using leisure time constructively. Field workers traveled from city to city, meeting with public officials and citizens' groups and helping in the development of playgrounds and recreation programs. In order to promote professional training, the association developed *The Normal Course in Play*, a curriculum plan of courses on play leadership on several levels.

In keeping with its broadening emphasis, the organization changed its name in 1911 to the Playground and Recreation Association of America, and in 1926 to the National Recreation Association. It sought to provide the public with a broader concept of recreation and leisure, and to promote recreation as an area of government responsibility.

Recreation Programs in World War I

The nation's rapid mobilization during World War I revealed that communities adjacent to army and navy stations and training camps needed more adequate programs of recreation. The Council of National Defense and the War Department Commission on Training Camp Activities asked the Playground and Recreation Association to assist in the creation of a national organization to provide wartime community recreation programs. The association established the War Camp Community Service (WCCS), which utilized the recreation resources of several hundred communities near military camps to provide wholesome recreation activities for both military personnel and civilians.

At its peak, WCCS employed a national staff of approximately 3,000 paid workers who organized programs in 755 cities with the help of more than 500,000 volunteers. At other military bases in the United States and Europe, organizations such as the Young Men's Christian Association sponsored canteens and other morale-boosting services.

Role of the Schools

As indicated earlier, a number of urban school boards initiated after-school and vacation play programs as early as the 1890s. This trend continued in the twentieth century. Playground programs were begun in Rochester, New York, in 1907; in Milwaukee, Wisconsin, in 1911; and in Los Angeles, California, in 1914. These pioneering efforts were strongly supported by the National Education Association, which recommended that public school buildings be used for community recreation and social activities.

With such support, public opinion encouraged the expansion of organized playground and public recreation programs in American communities. Between 1910 and 1930, thousands of school systems established extensive programs of extracurricular activities, particularly in sport, publications, hobbies, and social- and academic-related fields. In 1919, the first college curriculum in recreation was established at Virginia Commonwealth University.

In addition to playgrounds, other facilities of the schools that could be useful for recreational purposes were assembly rooms and gymnasiums, swimming pools, music and arts rooms, and outdoor areas for sport and gardening. Education for the "worthy use of leisure" was vigorously supported as an important goal for secondary schools throughout the United States.

Outdoor Recreation Developments

The role of the federal and state governments in promoting outdoor recreation was enlarged by the establishment of the National Park Service in 1916 and an accelerated pattern of acquisition and development of outdoor areas by the U.S. Forest Service. In 1921, Stephen Mather, director of the National Park Service, called for a national conference on state parks. This meeting made it clear that the Park Service was primarily to acquire and administer areas of national significance; it led to the recommendation that state governments take more responsibility for acquiring sites of lesser interest or value.

Park administrators began to give active recreation a higher priority in park design and operation. The founding of the American Association of Zoological Parks and

Aquariums in 1924 was an indication that specialized recreational uses of parks were becoming widespread in American communities.

The End of Shorter Hours

At the same time that the recreation movement continued to gain impetus, a reverse trend took place as the movement to shorten the workweek and provide workers with more free time gradually slackened. Benjamin Hunnicutt points out that the most dramatic increase in free time occurred in the period between 1901 and 1921, when the average workweek dropped from 58.4 hours to 48.4 hours, a decline never before or since equaled.[25]

Since the mid-nineteenth century, shorter hours and higher wages had been a campaign issue for progressive politicians. Union pressure, legislation, and court decisions achieved the eight-hour day in jobs under federal contracts, sections of the railroad industry, and certain hazardous occupations. The policy was supported by the findings of scientific management experts such as Frederick Taylor, who argued that workers' efficiency declined significantly after eight hours. It also responded to a trend in other industrialized nations, such as France, Germany, Italy, and Belgium, to approve legal restriction of working time, based on the eight-hour day or 48-hour workweek.

New problems began to arise in the American economy, though, as overproduction and "economic maturity" left the nation with an excess of goods and services. Many leading businessmen and economists began to promote a "New Gospel of Consumption" during the 1920s. They argued that the way to stimulate the economy was not to provide more leisure, but to increase productivity and public spending on a broad range of consumer goods.

IMPACT OF THE GREAT DEPRESSION

Following the flourishing 1920s, the Great Depression of the 1930s mired the United States—and much of the industrial world—in a period of almost total despair. The Depression resulted in mass unemployment and involuntary idleness for American workers. By the end of 1932, an estimated 15 million people, nearly one-third of the labor force, were unemployed. Individuals who were employed also experienced greater free time as the average workweek declined. During this period, scholars and public officials became concerned that leisure had become too commercial and passive and would contribute to the decline of American culture. Furthermore, there was widespread concern that excessive free time was linked to crime.

In response to these concerns and in conjunction with a broad plan to combat the effects of the Depression, the federal government soon instituted a number of emergency work programs related to recreation. The Federal Emergency Relief Administration, established early in 1933, financed construction of recreation facilities such as parks and swimming pools and hired recreation leaders from the relief rolls. A second agency, the Civil Works Administration, was given the task of finding jobs for four million people in 30 days! Among other tasks, this agency built or improved 3,500 playgrounds and athletic fields in a few months.[26]

Both the National Youth Administration and the Civilian Conservation Corps carried out numerous work projects involving the construction of recreational facilities.

During the five years from 1932 to 1937, the federal government spent an estimated $1.5 billion developing camps, buildings, picnic grounds, trails, swimming pools, and other facilities. The Civilian Conservation Corps helped to establish state park systems in a number of states that had no organized park programs before 1933. The Works Progress Administration allocated $11 billion or 30 percent of their budget to recreation-related projects that spanned the nation and included 12,700 playgrounds, 8,500 gymnasiums or recreation buildings, 750 swimming pools, 1,000 ice skating rinks, and 64 ski jumps.[27] These programs initiated under President Franklin D. Roosevelt's New Deal had a beneficial effect on the development of the recreation and park movement throughout the United States: They made it clear that leisure was an important responsibility of government.

Sharpened Awareness of Leisure Needs

The Depression helped to stimulate national concern about problems of leisure and recreational opportunity. For example, a number of studies in the 1930s revealed a serious lack of structured recreation programs for young people, especially African Americans, girls, and rural youth. In the early 1930s, the National Education Association carried out a major study of leisure education in the nation's school systems and issued a report, *The New Leisure Challenges the Schools*, that urged the educational establishment to take more responsibility for this function and advocated enlarging the school's role in community recreation.

Shortly thereafter, the National Recreation Association examined the public recreation and park programs in a number of major European nations with nationalized recreation programs, and published a detailed report that included implications for American policy makers. The American Association for the Study of Group Work studied the overall problem and in 1939 published an important report, *Leisure: A National Issue*. Written by Eduard Lindeman, a leading social work administrator who had played a key role in government during the Depression, the report stated that the "leisure of the American people constitutes a central and crucial problem of social policy."[28]

Lindeman argued that in the American democracy, recreation should meet the true needs of the people. Pointing out that American workers were gaining a vast national reservoir of leisure estimated at 390 billion hours per year, he suggested that the new leisure should be characterized by free choice and a minimum of restraint. He urged, however, that if leisure were not to become "idleness, waste, or opportunity for sheer mischief," a national plan for leisure had to be developed, including the widespread preparation of professionally trained recreation leaders.

A NATION AT WAR

World War II, in which the United States became fully involved on December 7, 1941, compelled the immediate mobilization of every aspect of national life: peoplepower, education, industry, and a variety of social services and programs. The Special Services Division of the U.S. Army provided recreation facilities and programs on military bases throughout the world, making use of approximately 12,000 officers, even more enlisted personnel, and many volunteers. About 1,500 officers were involved in the Welfare and

Recreation Section of the Bureau of Naval Personnel, and expanded programs were offered by the Recreation Service of the Marine Corps. These departments were assisted by the United Service Organizations (USO), which was formed in 1941 and consisted of the joint effort of six agencies: the Jewish Welfare Board, the Salvation Army, Catholic Community Services, the YMCA, the YWCA, and the National Travelers Aid. The USO functioned in the continental United States and outside of military camps and in clubs, hostels, and lounges throughout the western hemisphere. The American National Red Cross established approximately 750 clubs in wartime theaters of operations throughout the world and about 250 mobile entertainment units, staffed by more than 4,000 leaders. Its military hospitals overseas and in the United States involved more than 1,500 recreation workers as well.

Many municipal directors extended their facilities and services to local war plants and changed their schedules to provide programs around the clock. Because of the rapid increase in industrial recreation programs, the National Industrial Recreation Association (later known as the National Employee Services and Recreation Association) was formed in 1941 to assist in such efforts. Also, the Federal Security Agency's Office of Community War Services established a new recreation division to assist programs on the community level. This division helped set up 300 new community programs throughout the country, including numerous child-care and recreation centers, many of which continued after the war as tax-supported community recreation programs. The Women's Bureau of the U.S. Department of Labor developed guidelines for recreation and housing for women war workers, based on their needs in moving from their home environments into suddenly expanded or greatly congested areas.

By the end of World War II, great numbers of servicemen and servicewomen had participated in varied recreation programs and services and thus had gained a new appreciation for this field. Many people had been trained in recreation leadership (more than 40,000 people were in the Special Services Division of the U.S. Army alone) and were ready to return to civilian life as professionals in this field.

SUMMARY

This chapter shows the long history of recreation, play, and leisure by discussing their roles during the ancient civilizations of Assyria, Babylonia, and Egypt; then in the Greek and Roman eras; during the Middle Ages and the Renaissance in Europe: and from the pre-Revolutionary period in the North American colonies to the mid-twentieth century.

Religion and social class were major factors that influenced recreational involvement in terms of either prohibiting certain forms of activity or assigning them to one class or another. Leisure, seen as an aristocratic devotion to knowledge, the arts, athletics, philosophy, and contemplation in ancient Athens, took a different form in Rome, where it became a political instrument devoted to perpetuating the rule of the Roman emperors by entertaining and placating the common people.

During the Dark and Middle Ages, the Catholic Church placed a strong value on work and worship and sought to prohibit forms of play that had descended from pagan sources. However, such activities as sport and games, music, dance, the theater, and gambling persisted, even under the stern condemnation of the new Protestant sects that gained influence during the period of the Reformation. At this time, class distinctions in terms of appropriate forms of play became clearly evident in England, France, and other European nations. However, the value of play as a form of childhood education was championed in the writings of numerous educators and philosophers of that era.

In the pre-Revolutionary American colonies, New England Puritans were very strict in their condemnation of most recreational pursuits. After an initial conservative period, however, play and varied social pursuits flourished in the plantations of the southern colonies, which had been settled by members of the English gentry who used slaves and indentured servants to make their own leisure possible.

The chapter traces the influence of the Industrial Revolution, which brought millions of immigrants from Europe to America, where they lived in crowded tenements in large cities or in factory towns. It also led to increased attempts to impose the stern strictures of the Protestant work ethic on the nation's population.

By the middle of the nineteenth century, however, religious opposition to varied types of play and entertainment began to decline. Sport became more popular and accepted and, after reaching a high point at mid-century, work hours began to decline. Four major roots of what was ultimately to become the recreation and park movement appeared: (1) the establishment of city parks, beginning with New York's Central Park, and the later growth of county, state, and national parks; (2) the growing interest in adult education and cultural development; (3) the appearance of playgrounds for children, sponsored first as charitable efforts and shortly after by city governments and the public schools; and (4) the development of a number of nonprofit, youth-serving organizations that spread throughout the country.

Popular culture gained momentum during the Jazz Age of the 1920s, with college and professional sport, motion pictures and radio, new forms of dance and music, and a host of other crazes capturing the public's interest. Although the Great Depression of the 1930s had a tragic impact on many families, the efforts of the federal government to build recreation facilities and leisure services to provide jobs and a morale boost for the public at large meant that the Depression was a powerful positive force for the recreation movement in general.

By the early 1940s, organized recreation service was firmly established in American life, and both government officials and social critics began to raise searching questions about its future role in postwar society.

QUESTIONS FOR CLASS DISCUSSION OR ESSAY EXAMINATION

1. Contrast the attitudes toward sport and other uses of leisure that were found in ancient Greece with those found in the Roman Empire. How did their philosophies differ, and how did the Roman philosophy lead to a weakening of that powerful nation? Could you draw a parallel between the approach to leisure and entertainment in ancient Rome and that in the present-day United States?
2. Trace the development of religious attitudes and policies regarding leisure and play from the Dark and Middle Ages, through the Renaissance and Reformation periods, to the colonial era in seventeenth- and eighteenth-century North America. What

differences were there in the approach to recreation between the northern and southern colonies at this time?

3. In the second half of the nineteenth century, the roots of what was to become the modern recreation and park movement appeared. What were these roots (e.g., the adult education or Lyceum movement), and how did they relate to the broad social needs of Americans?

4. Three important pioneers of the early recreation movement in the United States were Lee, Gulick, and Addams. Summarize some of the key points of their philosophies and their contributions to the playground and recreation developments of the pre–World War I era. Describe the conflict between the traditional Victorian values and code of morality and the emerging popular culture, especially during the 1920s.

5. Trace the expanding role of government in terms of sponsoring recreation and park programs during the first half of the twentieth century, with emphasis on federal policies in wartime and during the Depression of the 1930s. What were some of the growing concerns about leisure during this period?

ENDNOTES

1. John Pearson, *Arena: The Story of the Colosseum* (New York: McGraw-Hill, 1973): 7.

2. Gary Cross, *A Social History of Leisure Since 1600* (State College, PA: Venture Publishing): 73.

3. Jonah Blank, "Playing for Keeps," *U.S. News and World Report* (28 June 1999): 64.

4. Zhang Juzhong and Lee Yun Kuen, "The Magic Flutes," *Natural History* (Vol. 114, No. 7, 2005): 43.

5. Plato, *The Laws*, translated by R. G. Bury (Cambridge, MA: Harvard University Press, 1926, 1961): 23.

6. Cited in Lincoln Kirstein, *Dance: A Short History of Classical Theatrical Dancing* (New York: G. P. Putnam, 1935): 57.

7. E. M. Hulme, *The Middle Ages* (New York: Holt, 1938): 604.

8. Cited in Fred Leonard, *A Guide to the History of Physical Education* (Philadelphia: Lea and Febiger, 1928): 55.

9. N. Miller and D. Robinson, *The Leisure Age* (Belmont, CA: Wadsworth, 1963): 66.

10. Cited in Paul La Croix, *France in the Middle Ages* (New York: Frederick Ungar, 1963): 346.

11. Michael Kraus, *The Atlantic Civilization: 18th Century Origins* (Ithaca, NY: Cornell University Press, 1949): 3.

12. Jearold Winston Holland, *Black Recreation: A Historical Perspective* (Chicago: Burnam, 2002).

13. Benjamin Hunnicutt, "The End of Shorter Hours," *Labor Review* (Vol. 3, 1984): 373–374.

14. J. Larkin, "The Secret Life of a Developing Country (Ours)," *American Heritage* (September–October 1988): 60.

15. George Will, review of G. Edward White, "Creating the National Pastime," *New York Times Book Review* (7 April 1996): 11.

16. John Adams to Abigail Adams, May 1780, *Adams Family Correspondence III* (Cambridge, MA: Harvard University Press, 1973): 342.

17. Paul Heintzman, "Wilderness and the Canadian Mind: Impact upon Recreation Development in Canadian Parks" (*NRPA Research Symposium*, 1997): 75.

18. Cited in H. H. Reed and S. Duckworth, *Central Park: A History and a Guide* (New York: Clarkson N. Potter, 1967): 3.

19. Walter Vrooman, "Playgrounds for Children," *The Arena* (July 1894): 286.

20. Luther H. Gulick, *A Philosophy of Play* (New York: Scribner, 1920): 125.

21. Mary Duncan, "Back to Our Radical Roots," in Thomas Goodale and Peter Witt, eds., *Recreation and Leisure: Issues in an Era of Change* (State College, PA: Venture Publishing, 1980): 287–295.

22. Kathy Peiss, *Cheap Amusements: Working Women and Leisure in Turn-of-the-Century New York* (Philadelphia: Temple University Press, 1986): 57.

23. James Rogers, "The Child and Play," *Report on White House Conference on Child Health and Protection* (1932): 27.

24. John Kasson, *Amusing the Millions: Coney Island at the Turn of the Century* (New York: Hill and Wang, 1978): 3–4.

25. Benjamin Hunnicutt, "Historical Attitudes Toward the Increase of Free Time in the Twentieth Century: Time for Leisure, for Work, for Unemployment," *Loisir et Societe* (Vol. 3, 1980): 196.

26. Richard Knapp, "Play for America: The New Deal and the NRA," *Parks and Recreation* (July 1973): 23.

27. Susan Currell, *The March of Spare Time: The Problem and Promise of Leisure in the Great Depression* (Philadelphia: University of Pennsylvania Press, 2005): 51.

28. Eduard Lindeman, *Leisure: A National Issue* (New York: American Association for the Study of Group Work, 1939): 32.

CHAPTER 4

RECREATION AND LEISURE IN THE MODERN ERA

◆ ◆ ◆

During the 1950s and 1960s, organized recreation had a marked impact on community life. The growing movement was advanced by an increasing concern for physical fitness; programs for the ill, aged, and disabled; an upsurge in outdoor recreation and park development; involvement in the arts; professional education; unification of the parks and recreation professional organization; and the impact of civil unrest and youth dissent. . . . During this time, recreation and leisure services . . . came to be seen as an opportunity system to improve the quality of life, reduce social pathology, build constructive values in citizens, and generally make communities better places to live.[1]

◆ ◆ ◆

INTRODUCTION

From the end of World War II to the turn of the twenty-first century, recreation, park, and leisure services evolved from a relatively minor area of government responsibility and nonprofit agency or business function to an enormous, complex enterprise. This chapter chronicles the expansion and diversification of the recreation movement, seen against the broader background of social and economic change in the United States. In addition to describing these elements, the chapter presents a number of trends in leisure involvement and professional services that were influenced by environmental, demographic, social, and economic trends in the postwar era.

These trends included (1) growing concern about the natural environment and government's role in protecting it; (2) stronger emphasis on recreation's role in combating poverty and racial tensions; (3) programs designed to serve girls and women more fully, along with people with disabilities and older adults; (4) the emergence of a number of specialized disciplines and professional groups serving the military, business, private-membership groups, and other interests; (5) a period of economic austerity during the 1980s and early 1990s, followed by a dramatic upsurge in the nation's economy during the last years of the century; and (6) the longest economic decline since the Depression as the United States entered the first years of the twenty-first century.

POST–WORLD WAR II EXPECTATIONS

Immediately after World War II, expectations for the growth of leisure in the United States were high. In the 1950s and 1960s, it was predicted that leisure—usually defined as nonwork or discretionary time—would expand dramatically and have an increasing influence on the lives of Americans in the years ahead.

Think tanks such as the Rand Corporation or the Hudson Institute and special planning bodies such as the National Commission on Technology envisioned futurist scenarios with such alternatives as lowering the retirement age to 38, reducing the workweek to 22 hours a week, or extending paid vacations to as many as 25 weeks a year. Other authorities predicted that the three-day or four-day workweek, which some companies had been experimenting with, would soon be widespread.

It was also assumed that leisure would become an increasingly important source of personal values and life satisfaction for many Americans. There was widespread agreement that the work ethic was declining sharply, with work in the industrial era having become more and more specialized, routine, and unfulfilling. Leisure was seen as having immense potential, and writers and educators such as David Gray and Seymour Greben suggested that it offered new possibilities for confronting such social problems as human misery and suffering, health and fitness concerns, environmental and energy problems, and worker dissatisfaction.

In the early and mid-1990s, widespread company downsizing and other business trends led to the firing of millions of employees and an atmosphere of economic pessimism. With the strong business recovery of the late 1990s, unemployment declined sharply, prosperity was widespread, and government budgets began to show surpluses on every level.

■ *Snowmobiling is one example of outdoor recreation that is expanding in the U.S.*

EXPANSION OF RECREATION AND LEISURE

Through it all, recreation and leisure witnessed an immense growth in participation. There was a steady increase in sport, the arts, hobbies, outdoor recreation, and fitness programs, along with a parallel expansion of home-based entertainment through the use of stereo, television, DVD players, and other electronic equipment.

Influence of National Affluence

An important factor in the growth of recreational participation was the national affluence of the postwar years. The gross national product rose from $211 billion in 1945 to over a trillion dollars annually in 1971. In the late 1950s, it was reported that Americans were spending $30 billion a year on leisure—a sum that seemed huge then but is dwarfed by the $756 billion spent in 2005.[2]

Involvement in varied forms of recreation exploded during this period. Visits to national forests increased by 474 percent between 1947 and 1963, and to national parks by 302 percent during the same period. Overseas pleasure travel increased by 440 percent, and attendance at sports and cultural events also grew rapidly. Sales of golf equipment increased by 188 percent, of tennis equipment by 148 percent, and use of bowling lanes by 258 percent. Hunting and fishing, horse-racing attendance, and copies of paperback books sold all gained dramatically and—most strikingly—the number of families with television sets grew by 3,500 percent over this 16-year period.[3]

Government recreation and park agencies dramatically expanded their budgets, personnel, facilities, and programs until the mid-1970s. Then, many federal, state, and local agencies were forced by funding cuts to cut back or freeze budgets. At the same time, the recreation and park profession continued to grow in numbers and public visibility. Preprofessional curricula were established in many colleges and universities during the 1960s and 1970s, and several national organizations, including the National Recreation Association, the American Recreation Society, and the American Institute of Park Executives, merged to form the National Recreation and Park Association—a stronger and more unified voice for the park and recreation field overall.

■ *Recreation participation continues to grow rapidly around the world. This 3-tiered driving range demonstrates the popularity of golf as well as a creative use of limited urban space to accomodate large numbers of users.*

Effect of Demographic Changes: Suburbanization and Urban Crises

In the years immediately after World War II, which had disrupted the lives of millions of servicemen and -women, great numbers of young couples married. Within a few years, many of these new families with young children moved from the central cities to new homes in surrounding suburban areas. In these suburban communities, recreation for growing families became an important concern. Most suburbs were quick to establish new recreation and park departments, hire personnel, and develop programs and facilities to serve all age groups—often in concert with local school districts.

At the same time, the population within the inner cities changed dramatically. With the rapid mechanization of agriculture in the South and the abandonment of the sharecropper system, millions of African Americans moved from the South to the cities and industrialized areas of the Northeast, the Midwest, and the West in search of jobs and better opportunities. Growing numbers of Hispanic immigrants surged into the cities from the Caribbean islands and Central America. Generally, these new residents faced economic hardships, including limited employment opportunities, that resulted in health, housing, and welfare concerns for cities.

TRENDS IN PROGRAM SPONSORSHIP

As a result of such population shifts and changes in lifestyle, a number of trends in recreation program functions and in the role to be played by government emerged. These included (1) programs aimed at improving physical fitness, (2) emphasis on environmental concerns, (3) activities and services designed to meet specific age group needs, (4) recreation for persons with disabilities, (5) increasing programming in the arts, (6) services for people living in poverty, and (7) programs concerned with the needs of racial and ethnic minorities.

Emphasis on Physical Fitness

Beginning in the 1950s, there was a strong emphasis on the need to develop and maintain the physical fitness of youth. In both world wars, a disappointingly high percentage of male draftees and enlistees had been rejected by the armed forces for physical reasons. Then, after World War II, comparative studies such as the Kraus-Weber tests showed that American youth were less fit than the youth of several other nations. Vice President Richard Nixon convened the President's Conference on the Fitness of American Youth at the United States Naval Academy in Annapolis, Maryland, in 1956. The recommendations from the conference included increasing public awareness, increasing public funding of community recreation, supporting nonprofit youth-serving agencies through private and public funds, increasing and improving community recreation facilities, improving fitness opportunities for girls, and improving leadership for physical activity. In 1956, President Dwight Eisenhower also established the President's Council on Youth Fitness to serve as a catalyst for motivating communities and individuals to adopt active lifestyles. In response to the conference, schools strengthened their programs of physical fitness, and many public recreation departments expanded their leisure activities to include fitness classes, conditioning, jogging, and sports for all ages.

Environmental Concerns

A key concern of the recreation field has been the environment. In the postwar period, it became evident that there was a critical need to preserve and rehabilitate the nation's land, water, and wildlife resources. U.S. citizens permitted the country's great rivers and lakes to be polluted by waste, forests to be ruthlessly razed by lumbering interests, and wildlife to be ravaged by overhunting, lack of adequate breeding areas, chemical poisons, and invasion of their environments. Greater and greater demands had been placed on the natural resource bank, with open space shrinking at an unprecedented rate.

In the late 1950s, President Dwight Eisenhower and the Congress formed the Outdoor Recreation Resources Review Commission to investigate this problem. The result was a landmark, heavily documented report in 1962 that helped to promote a wave of environmental efforts by federal, state, and municipal governments. The Federal Water Pollution Control Administration divided the nation into 20 major river basins and promoted regional sewage treatment programs in those areas. The Water Quality Act of 1965, the Clean Water Restoration Act of 1966, the Solid Waste Disposal Act of 1965, the Highway Beautification Act of 1965, and the Mining Reclamation Act of 1968 all committed the United States to a sustained program of conservation and protection of its natural resources. Another major piece of legislation was the Wilderness Act of 1964, which gave Congress the authority to declare certain unspoiled lands permanently off-limits to human occupation and development.

Many states and cities embarked on new programs of land acquisition and beautification and developed environmental plans designed to reduce air and water pollution. Nonprofit organizations such as the American Land Trust, the Nature Conservancy, and the Trust for Public Lands took over properties encompassing hundreds of thousands of acres—many of them donated by large corporations—for preservation or transfer to public agencies for recreational use. Such programs were accompanied by efforts within federal agencies such as the National Park Service, the Forest Service, the Fish and Wildlife Service, and the Bureau of Land Management to meet public needs for outdoor recreation.

■ *Baby boomers, who make up a large portion of the population, are staying active in recreation longer.*

In the early 1980s, federal expenditures for parks and environmental programs were sharply reduced, the rate of land acquisition was cut back, and government policies regulating the use of wild lands for mining, timber cutting, grazing, oil drilling, and similar commercial activities were dramatically relaxed.

Although national outdoor recreation planning ended in 1981, a number of major studies continued to assess the nation's natural resources and environmental concerns through the decades that followed.[4]

Meeting Age-Group Needs

In addition to the demographic trends cited earlier, three important changes in the nation's population that gathered force in the postwar decades were (1) the dramatic rise in the birth rate, with millions of children and youth flooding the schools and community recreation centers; (2) the lengthening of the population's life span, resulting in a growing proportion of older adults in society; and (3) the increasing pressures on families with children due to growing numbers of single-parent households and the entrance of millions of women into the workforce.

In response to these trends, thousands of governmental and nonprofit organizations expanded their programs for children and youth, and numerous youth sport leagues such as Little League, Biddy Basketball, and American Legion Football recruited millions of participants. At the other end of the age range, public and nonprofit organizations, including many municipal park and recreation agencies, developed golden age clubs or senior centers, often with funding from the federal government through the Administration on Aging.

Changing family households confirmed the need for recreation programs to provide day-care services for children of working parents and to meet other leisure-related needs. Religious organizations in particular are stressing family-oriented programming today in an effort to strengthen marital bonds and improve parent-child relationships.

■ *People with disabilities engage in a variety of sport and recreation activities today including such things as street hockey, tennis, and snow skiing.*

Special Recreation for Persons with Disabilities

An area of increased emphasis in the postwar era was the provision of supportive services for persons with physical and mental disabilities. As in the environmental field, this trend was strengthened by federal legislation. Various government agencies concerned with rehabilitation were expanded to meet the needs of individuals with physical disabilities, especially the large numbers of returning veterans who sought to be integrated into community life.

In order to better serve people with developmental disabilities, the federal government sharply increased its aid to special education. In recreation, assistance was given to programs serving children, youth, and adults with developmental disabilities. Beginning in the mid-1960s, there was an increased emphasis on developing social and recreational programs for aging persons in both institutional and community settings. Overall, the specialized field of what came to be known as therapeutic recreation service expanded steadily in this period. With the establishment of the National Therapeutic Recreation Society in the mid-1960s and the American Therapeutic Recreation Association in the 1980s, professionalization in therapeutic recreation service developed rapidly. The establishment of curriculum guidelines for courses in professional preparation, the setting of program standards, and the development of registration and certification plans all served to make this field a significant specialized area within the broad leisure-service field.

Increased Interest in the Arts

Following World War II, the United States embarked on an expansion of cultural centers, museums, and art centers. In part, this represented a natural follow-up to the stimulus that had been given to art, theater, music, and dance by emergency federal programs during the Great Depression. Another element, however, was that Americans now had come to respect and enjoy the arts as both spectators and participants. Through the 1970s and early 1980s, community arts activities continued to flourish, with the assistance of federal funding through the National Endowment for the Arts, which helped to support state arts units, choreographers and composers, and individual performers and companies.

In the mid- and late 1980s, some decline in attendance at music, drama, and dance events was noted, possibly due to declining federal support, increased ticket prices, and to the increasing public interest in home-based video entertainment. To meet this

In 1968, Eunice Kennedy Shriver organized the first International Special Olympic Games in Chicago, Illinois. The Special Olympics were an outgrowth of a day-camp program started in 1962 by Shriver for people with developmental disabilities. During the first international games, 1,000 athletes from the United States and Canada competed. In 1977, the first winter games were held in Steamboat Springs, Colorado, and included 500 athletes. Today, 2.25 million athletes in 160 countries compete in local, state, national, and international Special Olympics events. The Special Olympics movement and the tireless work of Shriver have had an extraordinary impact on the public's understanding of people with developmental disabilities and creation of supportive public policy.

challenge, many cultural organizations in the fine and performing arts, as well as many museums, libraries, and similar institutions, developed new methods of fundraising by diversifying their offerings and marketing them to a broader community audience. As an example, art, natural history, and science museums today offer lectures, tours, classes, films, innovative displays, special fundraising dinners, and other events designed to attract a wide spectrum of patrons. As a result of these creative programming efforts, attendence at community theaters has grown steadily over the past 15 years.

Recreation's Antipoverty Role

An important development of the 1960s was the expanded role given to recreation as an element in President Lyndon Johnson's "war on poverty." Initially, the nation's concern about the economically and socially disadvantaged had been aroused by a widely read book on poverty in America by Michael Harrington, published in 1962 at a time of great prosperity for most citizens.

During the 1930s and 1940s, a number of federal housing programs provided funding to support small parks, playgrounds, or centers in public housing projects. Now, a new wave of legislation, such as the Economic Opportunity Act of 1964, the Housing and Urban Development Act of 1964, and the Model Cities program approved in 1967, provided assistance for locally directed recreation programs to be conducted by disadvantaged citizens themselves in depressed urban neighborhoods. Other federal programs, such as the Job Corps, VISTA (Volunteers in Service to America), and the Neighborhood Youth Corps, also included recreation-related components.

Segregation and Integration in Recreation

The public recreation movement of the late nineteenth and early twentieth century did not equally benefit all Americans. Throughout most of the United States, separate recreation facilities had been built for African and Caucasian Americans. As with public education, the result of this segregation was highly disparate opportunities. The first widespread attempts at racial integration were in the late 1950s and early 1960s following the Supreme Court's landmark, *Brown vs. the Board of Education* decision.

Unfortunately, it was not until the late 1960s, following escalated racial tensions in many cities, that the federal government dedicated serious financial resources to serving African Americans, particularly those living in impoverished urban centers. Hundreds of millions of dollars were granted each year to local governments and to organizations of local residents to provide enriched recreation services aimed particularly at youth. These included sports and social activities, cultural pursuits, job-training and tutorial programs, and trips and similar recreation activities. On a national scale, the Job Corps, VISTA, Neighborhood Youth Corps, and an aggregate of special projects known as Community Action Programs continued into the 1970s but were gradually terminated in the years that followed.

COUNTERCULTURE: YOUTH IN REBELLION

During the late 1960s, what came to be known as the counterculture made its appearance in America. The term *counterculture*, as John Kelly points out, is generally applied to a movement that develops in opposition to an established and dominant culture—often in political, religious, or lifestyle terms—and that manifests itself in language, symbols, and behavior.

Rejection of the Work Ethic

A significant aspect of the counterculture movement was its rejection of work as the be-all and end-all of one's life and of the widely accepted goal of "making it" in the business or professional world. As Chapter 3 showed, a deep-rooted belief in the value of hard work, which was linked to an essentially conservative, industrious, and moralistic view of life, had long been a fundamental tenet of American society.

However, since World War II, there had been a retreat from the stern precepts of the Protestant work ethic. As establishment values and monetary success were undermined in the thinking of young people during the counterculture period, leisure satisfactions assumed new importance. Writers urged new, holistic approaches to the use of free time that would integrate varied aspects of human personality and lead to the self actualization spoken of by Maslow and other psychologists.

The counterculture movement in the United States during the 1960s was part of a larger youth movement that challenged the political, economic, and educational establishments in a number of other nations around the world. Here, it symbolized the rebellion of young people against parental authority and the curricular and social controls of schools and colleges. Much of it stemmed from mass protests against the Vietnam War as students initiated strikes and takeovers of administrative offices in a number of universities. Rock music and lyrics that challenged traditional values became popular, and some young people joined "hippie" communes or fled to neighborhoods like Haight-Ashbury in San Francisco or the East Village in New York City, where they experimented with drugs and a variety of alternative lifestyles.

DRIVES FOR EQUALITY BY DISADVANTAGED GROUPS

Another important aspect of the counterculture movement was that it provided a climate within which various populations in American society that had historically been disadvantaged were encouraged to press vigorously for fuller social and economic rights.

The rejection of the Protestant work ethic was widely expressed in the music, art, and literature of the 1960s. The historical record of the baby boomers of the 1960s, however, indicates that the demise of Americans' obsession with work is more myth than reality. A study published by the Families and Work Institute in 2006, indicated that baby boomers are more likely to live work-centric lifestyles than the generations that precede and follow them. A 2004 study by the same institute, indicated that baby boomers work longer hours and are more likely to feel overworked than employees of other generations.

■ *Youth lifestyles changed radically, from this formal college prom in the 1950s (left) to a swinging party in the 1960s (right).*

Racial and Ethnic Minorities

For racial and ethnic minorities, there was a strong thrust during the 1960s and 1970s toward demanding fuller recreational service in terms of facilities and organized programs. In response, many public recreation and park departments not only upgraded these traditional elements, but also began to provide mobile recreation units that would enter affected neighborhoods to offer cultural, social, and other special services. Building on projects that had been initiated during the war on poverty and in response to escalating racial tensions in cities, many departments initiated classes, workshops, festivals, and holiday celebrations designed to promote ethnic pride and intercultural appreciation.

Through legislation, Supreme Court decisions, other judicial orders, and voluntary compliance, public, nonprofit, and commercial facilities were gradually desegregated through the 1970s and 1980s. Major youth and adult social membership organizations such as the Girl Scouts and the YMCA, which had tended either to maintain segregated units for racial minorities or to not serve them at all, opened up their memberships and in some cases identified racial justice as a high-priority mission for the years ahead. In terms of the broader culture, greater numbers of racial and ethnic minorities began to achieve great success in such leisure-related areas as college and professional sports and popular entertainment such as music, television, and motion pictures.

Progress for Women

In the 1960s and 1970s, feminist groups mobilized to attack two major areas of gender-based discrimination in recreation and leisure: employment practices and program involvement. A number of studies showed that women tended to secure fewer high-level administrative positions and were paid lower salaries than men in recreation and park departments throughout the United States.

In response to equal opportunity laws and other pressures, governmental recreation and park departments and other agencies began to hire women in greater numbers than in the past. Several states hired their first women park rangers, naturalists, and park superintendents; in a number of cities women were appointed as directors of the recreation and park departments.

A fundamental principle in community recreation has been that all persons should be given an equal opportunity, regardless of sex, religion, race, or other personal factors. However, in the postwar decades, it became evident that this principle had not been applied to participation of girls and women in public recreation programs in the United States.

In 1972, growing pressure from women's groups led to the approval of groundbreaking legislation, Title IX of the Education Amendments Act. Title IX was the first legislation to prohibit sex discrimination in educational institutions. Although Title IX prevents discrimination in all aspects of public education, including recruitment, admission, and employment, the primary focus of public discourse over the past 30 years has been equality in athletics. The impact of Title IX is clear. The number of girls participating in high school athletics increased from 294,015 in 1971–1972 to 2,953,355 in 2005–2006—an increase of over 1,000 percent. During the same period, participation of boys increased from 3,666,917 to 4,206,549.

During the 1970s and 1980s, community recreation organizations joined the nationwide effort to offer equal opportunities for girls and women. A significant development at this time was the merger of formerly sex-separated organizations into organizations serving both sexes, such as the Boys and Girls Club of America. As a result of these changes, girls and women today have a far greater range of sport and physical recreation opportunities than they did in the past.

Gays and Lesbians

Gay, lesbian, and bisexual individuals compose a third group who traditionally have been disadvantaged in American society. During the counterculture era, gay activists began to mobilize as an economic and political force. In the 1960s and 1970s, many gay and lesbian groups began to organize and promote their recreational and social activities openly on college campuses and in community life. In a number of cities, they had to fight through the courts for the right to take part in community celebrations, parades, and other civic events.

In other cases, when homosexual groups sought to participate in big-city St. Patrick's Day parades, or when they held a huge gay festival at Florida's Walt Disney World, a number of conservative Christian organizations protested vigorously. In retaliation, when rural Cobb County, Georgia, passed a resolution condemning the gay lifestyle as incompatible with its values, gay groups and their allies pressured the International Olympic Committee to withdraw some of its featured events from the county after they had already been scheduled to take place there as part of the 1996 Olympics.

Older Adults in Community Life

Although the counterculture was primarily a youth movement in the United States and abroad, it also prompted many middle-aged and older persons to examine their value systems and their status in community life.

Older adults at this time represented a fourth group of disadvantaged persons in the sense that they were generally regarded and treated as powerless individuals who were both physically and economically vulnerable. However, under the leadership of such growing organizations as the American Association of Retired Persons and the much smaller Gray Panthers, elderly persons began to mobilize and exert political clout in order to obtain improved benefits. With support from various federal programs, including the Administration on Aging, senior citizens' groups and golden age clubs around the United States began to offer diversified programs of health care, social services, nutrition, housing and transportation assistance, and recreation.

Programming for Persons with Disabilities

Although significant progress had been made following World War II, both treatment-centered and community-based programming for persons with disabilities received a major impetus during the counterculture period. Like other disadvantaged groups that had essentially been powerless, persons with disabilities began to act as their own advocates, demanding their rights and opportunities. People with disabilities began to mobilize politically to promote positive legislation and increased community services for those with physical, mental, or social disabilities.

At the same time that therapeutic recreation specialists began to include a broader range of disabilities within their scope of service, numerous organizations went one step further and promoted such innovative programming as theater arts for people with physical disabilities, skiing for individuals with visual impairments, and a full range of sports and track-and-field events for the people with mobility impairments.

ERA OF AUSTERITY AND FISCAL CUTBACKS

Despite this general picture of positive progress, the recreation, parks, and leisure-service field faced a serious threat in the 1970s and 1980s as mounting costs of government led to tax protests and funding cutbacks in states and cities across the United States. As early as the mid-1970s, a number of older industrial cities in the nation's Rust Belt, an area of the Midwest where iron and steel are produced and manufactured, began to suffer from increased energy costs, welfare and crime problems, and expenses linked to rising infrastructure maintenance problems. Along with some suburban school districts confronted by skyrocketing enrollments and limited tax bases, such communities experienced budget deficits and the need to freeze expenditures.

In 1976, a tax limitation law was passed in New Jersey, and in 1978 California's much more radical Proposition 13 sharply reduced local property tax rates and assessment increases. A "tax revolt" soon spread rapidly across the United States. By the end of 1979, statutory provisions had been approved in 36 states that either reduced property, income, or sales taxes or put other types of spending limits in place. Austerity budgets had to be adopted in many communities, counties, and other governmental units. Typically, Proposition 13 resulted in major funding cutbacks for

No person in the United States shall, on the basis of sex, be excluded from participation in, or denied the benefits of, or be subjected to discrimination under any educational program or activity receiving federal assistance.
—Title IX of the Education Amendments of 1972 to the Civil Rights Act of 1964

parks, libraries, recreation, social services, and street sweeping and maintenance, while police and fire departments tended to be protected against cuts.

Expanding Use of Revenue Sources

Many local recreation and park agencies adopted the policy of instituting or raising fees and charges for participation in programs, for use of the facilities, for rental of equipment, and for other types of involvement in a wide range of leisure activities and services. In the past, it generally had been the practice to provide all basic play opportunities, particularly for children and youth, without charge and to impose fees only for classes with special expenses or for admission to facilities such as skating rinks, swimming pools, golf courses, or tennis courts—often with arrangements made for annual permits at modest cost.

Acceptance of Marketing Orientation   Directly linked to this trend was the widespread acceptance of an entrepreneurial, marketing-oriented approach to recreation and park programming and administration. It was argued by both educators and practitioners that it was necessary to be aggressive in seeking out new program opportunities and creative in responding to fiscal challenges rather than relying on past, and often outmoded, formulas or policies.

References were being made to recreation as an "industry" in both the popular and the professional literature. Typically, in 1986, the *American Association for Leisure and Recreation Reporter* described the recreation field as a mosaic of thousands of businesses woven directly or subtly into the American economy.

In other professional publications, it was argued that managers of recreation and park programs, directors of nonprofit youth organizations, and operators of commercial play facilities were all essentially in the same "business"—that of meeting the public's leisure needs and interests.

Trends, published by the National Recreation and Park Association and the National Park Service, agreed:

> Managed recreation is a profession that provides services to consumers of all demographic stripes and shades. Under this designation, a public park superintendent is in the same business as a resort owner . . . a theme park operator and the fitness directors of a YMCA.[5]

It was often argued that in order to compete effectively public recreation agencies had to adopt the philosophy and businesslike methods of successful companies. This meant that at every stage of agency operations—from assessing potential target populations and planning programs to pricing, publicizing, and distributing services—sophisticated methods of analysis and businesslike approaches to attracting and satisfying "customers" were to be used.

Privatization of Recreation and Park Operations

As a second type of response to the era of austerity that began in the 1980s, many recreation, park, and leisure-service agencies resorted to privatization—subcontracting or developing concession arrangements with private organizations—to carry out functions that they could not themselves fulfill as economically or efficiently.

Privatization has become a major thrust in American life as the role of government has been challenged. Many cities now rely on private businesses to construct or maintain facilities, provide food and health services, or manage a variety of other formerly public functions. In a number of cases, prisons and correctional institutions are managed by for-profit companies under contract with public authorities, and several cities have experimented with assigning private organizations the responsibility for running all or part of their school systems.

As for recreation and parks, numerous public departments have contracted with private businesses to operate golf courses, tennis complexes, marinas, and other facilities under agreements that govern the standards they must meet and the rates they may impose. Particularly in the construction of massive new facilities such as sports stadiums and arenas, similar arrangements have been made with commercial developers or businesses for private funding of all or part of construction expenses, with long-term leases being granted to owners of major sports teams.[6]

Impact of Funding Cuts

In 1978, the National Urban Recreation Study reported that hiring freezes and staff cutbacks had taken place in a majority of urban park and recreation departments during the preceding five years. Two years later, a study of U.S. cities having over 150,000 in population found that a majority of the responding recreation and park departments experienced major cutbacks that necessitated personnel freezes and staff discharges, program eliminations, rejection of bond issues, and reduced facility maintenance.

Some reports suggested that many municipal and county recreation and park agencies weathered the financial crisis that followed the tax revolt and reached a point of relative stability. A study of small-town public recreation departments in several Western and Midwestern states by Ellen Weissinger and William Murphy found that although these departments experienced somewhat similar cutbacks to those reported in larger cities, they generally avoided drastic reductions in staff and programs.[7]

However, the reality is that in many larger cities, which have the greatest number of poor families and are marked by high welfare statistics, school dropouts, drug and alcohol abuse, youth gangs, and random violence, recreation and park programs today offer only the most minimal opportunities. The facilities that are provided are often vandalized and covered with graffiti, staff members are threatened, and overall agency operations are extremely limited.

Beyond this, Jack Foley and Veda Ward point out that in the most severely disadvantaged communities, such as South Los Angeles, nonprofit sports groups like Little League, Pony League, AAU swimming, and gymnastic and track clubs (which use public facilities but rely on volunteer leaders and membership fees) do not exist. There is also no commercial recreation in the form of movie theaters, malls, skating rinks, or bowling alleys. They continue:

> Boys and Girls Clubs, YMCAs and YWCAs, Scouts, and so forth, which rely on business and community support, are under-represented and financed in poor communities. A market equity policy (one gets all the recreation one can buy) [has] created a separate, unequal, and regressive City of Los Angeles recreation system. Many city parks [in wealthier neighborhoods] raise from $50,000 to $250,000 annually from user fees and

donations for state-of-the-art services, while recreation centers in South Los Angeles exist on small city subsidies and what money they can squeeze out of the parents of poor children.[8]

EXPANSION OF OTHER RECREATION PROGRAMS

In sharp contrast with this negative picture, other forms of recreation services have flourished over the past three decades. Today, the largest single component of leisure services is the diversified field of commercial recreation businesses. Travel and tourism; fitness spas; professional sport and sport equipment; the manufacture and sale of hobbies, toys, and games; and varied forms of popular entertainment represent only part of this major sector of leisure involvement.

Similarly, most of the other areas of specialized recreation programming, such as therapeutic recreation, employee services, campus recreation, and private-membership and residential leisure services, have expanded steadily. In each case, these fields have sharpened their own identities and public images by developing professional societies or business associations, sponsoring national and regional conferences, publishing newsletters and magazines, and in some cases establishing continuing education and certification programs.

TRENDS IN THE 1990s AND EARLY TWENTY-FIRST CENTURY

This section describes several important demographic, social, economic, and technological trends beginning in the 1990s that influenced the provision of recreation and leisure services in the years immediately before and after the turn of the century.

Economic Stratification: Income Gaps and "Luxury Fever"

Historically, the United States was viewed as a land of opportunity, in which every individual might climb the socioeconomic ladder and in which the middle class represented the backbone of society. During the 1990s, these assumptions were sharply reversed. Several new studies on the growing concentration of U.S. wealth and income challenged the nation's cherished self-image. Bradsher writes:

> They show that rather than being an egalitarian society, the United States has become the most economically stratified of industrial nations. . . . Indeed the drive [under the so-called Contract with America] to reduce federal welfare programs and cut taxes is expected to widen disparities between rich and poor.[9]

In part, this development stemmed from the emergence of a winner-take-all mentality in American business and public life, as more and more Americans competed for ever fewer and bigger prizes, encouraging "economic waste, income inequality, and an impoverished cultural life."[10]

The growth of the number of wealthy families in the United States in the 1990s was not accompanied by reduction of families living in poverty. In 1993, the nation's poverty rate rose to a 10-year high of 15.1 percent. In 2005, 12.6 percent of U.S. citizens or 37 million people lived in poverty. Although the poverty rate fluctuates a few percentage points across each decade, there has been very little change since the mid-1960s when a number of antipoverty social programs were implemented.

Starting in the 1990s, there were growing concerns about the ability of the middle class to make ends meet. Meanwhile, the middle class was declining, both in terms of numbers, income, and morale. In 1995, Labor Secretary Robert Reich concluded:

> Today's middle class is split into three groups. An underclass largely trapped in center cities, increasingly isolated from the core economy; an overclass of those who are positioned to profitably ride the waves of change; and in between, the largest group, an anxious class, most of whom hold jobs but who are justifiably . . . uneasy about their own standing and fearful for their children's futures.[11]

The stratification between social classes is abundantly apparent in the discrepancy between CEOs and their employees. In 2004, at several large companies in the United States, the average CEO's salary was more than 170 times greater than the average workers. It is especially discouraging to note that the discrepancy existed even in companies with extraordinarily poor performance records.[12]

Implications for Leisure   What does this growing separation of U.S. society into rich and poor mean for recreation and leisure? First, a growing number of individuals became immensely wealthy. In 1999, it was reported that 4.1 million of the nation's 102 million households had a net worth of $1 million or more.

In what seemed to be a vivid replay of Thorstein Veblen's view of "conspicuous consumption" (see page 34), these individuals were caught up in what Cornell economist Robert Frank described as *luxury fever*—a rage to spend wildly on vehicles, clothing, toys and hobbies, and a host of other possessions.

> Multimillion-dollar megamansions were being built throughout the country, often on relatively small lots. Many of the newly rich were paying huge sums to build elaborate swimming pools or buy luxury yachts or giant motor homes for vacation travel. One billionaire's ex-wife demanded $4,400 a day to raise their daughter after divorce, and parents began paying sports coaches $70 an hour—sometimes more—to coach their youngsters in Little League baseball skills.[13]

Meanwhile, children in less-affluent neighborhoods or school districts often attended schools that lacked even the most minimal resources for play, as well as spaces and equipment for classes. Throughout the nation at the century's end, the growing gap between rich and poor evidenced itself in jarring contrasts in terms of recreation, parks, and leisure opportunities.

Growing Conservatism in Social Policy

Accompanying the nation's division into rich and poor social classes, there was a pronounced shift in the late 1980s and early 1990s toward more conservative social and economic policies. This trend took many forms, including a sharp withdrawal of assistance for welfare and for inner-city programs serving the economically disadvantaged. Particularly in the mid-1990s (and again in the early twenty-first century), there were renewed efforts to open the nation's parks and forests to economic exploitation and to reduce support for environmental education programs.

There were continuing assaults on federal support for the National Endowment for the Arts and other cultural programs. Funding for the National Endowment for the Arts was cut from $162 million in 1995 to $99 million in 1996. *Time* magazine's arts critic Robert Hughes described the all-out assault on federal funding as unenlightened, uneconomic, and undemocratic:

> The present [leadership in Congress means to sever] all links between American government and American culture. It wants the federal government to give no support at all to music, theater, ballet, opera, film, intelligent television, literature, history, archaeology, museum work, architectural conservation, and the visual arts. It intends to abolish federal funding for the National Endowment for the Arts, the National Endowment for the Humanities, and the Corporation for Public Broadcasting. And it wants to do it tomorrow.[14]

Throughout the past two decades, newspaper headlines illustrated the impact of conservative political thrusts on American life in such areas as mandates for child welfare, nursing home beds for the elderly, health care, environmental protection enforcement, legal help for the urban poor, and youth programs. The widespread decline in support for needed public services and the harsh resistance to government policies benefiting minorities and the poor inevitably posed a severe challenge to many public and nonprofit leisure-service organizations during the early and mid-1990s.

Commodification and Privatization of Leisure Services

The final years of the twentieth century saw a pronounced blurring of functions among different types of organizations in American society: governmental, nonprofit, private, and commercial. Instead of having clearly marked areas of responsibility and program operations in the leisure-service field, these separate kinds of organizations began to overlap each other through partnership or cosponsorship arrangements; by expanding their missions and undertaking new, innovative ventures; and by adopting new fiscal policies. This overall trend had two related components: commodification and privatization.

Commodification   Simply defined, *commodification* describes the process of taking any product or service and commercializing it by designing and marketing it to yield the greatest degree of financial return or profit. Political scientist Sebastian de Grazia described the fuller meaning of this trend:

> Commodification of leisure is understood as a necessary element in the subordination of the entire social system to the reproduction of capitalism and its institutional structure. The consequence to the worker is surrendering to forms of leisure which turn away from self-defining, creative experience and, instead, consume vast quantities of market-produced goods and services.[15]

On the national scene, as part of the effort to gain fuller financial support in an increasingly consumer-oriented society, art museums, libraries, and theater, orchestra, and ballet companies all have become centers of popular entertainment, offering chartered trips abroad, film series and lecture programs, social events, and jazz concerts.

Privatization   As described earlier in this chapter, *privatization* refers to the growing practice of having private corporations take on responsibility for providing services, maintaining facilities, or performing other functions formerly carried out by government agencies.

During the 1990s, privatization grew increasingly widespread in such areas as the so-called prison industry, in which growing numbers of commercial businesses gained contracts for managing prisons or correctional centers, and such civic functions as trash removal, building maintenance, or the operation of utility or water-supply systems. In terms of public recreation and park privatization, the most striking event was the 1998 contract for a private group, the Central Park Conservancy, to operate New York's famous and historic Central Park, with joint public and private funding.

New Environmental Initiatives

As this chapter has shown, the nation's support for environmental protection and the recovery of polluted lakes and streams, as well as the continuing acquisition and preservation of wilderness areas, faced a sharp challenge during the 1980s and early 1990s.

Several decades of neglect and overcrowding left the nation's park system and forests in a precarious state. In 1997, *Time* cited Yellowstone as a leading example:

> There is little doubt that the preservationists are losing ground. The ills that beset the nation's first and still most magnificent park affect the park system as a whole: underfunding and overcrowding, pollution, encroaching commercial development, invasion of exotic species, and the decline of natural, historical, and cultural treasures.[16]

With national concern mounting, park authorities and Congress moved ahead in the years that followed. In a number of the major parks, they instituted new fees to gather additional revenue and restricted automobile traffic into interior sections. Increasingly, corporate sponsors were recruited to assist in park maintenance, and major environmental organizations such as the National Park Trust provided support for the acquisition of new parks and wildlands.

Although public concerns focused chiefly on the ecological recovery of parks and wilderness areas, they also were directed to problems of clean air and water that affected major metropolitan areas. At the same time, as Chapter 7 will show, major efforts were made in such older cities as Baltimore and Boston to revive waterfront and disused industrial areas. In such settings, cities developed new harbor facilities such as aquariums, museums, sport stadiums, marinas, theme parks, and other cultural and entertainment attractions—both to improve their image and attract tourists and to serve their own residents with appealing leisure programs.

Technological Impacts on Leisure

Beyond the effects of technological innovation described in Chapter 3, a number of other scientifically based advances had a major impact on American leisure in the final decades of the twentieth century. Many of these had to do with forms of travel. Apart from the use of computers in tourism planning and reservations, electronic guidance systems became able to direct an automobile trip through every turn until reaching the desired destination. Electronic navigation simulators created by companies such as Maptech, Inc., provided piloting assistance for boating enthusiasts. For the vacationing family, movies and video games replaced license-plate Bingo, as cars became entertainment centers with the latest audio and video technology that was being displayed at consumer electronic shows.

Home environments became increasingly "smart," with "Nanny cams" to watch over sleeping babies or "intelligent" wallpaper that turned the wall of a room into a television screen, virtual aquarium, or other visual feature. Home theater systems can control lighting; stereo, CD, and MP3 systems; window shades; satellite service; and DVD players, while other lines accommodate the family's telephones, fax machines, and modems—all at a distance.

Television, video games, and children's toys represent impressive examples of technology's impact on family leisure. As of the late 1990s, almost 80 percent of homes had cable or satellite television, and many studies reported that about 40 percent of Americans' free time was spent watching the home screen. Seplow and Storm wrote:

> For half a century now, television has been gobbling up time the way a good running back gobbles up yardage. Regardless of income, education, or any major demographic indicator, Americans have made television the unrivaled consumer of their free time. [Apart from recent findings that television watching is beginning to decline among young people] nothing has remotely weakened its grip. Americans spend more time watching television than working out, reading, using the computer, working in the garden, and going to church—combined.[17]

Numerous critics bemoaned the cultural level of most television programs, from inane situation comedies or fake wrestling bouts to news broadcasts that endlessly reported crime and to the continuing emphasis on sex and violence in many rock and rap music shows. As a single example, many psychologists and sociologists regarded popular talk programs as "freak shows" that trivialized social issues and exploited troubled people who were often presented as pathetic losers.

RECREATION AND HEALTH REVISITED

Public health officials have recognized that the sedentary lifestyles led by a large percentage of adults and children in the United States are directly contributing to a prevalence of obesity in the population that approaches epidemic levels. According to a 2001 report of the Surgeon General's Office, fewer than one-third of adults engage in the recommended 30 minutes of moderate physical activity most days of the week. Forty percent of adults engage in no physical activity. Childhood obesity also is of significant concern. During the past two to three decades, the number of overweight and obese children in the United States more than doubled. As with adults, excessive

Even when recreation programs are provided by public local or nonprofit agencies, price tags are placed today on almost every kind of sponsored recreational opportunity. Typically, the annual or seasonal program brochures of public recreation and park agencies list varied classes, aquatic or sport facilities, camps, tournaments, or special events—invariably with attached fees and charges that may run into several hundreds of dollars.

caloric intake and inadequate physical activity are the primary contributors to obesity.[18] Unfortunately, the rise in childhood obesity has coincided with a decline in student time spent in physical education classes and recess.

During the early twenty-first century, recreation and leisure-service providers and the federal government recognized the role of community recreation in encouraging physical activity. Federally funded initiatives included the establishment of community trail systems and support of after-school programs. The Surgeon General's Office recommended the development of public policy that addressed community access to safe physical activity.

Community recreation agencies responded to this public health crisis with diverse initiatives. In Graham, North Carolina, a group of private and public organizations funded the Movin' Van program, a mobile fitness program that delivers physical activity programs to overweight children and adolescents in low-income neighborhoods. In Wausau, Wisconsin, a community coalition provides free ski lessons for approximately 250 children. Michigan Parks and Recreation sponsors the Walk Michigan program that encourages and facilitates utilization of parks and trails throughout the state. Agencies across the country developed educational and physical activity programs that promote the health of older adults.

Changing Demographics

The face of the United States began to change in the 1990s and will continue to change over the next several decades. As a result, the population served by recreation and leisure organizations in the twenty-first century will differ substantially from that of the twentieth century. Some of the primary changes include the following:

- The number of adults 65 and older grew from 25 million in 1980 to over 36 million in 2005. By 2050, the 65-and-over population is projected to grow to over 70 million.
- The composition of households in the United States will become increasingly diverse, as the number of households without children and single-parent households continue to grow.
- The growth of the Hispanic population in the United States will continue throughout the next few decades as Hispanic Americans become the largest ethnic minority group in the United States. This growth will occur throughout the country, including regions, such as the rural Midwest, that historically have had homogeneous populations.

A changing population will require new approaches to delivery of leisure services. Agencies are challenged to serve an older population that will include several cohorts with different values and views of aging. Traditional recreation programs for older adults may not appeal to baby boomers, who highly value independence and resist aging stereotypes. The range and number of programs targeted at older adults will have to increase to meet the demands of this growing population.

The changing ethnic composition of U.S. society will require leisure-service providers to examine the cultural framework that underlies programs and services. Agencies in certain geographic areas and some urban areas currently are responding to the need for truly multicultural programming. In other areas, particularly those with little history of ethnic diversity, significant work remains to be accomplished.

SUMMARY

The years following World War II represented a period of immense change in the lives of Americans. From 1945 to the early 1970s, it was a time of prosperity and optimism for most families. As great numbers of young people—generally white and working- or middle-class—moved into suburban areas, recreation and park programs flourished and leisure was seen as part of the good life.

Recognizing that a substantial part of the population continued to live in urban slums, with limited economic and social opportunities, the federal government launched a "war on poverty," in which recreation played a significant role. Under pressure from the civil rights movement, many recreation and park agencies began to give a higher level of priority to serving minorities. With the inner-city riots of the mid- and late 1960s, this effort was expanded throughout the country. At the same time, the counterculture movement, which saw young people rebelling against traditional authority and establishment values, transformed society with its resistance to the work ethic and its acceptance of drugs.

The late 1960s and 1970s were also a time when minority groups—including women, the elderly, persons with disabilities, and those with alternative sexual lifestyles—began to demand greater social, economic, political, and leisure opportunities. For them, recreation represented a means of gaining independence and achieving their fullest potential.

Beginning in the 1970s and intensifying during the decade that followed, recessions, inflation, rising costs of welfare and crime, and declining tax bases created an era of austerity that affected many government agencies. With sharp cutbacks in their budgets, many recreation and park agencies imposed severe staffing and maintenance cuts and relied more markedly on fees and privatization to maintain their programs. The entrepreneurial marketing strategy that prevailed widely at this time meant that many public departments were forced to give less emphasis to socially oriented programming.

At the same time, political conservatism in areas related to race relations, the criminal justice system, services for the poor, and environmental programs gained support. Studies in the 1980s and 1990s indicated that many Americans were working longer hours because of changes in family patterns and technological influences on business. At the end of the 1990s, with economic prosperity and more positive social and environmental concerns gaining acceptance, the place of recreation and leisure in contemporary life appeared to be more secure than ever.

Parks and recreation agencies face new challenges and opportunities in the twenty-first century. The population has started to change dramatically, requiring parks and recreation professionals to develop appropriate programs and services. Growing health concerns have provided an opportunity for agencies to play a greater role as public health advocates. The rapidly growing older population has time and resources for leisure, but may reject traditional senior programs for more youthful and diverse opportunities. Changing household composition, including an increase in the number of singles, has challenged agencies that have historically focused on providing programs for families with children. Increasing ethnic diversity provides an opportunity for agencies to increase multicultural programming. In addition to changing demographics, parks and recreation agencies have experienced growing pressure to provide evidence of financial accountability through outcomes assessment. In the early twenty-first century, the place of recreation and leisure as a cultural and social institution seems secure.

QUESTIONS FOR CLASS DISCUSSION OR ESSAY EXAMINATION

1. During the 1950s and 1960s, Americans became sharply aware of environmental problems, and the federal government took action to curb pollution and protect open spaces. What were some of the key events in this process, and how did it affect the recreation and park movement? Describe the changes that occurred with respect to federal environmental policy in the 1980s and 1990s.

2. Poverty, racial unrest, and the counterculture movement were important trends or concerns during the 1960s and 1970s. What actions did government take with respect to these problem areas, and how did they affect public values and behavior with respect to recreation? Some critics suggest that the breakdown in family values and social stability of the last several decades had its roots in this earlier period. Could you make a case for this argument?

3. Immediately after World War II, social forecasters predicted that free time would increase greatly by the turn of the twenty-first century and that society would adopt humanistic leisure interests and lifestyles, largely replacing the work ethic. From the perspective of the early twenty-first century, what has actually happened?

ENDNOTES

1. J. Murphy, E. W. Niepoth, L. Jamieson, and J. Williams, *Leisure Systems: Critical Concepts and Applications* (Champaign, IL: Sagamore Publishers, 1991): 94.

2. U.S. Census Bureau, "2007 Statistical Abstract." www.census.gov/compendia/statab/.

3. Richard Kraus, *Leisure in a Changing America: Multicultural Perspectives* (New York: Macmillan College Publishing, 1994): 61.

4. J. Zenger, "Leadership: Management's Better Half," *Trends* (Vol. 4, No. 3, 1987).

5. Ibid.

6. Richard Kraus, *New Directions in Urban Parks and Recreation: A Trends Analysis Report* (Temple University and Heritage Conservation and Recreation Service, 1980): 6.

7. Ellen Weissinger and William Murphy, "A Survey of Fiscal Conditions in Small-Town Public Recreation Departments from 1987 to 1991," *Journal of Park and Recreation Administration* (Vol. 11, No. 3, 1993): 61–71.

8. Jack Foley and Veda Ward, "Recreation, the Riots and a Healthy L.A.," *Parks and Recreation* (March 1993): 68.

9. Keith Bradsher, "Gap in Wealth in U.S. Called Widest in West," *New York Times* (17 April 1995): 1.

10. Robert Frank and Philip Cook, *The Winner Take All Society* (New York: The Free Press, 1995).

11. Robert Reich, cited in "A New Profile of Middle Class," *Employee Services Management* (May/June 1995): 4.

12. The Corporate Library, The Corporate Library's 2006 CEO Pay Survey.

13. Robert Frank, *Luxury Fever: Why Money Fails to Satisfy in an Era of Excess* (New York: The Free Press, 1999).

14. Robert Hughes, "Pulling the Fuse on Culture," *Time* (7 August 1995): 61.

15. Sebastian de Grazia, cited in J. S. Shivers and L. J. DeLisle, *The Story of Leisure: Context, Concepts, and Current Controversy* (Champaign, IL: Human Kinetics, 1996): 173.

16. Michael Satchell, "Parks in Peril," *U.S. News and World Report* (21 June 1997): 24.

17. Stephen Seplow and Jonathan Storm, "How TV Redefined Our Lives," *Philadelphia Inquirer* (30 November 1997): A1.

18. U.S. Department of Health and Human Services, *The Surgeon General's Call to Action to Prevent and Decrease Overweight and Obesity* (Rockville, MD: U.S. Department of Health and Human Services, Public Health Service, Office of the Surgeon General, 2001).

CHAPTER 5

PERSONAL LEISURE PERSPECTIVES
Motivations and Age Group Factors

◆ ◆ ◆

Soccer practice, dance class, play rehearsal, Boy Scouts. Be at Tuesday football practice or be benched in Saturday's game. First graders carry daily planners. Family vacations, not to mention family dinners, take a back seat to basketball. . . . Now some parents in Wayzata, Minnesota, a prosperous, purposeful community of high-achieving, energetic children and color-coded family calendars, have decided that it is all too much.

They are concerned that too little time with parents means that children are missing the stabilizing, character-shaping experiences of rituals like suppertime conversations and family outings. And, especially in the wake of school shootings in which the killers' parents often seemed to know little about their children's lives, they are worried that the influence of peers and the media and commercialism may be outweighing the influence of parents.[1]

◆ ◆ ◆

INTRODUCTION

Having reviewed the history of leisure on the world scene and over the past three decades in the United States, we now examine it from personal and societal perspectives. This chapter outlines the varied motivations that impel individuals in different age groups to take part in a wide range of recreational and play activities. It presents the values and benefits of leisure, as well as the constraints that limit participation.

MOTIVATION: WHAT IS IT?

Why do people choose to watch television for hours on end, play competitive sports, or conquer Mount Everest? The reasons are as varied as people are. Recreation enthusiasts derive different qualities from their activities, and these qualities are what drive them to participate. These driving factors are called *motivators*. Motivation can be defined as an internal or external element that moves people toward a behavior. A recreation-related motivator could be the desire to develop soccer skills or to learn about the visual arts.

There are two types of motivators to consider. First, *extrinsic motivators* are those things that cause a behavior but are controlled by an external force. Extrinsic motivators are oftentimes seen as rewards. For example, a professional athlete receives compensation for playing for his or her team. This compensation is an external reward, and is most likely one of the driving factors behind the athlete's participation. Another example of an extrinsic motivator is that of the golfer who plays with a regular foursome and bets $5 per hole with her friends. If she plays because of the money involved, this is an extrinsic motivator.

The second type of motivator is *intrinsic motivators*. These are elements that drive a person to behave in a certain way simply for the behavior itself and how it feels to the individual. Completing a 100-mile bike ride for the first time could lead to a sense of accomplishment and pride in the fact that a goal was reached. These feelings are intrinsic motivators. The bicycle ride was done because of the benefits of the activity and not because an external reward was dictating or influencing the person's behavior. The rewards are internal to the person, and the activity is done for its own sake.

Personal Influences on Leisure Motivations

Depending on the life stage of the individual, different kinds of recreational motivations may prevail. For example, systematic studies of the reasons why children engage in competitive sports programs have yielded the following kinds of ranked responses: (1) to have fun, (2) to improve my skills, (3) to stay in shape, (4) to do something the individual is good at, and (5) for the excitement of competition. In studies of the recreational motivations of adults, Kelly found that these included such elements as the need for rest and relaxation, excitement, self-expression, enjoying companionship, or to escape pressure from one's spouse.[2]

Gender obviously has a powerful impact on leisure needs and choices. In an extensive study of several thousand adult women in the province of Ontario, Canada, researchers Bolla, Dawson, and Harrington identified the basic meanings of leisure for women and described their subjective experiences reported during leisure involvement. These included such elements as the feeling of competence, security, or playfulness and the expression of serenity, femininity, or assertiveness. Clearly, such factors were closely tied to their motivations for taking part in leisure pursuits.[3]

The reasons for taking part in recreational activities also tend to be influenced by the nature of the activities themselves. In some cases, participation may be linked to a set of specific personal benefits. For example, Clough, Shepherd, and Maughan examined a sample of recreational long-distance runners and found that these marathoners had motivations linked to such underlying needs as health, challenge, and personal well-being. They listed the following kinds of benefits to be gained from running: (1) it keeps me fit; (2) it keeps me healthy; (3) it provides me with a physical challenge; (4) it gives me a sense of achievement; (5) it helps me relax; (6) it gives me more energy in my other activities; and (7) it increases my self-discipline.[4]

Still other research has identified the major purposes of an individual taking part in wilderness recreation such as extended hiking and camping, backpacking, rock climbing, or similar pursuits as including such elements as responding to the splendor of nature; resting and relaxing; enjoying adventure, challenge, and contact with others; escaping the pressures of modern, urban life; or living in simple and natural ways.

Simon Priest examined the function of privacy as part of camping in the Canadian wilderness and identified such personal needs and values as the following:

- *Personal autonomy:* The need to avoid being manipulated or dominated by others; to safeguard one's individuality
- *Emotional release:* Providing for respite from the psychological tensions and stresses of everyday life
- *Intimacy:* Being part of a small social unit, achieving a close personal relationship with others involved in the wilderness experience[5]

Often, leisure motivations are shaped by the interplay of both participants and activities at different levels of skill, experience, or difficulty. For example, Williams, Schreyer, and Knopf examined river floating as experienced by several different types of participants: beginners, novices, and those with both narrow and broad past floating adventures. They found that motivations included such categories as escape, challenge, action, autonomy, self-awareness, learning activity, and interest in nature. However, these motivations varied considerably according to the experience background of those studied. For example, less-experienced participants rated escape as a primary motivation, whereas more advanced floaters rated challenge or learning activity as primary goals.[6]

MOTIVATION FOR RECREATION PARTICIPATION

Although there are a plethora of ways to look at motivation, including by activity type, age, and gender, it is important to look at broad motivating factors that relate to leisure preferences. In describing the major areas of human development, behavioral scientists use such terms as *cognitive* (referring to mental or intellectual development), *affective* (relating to emotional or feeling states), and *psychomotor* (meaning the broad area of motor learning and performance). Because these terms are somewhat narrow in their application, this chapter will instead use the following more familiar terms: (1) *physical*, (2) *social*, (3) *psychological*, and (4) *emotional, intellectual,* and *spiritual*. Most, if not all, motivators of leisure participation can fit into one or more of these four categories.

Physical Motivators

Active recreational pursuits such as sport and games, dance, and even such moderate forms of exercise as walking or gardening have significant positive effects on physical

Youth baseball serves as a physical motivator where health, wellness, and other physical qualities are gained.

development and health. The value of such activities obviously will vary according to the age and developmental needs of the participants. For children and youth, the major need is to promote healthy structural growth, fitness, endurance, and the acquisition of physical qualities and skills. It is essential that children learn the importance of fitness and develop habits of participation in physical recreation that will serve them in later life. This is particularly important in an era of electronic gadgets, labor-saving devices, and readily available transportation, all of which save time and physical effort but encourage a sedentary way of life.

Physical motivators can best be summarized as (1) control of obesity, (2) preserving cardiovascular health, and (3) achieving wellness. Although each will be discussed separately, they are all intertwined. Most of what drives people who are motivated by the physical aspects of leisure is achieving wellness. A means to wellness is cardiovascular health and reduced obesity. Society is changing and starting to realize how important an active lifestyle is and parks and recreation play an active role in this.

Control of Obesity   Scientists agree that physical activity plays a major role in weight control. Obesity among American adults has grown steadily and is now a serious health problem in this country. Just over 65 percent of the U.S. population is overweight and of those 35 percent are considered obese. Children are not exempt from this weight problem because 15.8 percent of children ages 6–11, 16.1 percent of teens ages 12–19, and 10 percent of all preschoolers are overweight.[7]

The main reason for these obesity rates is inactivity. It is evident that inactivity is not just a youth or an adult problem. It stretches to all ages, races, genders, and income levels. In 2003, only 36.8 percent of adults ages 18–44 get regular physical activity which is up from 33.5 percent in 1998, and this activity rate decreases as people age. Of those 45–64 years old, only 31.3 percent and only 23.3 percent of those 65 and over get regular physical activity. Overall, men (35.4 percent) get more physical activity than women (30.6 percent). When looking at race Caucasians (33.9 percent) and biracial adults (32.6 percent) get the most regular physical activity followed by Asians (33.1 percent), African Americans (25.5 percent), and Hispanics/Latino Mexicans (24.4 percent). Education is also an indicator of regular physical activity levels. People without a high school diploma (18.1 percent) are least likely to get regular physical activity followed by those with a high school diploma (27.0 percent) and those with some college education (38.2 percent).[8]

The American Heart Association recommends that people over the age of two get at least 30 minutes of enjoyable, moderate-intensity activity every day and 30 minutes of vigorous physical activity three to four days per week. The benefits for both children and adults are decreased obesity, decreased incidences of coronary disease, diabetes, high blood pressure, and stroke. Although many of these diseases do not occur in children, obese children are more likely to become obese adults.

Because of these statistics, public, nonprofit, and commercial agencies have come together to offer programs and education to help people become more active. For example, Healthy People 2010 is an organization through the U.S. Department of Health and Human Services dedicated to helping people live longer and have a better quality of life. They have 10 indicators as to what makes a person healthy, and physical activity is at the top of the list.[9] This organization serves as an information clearinghouse as well as overseeing Steps to a HealthierUS, a program launched by the U.S. Department of Human Services. Money from this program has funded programs to get people to take small steps to becoming more active. For example, the Wenatchee Valley YMCA in Washington developed a program to address teen inactivity and poor nutrition through development of a fitness program and the purchase of portable fitness equipment.[10]

Preserving Cardiovascular Health   Of all the fitness-related aspects of active recreation, maintaining cardiovascular health may represent the highest priority. Cardiovascular diseases include such things as high blood pressure, heart failure, stroke, and coronary heart disease. Over 71.3 million people in the United States have cardiovascular diseases and it is the leading cause of death in Hispanics and Latinos. It was also an underlying or contributing factor in 58 percent of all deaths in 2002.[11]

Even with these known statistics, physical inactivity is the main culprit with a sedentary lifestyle being every bit as bad for one's heart as smoking, high cholesterol, or high blood pressure. On the basis of long-term population studies, authorities have generally recommended that a minimum of three half-hour periods of vigorous aerobic exercise with pulse-rate targets keyed to one's age is necessary to have a desired cardiovascular impact. However, recent research involving thousands of men and women indicates that even moderate forms of exercise, including such activities as walking, stair climbing, gardening, or housework have a beneficial long-term effect on one's health. Although high-intensity, pulse-pounding workouts yield the most dramatic benefits, more modest forms of exercise do yield significant benefits. Beyond these findings, other research has demonstrated that regular exercise reduces the incidence of other diseases such as diabetes, colon cancer among men and breast and uterine cancer among women, stress osteoporosis, and other serious illnesses.

However, exercise alone, in the form of solitary aerobic activity or body conditioning, is not likely to become a long-term health measure if it lacks sociability or recreational atmosphere. Summerfield and Priest point out that more than half of all adults exercise intermittently and that, of those who start an exercise program, less than half will still be exercising six months later.[12] Wankel found, in a study of adult fitness programs in a Canadian industrial setting, that the key factors associated with people continuing to engage regularly in group exercise had to do with the need for sociability, competition, and developing recreational skills. Thus, the most effective fitness activities are likely to be those with enjoyable recreational elements.[13]

If people are motivated to participate in park and recreation activities based on physical motivators, then there are plenty of opportunities to be found. More and more employers have fitness facilities, offer discounted memberships at local clubs, or give paid time off for employees to participate in fitness activities. Organizations such as YMCAs, YWCAs, local parks and recreation agencies, and hospitals all provide activities to get people moving. Even the travel industry is trying to help. Seeing the value of health and fitness, the travel industry is taking action by making health easier for guests. Many hotels are offering more healthy options on the room service menus, but more importantly, they are catering to the health conscious. For example, Omni Hotels brings a workout kit to the guest's hotel room. The Get Fit Kit arrives in a canvas bag and includes a mini radio headset, floor mat, dumbbells, exercise bands, and a workout booklet. Omni Hotels has expanded this program to include a mini-bar with healthy drinks and snacks, and a treadmill for a small additional cost.[14]

Wellness Concept of Health   Traditionally, health has been conceptualized as the absence of disease or, more positively, as the quality of personal physical fitness. Increasingly, however, the modern view of wellness holds that a variety of physical, emotional, social, and other factors underlie health in the fullest sense—and that these varied factors help to support and strengthen each other. McDowell writes that true wellness is a holistic state of being that is closely linked to one's leisure life.[15]

He goes on to say that leisure values, the breadth and depth of one's leisure interests, and the degree to which one uses leisure with purpose and joy are all part of holistic wellness. As indicated earlier, numerous research studies have confirmed that active and satisfying leisure experiences throughout one's life span contribute significantly to emotional and physical well-being and to successful aging. Such findings are reinforced by a growing body of evidence confirming the linkage of emotional, physical, and intellectual well-being.

Decreasing obesity, achieving physical fitness, and maintaining a healthy heart are just a few of the physical motivators that help people become more active and participate in recreation activities.

Social Motivators

The need to be part of a social group and to have friends who provide companionship, support, and intimacy is at the heart of much recreational involvement. It helps to explain why people join sororities, fraternities, or other social clubs, senior citizen centers, tour groups, or other settings where new acquaintances and potential friends may be met. It is an underlying element in sport in terms of the friendships and bonds that are formed among team members. There are a number of specific social motivators that must be mentioned, including being with others, overcoming loneliness, and developing social norms among children.

Being with Others and Reducing Loneliness   Many adults today find their primary social contacts and interpersonal relationships not in their work lives, but in voluntary group associations during leisure hours. Even in the relatively free environment of outdoor recreation, where people hike, camp, or explore the wilderness in ways of their own choosing, interaction among participants is a key element in the experience. Only 2 percent of all leisure activities are done alone. This indicates that people like to participate in activities with others.

■ *Two college friends take time away from their senior internships to walk the beach in Garrapata State Park in California.*

Social contact, friendship, or intimacy with others is key to avoiding loneliness. Loneliness is a widespread phenomenon among all ages. Typically, as many as three-quarters of all college students report being lonely during their first term away from home. As adults age, they begin to experience increased loneliness as significant others and friends begin to pass away and children leave home. Loneliness can have unpleasant and even life-threatening consequences and often is directly linked to alcoholism, physical illness, or suicide. In a poll taken by *Psychology Today*, loneliness was the most frequently mentioned personal problem, with 38 percent of female and 43 percent of male readers saying they often felt lonely. Involvement in recreation activities with others can alleviate feelings of loneliness. People can join the YMCA, YWCA, their local recreation center, or take classes at their local parks and recreation department where participants learn new skills or exercise while also meeting others who enjoy these same activities. Keep in mind there is a difference between loneliness and solitude. Russell suggests that time spent alone is an important part of our lives and can be a much desired state. People participate in certain activities to reduce loneliness, but they also do things to escape or focus totally on themselves such as the case with solitude.[16]

Clearly, different types of recreation groups and programs impose different sets of social norms, roles, and relationships that participants must learn to accept and that contribute to their own social development. For children, play groups offer a realistic training ground for developing cooperative, competitive, and social skills. Through group participation, children learn to interact with others to accept group rules and wishes, and, when necessary, to subordinate their own views or desires to those of the group. They learn to give and take, to assume leadership or follow the leadership of others, and to work effectively as part of a team.

As children age, their social groups increase in importance in their lives. Social peer groups for teens are a major sense of support and help them form their social identity. Into adulthood, social groups reflect our social status and position in society whether it is playing golf at the country club or camping with family and friends. As people reach senior adulthood (65+), social connections increase in importance as the social group starts to decrease in numbers due to life changes and death. Although social connections change throughout our lives, they always remain a significant part of our leisure lives.[17]

The social aspect of leisure is a significant motivator for many people. It may be a terrific opportunity to participate in activities with a friend or significant other or to participate in a setting to increase the possibility of meeting people for friendship or more.

Psychological Motivators

Oftentimes recreational activities are seen as a means of providing excitement and challenge, as a means of relaxation and escape, or as a way to relieve stress. These are psychological motivators that contribute to our mental health.

Excitement and Challenge   A great deal of recreational involvement today is based on the need for excitement and challenge, particularly in such outdoor recreation activities as skiing, mountain climbing, or hang gliding, or in active, highly competitive individual or team sports.

Risk recreation and outdoor adventure pursuits have become increasingly popular program elements, serving the needs of individuals who have a strong sensation-seeking drive. For many people, such urges are met through spectatorship—by watching action-oriented movies or television shows—or in the form of video games based on high-speed chase or conflict. For others, ballooning, skydiving, parasailing, amateur stock car racing, or scuba diving satisfy risk-related motivations. Although varied forms of deviant social behavior, such as gang fighting, vandalism, or other types of juvenile crime, are not commonly considered as leisure pursuits, the reality is that they often are prompted by the same need for thrills, excitement, and challenge that other, more respectable recreation pursuits satisfy.

Relaxation and Escape   Chubb and Chubb suggest that one of the most important psychological benefits of recreation is relaxation. Some people obtain this through physical activity, others from reading or other mental pastimes, and still others by dozing, day dreaming, or taking it easy. Relaxation, Chubb and Chubb write,

> provides a respite from life's worries and pressures, relieves feelings of tension and fatigue, and restores mental efficiency. Most people need it after a day's work, following an emotionally disturbing experience, or part way through a long period of involvement in one task.[18]

Kleiber suggested that leisure starts with relaxation. Only when we are relaxed are we able to forget about worries, feel comfortable with the conditions of our lives, and be receptive to the world around us.[19]

■ *Sisters relieve stress through laughter and recreation.*

Stress Management   A closely related value of recreation is its usefulness in stress reduction. A leading authority on stress, Dr. Hans Selye, defines *stress* as the overall response of the body to any extreme demand made upon it, which might include threats, physical illness, job pressures, and environmental extremes—or even such life changes as marriage, divorce, vacations, or taking a new job. Increasing amounts of stress in modern life have resulted in many individuals suffering from migraine or tension headaches, allergies, ulcers and ulcerative colitis, hypertension, and a number of psychosomatic illnesses, as well as accident proneness.

Once it was thought that the best approach to stress was rest and avoidance of all pressures, but today there is an awareness that some degree of stress is desirable and healthy. Today, researchers point out that physical activity can play a significant role in stress reduction. Typically, people work off anger, frustration, and indignation by taking long walks or engaging in some kind of physical activity such as exercise. All of the body's

For many individuals, strenuous physical activity does more than reduce tension; it may actually promote a state of elation or euphoria. The so-called runner's high results from chemicals called endorphins that are produced by the brain and pituitary gland following prolonged exercise. Endorphins help the body control pain and produce a strong sense of well-being. High-risk activities such as rock climbing, mountaineering, white-water canoeing, hang gliding, or wilderness backpacking may literally provide a sense of emotional release and an improved outlook, which help to overcome tension in daily life.

systems—the working muscles, heart, hormones, metabolic reactions, and the responsiveness of the central nervous system—are strengthened through stimulation. Following periods of extended exertion, the body systems slow, bringing on a feeling of deep relaxation. Attaining this relaxed state is essential to lessening the stress reaction.

Healthy Balance of Work and Play For most people, emotional well-being is greatly strengthened if they are able to maintain a healthy balance of work and recreation in their lives. Today, we recognize that there can be too much commitment to work, resulting in the exclusion of other interests and personal involvements that help to maintain mental health.

The emphasis on work and leisure is shifting in the United States. Much has been said in the news about the different generations and how the baby boomers (born 1940–1960) are impacting our lives. The baby boomers are today's upper management. They live to work and view themselves as having a strong work ethic. A strong work ethic is characterized by this group as working long hours and weekends to meet customer demands. This group likes recognition for a job well done and sees working long hours as a way of getting this reward. It was with this group that the divorce rates and stress levels skyrocketed and the number of latchkey kids increased.[20]

The tendency to place excessive emphasis on work, at the expense of other avenues of expression, has been popularly termed *workaholism*. For some people, work is an obsession and they are unable to find other kinds of pleasurable release. For those who find their work a deep source of personal satisfaction and commitment, this may not be an altogether undesirable phenomenon.

Generations are groups of people who share similar formative years by experiencing history, fads, and events. One way to divide the generations is as follows:

World War II generation—born 1928–1945, they experienced the Depression, World War II, Amelia Earhart's solo flight across the Atlantic, and the passage of the Social Security Act.

Baby boomer generation—born between 1946 and 1964, this group saw Woodstock, the Korean War, Jackie Robinson break into major league baseball, and the assassinations of Bobby and President John Kennedy and Martin Luther King.

Generation X or Gen X—born between 1965 and 1980 they experienced Watergate, the peak of Michael Jackson, break dancing, and Madonna.

Generation Y or Millennial generation—born between 1981 and 1997 this group experienced the technology boom with MP3 players, cell phones, and handheld computers.[21]

The idea of workaholism will always be prevalent in society but Generation X and the Millennial generation will most likely decrease this phenomenon. Generation Xers prefer a balance to work and play. They are today's middle and upper managers who were the latchkey kids coming home to find their parents still at work. They feel work productivity is important but not at the cost of what is most important to them—their leisure, family, and friends. The Millennial generation works to live. They have a job so they can make money to do the things they really want to do. They have been involved in a number of leisure activities their whole lives, from soccer to piano lessons, and they enjoy these things. This group sees the value of leisure and plans to take advantage of it rather than work excessive hours.[22]

Leading authorities on business management and personnel practices now stress the need for business executives to find outside pleasures that open up, diversify, and enrich their lives. The guilt that successful people too often have about play must be assuaged, and they must be helped to realize that, with a more balanced style of life, they are likely to be more productive in the long run—and much happier in the present. Generation X and the Millennial generation already know this and are probably better than their older supervisors and co-workers in taking advantage of the services offered by recreation professionals.[23]

Emotional, Intellectual, and Spiritual Motivators

What are the specific ways in which recreation contributes to emotional well-being? Millions of people who function within a presumable normal range of behavior tend to suffer from tension, boredom, stress, frustration, and an inability to use their leisure in satisfying ways. Mental depression afflicts an estimated 35 million people in the United States. The feeling of engagement and control over one's life that may be achieved in leisure is critical to sound mental health. Iso-Ahola and Weissinger point out that many psychologists base their treatment on this principle—seeking to help patients develop freedom and control in their lives, as well as the kind of engagement with others in leisure that contributes to psychological well-being.[24]

Leisure activity can provide strong feelings of pleasure and satisfaction and can serve as an outlet for discharging certain emotional drives that, if repressed, might produce emotional distress or even mental illness. The role of pleasure is increasingly recognized as a vital factor in emotional well-being. Some researchers have begun to analyze the simple concept of fun, defined as intense pleasure and enjoyment and an important dimension of social interactional leisure. In a review of studies on the "anatomy of joy," Natalie Angier reports that scientists are finding that sensations such as optimism, curiosity, and rapture—as opposed to puritanical condemnation of pleasure—"not only make life worth living, but also make life last longer. They think that euphoria unrelated to any ingested substance is good for the body, that laughter is protective against the corrosive impact of stress, and that joyful people outlived their bilious, whining counterparts."[25]

Linked to the issue of emotional well-being is *self-actualization*, a term that became popular in the 1970s chiefly through the writings of Abraham Maslow, who stressed the need for individuals to achieve their fullest degree of creative potential. Maslow developed a convincing theory of human motivation in which he identified a number of important human needs, arranging them in a hierarchy. As each of the basic needs

■ *A group of backpackers seek to achieve social, ego, and self-actualization needs through a backpacking trip on the Appalachian Trail.*

is met in turn, a person is able to move ahead to meet more advanced needs and drives. Maslow's theory includes the following ascending levels of need:

- *Physiological needs:* Food, rest, exercise, shelter, protection from the elements, and other basic survival needs
- *Safety needs:* Self-protection needs on a secondary level, such as protection against danger, threats, or other forms of deprivation
- *Social needs:* Needs for group associations, acceptance by one's fellows, and for giving and receiving affection and friendship
- *Ego needs:* Needs for enhanced status, a sense of achievement, self-esteem, confidence, and recognition by others
- *Self-actualization needs:* Needs for being creative and for realizing one's maximum potential in a variety of life spheres

Obviously, play and recreation can be important elements in satisfying at least the last three, the highest levels of need in Maslow's hierarchy. In his writing, Maslow stressed the need for individuals to be more spontaneous and creative and to find fulfillment in a variety of expressive activities—both work and play.[26]

Intellectual Values and Outcomes   Of all the personal benefits of play and recreation, probably the least widely recognized are those involving intellectual or cognitive development. Play is typically considered physical activity rather than mental, and has by definition been considered a nonserious form of involvement. How then could it

In the late 1990s, the findings of a long-term study of the effectiveness of high-quality early childhood day care demonstrated that children who had been exposed to such programs far outperformed others who had not, both on academic and cognitive tests, and were more likely to attend college or hold high-skill jobs. Games were an important element in these experimental day-care programs.[27]

contribute to intellectual growth? Researchers have slowly come to realize that physical recreation tends to improve personal motivation and make mental and cognitive performance more effective. Numerous studies, for example, have documented the effects of specific types of physical exercise or play on the development of young children. Other research studies have shown a strong relationship between physical fitness and academic performance. Although a number of these studies have focused on formal instructional programs, others have utilized less-structured experimental elements. Several studies have shown that playfulness as a personal quality is closely linked to creative and inventive thinking among children.

In the past, play was viewed as a frivolous activity, and children were discouraged from playing in order to devote fuller effort to serious learning activities. Today, we recognize that play contributes to cognitive growth and, indeed, may provide a uniquely effective way of learning. How does this happen?

The leading psychologist in the field of child development over the past several decades was Jean Piaget, once a professor at the University of Geneva and director of the Institut Rousseau. Piaget suggested that there are two basic processes to all mental development: assimilation and accommodation. *Assimilation* is the process of taking in, as in the case of receiving information in the form of visual or auditory stimuli. *Accommodation* is the process of adjusting to external circumstances and stimuli. In Piaget's theory, play is specially related to assimilation, the process of mentally digesting new and different situations and experiences. Anything important that has happened is reproduced in play, which is a means of assimilating and consolidating the child's emotional experiences.

Games also have been used to help children learn simple scientific, mathematical, and linguistic concepts. One firm provides game kits and visual aids that use playlike approaches to teach number relationships and mathematical symbols; puzzle boxes and equation games are just two of these approaches. Other games deal with civics, government, history and political science, banking, international trade, geometry, and physics. In the early age of games in North America, the sole purpose of playing was for intellectual stimulation. Although the focus has moved away from learning to that of a means of having fun, many games still hold an intellectual property. For example, Monopoly was first developed so people could begin to understand economic principles, and Snakes and Ladders (later renamed Chutes and Ladders) taught about morality and ethical behavior.

On another level, a reporter for *Forbes* magazine points out that business executives frequently enjoy high-level competitive play in games such as contract bridge, chess, or backgammon, and that they value competence in these pastimes in the people they employ. Investment advisors in particular recognize the risk-taking elements involved in such games and the need for strategic flair in taking calculated risks. Whether the game is poker, gin rummy, bridge, backgammon, or chess, the skills involved are all equally important in business.[28]

Spiritual Values and Outcomes   A final area in which recreation and leisure make a vital contribution to the healthy growth and well-being of human beings is within the spiritual realm. The term *spiritual* is commonly taken to be synonymous with *religion*, but here it means a capacity for exhibiting humanity's higher nature—a sense of moral values, compassion, and respect for other humans and for the earth itself. It is linked to the development of one's inner feelings, a sense of order and purpose in life, and a commitment to care for others and to behave responsibly in all aspects of one's existence.

How does recreation contribute in this respect? Pieper and others have suggested that in their leisure hours, humans are able to express their fullest and best selves. Leisure can be a time for contemplation, for consideration of ultimate values, for disinterested activity. This means that people can come together simply as people, sharing interests and exploring pleasure, commitment, personal growth, beauty, nature, and other such aspects of life.

In part, the use of outdoor settings for organized recreation experiences is based on the view of the natural world as "God's great temple," which has often been expressed in literature on the outdoors. Such settings often provide places for wilderness retreats, Bible study, or other religiously oriented programs. The Zen Buddhist view that sees God in every aspect of nature and in the relationships of human beings with the natural world underlies this concept. For men and women who accept the challenge of being alone in the natural world, even in perilous circumstances, the experience may often be a highly religious one.

Thus far this chapter has examined the important personal values of recreation and leisure involvement from four different perspectives: physical; social; psychological; and emotional, intellectual, and spiritual motivators. It is essential to recognize that these are not distinctly separate components of motivation, but are instead closely interrelated from a holistic perspective. Furthermore, it must be understood that leisure means different things to different people. The motivators behind one person bicycling may be completely different from what another gets out of it. The same is true for the outcomes from participation. The first individual may feel great after biking because of the exercise element, whereas the second person may not think about the exercise portion but the feeling of joy he or she gets from contributing to a healthy environment by biking to work rather than driving. Leisure motivators are as unique as the participants themselves.

INFLUENCE OF AGE GROUPS ON RECREATION

The influence of one's age on recreational values and motivators, and patterns of participation have been analyzed in numerous recreation and leisure-service programming textbooks. There are key states of the life span as well as growth processes and development tasks to be accomplished at each stage. Apart from differences in individual personalities within each age bracket, there is also the reality that developments in modern technology, economic and social trends, and shifts in family relationships have been responsible for major changes in age-related norms of human behavior. Our patterns of birth and parenthood have been radically altered by innovative technology in medical practice. We now have the potential for mothers to give birth to their own daughter's babies through the surgical implantation of fertilized ova. Similarly, men can now father babies for many years after their own deaths.

We have seen dramatic shifts in life experiences. Today, children are exposed to the realities of life and mature physically at a much earlier point than in the past. At the same time, paradoxically, they have a longer period of adolescence and schooling before entering the adult workforce. Adults now tend to marry later and have fewer children, and many adults are choosing not to marry at all. Older people have a much longer period of retirement, and a significantly greater number of elderly persons live more active and adventurous leisure lives today than in the past.

To fully understand the impact of societal trends on public involvement in recreation, park, and leisure-service programs, it is helpful to examine each major age group in turn. Rather than discuss the development stages of each age group, an overview of some important issues will be presented.

RECREATION IN THE LIVES OF CHILDREN

Childhood Play

Childhood is the age group that includes children from early infancy through the preteen years. Throughout this period, play satisfies important developmental needs in children—often helping to establish values and behavior patterns that will continue throughout a lifetime. Psychologists have examined the role of play at each stage of life, beginning with infancy and moving through the preschool period, middle and late childhood, and adolescence.

■ *Children develop physically, emotionally, and socially through play and recreation.*

Susanna Millar points out that children typically move through several stages: (1) solitary play, carried on without others nearby; (2) parallel play, in which children play side by side without meaningful interplay; (3) associative play, in which children share a common game or group enterprise but concentrate on their own individual efforts rather than group activity; and (4) cooperative play, beginning at about age three, in which children actually join together in games, informal dramatics, or constructive projects. By the age of six or seven, children tend to be involved in loosely organized play groups, leading to much more tightly structured and organized groups in the so-called gang age between eight and twelve.[29]

The important role of play in child development is illustrated by Lynn Barnett, who summarizes a number of the values and outcomes of constructive forms of leisure activity for children. These include play's demonstrated contribution to cognitive development, including problem solving and creative thinking, based on its flexible or experimental nature, which helps the child's transition from concrete experiences to abstract thought processes.[30]

Typically, we tend to think of childhood as a happy time, picturing it in literature or other forms of entertainment as a period of innocence, marked by a warm nostalgic glow. Television shows of the 1950s, for example, generally idealized the American family in terms of love, support, and security. Within this context, family play was presented as an experience that all could share, one with elements of companionship, humor, and self-discovery. Over the past three decades, however, a number of major changes have taken place that have radically changed the lives of children in terms of their family and neighborhood environments, the community services provided to meet their needs, and the commercial forces that entertain them and shape their personal values and view of the world.

Decline of the Family Structure

A major problem facing the American family involves the steadily growing divorce and separation rate, and the increasing employment of single parents or both parents. In the mid-1990s, the U.S. Census Bureau confirmed that the percentage of single parents raising children continued to rise dramatically: 54 percent of all children under the age of six now lived in families in which the sole parent or both parents worked. As a consequence, the number of "latchkey" children—who are twice as likely to abuse alcohol, tobacco, or marijuana as children with parental supervision—represents an increasing social problem.

Overscheduled Children

The overscheduling of children is becoming a problem in today's culture. For example, there are increasing opportunities for youth to participate in sport clinics, camps, and leagues for children as young as four. Many go on to be a part of traveling sport teams that go to different communities on the weekends to play in tournaments. Couple this with the demands of household chores, school assignments, and any number of other recreation activities, classes, and clubs and the result is dwindling free time for today's youth.

Although art and music lessons as well as sport and other educational activities may be beneficial to the child, there comes a point when the child has too many things going on in her life. This can result in damage to a child's self-esteem because she sees that her parents are always trying to improve her and she is not good enough the way she is. This overscheduling can add unnecessary stress to a child's life and quite possibly lead to escalated incidences of depression and substance abuse in the teen years.[31]

Economically Disadvantaged Children

Children in economically disadvantaged households tend to have few resources for constructive play. In the early 1990s, the National Commission on Children reported that there was ample evidence that the poverty rates for children had risen sharply over the past three decades. A Tufts University report showed that the proportion of children living in suburban settings whose family income fell below the poverty line had risen by 76 percent, compared with 56 percent in inner cities and 36 percent in rural areas.

The problem of inadequate recreational opportunities for the poor remains most severe in America's inner cities. Poor children have fewer toys, games, books, or trips to the zoo or beach; they seldom have access to special classes, vacation day camps, or well-equipped and staffed playgrounds. Recreation centers, playgrounds, or pools in these communities often have been vandalized or dominated by drug dealers or youthful gangs. At the same time, youngsters in such settings often are subject to pathologies that are made worse by poverty, such as alcoholism, drug abuse, violence, and other negative forces. Lacking the ability to provide for safe, supervised play after school or during vacation periods, many working parents in inner cities must choose between the enforced boredom of locking children in their apartments during free hours or exposing them to the dangers of an unsafe neighborhood.

Influence of Commercial Media: Violence and Sex

Another important influence on the lives of children today stems from the overwhelming barrage of violence and sexual content contained in the movies, television shows, video games, and music that saturate their environment.

Because children spend more time watching television than any other activity and 54 percent of all children have televisions in their bedrooms, it is not surprising that the shows impact their behavior. Two-thirds of all television shows contain sexual activity and/or violence. It is estimated that children are exposed to 14,000 sexual messages each year and by the age of 18, they will have seen 16,000 simulated murders and 200,000 acts of violence.[32] For the past 30 years, the American Psychological Association has posited that media increases aggressive behavior in children. Additionally, limiting violence seen on television will reduce aggressive behaviors in children toward their peers.[33]

Lack of Outdoor Play

Children are staying inside and spending more and more time with their computers, video games, and televisions rather than being outside experiencing all that nature has to offer. Richard Louv authored a book in which he explains how children do not have the same outdoor experiences previous generations had.[34] Parents keep a closer watch over children and limit where they can play and explore. They prefer the structured, supervised activities to free play in the outdoors. The radius that children are allowed to roam outside of their home is one-ninth of what it was 20 years ago. Much of this is due to safety concerns when in actuality child safety has steadily improved during the past decade, and they are far safer than they were 30 years ago.[35]

Louv reviewed research on the positive effects of children being close to nature. It was determined that nature can improve a child's emotional health. Furthermore,

■ *Outdoor recreation such as fishing can improve the emotional and physical health and creativity of children.*

nature helps relieve everyday stress that leads to depression, and children with nature near their home had fewer problems with behavior disorders, anxiety, and depression.[36] Nature also is seen as an intellectual enhancer. Moore and Hong suggest that natural settings will stimulate a child's senses and bring together informal play with formal learning and that these sensory experiences help a child grow intellectually.[37]

Attention Deficit Hyperactivity Disorder (ADHD) is a growing phenomenon among today's youth. More and more children are taking prescription drugs such as Ritalin to curb the symptoms of ADHD that include a difficulty in paying attention, focusing, listening, and following directions. Researchers have claimed that being in nature can boost a child's attention span and relieve symptoms of ADHD.[38] Something as simple as taking a walk in the woods, playing in an open space such as a park, or spending time in the backyard can have tremendous rewards, yet these types of activities are on the decline.

An Optimistic Picture

Despite the negative issues that have just been presented, it is encouraging to know that American children, by and large, are far more optimistic about the world and their place in it than one might have expected. A national survey in 1999 of 1,740 youngsters, aged 6 to 14, in 25 cities found the following:

> . . . [K]ids are very happy to be kids, and they don't view the world as the nasty place their parents perceive it to be. Nine out of 10 say they feel safe in their schools and neighborhoods. While parents list crime, violence, and guns as the worst aspects of being a child today, such concerns are way down the list for kids. Their gripes are the timeless laments of childhood: "getting bossed around," homework, chores.[39]

However, the study also found that most children were "in no rush to grow up" and were not in a hurry to become teenagers.

RECREATION IN THE LIVES OF ADOLESCENTS

The teenage population, which began to climb in the early 1990s following years of decline, is expected to keep growing until at least 2045, according to U.S. Census

Bureau projections. By then, it is projected there will be over 51 million Americans between the ages of 10 and 19.

Psychologists who have done extensive research into the lives of adolescents document a significant relationship between their recreational habits and their emotional and social development. Beth Kivel writes that in the past researchers have tended to focus on cognitive, emotional, social, and biological aspects of adolescent development and identity formation.

> Recently, however, researchers from all disciplines—psychology, social psychology, sociology—have broadened their focus to include the central contexts that contribute to a young person's identity—school, family, work, peers, and, more recently, leisure.[40]

Early studies found that the self-image of teenagers was closely related to their involvement in school activities. High school students with a high degree of self-esteem tended to take part in team sport, musical groups, publications, outdoor recreation, and social activities. Those with a low degree of self-esteem were much less involved.

In studies of high school subcultures, researchers have identified three distinct groups of adolescents: (1) the "fun" subculture, similar to the collegiate world of football, fraternities, sororities, dates, cars, and drinking; (2) the "academic" subculture of serious students who work hard, get the best grades, and are career oriented; and (3) the "delinquent" subculture, which rebels against the whole school enterprise and is associated with "negativism, hedonism, and violence."

Trends in Negative Adolescent Leisure Pursuits

Negative leisure pursuits by teens include such things as drug and alcohol use, gambling, and sexuality among others. Participation rates are changing with each one. For example, the National Institute on Drug Abuse is seeing a decline in teen drug use. This includes such drugs as marijuana, anabolic steroids, and ecstasy. However, the abuse of prescription drugs such as OxyContin and Vicodin are increasing as is the use of inhalants.[41]

Alcohol is also a major problem with adolescents that kills six and a half times as many teens as all other illicit drugs combined. Most of these deaths are due to alcohol-related car accidents.[42] This alcohol problem carries over to young adulthood when many teens go off to college. The problem is not so much social drinking as it is binge drinking. The Journal of Studies on Alcohol defines *binge drinking* as drinking for an extended period of time, usually two or more days, where a person repeatedly becomes intoxicated and disregards other activities and obligations.[43] The results or consequences of binge drinking are increased violence and aggressiveness, blackouts, driving under the influence, sexual aggression, and an indicator of mental health disorders, depression, anxiety, or compulsiveness.[44] Many researchers believe that adolescent binge drinking is a strong predictor of this same behavior in college.

Teen gambling is also on the rise. It is estimated that 60–80 percent of all teens have gambled at least once in the last year. That may include buying lottery tickets, small bets with friends, online gambling, or participating in an NCAA basketball tournament pool. If gambling becomes a problem among adolescents, suicide attempts escalate, and depression increases, as do petty crimes and delinquent activities.[45] Online gambling may be a major player in teen gambling behaviors because tens of thousands of websites are available to them as well as advertisements running on television. There is never a lack of exposure to gambling opportunities for this age group.

In 2003, the Planned Parenthood Federation reported that the United States had the highest rate of teen pregnancies among Western developed nations. Teen pregnancy rates are declining. However, an estimated one million teens get pregnant each year.[46] Other reports show that the percentage of sexually active teenage girls who have several partners has risen sharply, with a growing number of girls under the age of 14 reporting sexual involvement. Many children as young as 10 or 11 today are involved in mutual masturbation, oral sex, and similar activities as precursors to intercourse.[47] On a more positive note, however, reports by the U.S. Department of Health and Human Services and the National Center for Health Statistics indicated that the nation's teenage birth rate had fallen to near-record lows and that there was a clear decline in illicit drug use by young people in the late 1990s.[48]

Influence of Mass Media

As was the case with younger children, there is widespread concern about the influence of movies, television, mass media, and music on the values and behavior of teenagers. First, there is the conviction that excessive television watching may have serious outcomes. The thousands of hours that children and youth spend in passive contemplation of the screen during their formative years are hours stolen from the time needed to learn to relate to others and gain usable and enjoyable skills of active participation. It is believed that intensive exposure to television stifles creative imagination and encourages a passive outlook toward life.

As previously discussed, there is mounting evidence that television actually encourages violent, criminal, and sexual youth behavior. As early as 1969, the National Commission on the Causes and Prevention of Violence concluded that violence on television had to be reduced because it encouraged imitation and strengthened "a distorted, pathological view of society." Studies repeatedly have documented lowered inhibitions of aggressive behavior after exposure to violence on television, and there have been numerous examples of crimes committed shortly after similar crimes were shown on television. Research shows that teens ages 12–17 who watched more

Despite efforts at education and discipline, the College Alcohol Study by the Harvard School of Public Health found that binge drinking in American colleges continued at a high level in the late 1990s, with about two of every five students currently involved in drinking to excess.

television with sexual content were more likely to engage in sexual behaviors earlier and these behaviors would escalate.[49]

Boredom and the Need for Excitement

Since the last decades of the nineteenth century, the perceived need to provide positive recreation programs and facilities for children and youth has been based on the belief that constructive free-time alternatives not only keep youngsters off the street but also help prevent the kinds of delinquent play that otherwise might result from boredom. Again and again, adolescents apprehended for criminal activity use the excuse that they were bored, that there was nothing else to do, or that their delinquent actions were a form of fun. Often, however, such forms of thrill-seeking play end in tragic episodes of violence, clashes between different ethnic groups, drug- and alcohol-fueled accidents, or other self-destructive experiences.

Changing Teen Experiences

A report by the Carnegie Council on Adolescent Development suggests that the period between the ages of 10 and 14 is the least understood and "most neglected phase of the life span from conception to senescence." Young teens' mental and physical growth is accelerated, with puberty coming two years earlier than it did a century ago. It is argued by feminists that, because schools and society favor boys, adolescent girls seriously suffer from a lack of self-esteem. It has been documented that adolescent girls can be vulnerable to depression, eating disorders, and other addictions—yet boys make up 85 percent of special education students, with such diagnoses as learning disabilities or behavior disorders. They get lower grades and more punishment, commit suicide at a higher rate, and get into far more problems of delinquency than do girls. Given such problems, it is ironic that more than half of all adolescents will spend at least part of their lives in a single-parent family and that the total time that American children spend with their parents has decreased by at least one-third over the past 30 years. The Carnegie Council report concludes that the United States is neglecting its adolescent population.

At the same time that national concern is focused on many of the difficulties facing adolescents today, there is evidence that many teens hold conservative views and have traditional lifestyles. A nationwide poll reported in 1998 by the *New York Times* and CBS News found that teenagers today are worldly, shaped by exposure to a culture that has dropped many of its inhibitions. However, Goodstein and Connelly write:

> [I]n some ways they are as wholesome and devoid of cynicism as the generation that wore saddle shoes. They trust their government, admire their parents, and believe it is possible to start out poor and become rich. Ninety-four percent say they believe in God. Strong majorities say they never drink alcohol and never smoke cigarettes or marijuana.[50]

RECREATION IN THE LIVES OF ADULTS

The adult population in modern society, defined as those in their late teens to their early or mid-sixties, may logically be subdivided into several age brackets, lifestyle patterns, or generations. Although many life experiences occur in this broad age range, it is important to look at an overall picture of how people progress through these years.

Young Adults

The population of young adults, extending from late teens to early or mid-thirties, includes Gen X and a few of the older Millenial generation. For them, the single population has exploded. People are marrying later, if at all. In the past, the word *single* usually meant a lonely person, or a "loser" whose solitary status was a temporary sidetrack on the way to happy matrimony. However, in the decade of the "Me Generation," with its emphasis on narcissistic pleasure and self-fulfillment, singlehood came to be regarded as a happy ending in itself—or at least an enjoyable prolonged phase of postadolescence. When this trend became obvious, a vast number of singles-only institutions sprang up to meet the needs of this newly recognized population that had an estimated $40 billion of annual spending power. Singles apartment complexes, bars, weekends at resort hotels, social groups at local churches, cruises, and a variety of other leisure programs or services emerged—including computer-dating services and speed dating. *Speed dating* is an interesting phenomenon in which singles talk with each other one-on-one 5 to 10 minutes and then move on to the next person. In our hurried society, speed dating allows singles to connect with more people in a shorter amount of time.

As a subgroup of the young adult population, college students are usually strongly influenced in their choice of leisure activities by their status as students. Students living at home are likely to have relatively little free time, often holding jobs and traveling back and forth to school, and they often find much of their recreation with friends in their neighborhoods. Students living on college campuses generally take part in social or religious clubs, athletic events, fraternity or sorority functions, and college union programs, entertainment, or cultural activities. Many young college students regard their first experience in living away from home for a sustained period of time as an opportunity to engage in hedonistic forms of play without parental supervision. In part, this appears to be a response to the stress that challenges many first-year college students. A January 2000 national survey reported by researchers at the University of California at Los Angeles revealed that both male and female beginning students suffered from higher levels of anxiety than in past generations, with almost twice as many women as men reporting severe levels of stress.[51]

Despite the problems attached to alcohol and drug abuse previously discussed, the majority of young single adults are able to use their leisure time in positive and constructive ways. Particularly for those who have finished school and are financially independent, travel, participation in sport or fitness clubs, social clubs, or forms of popular entertainment and involvement in hobbies and creative activities enrich their lives, both in colleges and in community settings.

Although millions of men and women have joined the trend toward a continuing single lifestyle, a majority of young adults today choose marriage and family life. Leisure behavior is markedly affected when people marry and have children. Social activities tend to center around the neighborhood in which the couple lives, and the home itself becomes a recreation center for parent and child activities. The family takes part in social programs sponsored by religious agencies, civic and neighborhood associations, or PTAs. As children move into organized community programs, parents begin to use their leisure time for volunteer service as adult leaders for Scout groups, teachers in cooperative nursery schools, coaches and managers for sport teams, or in similar positions.

The group in this age bracket that is most deprived of leisure consists of single parents who often must work, raise a family under difficult economic and emotional circumstances, and try at the same time to find needed social outlets and recreational opportunities for themselves. A limited number of

■ *Leisure for young adults often encompasses both family and friends.*

municipal and school recreation agencies provide day-care or after-school programs to assist such single parents; in addition, some commercial and voluntary recreation agencies sponsor babysitting services in order to permit mothers of young children to take part in their programs during the day.

Middle Adults

The current middle adult age group is considered the baby boomers. They are approximately 45–65 years old and make up the largest section of the population. Paul Light comments that the baby boomers were remarkably homogeneous in terms of the widely accepted social values prevailing in their early childhoods. However, in the following turbulent period of social change, the members of this young generation shifted abruptly from the values of their parents and grandparents. Light writes:

> They may love their parents, but when it comes time to talk about politics, marriage, drugs, or sex, the baby boomers respectfully disagree. From questions on the government's role in creating jobs, religion in the schools, war and peace, political trust, and race, to questions on AIDS, homosexuality, drugs, pornography, and women's rights, the baby boomers maintain their distance from their parents and grandparents.[52]

Boomers Are Boosting the RV Market
Fifty percent of RV owners are part of the baby boomer generation. This $20 billion a year industry is seeing record numbers of people buying pop-up campers, travel trailers, and motor homes. The increasingly high gas prices have not deterred this group from spending an average of 26.5 nights per year in campgrounds and RV parks around the country.[53]

Studies show that baby boomers have immense diversity in their lifestyles as well. Some are devoted to their families; others remain unattached. Some boomers are sport minded or wilderness oriented, whereas others are committed to the arts, hobbies, or literary pursuits. Growing numbers of this age group have begun to place a high value on the creative satisfaction found in work or to devote a fuller portion of their time to family and personal involvements.

For parents in the middle adult years, patterns of leisure involvement begin to change as children become more independent and even establish their own families. Many nonworking parents, who have devoted much time and energy to the family's needs, begin to find these demands less pressing. They have more available time, as well as a need to find a different meaning and fulfillment in life through new interests and challenges.

In 1999, a portrait of the midlife years based on a 10-year study of nearly 8,000 Americans conducted by the MacArthur Foundation concluded that

> Far from being a time of turmoil, for most people the midlife years appear to be a time of psychic equanimity, good health, productive activity, and community involvement. . . . Between ages 35 and 65, and in particular between 40 and 60, people report increased feelings of well-being and a greater sense of control over many parts of their lives [with] just a third [describing the period] as a time of personal turmoil brought about by the realization that they were aging.[54]

Strikingly, in the late 1990s, the American Association of Retired Persons (AARP) reported that most baby boomers in the midlife years were optimistic about retirement and were planning for it financially. However, 80 percent of individuals surveyed by the AARP indicated that they planned to keep working in some capacity well after the traditional retirement age of their parents.

Numerous research studies have documented the importance of recreation and leisure during the middle and later years of life. Valeria Freysinger found that leisure had various connotations; it provides (1) an agent for change and an opportunity for exerting personal choice and freedom; (2) an opportunity for relaxation, enjoyment, and rejuvenation; (3) a means of affiliation and interaction with others; (4) an area for self-expression and gaining feelings of mastery and accomplishment; and (5) a time for maintenance of friendships and affirming family values.[55]

Many leisure-service providers are realizing the impact of the baby boomers and what it means for their agencies. As more of this group moves into retirement, they are going to be looking for activities to keep themselves busy. This group is going to retire with money to spend, and they are healthier than retirees in the past. Furthermore, baby boomers are not afraid to try new things and go to new places. They refuse to retire and go quietly to a senior citizens center to play passive games, because they do

Gail Sheehy, in her 1995 book *New Passages: Mapping Your Life Across Time,* suggests that middle age has been extended to a much later point in the life span, and that Americans can now look forward to what she calls the "Flourishing Forties," the "Flaming Fifties," and the "Age of Integrity" in their sixties.

not see themselves as seniors. They plan to stay active to show that they are not old and will need recreation and tourism services to do it.

RECREATION IN THE LIVES OF OLDER ADULTS

In a 1998 report, the United Nations Population Fund concluded that although overall population growth has been steadily declining, there will be an unprecedented increase in older persons—from 10 percent of the population in 2000 to 31 percent in 2150. *Older adults* are defined here as people in their mid-sixties and older, or the current World War II generation. Given the increase in life expectancy, this group is quite large and diverse. They pass through several stages, much like those in the adult category do.

Active Older Adults

Recreation and leisure assume a high priority in the lives of most elderly persons, particularly for those in their late sixties and beyond who have retired from full-time jobs. Without work to fill their time and often with the loss of partners or friends, such persons find it necessary to develop new interests and often to establish new relationships. Loneliness can be devastating to people who are aging. One study showed, for example, that the mortality rate rose dramatically for older men who had been widowed.

It is now popular to assert that older adults are far more active, vigorous, economically secure, and happier than had been assumed in the past. With improved financial support and pension plans, a much higher percentage of older persons are relatively well-to-do and able to enjoy a far longer period of retirement. Research has

■ *Older adults gather in New York City's Juniper Park daily to play bocce ball.*

shown that many older adults continue to enjoy sexual relations and to maintain active and creative lives well into their seventies and eighties.

Changes for Older Adults

The lives of older adults have changed dramatically over the past three or four decades. Not only can they expect to live much longer, but their living circumstances are likely to be radically different from those of past generations in terms of familial roles, social activities, economic factors, and other important conditions.

Changes in Family Structure   In the past, it was common for several generations of family members to live together. Older persons continued not only to receive the affection and support of their children and grandchildren, but also to play meaningful roles in family life. With the shift toward living in urban and suburban apartments and small one-family homes, increasing numbers of older adults must now live separately. Although many do not want to live in a nursing home, there is still need for some additional care as people age. The number of senior living communities, retirement communities, and assisted-living environments is growing. Depending on the level of care needed (from no care at all to full-time nursing care), these types of living situations can meet the needs of people as they age. These communities provide nursing care, daily living assistance, socialization, and recreation opportunities for the residents. Many see this as a better alternative than living with grown children and their families.

A second shift in the family structure is found in the growing number of cases where grandparents are forced to take responsibility for young children because their own children—the parents—are unable to maintain a stable household.

Positive Changes   Even though these negative trends must be acknowledged, the reality still is that most older people are living longer, happier, and healthier lives than in the past. Indeed, there is striking new evidence that the very old are enjoying remarkably good health in comparison with other age groups. The average annual Medicare bill for people who live to their late eighties and

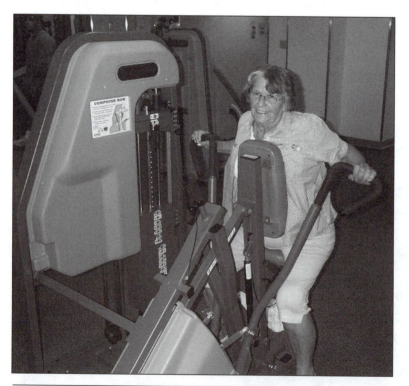

■ *Older adults remaining physically active later in life have led to improved quality of life for many.*

nineties is significantly lower than that for those who die sooner. Part of the reason is that older adults tend to be relatively robust. Cancer and heart disease, the two chief killers for retired persons in the younger age brackets, tend not to affect the very old, and Alzheimer's disease also attacks slightly younger men and women. Today, there are more and more centenarians—people who have made it to their 100th birthday—there is an estimated 30,000 to 50,000, according to demographers, which is a sharp increase from the 1980 estimate of 15,000.

There is growing evidence that aging need not be accompanied by mental deterioration. Although some losses in memory or other aspects of mental performance do commonly occur, studies have shown that from 20 percent to 30 percent of people in their eighties who volunteer for cognitive testing perform as well as volunteers in their thirties and forties, who are presumably at the peak of mental performance. Scientists have recently discovered that the adult brain can generate new cells even well into old age and that the network of connections among brain cells can strengthen over time. They concluded that intellectually challenging work boosts cognitive skills in older adults even more than in younger people:

> Not only can most healthy people function well mentally until the end of life, says the director of George Washington University's Center on Aging, Health and Humanities, but "they can do even better by staying mentally, physically, and socially active."[56]

With improved medical care, people are not just living longer, healthier lives—they are living them differently. Particularly in the so-called retirement states of New Mexico, Arizona, Nevada, and Florida, which have fast-growing populations of older men and women, they are engaging in active sports, volunteering, going back to school, and developing new networks of friends and relationships. Surprisingly, however, recent census reports indicate that only a small fraction of older persons—about 1 in 10—move at all when they retire. Of that number, about half remain in their home states. In many cases, as younger adults leave farming areas in search of jobs and cultural opportunities elsewhere, elderly men and women remain in rural districts of Nebraska, Iowa, Kansas, and the Dakotas and strive to maintain vital communities in these settings.[57]

Specific Contributions of Recreation and Leisure

Research confirms that recreational involvement meets a number of important physical, emotional, and social needs of older adults. Numerous studies have shown that regular physical exercise has immense health-related value for older persons, with a range of specific benefits that include preventing heart disease, stroke, cancer, osteoporosis, and diabetes; assisting in weight reduction; improving immunity against common infections; reducing arthritic symptoms; countering depression; and even helping to improve memory and the quality of the older individual's sleep.

In terms of social benefits, one of the key problems affecting older adults is that they tend to become isolated and lose a sense of playing a significant role in family life or in the community at large. Therefore, community service and volunteerism are useful leisure activities for older adults. In fact, volunteerism is frequently conceptualized as a satisfactory substitute for paid work for older persons. Older adults gain an important sense of recognition and self-worth through volunteerism. It provides structure in their lives in terms of regular time commitments and offers social contacts that often lead to friendship and other group involvement.

Another important leisure pursuit for older adults consists of continuing education— either on a fairly casual basis with classes or workshops in nearby after-school or community center programs or on a more formal basis in noncredit courses taken through Elderhostel or other college-sponsored programs. Robert Hopp writes:

> The hundreds of thousands of "Elderhostel alumni" reflect a positive, motivated, participatory attitude that directly refutes North America's attitude of "used-up elders." Elderhostel is an inexpensive, uncomplicated, and highly accessible experience, promising interaction with peers and interesting travel opportunities. The programs [involving varied cultural, historical, and creative subjects] are usually affiliated with universities, relying on them for residence hall and cafeteria space, as well as instructors, for some of their classes.[58]

Linked to such involvements, a growing number of older persons are traveling the "information superhighway," learning computer skills and exploring the Internet. Still others break new ground by entering a new period of creative development in the arts, writing, social service, or other unknown kinds of personal involvement. Much of today's increased life expectancy has been added, it seems, not to the end but to the middle of our lives—extending the opportunity for "late bloomers" to realize their dreams.

Many leisure activities of older persons are relatively simple close-to-home pursuits, such as reading for pleasure, talking on the telephone, gardening or raising plants, watching television, socializing with friends and family, and carrying on individual hobbies. Other activities may be more active and demanding, such as sport, outdoor recreation, fitness classes, and dancing. These may be enjoyed with people of all ages or in special senior citizens groups, golden age clubs, or retirement communities.

SUMMARY

Beyond the familiar motivations of seeking fun, pleasure, or relaxation, people engage in leisure pursuits for a host of different reasons. Recreational motivations include personal goals such as the need for companionship, escape from stress or the boredom of daily routines, and the search for challenge, a sense of personal accomplishment, physical fitness, or emotional release. In addition to being based on widely shared motivations, leisure involvement is also influenced by the age, gender, race, or other characteristics of participants, as well as by the unique nature of the play activities themselves.

The outcomes of recreational involvement may be classified under four major headings: physical; social; psychological; and emotional, intellectual, and spiritual.

Age and family status represent key factors that affect the recreational needs and interests of individuals throughout life. Human development experts have outlined a sequence of age groupings extending from infancy through old age, and recreational authorities have developed guidelines for program planning for each group based on the developmental characteristics at each stage.

Today, changes in family life and social environment have altered traditional models of development, with significant implications for recreation programmers. The chapter points out that children today grow up much earlier and are subjected to influences that they would have been shielded from in the past. Youth in affluent families often have lavish recreational goods and abundant opportunities for structured play, while children in poverty settings frequently lack recreation facilities or programs.

The chapter also discusses adult life, pointing out that while a higher percentage of individuals remain or become single than in the past, the majority tend to marry and raise families, with much of their recreation centering around the home and family unit. For older adults, who represent a steadily increasing proportion of the population, many of the negative stereotypes of the past no longer apply. People today live longer and tend to be more independent and active in the varied forms of recreation that promote their overall well-being and life satisfaction.

QUESTIONS FOR CLASS DISCUSSION OR ESSAY EXAMINATION

1. The physical benefits of exercise have been well documented. Vigorous use of exercise machines and treadmills, running, swimming, and bicycling all contribute greatly to cardiovascular health. Why is it desirable to approach such activities as recreation rather than as prescribed exercise carried on for fitness purposes alone? In addition to cardiovascular benefits, what other important health outcomes have been identified?

2. The chapter describes some of the specific contributions of recreation to emotional or mental health. What are they? On the basis of your own experience, can you describe some of the positive emotional outcomes resulting from recreational involvement?

3. Select one of the following age groups: children, teens, young adults, middle adults, or older adults. What are their special needs for recreation in modern society, and what barriers or problems do they face in the appropriate choice of satisfying leisure activity?

4. Older adults make up a rapidly growing segment of the population. How has society traditionally considered the aging process and the role of older persons in community life? What new views have developed in recent years? What are the implications of these changes for recreation practitioners working with older persons?

5. Select your five favorite recreational activities and then answer the following question: Why do you participate in these activities (motives)? Predict how this list will change in the next 10, 20, 30, and 50 years.

ENDNOTES

1. Pam Belluck, "Parents Try to Reclaim Their Children's Time," *New York Times* (13 June 2000): A18.

2. John Kelly, "Leisure Styles and Choices in Three Environments," *Pacific Sociological Review* (Vol. 21, 1978): 178–208.

3. P. Bolla, D. Dawson, and M. Harrington, "Women and Leisure: A Study of Meanings, Experiences, and Constraints," *Recreation Canada* (Vol. 51, No. 3, 1993): 223–226.

4. P. Clough, J. Shepherd, and R. Maughan, "Motives for Participation in Recreational Running," *Journal of Leisure Research* (Vol. 21, No. 4, 1989): 305.

5. Simon Priest et al., "Functions of Privacy in Canadian Wilderness," *Journal of Applied Recreation Research* (Vol. 17, No. 2, 1992): 234–254.

6. D. Williams, R. Schreyer, and R. Knopf, "The Effect of the Experience Use History on the Multidimensional Structure of Motivations to Participate in Leisure Activities," *Journal of Leisure Research* (Vol. 22, No. 1, 1990): 36–54.

7. A. Hedley et al., "Prevalence of Overweight and Obesity Among US Children, Adolescents, and Adults, 1999–2002," *Journal of the American Medical Association* (Vol. 291, 2004): 2847–2850.

8. National Center for Health Statistics, *Health, United States, 2005, with Chartbook on Trends in the Health of Americans* (Hyattsville, MD: 2005).

9. Healthy People 2010. www.healthypeople.gov/About/goals.htm.

10. HealthierUS, "YMCA/Steps Community Collaborative Projects." www.healthierus.gov/steps/YMCASteps.htm, 2005.

11. American Heart Association, *Heart Disease and Stroke Statistics–2006 Update* (Dallas, TX: American Heart Association, 2006).

12. L. Summerfield and L. Priest, "Using Play as Motivation for Exercise," *Journal of Physical Education, Recreation, and Dance—Leisure Today* (October 1987): 24.

13. Leonard Wankel, "Personal and Situational Factors Affecting Exercise Involvement: The Importance of Enjoyment," *Research Quarterly for Exercise and Sport* (3rd Quarter 1985): 275–282.

14. Andrew Cohen, "Real Room Services," *Athletic Business* (2002 June).

15. C. F. McDowell, "Leisure Integrating a Wellness Consciousness," in B. Riley, J. Shank, and S. Nichols, eds., *Therapeutic Recreation: A Holistic Approach* (Durham, NH: New England Therapeutic Recreation Consortium, 1987): 22.

16. R. Russell, *Pastimes: The Context of Contemporary Leisure*, 3rd ed. (Champaign, IL: Sagamore Publishing, 2005).

17. D.J. Jordan, *Leadership in Leisure Services: Making a Difference*, 2nd ed. (State College, PA: Venture Publishing, 2001).

18. M. Chubb and H. Chubb, *One Third of Our Time: An Introduction to Recreation Behavior and Resources* (New York: John Wiley and Sons, 1981): 51.

19. D.A. Kleiber, "The Neglect of Relaxation," *Journal of Leisure Research* (Vol. 32, No. 1, 2000): 82–85.

20. C. Raines, *Connecting Generations* (Menlo, CA: Crisp Publications, 2003).

21. Ibid.

22. Ibid.

23. Ibid.

24. S. E. Iso-Ahola and E. Weissinger, "Leisure and Well-Being: Is There a Connection?" *Parks and Recreation* (June 1984): 40–44.

25. Natalie Angier, "The Anatomy of Joy," *New York Times Good Health Magazine* (26 April 1992): 50.

26. Abraham Maslow, "A Theory of Psychological Motivation," *Psychological Review* (July 1943): 370–396.

27. Jodi Wilgoren, "Quality Day Care, Early, Is Tied to Achievements as an Adult," *New York Times* (22 October 1999): A16.

28. A. Hurd, "Board Games," in G. Cross, ed., *Encyclopedia of Recreation and Leisure in America* (New York: Charles Scribner's Sons, 2004).

29. S. Millar, *The Psychology of Play* (Baltimore: Penguin, 1968): 178–184.

30. Lynn Barnett, "Developmental Benefits of Play for Children," *Journal of Leisure Research* (Vol. 22, No. 2, 1990): 138–153.

31. A. Rosenfeld, and N. Wise, The Overscheduled Child: Avoiding the Hyper-Parenting Trap. www.connectforkids.org/node/296, 2001.

32. Parents Television Council. www.parentstv.org/PTC/facts/mediafacts.asp.

33. T. N. Robinson et al., "Effects of Reducing Children's Television and Video Game Use on Aggressive Behavior," *Archives of Pediatrics and Adolescent Medicine* (Vol. 155): 17–23.

34. R. Louv, *Last Child in the Woods: Saving Our Children from Nature-Deficit Disorder* (Chapel Hill, NC: Algonquin Books of Chapel Hill, 2005).

35. K. C. Land, *The Foundation for Child Development and Youth Well-Being Index (CWI), 1974–2004, with Projections for 2005* (Durham, NC: Duke University, 2006).

36. N. Wells and G. Evans, "Nearby Nature: Buffer of Life Stress Among Rural Children," *Environment and Behavior* (Vol. 35, 2003): 311–330.

37. R. C. Moore and H. H. Hong, *Natural Learning: Creating Environments for Rediscovering Nature's Way of Teaching* (Berkeley, CA: MIG Communications, 1997).

38. A. F. Taylor et al., "Coping with ADD: This Surprising Connection to Green Play Settings," *Environment Behavior* (Vol. 33, 2001): 54–77.

39. Claudia Wallis, "The Kids Are Alright," *Time* (5 July 1999): 56.

40. Beth Kivel, "Adolescent Identity Formation and Leisure Contexts: A Selective Review of Literature," *Journal of Physical Education, Recreation, and Dance* (January 1998): 36.

41. National Institute on Drug Abuse. www.drugabuse.gov/Infofacts/HSYouthtrends.html.

42. Teen Drug Abuse. www.teendrugabuse.us/teen_drug_use.html.

43. Marc A. Schuckit, "The Editor Responds," *The Journal of Studies on Alcohol* (1998): 123–124.

44. National Institute on Alcohol Abuse and Alcoholism, *College Students and Drinking, Alcohol Alert No. 29* (Bethesda, MD: U.S. Department of Health and Human Services, 1995).

45. K. Hardoon et al., "Empirical vs. Perceived Measures of Gambling Severity: Why Adolescents Don't Present Themselves for Treatment," *Addictive Behaviors* (Vol. 28, 2003): 933–946.

46. Planned Parenthood, "Reducing Teenage Pregnancy: Pregnancy and Childbearing Among U.S. Teens." www.plannedparenthood.org/library/TEEN-PREGNANCY/teenpreg_fact.html.

47. Anne Jarrell, "The Face of Teenage Sex Grows Younger," *New York Times* (2 April 2000): ST1.

48. Marc Lacey, "Teenage Birthrate in U.S. Falls Again," *New York Times* (27 October 1999): A16.

49. R. L. Collins et al., "Watching Sex on Television Predicts Adolescent Initiation of Sexual Behavior," *Pediatrics* (Vol. 114, 2004): 280–289.

50. L. Goodstein and M. Connelly, "Teenage Poll Finds a Turn to the Traditional," *New York Times* (30 April 1998): A20.

51. Jodi Wilgoren, "Freshman Year as Stress Test," *New York Times* (30 January 2000): WK2.

52. Paul Light, *Baby Boomers* (New York: W. W. Norton, 1988): 28.

53. National Association of RV Parks and Campgrounds, *National Association of RV Parks and Campgrounds Explores the Lives and Travels of Active Campers and RV Owners.* www.arvc.org/, (24 January 2006).

54. Erica Goode, "New Study Finds Middle Age Is Prime of Life," *New York Times* (16 February 1999): D6.

55. Cited in Gail Sheehy, *New Passages: Mapping Your Life Across Time* (New York: Random House, 1995).

56. Laura Tangley, "Aging Brains Need Fresh Challenges to Stay Agile," *U.S. News and World Report* (5 June 2000): 90.

57. Sara Rimer, "Rural Elderly Create Vital Communities as Young Leave Void," *New York Times* (2 February 1998): 1.

58. Robert Hopp, "Experiencing Elderhostel as Lifelong Learners," *Journal of Physical Education, Recreation, and Dance* (April 1998): 27.

CHAPTER 6

SOCIOCULTURAL FACTORS AFFECTING LEISURE

◆ ◆ ◆

If someone says, "you throw like a girl," take it as a compliment. Once thought of as an insult suggesting female weakness, the phrase now carries new meaning. Today, strong girls and women excel in many areas of athletics, even in traditionally male-dominated sports. Females reach their goals, break records, and win championships. Participating in sports creates champions on and off the field. These champions not only lead in their respective sports, they lead in their homes, in their schools, at their jobs, and in their communities.

They lead on a path that has been paved by skilled and accomplished women who have gone before them.[1]

◆ ◆ ◆

INTRODUCTION

This chapter deals with sociocultural factors that affect personal leisure values and involvement today: gender, sexual orientation, racial and ethnic identity, and socioeconomic status.

Progress in this field has been striking with respect to expanded recreational opportunities for girls and women in sport and outdoor recreation. Although the chief concern has been about females and leisure, the role of boys and men in contemporary leisure has also been an issue.

Sexual orientation affects leisure pursuits in a number of ways. Focus is changing from ignoring this group to seeing them as a viable market as the numbers of identified lesbian, gay, bisexual, and transgendered people increase.

Racial and ethnic identity also has limited many individuals from full participation in organized recreation in the past and continues to influence the leisure involvement not only of African Americans, but also of the growing number of Hispanics and those of Asian background. With continuing waves of immigration from other parts of the world, religion linked to ethnic identity will pose new policy questions as Muslims, as well as other people who are neither Christian nor Jewish, become part of the national landscape.

Socioeconomic status limits leisure participation as well as where people participate in leisure activities. Those who are in poor or working classes have fewer opportunities and get most of their services from the nonprofit and public sector, whereas the upper class has relatively unlimited access to services and utilize commercial services almost exclusively. This is only the beginning of the vast differences among classes.

GENDER FACTORS INFLUENCING LEISURE

Beyond the issue of one's age group, a second factor that plays an important role in leisure has to do with sexual or gender identity and values.

A distinction should be made between the two terms *sex* and *gender*. Although they are often used interchangeably, social scientists generally accept the principle that the term *sex* should be used to identify biological or physical classification in terms of the structure and functions that are possessed by one sex or the other. In contrast, the word *gender* is used to describe a broad range of characteristics, roles, or behaviors that society usually attaches to males and females. Stated simply, the words *male* and *female* apply to one's sex, whereas the words *masculine* and *feminine* are descriptive adjectives applying to gender traits.

Throughout history, distinctions between males and females have been made that extend beyond the procreative functions. These distinctions encompass family or marital roles, educational status, career opportunities, political influences, and all other aspects of daily life. In some societies, women have held considerable power; for example, women have been worshiped as gods or have headed nations. For the most part, however, women have been subordinate to men.

Among younger children, play has served to reinforce gender-related stereotypes. Little boys were given toy guns or cowboy outfits and encouraged to playact in stereotypically masculine roles such as doctors, firefighters, or airline pilots. Girls were given dolls or play equipment designed to encourage stereotypically feminine roles such as caring for babies, cooking and sewing, or playing as nurses or flight attendants. Only after the resurgence of the feminist movement following World War II did society begin to question these roles and assumptions and challenge such sexist uses of play in childhood.

Throughout the development of organized recreation and park programs in the United States, agency planners typically responded to prevailing societal attitudes regarding appropriate leisure activities for the sexes by developing community recreation programs that supported the traditional stereotypes.

Women and Leisure

During the early decades of the twentieth century, leadership roles and activities assigned to girls and women, as well as the expectations regarding their ability to work well in groups, reflected past perceptions of women as weak and inferior in skills and lacking drive, confidence, and the ability to compete. Victorian prudery and misconceptions

■ *By the millions girls and women today take part in varied sports from volleyball to cycling.*

about physical capability and health needs also limited programming for girls and women.[2] Physical activity was seen as detracting from womanliness, having a negative effect on motherhood, and being detrimental to women's mental health.[3]

Impact of the Feminist Movement Although times have changed since the Victorian age, there are still differences in experiences, attitudes, and expectations of women's participation in sport and recreation versus that of men. A major influential factor in the changes toward equality was the feminist movement.

Feminism is defined as political, social, and economical equality among men and women. This equality first came to light politically with women wanting the right to vote just as men could. With the passage of the nineteenth amendment in 1920 giving women this right, feminism virtually disappeared until women entered the workforce in large numbers starting in the 1950s. As women entered the workforce, they wanted equal pay as well as access to jobs that were stereotypically a "man's job." With this, the economic aspect of feminism was brought to the forefront. Although much has improved in the last 60 years, women still make on average 75 percent of what men make per year. Political and economic aspects of feminism still exist today, but it is the social aspect of feminism that is most impacted by leisure.

The feminist movement, which in earlier periods of American history resulted in women obtaining fuller legal and political rights, was revived with a stronger thrust toward obtaining equality with men in a wide range of societal roles. In addition to equality, feminists advocated for freedom of choice in recreation and life activities, as well as the elimination of all repression. This movement led to the creation of women's

Title IX, the section of the 1972 federal law that prohibits sex discrimination in education, has had an immense effect—primarily in college—in terms of providing fuller support for women's teams in varied sports. Greater numbers of participants and athletic scholarships and improved facilities, coaching, and transportation arrangements all have been part of this picture. There has been a move toward increasing equity in terms of participation at the collegiate Division I level. Ten years after the implementation of Title IX, there were 31,686 female athletes on 2,011 teams, compared with 75,491 male athletes on 2,829 teams. By 2000–2001, the gap had shrunk, with 63,508 female athletes on 3,141 teams compared with 85,483 male athletes on 2,897 teams.[4]

organizations and support groups and was responsible for legislation and court decisions that broke down the walls of gender discrimination in the 1970s and 1980s.

What did this mean for leisure? Feminism gave women an understanding that they had freedom in their choices of activities and participation. Limits and stereotypes could be removed. Furthermore, it gave women the same opportunities as men in terms of leisure.

Implications for Women's Leisure

Women's leisure has been a prominent topic in research for over 20 years. By examining what scholars have learned, Russell identified several conclusions regarding women's leisure.

1. Women experience inequity in leisure when compared with men. Even in households with two working adults, women do a disproportionate amount of the housework, and this leaves less time for leisure than men typically have.[5] In addition to time, women still have fewer choices in leisure activities. For example, outdoor recreation and sport have seen unequal participation from men and women. With sport in particular, women increasingly have become engaged in a wide range of individual and team sport, achieving a higher participation rate in secondary school and college competitive programs. As professional athletes or international competitors in such sports as tennis, golf, gymnastics, and skiing, they have been successful. Beyond this, many highly skilled women have achieved success as race car drivers, horse racing jockeys, dogsled racers, and triathletes. These changes have occurred not only in schools and colleges and at professional levels of sport participation, but also in many community-based programs. On another level, growing numbers of girls and women have been taking part in such formerly male pursuits as rugby, ice hockey, boxing, and even tackle football. With the emergence of women's professional basketball and softball leagues, the breakdown of gender-based barriers gathered momentum in recent years, yet there is still much inequality between men and women in terms of leisure.

2. Combining role obligations with leisure is a common focus for many women. Oftentimes, the family and a woman's role as wife and mother define her leisure.

Golf clubs in particular have stubbornly resisted opening their full memberships and playing schedules to women golfers. However, in December 1999, in a case rattling clubs around the country,

women members of the Haverhill Golf and Country Club in Massachusetts won a stunning jury verdict of $1.9 million in damages for being systematically denied full memberships and equal access to the golf course in prime playing times. The award, and the prospect that the court might now take control of the club, was sure to make clubs around the country review their policies.[6]

Women are more likely to set their leisure around their family and household responsibilities while men do not do this.[7] Women, particularly mothers, feel the need to put other's needs before their own and forego their own leisure, because it is perceived as more important to go to their child's soccer game than to spend time doing something that they truly enjoy as a leisure activity because of their role as the mother. Others feel that the family should take first priority. Family defines leisure for women. Women sometimes feel guilty participating in leisure because it takes time away from the family[8] so a woman's leisure should be part of the family and not her own.

3. Women's leisure is more likely to occur in the home, it will be unstructured, and it will be fragmented. With household and family obligations filling the lives of many women, leisure time outside the house is limited. Many women claim to find leisure at home with such activities as reading or gardening. Also because of these household obligations, leisure activities must fit into small windows of opportunities rather than requiring major blocks of time. This results in unstructured activities that can be "squeezed in" whenever a few free moments occur.

4. Many women do not feel entitled to leisure. This may be more prevalent with homemakers. Because they do not have a job outside the home, they perceive that they do not directly contribute financially to the household. Without this financial contribution, many women feel they have not "earned" the right to have leisure. Women also feel the pressure of the "second shift"; after the remainder of the family comes home from work, they have that second shift at night which consists of fixing dinner, getting the children ready for bed, and other household tasks. This second shift prohibits much time spent on their own leisure because this has to be their priority, and they feel they are not entitled to their own leisure because of these other obligations.

These issues make women's leisure quite complex. Their lives mean assuming several different roles over time that impact leisure choices.

Continuing Patterns of Exclusion In other leisure-related areas, there are growing efforts to break down long-established patterns of gender-based exclusion. An interesting example has been the effort to open exclusive private clubs in many of the nation's cities to female membership. While, nominally, these are social groups that should have the right to restrict their memberships, they are also places where influential people meet to do business and where exclusively male memberships mean that women are placed at a marked career disadvantage.

In terms of employment, growing numbers of women in the 1980s and 1990s rose to executive positions in major public recreation and park agencies and nonprofit organizations. In the late 1980s, after protracted legal challenges, the Boy Scouts of America agreed to let women become scoutmasters and hold all other leadership positions—a long-resisted policy change. Furthermore, in May 1995, California's Disneyland adopted a comprehensive unisex "casting" approach for all of its rides. On the downside, the number of women serving as head coaches of women's athletic teams is the lowest ever. When Title IX was enacted, more than 90 percent of women's teams were actually coached by women, compared with 44.1 percent in 2004.[9]

At the same time, some of the entertainment-oriented activities that portrayed women as sex objects have been removed or modified in recent years. Women are being projected as viable participants in both sport and recreation. Professional women's sports teams are taking advantage of quality players and their athleticism rather than downplaying these qualities as not feminine enough.

Men and Leisure

Although most of the professional literature and research studies dealing with gender in recreation and leisure focuses on past discrimination against girls and women and the efforts made to strengthen their opportunities today, it is essential to examine the changing role of males in this area as well. Generally, men have been portrayed as the dominant sex within most areas of community life and have been seen as responsible for denying women access to a full range of leisure pursuits and professional advancement. However, it would be misleading to assume that men's lives are invariably richer and more satisfying than those of women.

In the late 1990s, workshops, conferences, and a growing number of articles and books began to call attention to the woes of boys in current American culture. Psychotherapists point out that four boys are diagnosed as mentally disturbed for every one girl and that six boys are diagnosed with attention-deficit/hyperactivity disorder for every girl. Many young boys appear to face a crisis when they are confronted with pressures to conform to cultural constructions of masculinity and are forced to strike out on their own when they would rather still be clinging to their mothers' legs. Too often, to show vulnerability or sensitivity is to bring instant ridicule by others.

Shifting Masculine Identities   Boys and men respond in varied ways to such gender challenges. A growing number today strive to create powerful body images of themselves through relentless weight training. The image of the ideal male has been transformed, as illustrated in the shift from the relatively slender G.I. Joe (the Barbie doll's male counterpart) of 1964 to the immensely muscled G.I. Joe Extreme of 1998. Surprisingly, some men today are taking the opposite tack and doing battle with anorexia, resisting the image of the all-powerful male.[10]

Still other men cheerfully take part in war games to affirm their masculinity. Dressed in camouflage gear and war paint, reeking of bug spray, and armed with rifles and ammo, they replay the games of childhood. Jane Gross describes a typical scene:

From behind bunkers and thick trees, their escape slowed by gopher holes and knee high grass, two teams fired gooey pellets of paint at each other. The "dead" left the field with carbon dioxide-powered guns raised over their heads in surrender, then compared welts with those who had fallen before them.[11]

Many men are now making a strenuous effort to come to grips with their need to share with others, to get a better sense of their masculine identities, and to become warmer, more expressive individuals. Robert Bly's book *Iron John* encouraged men to join drumming groups and wilderness retreats where they explored their past relationships with their fathers and their own roles as fathers and providers.

Some studies show that more men are beginning to take on child-care responsibilities, for reasons ranging from rising day-care costs to the growth in the number of working women. A late-1990s study by the Families and Work Institute in New York indicates that men are spending substantially more time on household responsibilities and in carrying on activities with their children than in the past.[12] In addition, the stay-at-home dad is not quite so rare as he once was. The U.S. Census Bureau reports there are 98,000 stay-at-home dads in the United States. As women's salaries are rivaling men's, many families are finding it just as beneficial if the father stays home to raise the children.

Implications for Men's Leisure What are the implications of these trends in masculine identity and lifestyle values for recreation and leisure? In the first place, many boys and men who formerly felt pressured to be involved heavily in sports, both as participants and as spectators, may now feel free not to conform to this traditional masculine image. Further, growing numbers of males are increasingly likely to take part in domestic functions or hobbies, the creative arts, or other leisure pursuits that in the past might have raised questions about their degree of "maleness." This new freedom to engage in leisure pursuits once considered inappropriate for men also extends to attitudes toward women. Increasingly, many parents are becoming sensitive to the way they permit their sons to behave toward girls.

Constraints on Leisure It is evident that both men and women have issues that impact their leisure participation. These issues have been labeled as constraints to leisure. An entire body of research examines these constraints and their impact. Constraints on leisure occur when an individual is unable to participate in a leisure activity, unable to participate as much as the individual would like, or when the quality of the experience is diminished for some reason. Constraints are categorized as interpersonal, intrapersonal, and structural.

Interpersonal constraints are associated with the individual's relationship with others. The constraint occurs because of this relationship with friends, family, or even co-workers. An example of an interpersonal constraint would be lacking another person to participate with or participating in an activity because of the desires of others rather than an actual desire to do so. If a person goes along with friends to see a baseball game, but really has no interest in the game, this is considered an interpersonal constraint.

Intrapersonal constraints are factors that affect an individual's preference for, or interest in, an activity. For example, a person may not feel he or she is skilled at an activity and as a result will choose not to participate. Another example is having feelings of self-consciousness. Women in particular sometimes feel self-conscious about their bodies. If this self-consciousness leads to a woman not joining a gym, she is experiencing an intrapersonal constraint. Likewise, if a man has interest in improving his cardiovascular fitness, he will most likely avoid an aerobics class because it is seen as an activity for women even though he is interested in taking an aerobics class.

Finally, *structural constraints* are factors that intervene between the desire to participate and actual participation in an activity. The most common structural constraint is a lack of time. Other examples include lack of transportation, money, or opportunity.

While women face constraints to leisure, so do their male counterparts. A major constraint that men face more than women is the lack of companions with which to participate. Women are much more likely to find a friend for such things as taking a class or attending a cultural event than men are. Furthermore, men are more likely to feel the constraints of gendered activities than women. Traditionally female activities such as ballet or aerobics are often seen as prohibitive for male participants because of the fear of being perceived as less than masculine.

With respect to both sexes, it is important to note that many of the barriers that separated males and females in the past have been broken down in recent years. For example, a number of leading youth organizations that formerly were separate in terms of membership have now joined forces, as in the case of Boys and Girls Clubs of America. In other cases, national organizations such as the Young Men's Christian Association not only have substantial numbers of members who are girls and women, but also in some communities are directed by women executives and division heads.

SEXUAL ORIENTATION FACTORS INFLUENCING LEISURE

Leisure is affected by sexual orientation as well as by gender. Although everyone has a sexual orientation, whether it is heterosexual, homosexual or bisexual, the focus here is on those who identify themselves as lesbian, gay, bisexual, or transgendered (LGBT). This group of people faces additional situations, challenges, and obstacles in their leisure and their life as a whole.

Members of this group have had a difficult past in terms of acceptance by the mainstream population. In the 1930s and 1940s, a backlash developed against gay forms of entertainment, with state assemblies barring the performance of plays dealing with sexual "degeneracy" and Hollywood agreeing not to depict homosexuality in movies. State liquor authorities closed many bars that catered to gay and lesbian clientele and in the 1950s, homosexual government employees lost their jobs because it was assumed that they could be easily blackmailed into spying for other countries on the basis of their hidden identities.

In the 1960s and 1970s, the effect of the Stonewall Riot in New York City (a mass protest against police persecution of gays and lesbians), the impact of the counterculture movement with its emphasis on sexual freedom, and the militant action of other gender and racial minorities all converged to help homosexuals gain a greater measure of public acceptance.

Although today there are more identified LGBT people than ever before—an estimated 29 million—some must continue to hide their sexual orientation. In the last

20 years, tremendous strides toward acceptance have been made, including the following.

- Universities are increasingly hiring LGBT faculty members to institute courses and curricula in gay, lesbian, and bisexual studies and are approving student organizations that sponsor publications, events, and other programs for LGBT students.
- Gay and lesbian community centers are being established in a number of cities to promote LGBT issues and concerns.
- School curricula and textbooks are being adopted that provide information about homosexuality, gay and lesbian families, and related issues of prejudice and discrimination.
- Schools are allowing and encouraging students to establish Gay/Straight Alliances to show support for LGBT students. Increasingly, same-sex couples are being accepted at school proms and other functions.
- Gay and lesbian issues began to appear more positively in popular culture, with LGBT-related themes seen in books, theater, dance, fine arts events, and prime time television. Logo is the new cable television channel dedicated solely to programming for LGBT people.
- Vermont and Massachusetts allow civil unions.
- More and more companies are extending domestic partner health benefits to their employees and their partners.

Implications for Leisure

There are several issues to consider with this group in terms of recreation. First, LGBT people have been labeled a gold mine for recreation companies and agencies. This group is more highly educated and has a higher income level than the national average. It is estimated that they have $500 billion per year in buying power. Second, on a more negative note, teens who identify as LGBT have a higher-than-average suicide rate among their peers. They often feel isolated and rejected by family or friends and have very few outlets for social and recreational opportunities where they feel comfortable. Third, LGBT people are increasingly becoming parents through past marriages, adoptions, or other means. All of these factors affect their leisure in a number of ways.

The following are a few examples of how these issues have sparked leisure-service providers to welcome and support LGBT people.

- Golf clubs and fitness centers are recognizing the abundant LGBT dollars and granting equal membership and benefits to same-sex couples as are granted to heterosexual couples.
- In Boulder, Colorado, a play group has been established for young children of gay and lesbian couples.
- Olivia Cruise Lines focuses solely on cruises for gays and lesbians.[13] R Family Vacations offers family cruises for gays and lesbians with children.[14]
- The Monroe County Tourist Development Council in Key West, Florida, specifically targets gay and lesbian tourists by promoting the city as a tourism

destination and providing information on gay/lesbian-friendly hotels, resorts, restaurants, and recreational opportunities.[15]

- The Lavender Youth Recreation and Information Center (LYRIC) is a recreation center for youth aged 23 and younger. It was opened in 1988 and offers social and recreational programs and services for LGBT youth. The center currently has 19 staff members and a $1.5 million budget.[16]
- In New York City there is a nonprofit group called Senior Action in a Gay Environment (SAGE). SAGE started in 1977 for adults, serving as a drop-in center and offering discussion groups and various recreational activities such as arts, exercise, dances, and trips. SAGE has since become more widespread, with centers opening in California and Florida.[17]
- Fort Lauderdale, Florida, opened a federally funded day-care center for elderly gay and lesbians. Although the center is open to all adults, gays and lesbians are the primary target audience because of the special needs of this group in terms of family structure. The center is located on the church grounds of Fort Lauderdale's Sunshine Cathedral, a predominantly gay and lesbian church. A wide variety of recreational activities are planned for participants.[18]

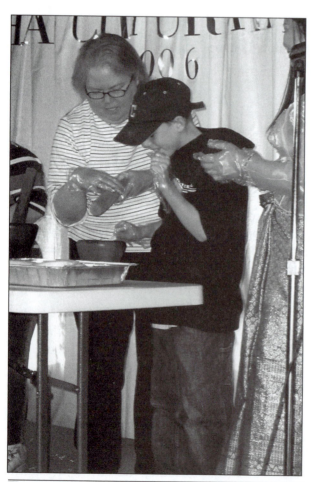

■ *Participants at the Thai Culture Night learn about Thailand traditions through food demonstrations.*

Given the growing numbers of LGBT people, the economic impact of this group, and the special issues faced by them, it is pertinent that recreation and leisure-service agencies understand the need to offer programs, activities, and events for this group from youth to adulthood.

RACE AND ETHNICITY FACTORS INFLUENCING LEISURE

A third major sociocultural factor is of key importance in determining leisure values and behaviors. A succession of past research studies shows that recreational involvement is heavily influenced by one's racial or ethnic identity. The provision of public, nonprofit, and other forms of recreation facilities and programs is also affected by these demographic factors, and the broader fields of popular culture—including the sport and entertainment worlds—continue to reflect their impact.

ncreasingly, the U.S. Census Bureau is confounded by the difficulty of classifying multiracial people who represent a blend of two or more family origins. The limited categories of "white," "black," "Asian and Pacific Islanders," and "American Indian or Alaskan native" used in the 1990 census cannot begin to convey the differences among different groups of Pacific Islanders or the immense number of markedly different Asian Americans. A major change in the 2000 census was the use of 18 races plus a category for "other" as well as an option to select more than one race.[19]

Meaning of Race and Ethnicity

Before examining the actual influence of race and ethnicity on recreation and leisure, it is helpful to clarify the meaning of the two terms. Although they are often used interchangeably, social scientists distinguish between them. *Race* refers to the genetic makeup of a person. The genetic makeup often results in biological characteristics that are exhibited among various groups. These characteristics include such things as the shape of one's eyes, texture of one's hair, and the color of one's skin.

In contrast, *ethnicity* involves having a unique social and cultural heritage that is passed on from one generation to another. Ethnic groups are often identified by patterns of language, family life, religion, recreation, and other customs or traits that distinguish them from other groups.

Within any particular population group, sizable segments of people may prefer to be identified by different labels. Typically, research shows that 44.2 percent of Americans of African origin prefer to be called *black*, whereas 28.1 percent prefer *African American*, 12.1 percent *Afro-American*, and only 3.3 percent *Negro* and 1.1 percent *colored*. The 2000 census labeled this group as black, African American, or Negro.[20] Similar variations of preferred labeling exist within other major racial and ethnic groups.

Implications for Recreation and Leisure

Despite the limitations of racial or ethnicity-based identification and its meaning in scientific terms, the reality is that the public continues to accept the concept of race and to apply it in terms of popular stereotypes about one group or the other. This is particularly significant for recreation and leisure because our traditional patterns of facility development and program planning were essentially based on the assumption that the public being served was predominantly a white, middle-class population familiar with the literature, traditions, and customs that came to North America from the British Isles.

Now, we are seeing the rapid growth of non-European populations in the United States as a consequence of recent immigration and birthrate trends. In a number of major cities throughout the country, nonwhites now outnumber those of European background, with the percentage of African American, Hispanic American, and Asian American children in the schools representing sizable majorities in some cases.

■ *May Pole Dancing is a featured activity at this festival reflecting the Scandinavian culture.*

This population trend has seen Hispanics become the largest minority group in the United States; it is estimated that by 2050 they will represent 25 percent of the U.S. population. Similarly, the number of Asian Americans has grown from 3.5 million in 1980 to over 10.2 million in 2000 and is expected to climb steadily in the decades ahead.[21]

Another striking trend has involved the growing number of Muslims; today, the United States is home to almost four million followers of Islam—five times as many as in 1970. The American Muslim population embraces American-born converts, mostly black, and a swelling immigrant tide from Asia, Africa, the Middle East, and the Indian subcontinent. Muslims are expected to outnumber American Jews, who have leveled off at 5.5 million adherents. In addition, two million Americans identify themselves as Buddhists, and the combined number of Hindus and Sikhs is over one million.[22]

The racial and ethnic composition in the United States is rapidly changing. Beyond the sheer numbers, it is evident that growing minority populations are also exerting powerful influences on the nation's cultural scene and recreational life. No longer is it acceptable to offer programs from a predominantly white, middle-class perspective and interest level. Leisure services need to be more inclusive than that. Programs can be offered from a "melting pot" perspective or a "mosaic" perspective. The melting pot perspective gives leisure-service providers the opportunity to merge groups to allow people to learn about different races, cultures, and ethnicities together, whereas the mosaic perspective allows programmers to offer activities, programs, and events tailored to the unique wants, values, attitudes, and beliefs of a particular group.

Focus on Race- and Ethnicity-Related Differences and Constraints

Beyond measuring the differences between or among various racial and ethnic groups in their leisure involvements, researchers have sought to develop a theoretical framework that would explain the reasons for the differences. The most prominent models used to explain such differences as "underparticipation" in varied leisure activities by African Americans are the marginality and ethnicity hypotheses. Floyd, frican Americans and other minority groups are underrepresented in jobs within collegiate athletics. Every two years, the NCAA collects race and gender data from member institutions. In 2003–2004, the percent of African American administrative positions was up from 5.1 percent in 1995 to 6.6 percent in 2003. Of these, 3.0 percent of all athletic directors in Division I are African American; 2.9 percent of all head coaches and 50 percent of the athletes were African American.[23]

Similarly, despite the growing number of racial and ethnic minority group athletes in the major professional sports, their representation among coaches and managers continues to be minimal. According to the Northeastern University Center for the Study of Sport, for example, only 20 percent of the players in the National Basketball Association are white, whereas 76 percent of the head coaches are.[24]

Shinew, McGuire, and Noe explain the marginality model in terms of the limited economic resources of and historical patterns of discrimination against African Americans. Stated differently, they write:

> [B]y occupying a subordinate class position, minorities have had limited access to society's major institutions which negatively affects life-chances and lifestyles, and which is reflected in reduced participation in certain types of activities.[25]

The marginality hypothesis further suggests that some groups are denied access or have limited access to some recreation opportunities because of such things as lack of money, transportation, and program availability.

The second idea, the ethnicity hypothesis, essentially says that different racial groups are influenced in their leisure choices by different norms, values, and socialization processes. This hypothesis suggests that if people are not socialized or do not have the opportunity to experience certain activities and places, then they do not participate as readily as someone who has had these experiences. An example of values and norms as related to leisure participation is the size of groups in which Hispanics and Asians participate. These two racial groups tend to participate in outdoor recreation in large groups. One explanation for these participation patterns is the cultural beliefs and value placed on participating with their extended families.[26]

In general, both models may serve as partial explanations of the distinctive behaviors of racial and ethnic minority populations—combined with continuing factors of social exclusion and self-segregation. A number of examples of race-based exclusion have continued to the present day. Well into the 1990s, a major chain of commercial health and fitness clubs covertly sought to exclude or discourage African American members, believing that their presence would have a negative effect on

acial antagonism and rejection represent a two-sided issue. When Marcus Jacoby, a white quarterback, was recruited and won the starting assignment on the football team at Southern University, a historically black institution in Louisiana, he was rejected by the student body and alumni and was ultimately pressured to leave the school, despite a winning record.[27]

Islam is a worldwide religion with over 1 billion followers. The Muslim population in this country was estimated in 2002 at 1.4 million individuals or 3.7 percent of the U.S. population.[28] Leisure is closely connected with religious activities for Muslims as free time is allotted to be spent with family and on religious activities and festivals.[29] Activity and sport are encouraged in Islamic countries for the purpose of a healthy body and mind. Livengood and Stoldolska found that Muslim Americans participate in the same mainstream leisure activities that the rest of Americans do but their leisure style, location of leisure, and the individuals whom they participate with were different.[30] Lack of participation by Muslims in leisure has been attributed to such things as disapproval from family, concern over contact with the opposite sex which is discouraged, unacceptable facilities, immodest sport clothes, agency dress codes for participation that go against religious beliefs about what parts of the body should be covered, lack of experience in an activity, and obligations to family.

white club members. Private-membership golf clubs systematically excluded African American or other minority group members until forced to accept them by public pressures relating to the sponsorship of major tournaments—an ironic circumstance when Tiger Woods (who is actually a mix of several racial strains, but who would clearly have been perceived as black and barred from most golf clubs a decade before) emerged at century's end as a record-breaking golf champion and possibly the greatest of all time.

■ *A Muslim family plays cricket in London's Kensington Park.*

Including Racial and Ethnic Groups

Chavez suggests a three-pronged approach to ensuring that all groups feel welcome to participate in leisure services. She posits that groups must be (1) invited, (2) included, and (3) involved.[31] The first step is to invite racial and ethnic groups to participate in programs, activities, and events and to use available facilities. This may mean printing brochures in languages reflecting the makeup of the community as well as showing pictures of people from the different racial and ethnic groups, among other things. Second, include members of different groups in planning activities for their group or neighborhood. The Skokie, Illinois, Park District does this by inviting representatives from over 24 different racial and ethnic groups residing in the community to serve on the planning committee for the Skokie Festival of Cultures. Each group is represented and plans its facet of the event, including food, art, entertainment, and activities. Third, involve people in the organization as a whole, from the board to full-time staff members at all levels.

Obviously, racial and ethnicity issues go beyond what recreation and park professionals are expected to deal with. However, within the total field of intergroup relations, it is essential that leisure-service managers plan programs that will contribute to intergroup understanding and favorable relations. This may be done through community celebrations, holidays, ethnic and folk festivals, friendly sport competition, and a host of other activities. It is also essential that leisure-service managers continue to strive to overcome the long-standing patterns of prejudice and racial discord that linger in many communities today.

SOCIOECONOMIC STATUS

Socioeconomic status (SES), or *social class*, is a means of classifying people based on their income, education, occupation, and wealth. Although sociologists have developed several labels for the different social classes, there are five common ones: poor, working class, middle class, upper middle class, and upper class. Most people have no difficulty determining what class they belong in.[32] People within a class have similar attitudes, values, and interests, and these things impact leisure activity choices.[33]

Social class affects leisure in a number of ways. The amount of education and/or the amount of money a person has dictates the amount of free time and discretionary income available for leisure. Traditionally, lower classes are underrepresented in recreation activity participation. It was seen in the previous chapter that this was particularly true for health and fitness programs. On the other hand, those in higher classes usually have more education and money and look for more refined and prestigious leisure.[34]

In the United States, the poor, the working class, and the middle class have been the dominant users of public and nonprofit services. Depending on the agency, these sectors provide programs for all income levels, but target the lower and middle classes in particular. Logically as income increases, so does the ability to pay more for services; thus, the upper class will use commercial services almost exclusively. This could be for a number of reasons. For example, it may be an attitude of "you get what you pay for" where the commercial sector is seen as higher quality. Arguably this is not an accurate assessment at all because many public and nonprofit agencies offer recreation services that rival commercial agencies. Another reason for using commercial services over the other two sectors may be a prestige or status issue. Status is assigned to such things as exclusive club memberships or exotic travel destinations booked through a travel agency.

Implications for Recreation and Leisure

Although there are several activities that transcend all social classes such as watching television, reading, or socializing, many others could be placed within each social class almost exclusively. For example, yachting, attending the symphony, or having a second home in the Hamptons would most likely be assigned to the upper class, whereas a trip to Disney World, golfing at a public course, or a camping trip would more likely be activity choices of the middle classes.

Sometimes there are activities that are popular among all classes, but the way in which they are enjoyed differs. Travel is a common activity to all classes. However, the poor and lower class may take short day or overnight trips and stay with family and friends; the middle class may vacation to a popular tourism destination in the United States and stay at a Holiday Inn; whereas the upper class may take an extended cruise, travel abroad, or stay in a luxury hotel where a night's stay is equal to a month's rent for people in the lower classes.

In ancient Greece, leisure and upper class were supported by the poor, slaves, and women. In some ways, this has not changed in modern society. The leisure of the middle and upper classes is also supported by the poor and working classes. Take tourism, for example. The economically stable classes travel to destinations and enjoy activities where the workers are making minimum wage. In today's economy, minimum wage is below the poverty level. In addition, when an area is tourism dependent, there is a tendency to drive up the cost of living including housing and food. This makes it difficult for the workers to live in these communities that provide leisure for the middle and upper classes.[35]

Gender, race, and socioeconomic status all have some impact on leisure activity choices, and it is the responsibility of leisure professionals to understand these impacts and provide services that meet the needs of the community. Because it is not feasible for all agencies to provide services to all people, the different segments and agencies must find their niche and work to understand the needs, leisure patterns, and preferences of their intended population so no group is underrepresented or denied leisure opportunities.

PROGRESS IN THE NEW MILLENNIUM

Although this chapter has dealt in detail with many of the past limitations that have affected the genders, people of different sexual orientation, racial and ethnic minorities, and people with different socioeconomic status with respect to recreation and leisure, it must also be stressed that immense progress has been made over the past several decades. Both women and members of sexual minorities are treated today with far greater respect and have achieved impressive levels of public support and access to a wide range of recreational opportunities that were not accessible to them in the past.

In terms of race, similar gains have been achieved—particularly for African Americans—since World War II. Certain injustices and forms of discrimination continue. However, overall, African Americans at the beginning of the twenty-first century progressed markedly with respect to education, employment, home ownership, and similar measures.

Beyond these advances, a July 2000 Urban League report stressed that U.S. blacks are clearly divided into two classes: (1) those who have successfully entered the middle and upper socioeconomic groups and (2) a large, depressed underclass. The Urban League report also focused on the interplay between racial and gender factors:

> [There is a] gulf between black men and black women in educational attainment. The number of blacks in college has surged by 43 percent since the 1970s. But black women have far outpaced black men in both undergraduate and graduate school settings [and hold twice as many advanced degrees]. . . . The implications are far-reaching. If few black men enter higher education, they will continue to be rare in corporate boardrooms and other spheres of power.[36]

In many cities, particularly in such states as Florida, Texas, and California, large Hispanic American populations have begun to achieve economic success and a degree of political power.

Among the nation's Native Americans, although the majority of tribes still suffer from extreme levels of poverty, unemployment, and other social ills, many Native Americans have experienced an unexpected wave of prosperity stemming from such things as tourism and successful tribal casinos. Gambling revenues have helped a number of Native American tribes establish successful new businesses and in some cases give all tribal members generous annual allowances. In a striking illustration of such casino-based wealth, the Florida Seminoles, who pioneered the Native American gambling business in the late 1970s, earned about $110 million in 1997 from gambling.

Strikingly, racist attitudes appear to have declined sharply among young Americans. A 1997 *Time*/CNN poll showed that a significant group of teenagers, both black and white, had moved "beyond their parents' views of race." These young people

> say race is less important to them, both on a personal level and as a social divide, than it is for adults. [Whereas many still consider it a problem in America,] a startling number of black teens call it a "small problem" or "not a problem at all." Indeed, nearly twice as many black kids as white believe "failure to take advantage of available opportunities" is more of a problem for blacks than discrimination.[37]

Ability to pay for leisure services by individuals and the ability of agencies to fund free programs for low-income people are issues faced by many. With the economy the way it is today, many agencies have to generate income to stay in business, even the nonprofit and public entities. So, "pay to play" becomes the norm and in turn, eliminates the poor and working classes. However, great strides have been made by nonprofit and public agencies to offer services to those who cannot afford them. Many agencies offer program scholarships, programs that are free to the public and supported by sponsors or tax dollars, or they seek local, state, and federal grants to pay for much-needed programs. Although access to leisure is not equal, and probably never will be, much improvement is being made.

SUMMARY

Major influences on recreation and leisure in contemporary society are the sociocultural factors of gender, sexual orientation, race and ethnicity, and socioeconomic status. This chapter defines these terms and shows how they have affected recreational participation in the past and continue to do so today.

As the chapter notes, women and girls have historically been denied many of the leisure opportunities open to men and boys. However, the feminist movement has succeeded in urging colleges, school systems, and community recreation agencies to provide more support to female participants in a wide range of sports and physical activities. This helps women to develop positive self-images and feelings of empowerment. In addition, many women have overcome barriers to professional advancement in various types of agencies in the leisure-service field. Women are also being admitted to business and social groups that had excluded females in the past.

The status of males with respect to recreation and leisure is also discussed. In the past, many men were pressured to adopt stereotypical "macho" roles in leisure activities. Today, they are being encouraged to play a more open, sensitive, and creative role in their recreational pursuits, as well as in domestic life and their relationships.

The issue of sexual orientation is dealt with as well. LGBT people have developed a wide range of recreational groups and are beginning to be courted as patrons by different sectors of the commercial recreation field.

There is rapid change going on in the United States in relation to race and ethnicity. Given that not all forms of discrimination have been erased, it is essential that organized recreation service contribute to positive intergroup relations in community life. This can be done through inviting, including, and involving all racial and ethnic groups.

Socioeconomic status plays a powerful role in what leisure opportunities are available to people. There is a major difference in the leisure lives of the poor versus the leisure lives of the upper class; as with most other things in society, the upper class has more access than the poor. However, the public and nonprofit sectors understand their responsibility in providing services to a group of people who have a great need for quality recreation near their homes and at a price they can afford.

QUESTIONS FOR CLASS DISCUSSION OR ESSAY EXAMINATION

1. How have women's roles with respect to recreation and leisure differed from those of men, in terms of societal attitudes and constraints, throughout history? How have they changed from the past? As a class, have male and female students analyze and compare their gender-related patterns of leisure interests and involvement.

2. Why is the area of sport and active physical recreation particularly important to girls and women from a feminist perspective? What has been the impact of legislation, court cases, and similar factors in terms of programming policies and other leisure-related areas?

3. Although there is still some resistance to considering LGBT people as a minority population, there has been major progress in terms of their legal standing and status in community life. What issues do you perceive as critical in terms of involving gays

and lesbians as identifiable groups in community recreation programs, and what policies would you support in this area?

4. The United States has traditionally regarded itself as a leading example of democracy. With respect to racial prejudice and discrimination, has this actually been the case? Specifically, how have racial or ethnic minorities been treated in terms of recreation and leisure? What progress has been made recently, and what problems continue to exist?

5. In terms of the general cultural scene, members of different racial and ethnic minorities have gained prominence in recent years in film, television, and other artistic or literary areas. What images are generally presented?

6. How do you think race, ethnicity, and socioeconomic status interrelate? How is leisure impacted by these sociocultural factors?

7. Although LGBT people are increasingly gaining acceptance in the United States, there are still a large number of people who disagree with alternative sexual orientations. Should public agencies, which are supported with public tax dollars, provide programs for LGBT people? Should these same agencies provide programs specifically targeted at specific ethnic or religious groups such as Muslims?

ENDNOTES

1. American Alliance for Health, Physical Education, and Dance, "Throw like a Girl—Lead like a Champion." www.aahperd.org/ngwsdcentral/2007_CAK.pdf.

2. F. R. Dulles, *A History of Recreation: America Learns to Play* (New York: Appleton-Century-Crofts, 1965): 96.

3. K. A. Henderson et al., *Both Gains and Gaps: Feminist Perspectives on Women's Leisure* (State College, PA: Venture Publishing, 1996).

4. National Collegiate Athletic Association, "NCAA Year-by-Year Sports Participation 1982–2001." www.aahperd.org/nagws/pdf_files/Yearyearsportsparticipation.pdf.

5. R. Russell, *Pastimes: The Context of Contemporary Leisure*, 3rd ed. (Champaign, IL: Sagamore Publishing, 2005).

6. "Equality on the Golf Course," *New York Times* (29 December 1999): A24.

7. T. Kay, "Having It All or Doing It All? The Construction of Women's Lifestyle in Time Crunched Households," *Society and Leisure/Loisir et Societe* (Vol. 21, 1998): 435–454.

8. S. Thompson, "Playing Around the Family: Domestic Labour and the Gendered Conditions of Participation in Sport," *ANZALS Leisure Research Series* (Vol. 2, 1995): 125–136.

9. R. Vivian Acosta and Linda Jean Carpenter, "Women in Intercollegiate Sport: A Longitudinal Study— Twenty Five Year Update, 1977–2004." http://webpages.charter.net/womeninsport/acostacarp_2004.pdf.

10. Erica Goode, "Thinner: The Male Battle with Anorexia," *New York Times* (25 June 2000): MH8.

11. Jane Gross, "Male Bonding, but No Strippers," *New York Times* (7 July 1998): B1.

12. Tamar Lewin, "Men Assuming Bigger Share at Home, New Survey Shows," *New York Times* (15 April 1998): A18.

13. Olivia Cruises and Resorts. www.olivia.com/.

14. R Family Vacations. www.rfamilyvacations.com/.

15. Monroe County Tourist Development Council. www.fla-keys.com/gaykeywest/index.htm.

16. Lavender Youth Recreation and Information Center. www.lyric.org.

17. SAGE. www.sageusa.org.

18. Deborah Sharp, "Florida Church Plans Gay Senior Center," *USA Today* (21 January 2002).

19. Elizabeth M. Grieco and Rachel C. Cassidy, "Overview of Race and Hispanic Origin," *Census 2000 Brief*. www.census.gov/prod/2001pubs/c2kbr01-1.pdf, March 2001.

20. Ibid.

21. Ibid.

22. Mary Rourk, "Many Keep the Faith(s) in 'New' U.S.," *Los Angeles Times* (5 July 1998).

23. "The 2003–2004 Race and Gender Demographics of NCAA Member Institutions' Athletics Personnel Study," The National Collegiate Athletic Association. www2.ncaa.org/portal/media_and_events/association_news/ncaa_news_online/2004/08_30_04/association_wide/4118n08.html.

24. Gerald Eskenazi, "Study Faults Teams' Efforts in Hiring Minority Coaches," *New York Times* (25 February 1998): C2.

25. M. Floyd et al., "Race, Class, and Leisure Activity Preferences: Marginality and Ethnicity Revisited," *Journal of Leisure Research* (Vol. 26, No. 2, 1994): 159.

26. D. J. Chavez, "Invite, Include, and Involve! Racial Groups, Ethnic Groups, and Leisure," in M. T. Allison and I. E. Schneider, eds., *Diversity and the Recreation Profession: Organizational Perspectives* (State College, PA: Venture Publishing, 2000).

27. Ira Berkow, "The Minority Quarterback," *New York Times* (2 July 2000): 1.

28. D. Kahan, "Islam and Physical Activity: Implications for American Sport and Physical Educators," *Journal of Physical Education, Recreation & Dance* (Vol. 74, 2003): 48–54.

29. W. Martin and S. Mason, "Leisure in Three Middle Eastern Countries," *World Leisure* (Vol. 1, 2003): 37–46.

30. J. Livengood and M. Stodolska, "The Effects of Discrimination and Constraints Negotiation on Leisure Behavior of American Muslims in the Post-September 11 America," *Journal of Leisure Research* (Vol. 36, 2004): 183–208.

31. D. J. Chavez, "Invite, Include, Involve!" in M. T. Allison and I. E. Schneider, eds., *Diversity and the Recreation Profession: Organizational Perspectives* (State College, PA: Venture Publishing, 2000).

32. M. R. Jackman, "The Subjective Meaning of Social Class Identification in the United States," *Public Opinion Quarterly* (Vol. 43, 1979): 443–462.

33. M. F. Floyd et al., "Race, Class, and Leisure Activity Preferences: Marginality and Ethnicity Revisited," *Journal of Leisure Research* (Vol. 26, 1994): 158–173.

34. K. van Eijck, "Leisure, Lifestyle, and the New Middle Class," *Leisure Sciences* (Vol. 26, 2004): 373–392.

35. J. R. Kelly and V. J. Freysinger, *21st Century Leisure Current Issues* (Boston: Allyn and Bacon, 2000).

36. "Report on Black America Finds a College Gender Gap," *Associated Press* (25 July 2000).

37. Christopher Farley, "Kids and Race," *Time* (24 November 1997): 89.

CHAPTER 7

SOCIAL FUNCTIONS OF COMMUNITY RECREATION

◆ ◆ ◆

When a nation abandons a tradition that has served it well, adopts a course that ignores what its citizens value most, allows indifference to a cherished part of its heritage, and diminishes the ways we can make a difference in the lives of Americans—then it is time to act.

Urban parks enrich our lives. They educate, protect, and enrich America's young people. They provide places to play after school and during summer vacations, and give individuals and families countless hours of recreation and relaxation.

Parks produce clean air and protect cities from floodwaters. They help to increase property value, grow the local tax base, contribute to education, reduce crime, attract businesses, and create jobs.[1]

◆ ◆ ◆

INTRODUCTION

As Chapter 2 shows, earlier definitions of recreation suggested that it served to restore participants' energy for renewed work but did not seek to achieve other, extrinsic purposes. Today, it is quite clear that this is no longer the case. Contemporary recreation programs and services—whether sponsored by public, nonprofit, educational, therapeutic, or other types of agencies—are goal oriented and intended to achieve constructive outcomes for both participants and the community at large. These outcomes range from improving the quality of life for all community residents and reducing antisocial and destructive uses of leisure to promoting the arts, serving special populations, and protecting the environment. This chapter outlines the societal benefits of organized recreation service in detail and provides a strong rationale for supporting recreation as an essential community function.

169

NEW EMPHASIS ON COMMUNITY BENEFITS

Thus far in this text, recreation and leisure have been described conceptually as important aspects of human experience. We now examine their contribution to community well-being on a broader scale. The term *community* is used here to mean a significant clustering of people who have a common bond, such as the residents of a city, town, or neighborhood. It may also refer to other aggregations of people, such as the employees of a company or those who live and work on an armed forces base.

Until recently, there was little concerted effort to identify the values and outcomes of community recreation. However, beginning with the period of fiscal austerity that affected many units of government and nonprofit social agencies during the 1980s and then again after September 11th, it became necessary to document the positive benefits derived from organized recreation programs and services in order to secure support for them. While communities called for more police protection, park and recreation agencies had to show how they contribute to communities and how they can make their community a better place to live, work, and play.

A number of major reports have been issued that present the demonstrated outcomes of organized recreation. One report by the Parks and Recreation Federation of Ontario, Canada, and several cooperating Canadian organizations concluded that the benefits of community recreation fell under four major headings: personal, social, economic, and environmental.[2] The National Recreation and Park Association undertook a similar charge and titled their benefits categories as individual, community, economic, and environmental. These benefits aided parks and recreation service providers in repositioning themselves from being the people who provided

Benefits of Parks and Recreation

Individual benefits are attributed to the person who is actually experiencing leisure activities. These benefits may include such things as increased self-esteem, improvement of physical and mental health, and relaxation and stress relief.

Community benefits impact both the community as a whole and as clusters of people including our friends, family, and neighbors. Stronger families, social support for the aging population, reduced crime and delinquency, and increased cultural understanding are just a few of the community benefits resulting from recreation.

Economic benefits improve the lives of individuals and community members by being an investment in the future rather than an expenditure of resources. Parks and recreation generates revenue for communities and provides jobs, parks enhance land value, and health-care costs are reduced when people are active.[3]

Environmental benefits result when beautification, conservation, and preservation are outcomes of leisure. For example, preserving green space, planting trees, and building ecologically sound parks and play areas result in cleaner air and water, enhanced property values, and serve as an attractive place for people to relocate.

softball leagues, dance lessons, or resorts to organizations that provided outcomes that improved the quality of life for people. The benefits movement helped agencies focus less on the activities offered and more on the experiences that people have.[4]

In a detailed text in the early 1990s, Driver, Brown, and Peterson outlined the overall benefits of organized recreation services, with an emphasis on recreation and park functions.[5] Similarly, a major study supported by the National Institute on Disability and Rehabilitation Research of the U.S. Department of Education summarized hundreds of research reports showing the benefits of therapeutic recreation, chiefly in a medical or rehabilitative context.[6] Furthermore, in the mid-1990s, a task force affiliated with the National Recreation and Park Association initiated a systematic analysis of the social functions of community recreation in dealing with major community needs, including problems involving ethnic or racial relations, the environment, disability, family life, and poverty.[7]

Given this understanding, we now examine 10 major areas of recreation's contribution to community life, drawing documentation from formal research studies and from anecdotal or qualitative evidence. In several cases, the benefits cited are similar to those presented in preceding chapters dealing with the personal values of recreation. However, here they apply to broader community needs and benefits.

Agencies like the YMCA of Greater Des Moines offer programs for preschool, youth, and adults that focus on values, building character, and enhancing creativity.

FUNCTION 1: ENRICHING THE QUALITY OF LIFE

Purpose: To enrich the quality of life in the community setting by providing pleasurable and constructive leisure opportunities for residents of all ages, backgrounds, and socioeconomic classes.

Quality of life can be looked at as what makes living in a community good.[8] In terms of recreation, this includes such things as available social opportunities, cultural activities, special events, parks, trails, lakes, flowers, streetscaping, and facilities to enjoy ample recreation programs. Recreation's most obvious value is the opportunity that it provides for fun, relaxation, and pleasure through active participation in leisure involvements.

For many individuals, the quality of life is directly linked to the individual's level of happiness. Psychologist Mihaly Czikszentmihalyi contends that creative experiences involving discovery contribute to one's zest for life and sense of well-being:

■ *Parks, activities, and special events enhance the quality of life for community members of all ages and abilities.*

When people are given a list and asked to choose the best description of what they enjoy about doing what they enjoy most—reading, climbing mountains, playing chess—the answer most frequently chosen is "designing or discovering something new." At first, it seems strange that dancers, rock climbers, and composers all agree that their most enjoyable experiences resemble a process of discovery. But the evidence suggests that at least some people . . . enjoy discovering and creating above all else.[9]

Parks provide a vivid illustration of the social value of leisure. During the warmer months of the year, they provide outdoor living spaces that are used by people of all ages and backgrounds. In swimming pools, zoos, playgrounds, nature centers, and sports facilities, community residents enjoy vigorous and sociable forms of group recreation. In community centers, children and adults can join clubs and special interest groups, take courses in a variety of enriching hobbies or self-development skills, and find both relaxation and challenge. Thus, in many ways, organized leisure service contributes significantly to the overall quality and enjoyment of community life.

A number of research studies have examined the degree to which recreation and leisure contribute to residents' satisfaction with community life. Lawrence Allen, for example, demonstrated the importance of recreation by citing evidence to show that, of seven dimensions of community life, recreation was the best predictor of overall satisfaction among residents surveyed.[10] In their view, recreation, parks, and leisure services made an important contribution to the quality of life in their communities.

FUNCTION 2: CONTRIBUTING TO PERSONAL DEVELOPMENT

Purpose: To contribute to a person's healthy physical, social, emotional, intellectual, and spiritual development, as well as to family cohesion and well-being.

As earlier chapters in this text illustrate, recreation does far more than simply provide fun or pleasure for participants. It also makes an important contribution to their growth and development at each stage of life. While we often tend to focus on such obvious goals as improving physical fitness or social adjustment, recreation participation also can help people to reach their full potential as integrated human beings. For example, psychologists point out that many individuals have vivid memories of sports experiences in their childhood. Such experiences often play a key role in developing positive self-concepts and, beyond this, help to strengthen the bonds between parents and their children. In addition to providing benefits for children, these experiences may also contribute to the parent's own sense of well-being and mental health.

Varied types of community-sponsored recreation programs provide a rich setting in which children and youth are able to explore and confirm their personal values, experience positive peer relationships, discover their talents, and achieve other important personal benefits. Organized camping represents a useful example of the role of recreational experiences in the personal development of children and youth. As an intensive, sustained experience, Marta Moorman writes, it

> provides a creative, recreational and educational opportunity in group living in the outdoors. It uses trained leadership and the resources of the natural surroundings to contribute to each camper's mental, physical, social, and spiritual growth.[11]

Camp Fire USA, originally called the Campfire Girls of America, has expanded its services, mission, and goals

■ *The Children's Discovery Museum of Central Illinois promotes the benefits of recreation in a learning environment. It offers programs designed to strengthen families and communities, allows children to grow and develop, and stimulates imagination and wonder.*

from its inception in 1912. Today Camp Fire USA is committed to providing activities and services to all children and families in the United States. The organization is dedicated to enhancing the lives of adults and children. It describes itself as follows:

> We are inclusive, open to every person in the communities we serve, welcoming children, youth and adults regardless of race, religion, socioeconomic status, disability, sexual orientation or other aspect of diversity. Camp Fire USA's programs are designed and implemented to reduce sex-role, racial and cultural stereotypes and to foster positive intercultural relationships. Camp Fire USA's mission is to build caring, confident youth and future leaders.[12]

Similarly, the Girl Scouts of America strives to help young girls grow up in a healthy and positive way, able to face the stresses and challenges that threaten all children and youth today. Many of its programs and activities promote self-knowledge, creative thinking and problem solving, feelings of self-worth, skills in relating to people, and other important areas of personal growth. Illustrative of its mission with respect to the emotional and social development of its members are the four goals of Girl Scouts, which focus on developing self-potential, relating to others, developing values, and contributing to society.[13]

How effective are such programs? Although it is difficult to demonstrate their effectiveness through rigorous experimental research studies, there is a wealth of information regarding the positive benefits of membership in youth organizations. For example, a detailed study of the outcomes of youth involvement in a Boys and Girls Club in a large city in the Southwest showed that this agency was able to meet important youth development needs. Carruthers and Busser point out:

> [I]n the past few decades, the well-being of children has come to be regarded narrowly as the responsibility of the family and select child welfare agencies, rather than all citizens and socializing institutions within a community. [However,] the healthy development of youth is dependent on the broad support of a rich and varied network of constructive relationships and environments within the family and community. [It is also recognized that] the after-school hours, when children are not under the direct supervision of parents and schools [represent] a potentially dangerous time for youth.[14]

Systematic evaluation showed that the club that was studied made important contributions within several core areas, including cultural enrichment, developing conflict resolution skills, developing citizenship and leadership skills, accepting positive adult role models, and resisting negative or antisocial forms of play.

In other studies, youth participation in sports and other extracurricular activities results in increased self-image and decreased levels of emotional distress, alcohol consumption, marijuana use, and vandalism.[15] Furthermore, the Child Trends Data Bank summarized the effects of participation in the arts by youth to decrease negative social behaviors,[16] increase student participation and attendance, increase self-esteem and motivation,[17] and have higher cognitive skills.[18] All of these are considered individual benefits.

■ *The gardens at Temple Square in Salt Lake City, UT, serve as an attraction for both residents and visitors.*

FUNCTION 3: MAKING THE COMMUNITY A MORE ATTRACTIVE PLACE TO LIVE AND VISIT

Purpose: To improve the physical environment and make the community a more attractive place to live and visit by providing a network of parks and open spaces, incorporating leisure attractions in the redesign and rehabilitation of run-down urban areas, and fostering positive environmental attitudes and policies.

In local governments, the recreation function is closely linked to the management of parks and other open spaces, historical sites, and cultural facilities. Together, they help to make cities and towns more physically appealing as places to live. In the post–World War II decades, it was recognized that many U.S. cities deteriorated greatly. Gradually, we have come to realize that we no longer can permit our urban centers to be congested by cars, poisoned by smog, cut off from natural vistas, and scarred by the random disposal of industrial debris, ugly signs, auto junkyards, decaying railroad yards, and burned-out slum tenements. It is essential to protect and grace rivers with trees, shaded walkways, boating facilities, and cafes; to eliminate auto traffic in selected areas by creating pedestrian shopping centers; and to provide increased numbers of malls, playgrounds, and sitting areas that furnish opportunities for both passive and active uses of leisure.

Over the past few decades, numerous cities throughout the world have adopted ambitious projects of promoting recreation and tourism through the revitalization of their waterfronts—both in the redevelopment of decayed harbor areas and in the recreational uses of formerly polluted rivers.[19] In a number of American cities, once-abandoned freight yards, wharves, waterfront ports, or junk-filled streams winding through inner-city slums have been dramatically transformed into new, attractive open plazas and parklike settings. Frequently with the help of the business community, these eyesores have been rebuilt into condominium housing, offices, up-scale shopping centers, marinas for boating or waterfront play, and outdoor amphitheaters for various forms of entertainment throughout the year. Run-down architectural masterpieces have been restored, and older ethnic neighborhoods preserved while adding restaurants, art galleries, and other cultural activities that appeal to tourists and residents.

In some cases, cities have been farsighted enough not to have to reclaim their waterfronts. Chicago, for example, thanks to a series of turn-of-the-century lawsuits initiated by A. Montgomery Ward (a leading businessman who was also a strong conservationist), never had to reclaim its priceless lakefront from rotting wharves and warehouses:

> It has preserved the area as practically a 20-some-mile-long park lined with smooth, paved bicycle and jogging paths, marinas, parks, picnic grounds, barbecue pits and beaches whose fair-weather scenes, smells, and patrons provide revealing insights into the ethnic mix of the Midwest's capital. . . . Sport fishing is coming back on [Lake Michigan]. And boating never left. Few cities can rival Chicago's view on summer Sundays when the yellow sun burns brightly on the azure lake, dotted by hundreds of brightly colored sails and pleasure craft on comfortable cruises and in regular regattas.[20]

Beyond recreation's role in helping to maintain and improve the environment in the central cities themselves, it also is a key player in helping to reclaim or protect natural areas within the larger framework of surrounding county or metropolitan regions. Environmental planners and park authorities are collaborating in many communities on remodeling abandoned railway corridors and establishing greenways to permit outdoor play or environmental education, provide hiking trails, or protect historic sites.

There are numerous examples of redeveloping land into usable space across North America. The Rio Salado Habitat Restoration Area managed by the City of Phoenix, Arizona, Parks, Recreation, and Library Department is a five-mile stretch of land running along the Salt River. This space was once a deteriorated dumping site where hundreds of tons of old tires were removed and recycled as well as other debris. This area was transformed into a trail system that winds through various habitats including a wetland area, a mesquite Bosque habitat, and a waterfalls area.[21]

In Boston, Massachusetts, the 1.7 acre Norman B. Leventhal Park at Post Office Square was constructed on top of a 1,500-car parking garage. Before its construction it was a dilapidated parking garage that was an eyesore to high-end office buildings. The new parking garage has 54 inches of soil and drainage materials on the garage roof which now allows 125 species of trees, bushes, plantings, and flowers to make a once ugly area a thriving and beautiful park.[22]

In order to foster environmental attitudes, the City of Boulder, Colorado, Parks and Recreation Department remodeled and opened the North Boulder Recreation Center, which was renovated with environmental impacts as a driving force behind the design. The construction promoted environmental responsibility by reducing the amount of landfill waste generated by the renovation, reducing the consumption of natural resources for facility operation, and improving the efficiency of the heating, ventilation, and air conditioning systems. Specifically, this was accomplished by doing such things as reassigning air conditioning units, counter tops, and flooring to other facilities, installing low-flow showers, and using solar power and materials made of recycled plastics.[23]

■ *Keeping youth engaged in recreation activities can reduce incidence of delinquent behavior.*

FUNCTION 4: PREVENTING ANTISOCIAL USES OF FREE TIME

Purpose: To prevent or reduce antisocial or destructive uses of free time, such as delinquency or substance abuse, by providing challenging programs that offer young people constructive and enjoyable recreational opportunities linked to other needed services.

As Chapter 3 shows, one of the major objectives of the early recreation movement in the United States was to help prevent or reduce juvenile delinquency. Indeed, during the last decades of the nineteenth century and for much of the first half of the twentieth century, it was widely accepted that vigorous group activities were helpful in burning up the excess energy of youth, diverting their aggressive or antisocial drives, and "keeping them off the streets" and sheltered from exposure to criminal influences.

In the United States, there was widespread support for playgrounds, community centers, and other recreation programs for city youth by the police, juvenile court judges, and other youth authorities (see Chapter 3). A number of sociologists pointed out that much delinquent behavior on the part of younger children stemmed from the search for excitement, risk taking, and the need to impress their peers. It was argued that if other, more challenging, forms of constructive play could be offered to youngsters at this stage, it would be possible to divert them from more serious involvement in criminal activities. Other investigators pointed out that much juvenile crime was committed for "the heck of it"—apart from considerations of gain or profit.

Gradually, however, social workers and other experts on juvenile crime sought other explanations for youth delinquency. One school of sociologists developed psychological theories that emphasized the impact of the child's personality: Children from broken homes with unstable, high-impulse behavior patterns, with a need for excitement, and with poor tolerance for delayed gratification were seen as delinquent-prone types. Other behavioral scientists held that juvenile delinquency was a cultural problem whose real roots were in the society itself.

Clearly, poverty and depressed neighborhood social conditions are key factors leading to gang involvement by children at risk. Lobo and Olson write:

> [B]ehind the facade of the promotional material showing children playing on glistening playgrounds in well-groomed parks is another world, a world in which children don't swim in sparkling pools or scamper over clean, bright grass. In the underbelly of every society are children who had little opportunity to personally come to understand and appreciate leisure and recreation. . . . Children living in the shadow of society subsist in poverty, are targeted with violence, suffer hunger and disease, receive little education, and swing between anger and hopelessness. For these children, adulthood holds few promises. These are children at risk.[24]

It is important to recognize that deviant behavior is found across all socioeconomic class lines. Only a portion of today's delinquents are lower-class urban youth involved in gangs. A considerable amount of crime is carried on by teenagers, often of middle- or upper-class backgrounds, in well-to-do suburbs. There has been an increase in amateur shoplifting, auto theft, and vandalism by such youth. Thrill-seeking and joyriding are cited as the primary reasons for car theft by juveniles, and vandalism is obviously motivated by reasons other than economic gain. In addition to such forms of delinquent behavior, many other acts reveal a search for excitement on the part of modern teenagers. Drag-racing or pranks involving desperate risks (like playing "chicken" and risking head-on collisions on highways or in tunnels) are examples of such thrill-seeking stunts.

Linkage Between Recreation and Delinquency

Although it is difficult to prove the specific benefits of organized recreation services for at-risk youth, a number of studies have demonstrated positive outcomes. Some examples are as follows.

- A research report sponsored by Fight Crime, an anticrime group of law enforcement professionals, found that housing projects without Boys and Girls Clubs had 50 percent more vandalism and scored 33 percent worse on drug use. The group also studied an after-school and summer program in Canada and found that juvenile arrests declined by 75 percent over the two years of the program.[25]

- In the three years after the Baltimore Police Department started the Police Athletic League (PAL) after-school program in a high-crime neighborhood, juvenile crime dropped 10 percent in the neighborhood. Crime rates dropped three times faster in this neighborhood than any others in the city.[26]

- A national study of 10th graders reported that children who did not participate in activities outside of school were six times more likely to drop out of school, three times more likely to be suspended from school, twice as likely to be arrested by their senior year, and 75 percent more likely to smoke cigarettes or use drugs.[27]

- Carruthers and Busser looked at Boys and Girls Clubs and found that participation in these programs resulted in youth developing leadership skills that increased their self-esteem and perception of competence, resulting in their ability to stay out of trouble.[28]

A number of cities and professional recreation and park societies have taken action to overcome the influence of gangs and other deviant behavior. Some examples are as follows.

- Austin, Texas, has experimented successfully with the use of roving leaders, although they have experienced difficulty in some cases in integrating at-risk youth into community recreation centers.[29]

On school days, most violent crime and other antisocial uses of free time occur between the hours of 3–6 P.M. Eleven million youth and teens are home alone during these high-risk hours. During these hours, youth are more likely to:

> Become victims of violent crimes.
> Be in or cause a car crash (the leading cause of death for teens).
> Experiment with drugs and cigarettes.
> Engage in sexual intercourse.
> Become pregnant teens.

Quality after-school programs and other recreational opportunities can deter youth and teens from becoming involved in crime. When this group avoids becoming involved in delinquent behaviors as youth, they are more likely to avoid this behavior as adults, resulting in short- and long-term benefits of recreation programs.[31]

- The Chicago Housing Authority initiated a highly successful Midnight Basketball League designed to serve older youth and young adults by providing exciting league play during the hours of the night when a lot of criminal activity takes place.
- Rincon Park in San Francisco is green space along the waterfront. The park contains two restaurants, public art, and a walking path, and was designed to attract people and make this a much used area that would help eliminate opportunities for undesirable behavior at night.[30]

A number of other cities have begun similar programs, as have county recreation agencies. Furthermore, in some cases, both nonprofit agencies and private organizations have developed "wilderness therapy," borrowing from Outward Bound models, which seek to

> strip away bad habits, build character, and restore self-esteem by forcing teenagers to fend for themselves and one another through a daily routine of hiking, campfire building, food preparation [and campground responsibilities, along with "survival" and challenge activities].[32]

Probably the leading example of such at-risk youth programs is to be found in Phoenix, Arizona, where the public Parks and Recreation Department sought special funding from a variety of sources to sponsor the following innovative services:

- The South Phoenix Youth Center opened in 1980 in response to a Youth Town Hall recommendation. The center currently provides programming daily for over 150 youth ages 12–21. The center provides a variety of programs, special events, school activities, information, and referral. Another major component of the South Phoenix programming is groups. These are not only fun but also enhance self-image and increase awareness and develop positive relationships and peer interaction. The groups provide positive alternative activities in a safe environment. Each group has a staff person who assists in processing of group dynamics, problem solving, teamwork, and decision making. Groups include such things as: boys' dance, theatre troupe, modeling, and speech and debate.[33]
- Project BRAVE (Bringing Reality to Adolescents about Violence Education) follows a curriculum that provides information to teens about violence prevention, decision-making skills, communication, choices, relationships, friendships, bullying, and related topics. This program provides information to over 2,000 youth weekly during the school year.
- There is an annual teen conference sponsored by the Teen Parks and Recreation Board that offers educational workshops and recreational activities that empower youth to make changes in their lives and their community.
- The Youth Development Division offers the Recreation Internship Program (RIP) funded through the Golf Enterprise fund utilizing $.25 per every round of golf played in the city. *RIP* began in 1992 offering assistance for youth (15–19) to gain valuable work experience, making them more competitive with adults in obtaining summer and year-round employment.

- In 1995, the Youth Development Division of the Parks and Recreation Department teamed up with the Arizona Society of Plastic and Re-constructive Surgeons to help young people who have chosen to turn away from gang life through a program called X-Tattoo. For former gang members trying to begin a new life, gang-oriented tattoos on their face, neck, and hands pose a significant barrier. Not only do tattoos scare off potential employers, they mark former gang members for reprisals from rival gangs. The primary goal of X-Tattoo is to help participants become employable without the barrier of gang-related tattoos. Of course, removing tattoos does not necessarily mean the participants understand how to look or apply for a job. Thus, staff added a requirement that program users between the ages of 13 and 22 attend educational workshops.[34]

FUNCTION 5: IMPROVING INTERGROUP AND INTERGENERATIONAL RELATIONS

Purpose: To help improve intergroup relations among community residents of different racial, ethnic, or religious backgrounds, and among different generational groups, through shared recreational and cultural experiences.

Racial and ethnic identity plays an important role in shaping the leisure-related values and behavior patterns of community residents throughout the United States. Clearly this presents a challenge to recreation and park professionals in terms of the need to provide program opportunities suited to the tastes and traditions of different racial and ethnic groups, while at the same time maintaining a core of shared values and interests.

As discussed in Chapter 6, Chavez suggests that if agencies want to make all groups feel welcome and want to participate in recreation activities, agencies need to (1) invite, (2) include, and (3) involve these groups.[35] Providing activities and events for different cultures serves as a means to educate the community about differing cultures, races, and ethnicities.

Special events in particular represent a major area of opportunity for sharing cultural traditions and increasing the self-knowledge and pride of different racial and ethnic populations. These events are designed to celebrate culture because they are planned by people within the specific culture, but they are designed for everyone regardless of race or ethnicity. As an example, the Wisconsin Department of Tourism promotes 37 ethnic festivals held in the state from May through November. They include such events as Syttende Mai, a Norwegian independence day festival; Fyr Bal Festival, a Scandinavia

Arab World Fest, held in Milwaukee, Wisconsin, showcases the histories, values, and cultures of over 20 Arabian nations. Activities include Arab art, food, educational programs, and entertainment. The event is planned by Arabian Festivals, Inc. They describe the organization as "a non-political, non-religious, nonprofit organization dedicated to fostering a better understanding and appreciation of Arab people and their rich cultural heritage."[37]

midsummer's eve celebration of heritage; an Irish Fest; and the African World Festival.[36] The Skokie, Illinois, Park District sponsors the Skokie Festival of Cultures, which features food, music, merchandise, and activities representing many of the 80 languages spoken in Skokie. Cultures represented at the festival include Armenian, Assyrian, Bangladeshi, Chinese, Cuban, Danish, Filipino, Finnish, Hellenic, Indian, Israeli, Japanese, Korean, Lebanese, Mexican, Pakistani, Scottish, Swedish, Thai, Turkish, West Indian, and more.

The Franklin, Indiana, Parks and Recreation Department features several cultural special events such as the Ethos Art Show as well as ongoing programs. For example, the department offers a preschool program with the head of the program from Wales and an

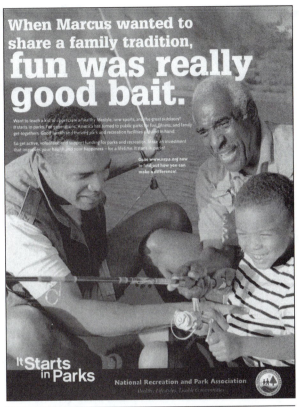

The National Recreation and Park Association promotes the social benefits of being active participants in parks and recreation through intergenerational activities.

assistant instructor from Palestine. This attracts many different youth culturally because the ethnically diverse preschoolers include Russian, Latin American, Hispanic, German, Palestinian, Romanian, and others. These programs and events are promoted as learning experiences for the community, while also trying to make those members of the community who have culturally diverse backgrounds and heritage feel welcome in Franklin.

In some cases, leisure-service agencies and programs may focus on problems of intergroup hostility and prejudice through meetings, staff training programs, workshops, and similar efforts. Organizations such as the YWCA have focused on the elimination of prejudice and discrimination as a key program goal, and in some cases youth camping programs have been established to promote intercultural friendship and understanding. In one such camp, the Seeds of Peace camp in Wayne, Maine, 300 teens from Egypt, Israel, Jordan, Palestine, and others are selected each year from their respective governments to participate in the camp that is based on academic achievement and leadership abilities. The youth come together to share cultural traditions and to begin to build respect, friendship, and leadership skills.[38]

FUNCTION 6: STRENGTHENING NEIGHBORHOOD AND COMMUNITY TIES

Purpose: To strengthen neighborhood and community life by involving residents in volunteer projects or service programs and events to enhance civic pride and morale.

An important tenet of the early recreation movement was that shared recreational experiences helped to strengthen neighborhood and community ties by giving residents of all backgrounds a sense of belonging and common purpose, helping them to maintain social traditions and cultural ties, and enabling them to join together in volunteer service roles. Recreation's role in strengthening neighborhood and community ties lies in the concepts of human and social capital. Human capital is the tools and training that can enhance an individual or collective productivity. When people give their time and talent to the workforce or the community, they are using human capital. While human capital is important, using it with social capital enriches the lives of those in the community. Social capital is defined as "connections among individuals—social networks and the norms of reciprocity and trustworthiness that arise from them."[39] Communities are made up of networks of people through such things as schools, employment, the neighborhoods we live in, and of course recreation. These networks of people form valuable relationships that bond them together. Recreation and parks provide a plethora of opportunities for the human and social capital to merge and strengthen the community. Here are a few examples of how recreation and parks strengthens and improves communities:

Groups of people can make a difference in a community simply by building networks for a good cause. For example, a group called Save the Bay, located in Rhode Island, has as its main purpose to educate residents and visitors about acting in an environmentally responsible manner. Save the Bay's Narragansett Bay project helped the community establish an estuary protection program, involve citizens in bay-water quality testing, and educate and lobby local business owners to become more environmentally responsible.[40]

The New York Restoration Project (NYRP), founded by actress Bette Midler, strives to reclaim, restore, and redevelop parks, open space, and community gardens in New York City primarily in economically disadvantaged neighborhoods.[41] NYRP volunteers, working with Rolling Stones keyboardist Chuck Leavell, New York Giants wide receiver Amani Toomer, and local school children, transformed a long-forgotten Bronx park into an urban forest. They did this by cleaning up the area that was used as a dumping ground, planting trees and shrubs, and building a walking path through the park.[42]

More and more leisure-service providers are realizing the value of volunteers to the agency, the individual, and the community. For example, Champaign Park District in Ilinois, which was one of the first public parks and recreation agencies to hire a volunteer coordinator, uses volunteers in all aspects of its operations, from recreation to maintenance. Each year, volunteers spend over 100,000 hours working in day camps, at special events, planting flower beds, and coaching youth sports. In addition, the Champaign Park District has an adopt-a-park program in which neighborhoods take ownership of their area parks through such things as building flowers beds, planting flowers, holding their own special events, raising money for playground equipment, and working with staff on park decisions. The adopt-a-park program allows the parks to be maintained at a higher level than ordinarily possible.

The unique role of recreation in helping to boost community togetherness and morale is illustrated in Toms River, New Jersey, which has suffered from an inordinately high rate of cancer among its children. In what some say is a response to this tragedy, parents in Toms River have given tremendous support to the tiny town's Pop Warner football teams and Little League baseball teams, winning national championships in both sports.[43]

In many other communities, recreational projects related to sports, the environment, the arts,

■ *Street rod owners form their own social community through a common hobby.*

people with disabilities, and similar concerns serve to promote civic pride and neighborhood cooperation. In some cases, municipal recreation and park departments have mobilized community volunteers to provide emergency relief and survival assistance at times of disaster, such as hurricane or tornado situations.[44] After Hurricane Katrina ravished Mississippi, a National Recreation and Park Association staff member and long-time Mississippi resident stated:

> One thing that I realized on my trip was just how much parks and recreation is a thread in every community. It's a common stabilizer and when people see it returning, they know their community is healing. The emotional impact we have on our communities is immeasurable. In this tragedy I believe that parks and recreation stood up quicker than anyone because we could. Parks and recreation is not about facilities and fields—we are about people and a sense of community.[45]

Unselfish involvement in civic-betterment activities is particularly important today, when many Americans see the signs of a spreading social and moral breakdown around them. At such a time, it is critical that every means be explored to develop a true sense of community, of sharing and mutual support in neighborhood life. Clearly, volunteerism and the kinds of projects just described help to promote such values and positive interactions among community residents.

FUNCTION 7: MEETING THE NEEDS OF SPECIAL POPULATIONS

Purpose: To serve special populations such as those with physical or mental disabilities, both through therapeutic recreation service in treatment settings and through community-based programs serving individuals with a broad range of disabilities.

All people need diversified recreational opportunity; those with disabilities are no different. It is estimated that one in five people in the United States has a disability, and as adults age, this number is likely to increase.[46] Add to these the number of men and women who are returning from serving in the Iraq war with disabilities ranging from amputations and visual impairments to traumatic head injuries and posttraumatic stress syndrome. As such, it is important to focus special attention on providing leisure services to this group.

Recreation for people with disabilities is provided from three different standpoints. First, recreation can be used as a form of treatment and delivered in a hospital, a residential facility, or outpatient programs that focus on the therapeutic values of recreation. This form of recreation is often referred to as *therapeutic recreation.* Therapeutic recreation programs have been used to assist clients to become self-sufficient, increase self-esteem, improve functional states, learn social skills, or learn to use leisure wisely. A second form of recreation for people with disabilities focuses on participation for the activity itself rather than as a means of therapy. This form of recreation is called *inclusive recreation.* Inclusive programs provide opportunities for people with and people without disabilities to interact together. The last form focuses on recreation programs designed for people with disabilities and is called *special recreation.* Opportunities for people with disabilities are as varied as the agencies that provide these services: Easter Seals, Special Olympic, or Disabled Sports USA.

Many of the opportunities for people with disabilities arose because of federal legislation. The Americans with Disabilities Act (ADA), passed in 1990, mandated that people not be denied opportunities, segregated, or discriminated against because of their disability. Recreation service providers had to ensure that equal opportunities were available for all constituents and that if some specialized services were available that people with disabilities had a choice of participating in the general or the special program. ADA also stipulated that facilities should be accessible and that programs be offered for all residents regardless of abilities. Furthermore, if a person has a disability, reasonable accommodations for participation must be made for that individual.

In January 2000, the official policy of the National Recreation and Park Association affirmed that diversity was a cornerstone of American life, and noted that it was essential to include people with disabilities in the fabric of society to strengthen both the community and its individual members:

Inclusive leisure experiences encourage and enhance opportunities for people of varying abilities to participate and interact in life's activities together with dignity. It also provides an environment that promotes and fosters physical, social, and psychological inclusion of people with diverse experiences and skill levels . . . enhancing individuals' potential for full and active participation in leisure activities and experiences.[47]

To coordinate the various types of agencies that serve people with disabilities, some communities have formed special committees or task forces to promote or sponsor leisure-service programs. Often representatives of wheelchair sports associations, local branches of the Easter Seal Society, service clubs, fraternal organizations, the Boy Scouts and Girl Scouts, and similar organizations are members of such bodies.

Throughout this process, it is essential that people with disabilities themselves be involved in determining needs and in planning programs, so that they are no longer kept in a dependent or subordinate role but are empowered to take control over their own lives.

FUNCTION 8: MAINTAINING ECONOMIC HEALTH AND COMMUNITY STABILITY

■ *Rockefeller Center Ice Rink is an economic stimulant for the city of New York because of the large number of visitors throughout the winter and the holidays in particular.*

Purpose: To maintain the economic health and stability of communities by acting as a catalyst for business development and a source of community or regional income and employment and by keeping neighborhoods desirable places to live.

Recreation has become a major focus of business investment and an essential element in the total national economy. It is estimated that leisure is a $400 billion dollar industry annually; it is the nation's third largest retail industry, and the second largest employer behind the health industry. Communities with commercial, public, and nonprofit agencies have benefited economically from recreation. Such economic benefits may arise through taxes, such as bed taxes at hotels, gas tax, or taxes from the lottery that go to support local parks and recreation. Furthermore, recreation increases property values, such as for homes on lakes, by parks, or on golf courses. For example, living on a golf course can increase property value from 5–19 percent although only 30–40 percent of the residents even play golf. This increase in property value may be attributed to the desire to live near green space and/or the natural beauty associated with many golf courses.[48]

Some cities have set out deliberately to transform themselves into centers of entertainment and sports. San Jose, California, for example, has built a huge downtown arena that has housed circuses, ice shows, concerts, amateur and professional sports (including the city's professional ice hockey team, the San Jose Sharks), tractor pulls, and numerous expositions. It is moving ahead on the development of varied arts institutions, including a symphony, opera company, repertory theater, and art, technology, and children's museums—all designed to breathe new life and appeal into a formerly dull and charmless city. In other cases, cities depend on special events and attractions to stimulate economic activity. For example,

- The St. Louis Zoo, which has free admission, generates $67,743,443 for the local economy. This includes revenues from food, lodging, programs, and souvenir sales from its 2,922,130 annual visitors; its 296 full-time employees and 650 part-time employees; and its $16,151,561 indirect revenue to local businesses.[49]
- The Portland, Oregon, Rose Festival attracts over 2 million people and generates an estimated $80 million annually for the local and state economies.[50]
- The National Football League estimates a Super Bowl will have a $400 million dollar economic impact on the hosting city.[51] A major league baseball All-Star game generates $75 million for a community.[52]
- The Key Arena in Seattle, Washington, boasted an economic impact of over $353 million for the city in 2005. This included 3,252 jobs and over $33 million in tax revenue. In addition, 4,370 of all Key Arena visitors come from outside of Seattle which means nonresidents are generating a large amount of tax money to sustain the city for its residents.[53]
- The Yerba Buena center in San Francisco is an 87-acre mixed development covering 12 blocks. This area once housed decrepit hotels and buildings. The Yerba Buena Gardens section of this area has been redeveloped to include museums, cultural attractions, a 5-acre park atop the underground convention center, and is home to over 270 outdoor events each year. The surrounding area has luxury hotels, apartments, and retail businesses. The revitalization has improved the aesthetics of the area as well as served as a catalyst for economic development because of the number of visitors using the park, museums, and business areas.[54]

Interest in wildlife and nature has become a powerful attraction for many regions of the country. Even as specialized a hobby as wildlife watching (actually, one of the more popular forms of outdoor recreation) sends millions of ecotourists to local, state, and national parks. In 2001, this generated $1.78 billion dollars in the state of Washington alone.[55]

What is less-easily measured is the importance of such elements as cultural attractions, outdoor recreation opportunities, sports teams, and similar leisure-related features in terms of attracting middle-class homeowners to cities, or persuading them to resist the lure of suburban life. Having major professional sports teams, for example, is believed to contribute to the image and overall morale of many communities and to make them more exciting places in which to live.

In summary, evidence shows that public, private, and commercial leisure attractions and resources of cities are key elements in their economic health and stability, not only in bringing tourism revenues but also in the positive picture they present to potential residents and companies that are seeking to relocate.

FUNCTION 9: ENRICHING COMMUNITY CULTURAL LIFE

Purpose: To enrich cultural life by promoting fine and performing arts, special events, and cultural programs and by supporting historic sites, folk heritage customs, and community arts institutions.

It is generally recognized that the arts provide a vital ingredient in the culture of nations. Through the continued performance and appreciation of the great works of the past, in the areas of symphonic and choral music, opera, ballet, theater, painting, and sculpture, or through contemporary ventures in newer forms of expression, such as modern dance or experimental art forms, people of every age and background gain a sense of beauty and human creativity. Arts and culture manifest themselves in many different ways in

■ *This sculpture park in Skokie, IL, provides high quality art free to the public.*

communities. Art and culture can be found in the architecture of buildings, the design of parks, in museums, through educational programs, or by attending concerts. Enriching a community through art and culture does not require that you be an artist or have talent in the areas of drawing, painting, or music. A community benefits when art and cultural opportunities are available to be appreciated or to educate the community. In addition, art and culture are not just for the rich; opportunities should be available for all ages and income levels.

As such, it is imperative that community agencies, both public and nonprofit, play a strong role in presenting programs in the arts that improve the level of popular taste and provide an opportunity for direct personal expression through music, dance, theater, and arts and crafts. One such program is found in Austin, Texas, at the Dougherty Arts School. The Dougherty Arts School is operated through the city of Austin and is a community-based arts organization that offers classes in such things as photography, drawing, jewelry making, and computer graphics and animation for students ages 3 and up.[56]

On February 12, 2005, artists Christo and Jeanne-Claude completed installation of their temporary work of art: *The Gates, Central Park, New York, 1979–2005.* The 7,503 gates were 16 feet tall and anywhere from 5'6" to 18' wide. The saffron-colored gates stretched 23 miles through the sidewalks of New York's Central Park. This $21 million art project was underwritten by the artists and remained in the park for 16 days. The exhibit served as a public art installation for New York City residents as well as a tourist attraction for people all over the world.[60]

■ *The* Gates Installation *is one example of public art that can be enjoyed by all residents free of charge.*

In Kansas City, Missouri, visitors can stroll through the 22-acre park that was a collaboration between the Hall Family Foundation, the Kansas City Board of Parks and Recreation Commissioners, and the Nelson-Atkins Museum of Art. In addition to the 34 sculptures located throughout the park, the impeccable landscape is carefully planned and maintained to reflect the art and culture of the entire park.[57]

Seattle, Washington, has the Olympic Sculpture Park that was opened in 2006. This 8.5-acre park on the waterfront contains classic, modern, and contemporary permanent sculptures, temporary art installations, art-related musical and theatrical performances, and year-round educational programming in the arts. Without parks such as these, many people would never be exposed to art at this level.[58]

Finally, some communities have directly linked the arts to current social needs, such as serving at-risk youth or promoting racial and ethnic pride among varied subcultural groups. Art agencies across the country have claimed for years that art can decrease youth delinquency and other negative behaviors. In 1996, the Regional Arts & Culture Council in Portland, Oregon; the Fulton County Arts Council in Atlanta; and the City of San Antonio, Texas, Department of Arts and Cultural Affairs—along with Americans for the Arts, began a collaborative research effort on arts programming for youth at risk.

This group examined best practices in art for youth, the impact of art on risk behaviors in youth, and created best practices for youth serving art agencies. This project resulted in YouthARTS—a program designed to "reduce risk factors, while increasing protective factors. One program to evolve from the YouthARTs project that continues today is Urban smARTS offered through the City of San Antonio, Department of Arts and Cultural Affairs, the Department of Community Initiatives, and the San Antonio Independent School District. The program is designed to divert youth away from drugs, gang activity, and contact with the juvenile justice system. A team of artists, caseworkers, and teachers work with youth on such things as music, theatre, drama, and visual and literary arts.[59]

In the tension between mass-produced, commercially dominated forms of entertainment and leisure experience and more authentically involving kinds of personal expression, such artistic ventures and projects play an important role.

FUNCTION 10: PROMOTING HEALTH AND SAFETY

Purpose: To promote community health and safety by offering needed services and programs, including leadership training and certification courses and supervision or regulation of high-risk activities.

A little-recognized but extremely important value of community recreation is its role in promoting public health and safety. As shown in Chapter 5, community recreation's most obvious value is the effect that its varied programs

■ *Parks offer unlimited opportunities for both children and adults to be physically active to improve their health.*

of sports and other physical activities have in promoting fitness. Many communities have developed programs such as fitness classes, dance programs, and sports leagues for all abilities to promote health and fitness. Although these programs most likely have a fee attached to them, these same communities also are promoting free opportunities for health through their parks and trails so that all residents can become physically active and healthier. Parks and trails allow for close-to-home, low-cost activities for people. With any community, the key is to get people to use the parks. It has been discovered that 70 percent of all park visitors are engaged in moderate to vigorous physical activity while they are in the park, demonstrating the relationship between health and use of local parks.[61] A National Recreation Foundation study found that people living near a park were twice as likely to use the park than those who do not live near one.[62]

In addition to parks, trails are also an important part of many cities. Walking and biking trails have been built through and around cities all over the United States. Trails have been built along rivers and streams, where railroads once stood, and on utility right of ways. These trails are used for fitness purposes as well as for transportation on foot, bike, or rollerblades. A study done by the Eppley Institute for Parks and Public Lands found that 70–95 percent of people living near a trail actually use it.[63]

Whether it is playing tennis with a friend, participating in a sand volleyball league, playing with a child on the playground, or biking on a trail, people who are in parks are physically active. There are thousands of examples of what local parks and recreation agencies are able to do in their communities to make their residents healthier. Here are a few examples:

- Many cities boast of their extended bike/walking trails built for residents as well as visitors to communities. For example, what once was a railroad bed connecting Chicago and Milwaukee has now become a continuous 100-mile bike trail that is promoted as a healthy tourism destination.

■ *Park and recreational professionals are instrumental in keeping children safe on playgrounds by adhering to national safety standards.(left) Children learn proper kayaking skills from a qualified instructor at REI's flagship store prior to attempting the sport on their own.(right)*

- Indy in Motion is a joint program with the Indianapolis Parks and Recreation Department, the City of Indianapolis, the National Institute for Fitness and Sport, and the Marion County Health Department. The objective of this program is to promote physical activity with an emphasis on families, children, seniors, and people with disabilities. Programs include a Walk in the Park with regularly scheduled walks in 12 parks throughout the city, Fit City Challenge designed for corporate wellness, fitness programs designed for the entire family to enjoy together, and the publication of Fitness Guide detailing free and low-cost activities available in the parks.[64]
- Carmel Clay Parks and Recreation Department in Indiana constructed a 150,000-square-foot facility that focuses on health and wellness programming including a space dedicate just to youth fitness programming. The room has youth-sized fitness equipment as well as state-of-the-art technology such as dance revolution to keep kids moving.

In addition to health factors, parks and recreation departments affect the safety of youth and adults. In terms of popular activities like swimming, which remains a leading

Each year *Men's Fitness Magazine* ranks the 50 largest cities in the United States from the fittest to the fattest. Rankings are determined by such indicators as the number of gyms and sporting goods stores, participation in exercise and sports, the number of parks, the amount of open space, and the number and types of recreation facilities available. In 2006, Baltimore and Honolulu were at the top of the fittest list and Chicago and Las Vegas topped the fattest cities list.[65]

cause of accidents for children, hundreds of thousands of youngsters receive water safety and skills instruction each year.

In numerous other ways, public, private, and nonprofit agencies are working to reduce the injuries and deaths that frequently result from high-risk recreational activities. For example, many state commissions today regulate the use of boats—requiring that children or adults operating them have boating safety certificates—govern the use of jet skis, and maintain strict controls by prohibiting the use of alcohol while boating. Twenty-seven states have skiing safety acts that define skiers' and ski area operators' responsibilities on the slopes. Commercial companies and business associations provide safety education and guidelines along with training programs in such areas as scuba diving, rollerblading, skateboarding, and other popular forms of outdoor play. At the same time, it is necessary to recognize that many accepted, even traditional, activities contain a high-risk component. For example, it is estimated that 200,000 children annually are hurt playing on playgrounds. This number would be a lot higher if it were not for NRPA's National Playground Safety Institute that is dedicated to training certified playground inspectors. These people inspect the playgrounds in their communities—often on a daily basis—to keep children safe.[66]

Although it is the goal of recreation agencies to provide a safe and enjoyable experience, not all activities can always be safe. Many people like an activity because of its real or perceived danger. Any outdoor recreation activity has an element of danger. Recreation service providers need to reduce as much risk as possible without changing the experience so much that it becomes a completely different experience. For example, whitewater rafting will always have an inherent danger to it. Rather than not offer this experience, rafting companies have found ways for people to still experience whitewater rafting while taking every precaution possible to make it safer. These safety precautions include such measures as requiring skilled and highly trained guides or ensuring that all participants wear safety helmets.

In addition to providing a safe atmosphere for participation in activities, many community programs are focused on teaching safety skills through programs and events. These programs include such things as swim lessons, basic water safety programs, and boater and hunter safety programs. For example, Clinton Township, Michigan, Parks and Recreation Department offers a program called Safety Town for children ages 4–6. The children learn about bike, car, and fire safety as well as stranger awareness. The children have replica pedal cars and a miniature city complete with miniature buildings, street signs, power lines, and traffic signals.[67]

Although health, and particularly safety, is not always at the forefront on many people's minds as a function of community recreation, it is a major player. Community recreation is a vital part of keeping people healthy in their communities, providing safe and enjoyable experiences, as well as offering programs that teach people to live safe lives.

NEED FOR A COHERENT PHILOSOPHY OF SERVICE

This chapter has presented 10 major areas of social concern in which community recreation may satisfy important needs, constituting a strong justification for providing socially oriented recreation programs and facilities. However, if such programs and facilities are not based on a sound philosophy of service, they may not achieve the desired ends. Chapter 13 discusses a number of issues or problems facing this field today and suggests guidelines for developing a coherent philosophy for solving these issues.

SUMMARY

Far from simply providing casual or superficial amusement, organized recreation services help to satisfy a number of significant community needs, including the following:

1. *Quality of life.* Constructive and enjoyable leisure for people of all ages and backgrounds contributes significantly to their quality of life and satisfaction with their communities.
2. *Personal development.* As described in Chapter 5, organized recreation promotes healthy personal development in physical, emotional, social, intellectual, and spiritual terms, thus contributing to overall community well-being.
3. *Environmental attractiveness.* Recreation and park agencies maintain parks, nature reserves, riverfronts, and other natural areas and may assist in rehabilitating or sponsoring historic and cultural settings.
4. *Combating juvenile delinquency.* As an important element in the community's educational, social, and other services for youth, organized recreation assists in preventing or reducing delinquency and other deviant forms of play.
5. *Improving intergroup relations.* Recreation serves as a useful tool in promoting ethnic, racial, and intergroup understanding and cooperation.
6. *Strengthening community ties.* Volunteerism and taking part in neighborhood efforts to improve the community environment, assistance programs for children or people with disabilities, and similar involvements help to build civic togetherness.
7. *Needs of special populations.* In both treatment settings and in the community at large, therapeutic recreation service promotes inclusion and independence for persons with physical, mental, or social disabilities.
8. *Maintaining economic health.* As a growing form of business enterprise, recreation employs millions of people today. By helping to attract tourists, industries that are relocating, or new residents, it also provides income and promotes community stability.
9. *Enriching cultural life.* Many public and nonprofit leisure-service agencies today assist or sponsor programming in the various artistic and cultural fields, strengthening this important dimension of community life.
10. *Promoting health and safety.* Increasingly, recreation is recognized as a health-related discipline by helping individuals to maintain sound lifestyles and by helping to promote safety in outdoor recreation and other risk-related leisure pursuits.

QUESTIONS FOR CLASS DISCUSSION OR ESSAY EXAMINATION

1. This chapter presents 10 different areas in which recreation, parks, and leisure services contribute to community life. If you had to present a positive argument for

establishing or expanding a community recreation and park department, which of these areas would you emphasize, and why?

2. Prevention of juvenile delinquency has been a long-standing purpose of many public and voluntary leisure-service agencies. Recognizing that there is limited research evidence to support the effectiveness of recreation in this area, could you sum up the evidence that exists, search for other research findings, and make a logical case for recreation's antidelinquency role?

3. Explain and discuss the importance of community recreation within one of the following areas: (1) economic contribution; (2) health-related benefits; (3) promoting the cultural arts; or (4) improving intergroup relations among residents of different socioeconomic, racial, or cultural backgrounds.

ENDNOTES

1. Rachel Roberts, "Urban Legends," *Parks & Recreation* (Vol. 41, No. 7, 2006): 58.

2. Ontario, Canada, Parks and Recreation Federation, *The Benefits of Parks and Recreation.* See Programmers Information Network, *National Park and Recreation Association* (Vol. 4, No. 4, 1993): 1.

3. O'Sullivan, *Setting a Course for Change—The Benefits Movement in Parks and Recreation* (Arlington, VA: National Recreation and Park Association, 1999).

4. Ibid.

5. B. L. Driver, P. Brown, and G. Peterson, eds., *Benefits of Leisure* (State College, PA: Venture Publishing, 1991).

6. C. Coyle, W. W. Kinney, and J. Shank, *Effect of Therapeutic Recreation and Leisure Lifestyle on Rehabilitation Outcomes and on the Physical and Psychological Health of Individuals with Physical Disability* (Philadelphia: Temple University and U.S. Department of Education, Office of Special Education and Rehabilitative Services, 1993).

7. "New Study Reveals Recreation, Parks' Impact on Serious Social Issues," *Dateline: NRPA* (December 1994): 1–2.

8. K. A. Henderson et al., "It Takes a Village to Promote Physical Activity: The Potential for Public Park and Recreation Departments," *Journal of Park and Recreation Administration* (Vol. 19, No. 1, 2001): 23–41.

9. Mihaly Czikszentmihalyi, "Happiness and Creativity: Going with the Flow," *The Futurist: Special Report on Happiness* (Vol. 31, No. 5, 1997): 8–13.

10. Lawrence Allen, "Benefits of Leisure Attributes to Community Satisfaction," *Journal of Leisure Research* (Vol. 22, 1990): 183–196.

11. Marta Moorman, "Satisfaction in Organized Camping," *Parks and Recreation* (April 1999): 41.

12. Camp Fire USA, "All About Us," www.campfire.org/all_about_us/. Accessed 11 July 2003.

13. Girl Scouts of the United States of America, "Girl Scout Program," www.girlscouts.org/program/index.html#leadership. Accessed July 11, 2003.

14. C. Carruthers and J. Busser, "A Qualitative Outcome Study of Boys and Girls Club Program Leaders, Club Members and Parents," *Journal of Park and Recreation Administration* (Vol. 18, No. 1, 2000): 50–67.

15. Patricia A. Harrison and Gopalakrishnan Narayan, "Differences in Behavior, Psychological Factors, and Environmental Factors Associated with Participation in School Sports and Other Activities in Adolescence," *Journal of School Health* (Vol. 73, No. 3, 2003): 113–120. Abstract available at:

www.ncbi.nlm.nih.gov/entrez/query.fcgi?cmd=Retrieve&db=PubMed&list_uids=12677730&dopt=
Abstract.

16. E. Winner and L. Hetland, eds., "Arts and Academic Improvement: What the Research Shows," *Journal of Aesthetic Education* (Vol. 34, 2000): 3–4. Executive summary available online at: www.pz.harvard.edu/Research/REAP.htm.

17. Robin Rooney, *Arts Based Learning and Teaching. A Review of the Literature.* Literature prepared for VSA Arts, Washington, D.C. www.vsarts.org/documents/resources/research/VSAarts_Lit_Rev5-28.pdf, May 2004.

18. Francis H. Rauscher, *Can Music Instruction Affect Children's Cognitive Development?* Champaign, IL: ERIC Clearinghouse on Elementary and Early Childhood Education. Available at: www.ericdigests.org/2004-3/cognitive.html, 2003.

19. S. Craig-Smith and M. Fagence, eds., *Recreation and Tourism as a Catalyst for Urban Waterfront Redevelopment* (Westport, CT: Praeger, 1995).

20. "The Midwest's Brawny Capital," *New York Times* (5 May 1985): X14.

21. Rio Salado Restoration Project, http://phoenix.gov/RIOSALADO/index.html.

22. "Boston—Beyond the Big Dig," www.boston.com/beyond_bigdig/cases/post_office.htm.

23. City of Boulder, "City Receives National Environmental Certification for North Boulder Recreation Center Renovation," www.ci.boulder.co.us/comm/pressrelease/2003/0307.html.

24. F. Lobo and E. Olson, "Leisure Services and Children at Risk: Against All Odds," *Journal of Park and Recreation Administration* (Vol. 18, No. 1, 2000): 5.

25. S. A. Newman, J. A. Fox, E. A. Flynn, and W. Christeson, *America's After-School Choice: Juvenile Crime or Safe Learning Time*, www.fightcrime.org/reports/asTwopager.pdf.

26. S. A. Newman et al., "America's After School Choice: The Prime Time for Juvenile Crime, or Youth Enrichment and Achievement," www.fightcrime.org/reports/as2000.pdf, 2000.

27. N. Zill et al., *Adolescent Time Use, Risky Behavior, and Outcomes: An Analysis of National Data.* (Rockville, MD: Westat, 1995).

28. C. Carruthers and J. Busser, "A Qualitative Outcome Study of Boys and Girls Club Program Leaders, Club Members and Parents," *Journal of Park and Recreation Administration* (Vol. 18, No. 1, 2000): 50–67.

29. J. Baker and P. Witt, "Backstreet Beacons: Austin's Roving Leaders," *Journal of Park and Recreation Administration* (Vol. 18, No. 1, 2000): 87–105.

30. "Boston—Beyond the Big Dig," www.boston.com/beyond_bigdig/cases/rincon.htm.

31. S. A. Newman et al., "America's After School Choice: The Prime Time for Juvenile Crime, or Youth Enrichment and Achievement," www.fightcrime.org/reports/as2000.pdf, 2000.

32. Michael Janofsky, "Deep in the Wilderness, a Growth Industry Is Blooming," *New York Times* (11 December 1999): A12.

33. City of Phoenix Parks & Recreation Department, http://phoenix.gov/PRL/arythctr.html.

34. Ibid.

35. D. J. Chavez, "Invite, Include, and Involve! Racial Groups, Ethnic Groups, and Leisure," in M. T. Allison and I. E. Schneider, eds., *Diversity and the Recreation Profession: Organizational Perspectives* (State College, PA: Venture Publishing, 2000).

36. Wisconsin Department of Tourism, http://agency.travelwisconsin.com/PR/Travel_News/OtherKits/Heritage%20-WI%20Ethnic%20Festivals.shtm.

37. Arab World Fest, www.arabworldfest.com/. Accessed 4 April 2007.

38. Seeds of Peace, www.seedsofpeace.org/. Accessed 4 April 2007.

39. R. D. Putnam, *Bowling Alone: The Collapse and Revival of American Community* (New York: Simon & Schuster, 2000): 19.

40. Civic Practices Network, www.cpn.org/topics/environment/savebay.html. Accessed 4 April 2007.

41. New York Restoration Project, https://nyrp.org/about.htm. Accessed 4 April 2007.

42. New York Restoration Project, https://nyrp.org/news_pr.htm#para2. Accessed 4 April 2007.

43. Jon Stenzler, "Town's Triumphs, Tragedy, May Be Linked, Some Say," *Philadelphia Inquirer* (30 January 2000): A1.

44. Sheila Franklin, "Operation Recreation Relief," *Parks and Recreation* (October 1999): 78.

45. T. McAdory, "A Sad Journey Home," *Parks & Recreation* (Vol. 41, No. 2, 2000): 71.

46. U.S. Census Bureau, www.census.gov/population/pop-profile/2000/slideshow/sld008.htm. Accessed 4 April 2007.

47. *National Therapeutic Recreation Society Report* (Vol. 25, No. 1, January 2000): 19.

48. Sarah Nichols, "Measuring the Impact of Parks on Property Values," *Parks and Recreation* (Vol. 39, 2004): 24–32.

49. St. Louis Zoo, www.stlzoo.org/home/economicimpact/. Acccessed 4 April 2007.

50. Portland Rose Festival, www.rosefestival.org/support/sponsorships.shtml. Accessed 4 April 2007.

51. National Football League, "Super Bowl XXXIII Generates $396 Million for South Florida," *NFL Report* (Vol. 58, 1999): 7.

52. B. Selig et al., "New Ballpark Press Briefing: July 12, 1999," www.asapsports.com/baseball/1999allstar/071299BS.html.

53. W. B. Beyers, "Key Arena Economic Impact Assessment," www.seattlecenter.com/images/media/pdf/KeyArenaEconomicImpactAssessment.pdf.

54. "Boston—Beyond the Big Dig," www.boston.com/beyond_bigdig/cases/yerba.htm.

55. Municipal Research and Services Center of Washington, www.mrsc.org/Subjects/Econ/ed-TourEco.aspx#Value. Accessed 4 April 2007.

56. Austin Parks and Recreation Department, www.ci.austin.tx.us/dougherty/programs.htm. Accessed 4 April 2007.

57. The Artnut, www.artnut.com/frusa.html. Accessed 4 April 2007.

58. Seattle Parks and Recreation, www.seattle.gov/parks/parkspaces/OlympicSculpturePark.htm. Accessed 4 April 2007.

59. Americans for the Arts Youth Arts Program, www.americansforthearts.org/youtharts/about/sites.asp#urbansmarts. Accessed 4 April 2007.

60. Christo and Jeanne-Claude, http://christojeanneclaude.net/tg.html#statement. Accessed 4 April 2007.

61. G. Godbey et al., "Final Report on Health and Park Use Study for NRPA Board of Trustees," (Arlington, VA: NRPA).

62. R. C. Brownson et al., "Environmental and Policy Determinants of Physical Activity in the United States," *American Journal of Public Health* (Vol. 91, No. 12, 2003): 1995–2003.

63. Indiana University, School of Health, Physical Education and Recreation, *Summary Report Indiana Trails Study: A Study of Trails in 6 Indiana Cities* (Bloomington, IN: Eppley Institute for Parks and Public Lands, 2001).

64. Indy in Motion, www.indyfitness.net/home.htm. Accessed 4 April 2007.

65. "Baltimore Surprised by New Title: America's Fittest City," http://www.usatoday.com/news/health/2006-01-06-fittest-city_x.htm, 2006.

66. National Playground Safety Institute, www.nrpa.org/content/default.aspx?documentId=5129. Accessed 4 April 2007.

67. Clinton Township Gratiot Cruise, www.ctgratiotcruise.com/Sponsor-a-Kid.cfm. Accessed 4 April 2007.

CHAPTER 8

THE LEISURE-SERVICE SYSTEM

Governmental, Nonprofit, and Commercial Recreation Agencies

◆ ◆ ◆

America is a land of majestic beauty, and we are blessed with immeasurable natural wealth. Americans are united in the belief that we must preserve this treasured heritage and conserve these natural resources for the benefit and enjoyment of the American people.

As a nation, we can be proud of our diverse parklands, ranging from the rugged wilderness of snow-capped mountains, thick forests, sweeping desert sands, and remote canyons to national symbols such as the Statue of Liberty and the Lincoln Memorial. Our National Park Service has a long and important history. In 1864, the Federal Government ensured a grand natural landscape for generations to come when it designated Yosemite Valley and the Mariposa Grove of giant sequoias to be "held for public use, resort, and recreation . . . inalienable for all time." Eight years later in 1872, Congress created the first national park in the Yellowstone region of the Territories of Montana and Wyoming. Finally, in 1916, the National Park Service was established to efficiently administer our growing number of parks, which today includes 388 national parks on more than 84 million acres of public lands. These lands continue to be cherished by all our citizens.[1]

◆ ◆ ◆

INTRODUCTION

We now turn to a detailed examination of the overall leisure-service system in the United States at the turn of the twenty-first century. This chapter deals with three major types of recreation providers that share a broad responsibility for sponsoring recreation, park, and related leisure facilities and programs for the public at large: governmental agencies, nonprofit community organizations, and commercial recreation businesses. In each case, the background, mission, and chief program elements of sponsoring agencies are described, with numerous examples drawn from the field that illustrate recreation and leisure services today.

KEY ELEMENTS IN THE LEISURE-SERVICE SYSTEM

There are 10 different types of leisure-service organizations in modern society, as shown in Table 8.1. Of these, three of the major types that meet a broad range of public needs are described in this chapter, with the other seven in the two chapters that follow.

PUBLIC RECREATION, PARK, AND LEISURE SERVICES

Public, or government, leisure-service agencies have the following characteristics: (1) They were the first type of agency to be formally recognized as responsible for serving the public's recreation needs and, as such, have constituted the core of the recreation movement; (2) the primary means of support for most government recreation and park agencies traditionally has been tax funding, although in recent years other revenue sources have begun to be used more fully; (3) government agencies have a major responsibility for the management of natural resources; and (4) they are obligated to serve the public at large with socially useful or constructive programs because of their tax-supported status.

ROLE OF THE FEDERAL GOVERNMENT

The federal government's responsibility for managing parks and recreation areas and providing or assisting other leisure services evolved gradually. The growth of the parks and recreation movement began with the early immigrants to New England, with Boston Common being an archetype of future park development across the United States. National and state parks grew differently from urban parks, and recreation evolved still differently—yet people talk of parks and recreation as if they were one. This is a U.S. institution ranging from Central Park in the late 1850s to the formation of the first national park in 1872. The growth of government and nonprofit involvement, beginning with experience such as the Boston Sand Gardens and expanding dramatically under Franklin Roosevelt's New Deal policies, solidified government's role in parks and recreation.

The federal government in the United States developed a great variety of programs related to recreation in dozens of different departments, bureaus, or other administrative units. Typically, recreation functions evolved in federal agencies as secondary responsibilities. For example, the initial purposes of the Tennessee Valley Authority lakes and reservoirs were to provide flood control and rural electrification; only over time did recreation uses become important. The following list examines the responsibilities and role of the federal government.

- *Direct management of outdoor recreation resources:* The federal government, through such agencies as the National Park Service, the National Forest Service, and the Bureau of Land Management, owns and operates a vast network of parks, forests,

TABLE 8.1

TEN MAJOR ELEMENTS IN THE MODERN LEISURE-SERVICE SYSTEM

Types of Recreation-Sponsoring Organizations	Assisted by Support Groups and Services	Provide Leisure Programs Consisting of	To Satisfy Public Needs for	Yielding Major Benefits in Four Areas
Public agencies	Trade associations	Direct program leadership	Full spectrum of involvement in:	Personal values (health, emotional wellness, mental development)
Nonprofit organizations	Professional associations	Provision of facilities for undirected public use	Games and sport	Social and community-based outcomes
Commercial recreation businesses	Special-interest groups	Education for leisure	Outdoor recreation	
Employee service and recreation programs	Sponsors of special programs and events	Information referral services	Cultural activities	Economic benefits, employment, taxes, other fiscal returns
Armed forces morale, welfare, and recreation units	Professional preparation institutions	Enabling facilitation	Creative arts	Environmental values, both natural and urban settings
Private-membership organizations	Private groups that subcontract leisure functions	Advocacy and leadership in special areas	Hobbies	
Campus recreation programs	Other civic agencies and citizens groups	Jointly sponsored campaigns and events	Special events	
Therapeutic recreation service			Club and other social groups	
Sport management organizations			Personal enjoyment	
Tourism and hospitality industry			Travel	
			Other social services	
			With needs influenced by:	
			Age group	
			Gender	
			Socioeconomic status	
			Educational background	
			Racial/ethnic factors	
			Residential and regional factors	
			Physical and emotional health	
			Ability/Disability	
			Family status	

Note: The same program elements, facilities, leisure needs, and outcomes may be found in all 10 types of agencies. Each column should be read vertically rather than across the page.

lakes, reservoirs, seashores, and other facilities used extensively for outdoor recreation.

- *Conservation and resource reclamation:* Closely related to the preceding function is the government's role in reclaiming natural resources that have been destroyed, damaged, or threatened and in promoting programs related to conservation, wildlife, and antipollution control.

- *Assistance to open space and park development programs:* Chiefly with funding authorized under the 1965 Land and Water Fund Conservation Act, the federal government has provided billions of dollars in matching grants to states and localities to promote open-space development. Also, through direct aid to municipalities carrying out housing and urban development projects, the federal government subsidized the development of local parks, playgrounds, and centers.

- *Direct programs of recreation participation:* The federal government operates a number of direct programs of recreation service in Veterans Administration hospitals and other federal institutions and in the armed forces on permanent and temporary bases throughout the world.

- *Advisory and financial assistance:* The federal government provides varied forms of assistance to states, localities, and other public or voluntary community agencies. For example, many community programs serving economically and socially disadvantaged populations have been assisted by the Departments of Health and Human Services, Housing and Urban Development, Labor, and others.

Providing interpretive services to visitors is essential to individuals understanding park and natural settings.

- *Aid to professional education:* Federal agencies concerned with education and the needs of special populations have provided training grants for professional education in colleges and universities throughout the United States.

- *Promotion of recreation as an economic function:* The federal government has been active in promoting tourism, providing aid to rural residents in developing recreation enterprises, and assisting Native American tribes in establishing recreational and tourist facilities on their reservations. Such agencies as the Bureau of the Census and the Coast Guard also provide needed information for those interested in travel, boating, and similar pastimes.

- *Research and technical assistance:* The federal government has supported a broad spectrum of research on topics ranging from outdoor recreation trends and needs and the current status of urban recreation and parks to specific studies of wildlife conservation, forest recreation, or the needs of special populations.

- *Regulation and standards:* The federal government has developed regulatory policies with respect to pollution control, watershed production, and environmental quality. It has also established standards with respect to rehabilitative service for those who are ill or those with disabilities and architectural standards to guarantee access to facilities for people with disabilities.

The first two areas of responsibility are carried out by seven major federal agencies that are either service units or bureaus in cabinet departments or separate authorities. They are the National Park Service, the Forest Service, the Bureau of Land Management, the Bureau of Reclamation, the U.S. Fish and Wildlife Service, the Tennessee Valley Authority, and the U.S. Army Corps of Engineers.

The National Park Service

The leading federal agency with respect to outdoor recreation is the National Park Service (NPS), housed in the Department of the Interior. Its mission has been stated as follows:

> The National Park Service preserves unimpaired the natural and cultural resources and values of the national park system for the enjoyment, education, and inspiration of this and future generations. The Park Service cooperates with partners to extend the benefits of natural and cultural resource conservation and outdoor recreation throughout this country and the world.

Most of the property administered by the NPS in its early years was west of the Mississippi, and has since added major seashore parks and other areas throughout the country and closer to urban centers. For example, East Coast sites now include the Fire Island National Seashore on Long Island, Acadia National Park in Maine, Assateague National Seashore on the Maryland coast, Cape Hatteras National Seashore in North Carolina, and Gateway East in the New York and New Jersey harbor area.

The national park system consists of over 79 million acres (31.9 million hectares) of land, about 5 percent of which remains in private ownership. The system generates a huge volume of tourism, with appeal for both domestic travelers and foreign visitors that yields major benefits for the nation's economy and the balance of trade with other countries. In 2005, the national park system experienced 273.5 million visitors, spread across the 388-unit system. The level of usage in the national parks has created overcrowding at what are frequently called the "crown jewels." The NPS in its Natural Resource Challenges acknowledges that the business of parks cannot continue in its current form; "Parks are becoming increasingly crowded remnants of primitive America in a fragmented landscape, threatened by invasions of nonnative species, pollution from near and far, and incompatible uses of resources in and around parks." Critical issues impacting the National Park System include contradictory mandates, global climate change, Yellowstone's northern range, invasive species, snowmobiles, and endangered species.

The Appalachian Trail is an example of a national trail used by tens of thousands of people annually for one-day to multiple-day trips.

In December 1999, the director of the NPS asked the National Park System Advisory Board to "develop a report that should focus broadly on the purposes and prospects for the National Park System for the next 25 years." The National Park System Advisory Board, therefore, recommends that the National Park Service:[2]

• Embrace its mission, as educator, to become a more significant part of the country's educational system by providing formal and informal programs for students and learners of all ages inside and outside park boundaries.

• Encourage the study of the U.S. past, developing programs based on current scholarship, linking specific places to the narrative of its history, and encouraging a public exploration and discussion of the American experience.

• Adopt the conservation of biodiversity as a core principle in carrying out its preservation mandate and participate in efforts to protect marine as well as terrestrial resources.

• Advance the principles of sustainability, while first practicing what is preached.

• Actively acknowledge the connections between native cultures and the parks, and assure that no relevant chapter in the U.S. heritage experience remains unopened.

• Encourage collaboration among park and recreation systems at every level—federal, regional, state, local—in order to help build an outdoor recreation network accessible to all Americans.

• Improve the service's institutional capacity by developing new organizational talents and abilities and a workforce that reflects America's diversity.

The Forest Service

A second federal agency that administers extensive wilderness preserves for public recreation use is the Forest Service within the Department of Agriculture (USFS). The resource management responsibilities of the NPS and USFS have blurred in recent years, even though their management mandates have not. Both agencies had responsibilities for managing national monuments, recreation areas, trails, and wild and scenic rivers. The USFS is best known for its management of huge areas of forests and grasslands. The USFS was a predecessor to the National Park Service (NPS) and had a very different role. It adopted the multiple-use concept of federally owned land under its control; mining, grazing, lumbering, recreation, and hunting are all permitted in the national forests.

The recreation function of the USFS has continued to grow steadily. In 2005, it oversaw a total forest system of 192.9 million acres (78 million hectares), which included 35 million acres (14.2 million hectares) of wilderness as well as major elements of the National Scenic Byways and National Wild and Scenic Rivers Systems, national volcanic areas, wildlife and fish habitats, and numerous other special-use areas. In the same year, the USFS recorded 205 million visits, as well as permitting extensive commercial uses with respect to timber harvesting, grazing, and mining operations. Its major recreational uses in 2004 were for relaxation and viewing scenery; camping, picnicking, and swimming; hiking, horseback riding, and water travel; winter sports; and hunting and fishing.

Many threats are on forest service–administered lands. The USFS identified four main threats: fires and fuels, invasive species, loss of open space, and unmanaged recreation. Data suggests the loss of over 3,000 acres a day over a six-year period, mostly to development, in lands near or adjacent to USFS areas. The loss of open space will place greater stress on forest service lands. Unmanaged recreation comes mostly in the form of off-highway vehicles (OHV). There were a reported 36 million OHV owners in 2000. The use of OHVs in USFS lands has resulted in increased erosion, creation of new unplanned roads, and watershed and habitat degradation. The USFS has established action plans for each of the threats.

Other Federal Agencies

The Bureau of Land Management (BLM) administers over 260 million acres (105 million hectares), chiefly in the western states and Alaska. Its properties are used for a variety of resource-based outdoor recreation activities (including camping, biking, hunting and fishing, mountain climbing, and cycle racing), as well as mining, grazing, and lumbering activities that yield over $800 million a year in revenues, much of it returned to state and local governments.

The U.S. Fish and Wildlife Service (USFWS) originally consisted of two federal bureaus, one dealing with commercial fisheries (which was transferred to the Department of Commerce) and the other dealing with sports fisheries and wildlife (which remained in the Department of the Interior). Its functions include restoring the nation's fisheries, enforcing laws, managing wildlife populations, conducting research, and operating the National Wildlife Refuge System. This system includes 520 units comprising 93 million acres (37.61 million hectares). In addition to meeting the ongoing needs of hunters and fishermen, the USFWS particularly has been active in helping to ensure the survival of endangered species, conserving migratory birds, and administering federal aid programs that assist state wildlife programs and tribal lands programs.

The federal Bureau of Reclamation (BOR) is responsible for water resource development, primarily in the western states. Although its original function was to promote irrigation and electric power, it has accepted recreation as a responsibility since 1936. The policy of the Bureau of Reclamation is to transfer reservoir areas wherever possible to other federal agencies; often these become classified as National

Recreation Areas and are assigned to the NPS for operation. The emphasis is on active recreational use such as boating, camping, hiking, hunting, and fishing rather than sightseeing. The National Park Service, Forest Service, Fish and Wildlife Service, and the Bureau of Reclamation have provided employment opportunities for thousands of young men and women through the Youth Conservation Corps (YCC) which has habilitating or building campgrounds and boating facilities at recreation areas throughout the West.

The Tennessee Valley Authority (TVA) operates extensive reservoirs in Kentucky, North Carolina, Tennessee, and other southern or border states. The TVA does not manage recreation facilities itself, but makes land available to other public agencies or private groups for development. Today the visitor-day total is reported to be approximately 14 million a year, but this includes those involved with the more than 20 universities and colleges that participate in resource management, environmental education, and campground operation through a consortium program at the Land Between the Lakes, an outstanding natural facility of more than 170,000 acres (68,796.6 hectares) located in west Kentucky and Tennessee.

The U.S. Army Corps of Engineers is responsible for the improvement and maintenance of rivers and other waterways to facilitate navigation and flood control. It constructs reservoirs, protects and improves beaches and harbors, and administers over 11 million acres (4.5 million hectares) of federally owned land and water impoundments. This includes 460 reservoirs and lakes; the majority of these are managed by the corps, and the remainder are managed by state and local agencies under lease. Army Corps of Engineers recreation sites are heavily used by the public for boating, camping, hunting, and fishing.

Several other agencies in the Department of Agriculture have important recreation functions. The Agricultural Stabilization Service assists farmers in developing ponds and reservoirs on private land and stocking them with fish. The Farmers Home Administration gives credit and management advice to rural organizations and farmers in developing recreation facilities. The Extension Service aids community recreation planning in rural areas and advises states on outdoor recreation development, working in many states through extension agents at land grant agricultural colleges.

The Bureau of Indian Affairs exists primarily to provide service to Native American tribes in such areas as health, education, economic development, and land management. However, it also

■ *Participation in outdoor recreation continues to hold steady. The variety of outdoor recreation activities demands diversity in the provision of natural and outdoor recreation agencies.*

operates (under civilian control in the Department of the Interior) Native American–owned properties of about 56 million acres, with more than 5,500 lakes that are used heavily for recreational purposes, including camping, museum visits, hunting, and fishing.

Programs in Health and Human Services, Education, and Housing

A number of federal agencies related to health and human services, education, and housing and urban development have provided funding, technical assistance, and other forms of aid to recreation programs designed to meet various social needs in U.S. communities. Within the federal Department of Health and Human Services, such units as the Administration on Aging, the Children's Bureau, and the Public Health Service have been active in this area. For example, the Administration on Aging, authorized by the Older Americans Act of 1965 and reauthorized in 2006, promotes comprehensive programs for elderly persons and supports training programs and demonstration projects intended to prepare professional personnel to work with older people. It also gathers information on new or expanded programs and services for the aging and supports research projects in this field.

The Rehabilitation Services Administration administers the federal law authorizing vocational rehabilitation programs designed to help persons with physical or mental disabilities gain employment and lead fuller lives. It has oversight of formula and discretionary grant programs. Other federal legislation, such as Section 504 of the Rehabilitation Act of 1975 (often called the "nondiscrimination clause") and the Americans with Disabilities Act of 1990, has been instrumental in pressuring school systems, units of local government, and other agencies to provide equal opportunity for people with disabilities in a wide range of community opportunity fields.

The federal Department of Housing and Urban Development (HUD) was established in 1965, with responsibility for a range of federally assisted programs, including urban renewal and planning, public housing, and open space. HUD's primary responsibility lies with urban development. Its mission is to increase homeownership, support community development, and increase access to affordable housing free from discrimination. Through its $35 billion budget, it administers a wide variety of programs focusing on community development. The Community Development Block Grant (CDBG), first authorized in 1974, is HUD's most valuable and effective community development program. Examples of use of CDBG funds include roads, sewers, and other infrastructure investments, or for community centers and parks. HUD also funds housing development and rehabilitation through CDBG, HOME, Youthbuild, and Lead Hazard Control grants.

Arts and Humanities Support

Another area of federal involvement in leisure pursuits in the United States has reflected public interest in the arts and a wide range of cultural activities. The National Foundation on the Arts and the Humanities Act of 1965 resulted in the creation of the National Endowment for the Arts (NEA), which functions as an independent federal agency supporting and encouraging programs in the arts (including dance, music, drama, folk art, creative writing, and the visual media) and humanities (including literature, history, philosophy, and the study of language).

■ *Attendance at cultural events is an important component of public services provided by leisure service and cultural arts agencies.*

Although there was strong conservative resistance to some controversial programs in the 1990s, the NEA had its highest appropriation ever in 2002 and by 2006 administered a $125.6 million budget. Over its 40-year history, NEA has awarded over 120,000 grants to communities, arts groups, and artists. In 2002, the NEA initiated the National Initiative program and by 2006 eight initiatives had commenced. They include both short- and long-term initiatives lasting from a single year to many years. The initiatives include NEA arts journalism institutes, Operation Homecoming: Writing the Wartime Experience, American Masterpieces, Shakespeare in American Communities, NEA Jazz Masters, Great American Voices Military Tour, Poetry Out Loud, and the Big Read. All of the initiatives follow the NEA model of working with local communities and arts organizations.

Physical Fitness and Sports Promotion

Another recreation-related federal program has been the President's Council on Physical Fitness and Sports. Created in 1956 to help upgrade the fitness of the nation's youth, and broadened in 1968 to include the promotion of sport participation, the Council has operated to encourage public awareness of fitness needs and to stimulate school and community-based sport and fitness programs. It has conducted nationwide promotional campaigns through the media and sponsored many regional physical fitness clinics. This effort continued through the 1990s, with a President's Challenge Physical Fitness Program providing for state and federal goals and guidelines, school championships, and participant fitness awards. Along with community school systems, many local recreation and park agencies and professional groups have assisted in such fitness programs.

RECREATION-RELATED FUNCTIONS OF STATE GOVERNMENTS

The role of state governments in recreation and parks generally has rested on the Tenth Amendment to the Constitution, which states, "The powers not delegated to the United States by the Constitution, nor prohibited by it to the States, are reserved to the States respectively, or to the people." This amendment, commonly referred to as the "states' rights amendment," is regarded as the source of state powers in such areas as public education, welfare, and health services.

Outdoor Recreation Resources and Programs

Each state government today operates a network of parks and other outdoor recreation resources. The National Association of State Park Directors developed categories of facilities and areas:[3]

- *State parks areas:* containing a number of coordinated programs for the preservation of natural and/or cultural resources and provisions of a variety of outdoor recreation activities supported by those resources.
- *State recreation areas:* where a clear emphasis is placed on the provision of opportunities for primarily active recreation activities; this category includes recreational beaches, water theme parks, and so forth.
- *State natural areas:* where a clear emphasis is placed on protection, management, and interpretation of natural resources of features; this category includes wilderness areas, nature preserves, natural landmarks, and sanctuaries.
- *State historic areas:* where a clear emphasis is placed on protection, management, and interpretation of historical and/or archaeological resources or features; this category includes monuments, memorials, shrines, museums, and so forth dealing with historical and/or archaeological subjects, as well as areas that actually contain substantive remains (forts, burial mounds, etc.) and areas where historic events took place (battles, discoveries, meetings, etc.).
- *State environmental education sites:* used exclusively or primarily for conducting educational programs on environmental subjects, natural resources, and conservation; this category includes nature centers, environmental education centers, "outdoor classrooms," and so forth.
- *State scientific areas:* set aside exclusively or primarily for scientific study, observation, and experimentation involving natural objects, processes, and interrelationships; any other allowable uses are secondary and incidental.
- *State trails:* linear areas outside any other unit of the state park system that provide primarily for trail-type recreational activities (hiking, cycling, horseback riding, etc.); they normally do not contain any land areas large enough to support nontrail activities.

During the 1960s and early 1970s, most state governments expanded their recreation and park holdings, primarily with funding assistance from the Land and Water Conservation Fund but also through major bond issues totaling hundreds of millions of dollars in many cases. In the 1990s, many states again secured major bond issues for park renovation, new construction, and land acquisition. Open space and natural beauty were widely supported concepts, and the public enthusiastically supported programs of land acquisition and water cleanup. State parks are perceived as a close-to-home outdoor recreation experience available to most residents. Attendance at state parks exceeds all national agencies except the USFS. Attendance at state parks in 2005 was 708.6 million on 14.1 million acres (5.7 million hectares). State park acreage is only 18 percent of the size of the National Park system and yet state parks have 2.6 times as many visitors. State parks are essential to outdoor recreation activities of many citizens.

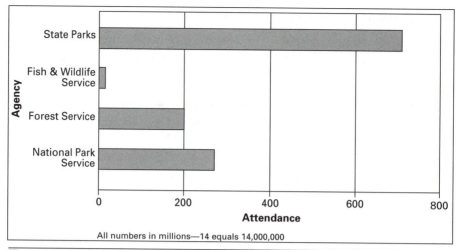

All numbers in millions—14 equals 14,000,000

Comparison of Attendance at Outdoor Areas

Other State Functions

An important function of state government is to assist and work with local governments in environmental efforts. Just as no single municipality can clean up a polluted stream that flows through a state, so in the broad field of urban planning, recreation resource development, and conservation, problems must be approached on a statewide or even a regional basis. In such planning, as in many other aspects of federal relationships with local communities, the state acts as a catalyst for action and as a vital link between the national and local governments.

Many state governments have offices or sponsor arts councils that distribute funds to nonprofit organizations and performing groups or institutions in various areas of creative and cultural activity. A unique aspect of state-sponsored or state-assisted recreation is the state fair. This term covers a wide variety of fairs and expositions held each year throughout the United States and includes carnivals and midways, displays and competitions of livestock and produce, farm equipment shows, and a host of special presentations by corporations of every type. The majority of such fairs are run by nonprofit organizations that are publicly owned and operated, including a number of bona fide state agencies. Attended by about 160 million persons each year, they promote civic and state boosterism, offer a showcase for agricultural and other regional industries or attractions, and provide varied forms of entertainment.

An important function of state governments is to promote all aspects of leisure involvement that support economic development. Many states assist or coordinate outdoor recreation ventures, tourism campaigns, regional recovery projects, and other efforts to attract visitors and revive local economies. Travel and tourism to urban and rural areas have become increasingly important to economies. States are providing leadership, assistance, and funding to local levels.

Therapeutic Recreation Service   Each state government provides direct recreation services within the institutions or agencies it sponsors, such as mental hospitals or mental health centers, special schools for people who are mentally retarded, and penal or correctional facilities. Many of the largest networks of facilities that employ therapeutic recreation specialists are tax-supported state mental health systems or similar organizations, although their overall numbers have been reduced because of deinstitutionalization policies.

Promotion of Professional Advancement   Although states promote effective leadership and administrative practices in recreation and parks by developing personnel standards and providing conferences and research support, their major contribution lies in the professional preparation of recreation practitioners in state colleges and universities. Of the colleges and universities in the United States with professional recreation and park curricula, a substantial majority are part of state university systems.

Many state agencies also assist professional development by conducting annual surveys of municipal and county recreation and parks departments and publishing their findings on facilities, fiscal practices, and personnel.

Development and Enforcement of Standards   States also have the function of screening personnel by establishing standards and hiring procedures, or by requiring Civil Service examinations, certification, or personnel registration programs in recreation and parks.

Many states also have developed standards relating to health and safety practices in camping and similar settings. State departments enforce safety codes, promote facilities standards, ensure that recreation resources can accommodate persons with disabilities, regulate or prohibit certain types of commercial attractions, and in some cases carry out regular inspections of camps, pools, or other facilities.

■ *Individuals with disabilities actively engage in sport, sometimes with individuals without disabilities.*

THE ROLE OF COUNTY AND LOCAL GOVERNMENTS

Although federal and state governments provide major forms of recreation service in the United States, the responsibility for meeting year-round day-to-day leisure needs belongs to agencies of local government. These range from counties, special park districts, and townships (which embrace larger geographical areas) to cities, villages, and other political subdivisions.

For recreation and parks in the United States, all powers that are not vested in the federal government belong to the states. In turn, local governments must get their authority through enabling laws passed by state legislatures or through other special charter or home rule arrangements. Of all branches of government, the local government is closest to the people and therefore most able to meet the widest range of recreation needs.

County and Special Park District Programs

As an intermediate stage between state and incorporated local government agencies, county or special district park and recreation units provide large parks and other outdoor recreation resources as a primary function. They may also sponsor services for special populations; that is, programs for those aging or having a disability as well as services for all residents of the county, such as programs in the fine and performing arts.

During the early decades of the century, county governments had relatively limited functions. However, since World War II, the rapid growth of suburban populations around large cities has given many county governments new influence and power. Counties have become a base for coordinating and funneling numerous federal grants-in-aid programs. As a result, county park and recreation departments expanded rapidly.

Regional and Special Park Districts

Several states, including California, Illinois, Oregon, and North Dakota, have enabling legislation that permits the establishment of special park and recreation districts. Illinois has over 300 such districts, including forest preserve and conservation districts. North Dakota has 225 park districts, California 118, and Ohio 26, while Oregon has 17 park and recreation districts.

Many special recreation and park districts are in heavily populated areas; in some cases, they may encompass a number of independent, separate counties and municipalities in a single structure. Frequently, special park districts and counties are able to carry out vigorous programs of land acquisition in a combined effort or to impose other means of protecting open space. Many counties enacted laws requiring home developers to set aside community recreation areas. One such example is Anne Arundel County, Maryland, which since 1957 has required all developers to allocate 5 percent of the land to be developed as park areas. Another common approach used by cities and counties to secure funds and lands is to require owners of new homes to pay an impact fee. The impact fee is based on the concept that current tax payers should not have to pay for new development; it should be the responsibility of the new owner to pay for community improvements to the neighborhood. Park and recreation departments have

Two similar examples of leading county park agencies are Miami–Dade County Park and Recreation Department in south Florida and the East Bay Regional Park District, comprising Alameda and Contra Costa on the eastern side of San Francisco Bay, California. Miami–Dade County Park and Recreation Department operates 12,000 acres of carefully planned and developed park and recreation facilities, serving 25 million plus visitors annually. The Crandon Zoo, Dade County Auditorium, and other facilities are important elements in this recreation-oriented metropolitan area, which depends heavily on its tourists. In addition, the Miami–Dade County department promotes numerous other privately owned or nonprofit attractions and leisure facilities, such as an impressive array of art museums, galleries, and collections in the metropolitan area that are sponsored by universities, individuals, and civic groups.

The East Bay Regional Park District's vision statement says "The East Bay Regional Park District will preserve a priceless heritage of natural and cultural resources open space, parks and trails for the future and will set aside park areas for enjoyment and healthful recreation for generations to come. An environmental ethic guides us in all that we do." The system started with three parks and two employees and now includes 97,000 acres (39,254 hectares) and operates an outstanding network of 65 regional parks, recreation areas, wilderness, shorelines, preserves and land bank areas, 29 regional interpark trails, 1,150 miles of trails within parklands, 11 freshwater swimming areas, boating and/or stocked fishing lakes and lagoons, a disabled-accessible swimming pool, 40 fishing docks, 3 bay fishing piers, 235 family campsites, 42 youth camping areas, 2 golf courses, 9 interpretive and education centers, 18 children's play areas, and over 600 employees. Consistent with the vision, 90 percent of the district's lands are protected and operated as natural parklands.

been recipients of these funds. Some county governments are establishing permanently protected green belts to halt or lessen the tide of construction. Strengthened zoning policies and more flexible building codes that permit cluster zoning of homes with larger and more concentrated open spaces are also helpful.

MUNICIPAL RECREATION AND PARK DEPARTMENTS

Municipal government is the term generally used to describe the local political unit of government, such as the village, town, or city, that is responsible for providing the bulk of direct community service such as street maintenance, police and fire protection, and education. Most areas depend on municipal government to provide many important recreation and park facilities and program opportunities, in addition to those provided by voluntary, private, and commercial agencies.

With the widespread recognition of this responsibility, municipal recreation and park agencies expanded rapidly in the United States during the period following World War II, with a steady increase in the number of departments, amount of acreage in park and recreation areas, number of full- and part-time or seasonal personnel, and total expenditures.

Functions and Structure of Municipal Agencies

The most common structure for delivery of services is a combined parks and recreation department. In some few cases, parks and recreation may include other social service organizations such as libraries, assistance agencies, and the like. Some remain separate parks and recreation departments.

Other municipal agencies may also sponsor special leisure services that are linked to their own missions. They may include (1) police departments, which often operate youth service centers or leagues; (2) welfare departments or social service agencies, which may operate day-care centers or senior centers; (3) youth boards, which tend to focus on out-of-school youth or teen gangs; (4) health and hospital agencies, which sometimes operate community mental health centers or similar services; (5) public housing departments, which sometimes have recreation centers in their projects; (6) cultural departments or boards, which frequently sponsor performing arts programs or civic celebrations; and (7) school systems and local community colleges.

Programs of Municipal Agencies

Municipal recreation and parks departments operate programs within several categories of activity: games and sports, aquatics, outdoor and nature-oriented programs, arts and crafts, performing arts, special services, social programs, hobby groups, and other playground and community center activities.

In addition, public recreation and parks departments often sponsor large-scale special events such as holiday celebrations, festival programs, art and hobby shows, and sport tournaments. These departments also assist other community agencies to organize, publicize, and schedule activities. Frequently, sport programs for children and youth, such as Little League or American Legion baseball, are cosponsored by public departments and associations of interested parents who undertake much of the actual management of the activity, including coaching, fundraising, and scheduling. Similarly, many cultural programs, such as civic opera or little theater associations, are affiliated with and receive assistance from public recreation departments.

Varied Program Emphases

Cities tend to have common and unique emphases in their recreation and park operations. Omaha, Nebraska, for example, has an established department that operates a major auditorium and stadium complex, extensive boating facilities, and other unusual physical facilities, including an outstanding indoor tennis complex and a trap and skeet shooting facility. With revenues from these sources, it is able to support a substantial portion of its overall recreation operations.

Vancouver, British Columbia, has given high priority to developing and maintaining an extensive network of parks, beaches, pools, golf courses, conservatories, ice rinks, community centers, and an outstanding zoo in famed Stanley Park. This landmark, established more than 100 years ago, has a remarkable seawall promenade, a

■ *Municipal parks and recreation agencies offer a wide variety of programs ranging from special events and arts to sports, fitness, and outdoor recreation.*

zoo, an aquarium, outstanding sports facilities, and other sites for leisure participation. A section of Stanley Park was named a Heritage Park Site in 1980, and its meadows and forests are carefully preserved as magnificent examples of relatively untouched natural environments.

Fitness Programming   Many cities have undertaken special programs to promote health, fitness, and sport. This effort has been assisted by the Step up to Health program, sponsored by the National Recreation and Park Assocation. The NFL Youth Football fund supported a series of summits to train communities on Step up to Health in 2006. The program continues park and recreation department efforts to be in the forefront of the healthy lifestyle movement. Linked to this program emphasis is the recent trend by many city and county recreation departments to build outstanding new aquatic facilities that include extensive exercise and sport components. Littleton, Colorado, for example, completed in March 2005, a 53,000-square-foot (4,924 square meter) recreation center with separate community and recreation wings. The community wing includes classrooms, commercial kitchen, a child-care area, and the recreation wing including an aquatic center, fitness room, aerobics and dance studio, and gymnasium. The cost was $9.98 million. In Dickinson, North Dakota, a new 80,452-square-foot (7,474 square meter) recreation center was constructed to include a lounge, climbing wall, lap pool, leisure pool, child-care area, and fitness room.

ndianapolis, Indiana, is an excellent example of a city that has combined vigorous expansion of its sports and cultural facilities and programs with a sound public recreation and parks program to enhance its appeal to new businesses, residents, and tourists. Once viewed as a less-than-lively midwestern town, Indianapolis is fast becoming known as the amateur sports capital of the nation. In addition to its famed Indianapolis 500 auto racing event, the track has added the Brickyard 400 and a major Formula One race. The city now has three major league sports teams—the Pacers, Fever, and the Colts—and several minor league teams. It built multiple major sports facilities, including the RCA Dome, Conseco Fieldhouse, Victory Field, and other athletic stadiums including a world-class tennis center, velodrome, and a natatorium. In 2006, construction began on a new $500-million football stadium with a retractable roof.

The National Collegiate Athletic Association moved to Indianapolis in the late 1990s. Other national sports associations have moved their headquarters to Indianapolis, including the Amateur Athletic Union, the U.S. Rowing Association, U.S. Track and Field, and the American College of Sports Medicine. In addition, the city boasts new art galleries, theaters, museums, performing companies, a zoo, and the world's largest children's museum.

Human Service Functions Many local recreation and park agencies have moved vigorously into the area of programming to meet human and social service needs. The Recreation and Human Services Department of the city of Gardena, California, for example, offers many services, including youth services; individual, family, and group counseling; tutoring workshops; alcohol and drug abuse programs; after-school activities; licensed family child care; youth and adult counseling; senior citizen outreach and meals programming; and care for those suffering from Alzheimer's or mental disease.

A trend of the last two decades has been to develop multiservice departments in which recreation and park programs play a leading role. Thus, a merged department of community services might have responsibility for beaches, parking meters, special housing units, libraries, and other special public facilities or programs. Larger urban recreation and park departments may include management responsibilities for stadiums, convention centers, piers and marinas, or even municipal airports.

■ *Aquatic centers with a variety of amenities have become popular year-round activities incorporated into public park and recreation agencies, commercial enterprises, and resorts.*

Fee-Based Programs

In response to government efforts to become more business oriented, including seeking expanded revenue sources, fee-based programs have gained popularity with recreation and park departments. The trend toward imposing substantial fees for many program elements or facilities membership in public recreation and parks is firmly established. Those who favor it argue that it provides a logical means of developing rich programs and services and strengthens the role of the recreation and agency in community life. As tax revenues available for recreation and parks continue to decline, many agencies find fee-based programs a survival tool. Other agencies have implemented fee-based programs to offer services that would otherwise not be available through government funding.

Some critics argue that placing heavy reliance on fee structures discriminates against children and youth, people who are elderly, people with disabilities, and the poor, who cannot afford to pay significant fees for participation in public recreation programs. As such, it represents a retreat from the fundamental mission of public recreation and leisure programs. In some cases, cities or other public recreation and park agencies have provided fee discounts, "scholarships," or variable pricing policies to enable participation by poorer families. Although such policies are generally acceptable in well-to-do towns or suburban areas, they are obviously not workable in socially and economically disadvantaged inner-city neighborhoods or in less-affluent communities. Some cities developed models in which they assess the social priority that should be attached to recreation facilities or programs and base fee-charging policies on this assessment.

Innovative Developments in Larger Cities

As earlier chapters in this text have shown, problems related to inadequate budgets, increasing crime, and declining infrastructure and maintenance services tend to be most severe in older cities with limited public, nonprofit, and commercial leisure resources—yet, even in these communities, recreation and park administrators are working to expand and improve leisure facilities, programs, and maintenance. New York City, which experienced major cuts in recreation and park operations at the start of the twenty-first century, has been able to mount aggressive campaigns to improve the care of its major parks, such as Central Park and Prospect Park, through the contributions of thousands of businesses and individual residents who joined park foundations or conservancy organizations. Additionally, some operations have been contracted to private vendors. The American Golf Corporation announced a $24-million investment in golf course renovation for six historic courses. Privatization efforts similar to New York's allow cities to use limited capital dollars for other needed improvements in parks and recreation facilities.

New York also successfully moved ahead with plans to develop its waterfront areas, as other cities like Baltimore have done, with mixed public, private, and commercial recreational uses. With the state's approval, four huge piers jutting into the Hudson River, which had been built in the early 1900s to accommodate a generation of giant ocean liners, were converted into a major sports and entertainment complex. Costing over $100 million, the waterfront, known as Chelsea Piers, boasts an 80,000-square-

■ *Many cities, such as Carmel, IN, offer recreational opportunities for all ages and abilities.*

foot (7,432 square meters) field house, year-round heated hitting stalls, a 200-yard (185.8 meter) artificial golf fairway, and a twin rink ice arena that is open 24 hours a day/7 days a week.

Extending such efforts, New York's Lower Manhattan Redevelopment Project allocated $24 million toward renovation and new development in 24 existing park sites. In another example of recreation's role in the recovery of older, major cities, the Boston, Massachusetts, harbor area continues an $11 billion transformation, which will include water-based recreation in the city's newly clean seaport and bay waters.[4]

Along with such environmental and marketing-based efforts, many municipal recreation and park agencies also have moved vigorously in the direction of benefits-based programming as a means of documenting and providing direction to their overall services.

NONPROFIT ORGANIZATIONS: ORGANIZING THE VOLUNTARY SECTOR

While government recreation and park agencies are responsible for providing a floor of basic leisure services for the public throughout the United States, a major segment of recreational opportunities is sponsored by nonprofit organizations, often called *voluntary agencies.* These consist of several different types of youth-serving, special-interest, and charitable organizations.

Organizations in this category may be completely independent or may be part of national or regional federations. Often they are described as "quasi-public" or "public/private." In some cases, they must meet government-imposed standards as charitable organizations to retain tax-exempt status. They tend to share the following characteristics:

- Usually established to meet significant social needs through organized citizen cooperation, community organizations represent the voluntary wishes and expressed needs of neighborhood residents. Thus, they are voluntary in origin.
- Governing boards of directors or trustees are usually public-spirited citizens who accept such responsibilities as a form of social obligation; thus, membership and administrative control are voluntary.
- For funding, voluntary agencies usually rely on public contributions, either directly to the agency itself or to Community Chest, United Way, or similar shared fundraising efforts. Contributed funds are usually supplemented by membership fees and charges for participation. In recent years, many voluntary organizations also have undertaken special projects for which they receive government funding.

- Leadership of voluntary agencies is partly professional and partly voluntary. Management is usually by directors and supervisors professionally trained in social work, recreation, education, or other related areas. At other levels, leadership is by nonprofessionals, part-time or seasonal personnel, and volunteers.
- In some cases, nonprofit organizations in the overall leisure-service system do not sponsor recreation activities directly, but represent organizations that do or that manufacture equipment or provide services, often on a for-profit basis. However, as in the case of educational institutions or professional societies in this field, they are nonprofit and tax exempt.

Nonprofit voluntary agencies regard recreation as part of their total spectrum of services, rather than their sole function. Typically, they recognize the importance of creative and constructive leisure and see recreation as a threshold activity that serves to attract participants to their agencies. In addition, they see it as a means of achieving significant social goals, such as building character among youth, reducing social pathology, enriching educational experience, strengthening community unity, and similar objectives. In general, even though voluntary agencies do not describe themselves as recreation agencies, this often tends to be the largest single component in their programs.

Nonprofits rely on volunteers for much of their work. Americans provide more volunteer service than any other society. In 2004, 28.8 percent of all Americans volunteered to serve organizations or other programs. Women represented 31 percent of all volunteers and those aged 35 to 54 provided 65 percent of all volunteers. Volunteers' median time spent was 50 hours.[5]

Nonprofit but Fee Charging

Many voluntary organizations, though they are nonprofit and interested in meeting important social goals, may charge substantial fees. For example, YMCAs or YWCAs in suburban areas are likely to have fees that are as high as several hundred dollars a year for full family memberships and charge impressive sums for varied program activities. However, such fees are intended simply to help the organization maintain financial stability, without making a profit, and are frequently used to subsidize other services to marginalized populations who cannot afford to pay fees for membership or participation.

Because of the word *voluntary*, some assume incorrectly that such agencies are staffed solely by volunteer workers. The reality is that, although some nonprofit organizations such as the Boy Scouts and Girl Scouts rely heavily on volunteer leaders, most of them have full-time, paid professionals in their key management or supervisory posts.

It was estimated in 2002 that nonprofit organizations employed 8.3 percent of working Americans, involving 11.6 million people. Salaries for professional employees of such bodies as Boy Scouts and Girl Scouts, the YMCA and YWCA, Junior Achievement, and Big Brothers/Big Sisters of America all have risen steadily in recent years. Indeed, during the early and mid-1990s, a wave of public criticism was directed at the executives of some major nonprofit, charitable organizations who received exorbitant salaries and benefits.

TYPES OF NONPROFIT YOUTH-SERVING AGENCIES

While voluntary nonprofit organizations fit under many headings—including the arts, education, health, and social service—the largest segment of such groups with strong recreational components is generally youth oriented. Included in this segment are

- nonsectarian youth-serving organizations
- religiously affiliated youth-serving or social agencies
- special interest organizations in such fields as sport, outdoor recreation, and travel
- conservation and outdoor recreation
- organizations promoting youth sports and games
- arts councils and cultural organizations
- service and federal clubs
- promotional and coordinating bodies

Nonsectarian Youth-Serving Organizations

Nationally structured organizations that function directly through local branches, nonsectarian youth-serving groups have broad goals related to social development and good citizenship and operate extensive programs of recreational activity. There are hundreds of such organizations: Many of them are junior affiliates of adult organizations, whereas others are independent. Sponsorship is by such varied bodies as civic and fraternal organizations, veterans' clubs, rural and farm organizations, and business clubs. Several examples follow.

Boy Scouts of America   Founded in the United States in 1910, the Boy Scouts of America is a powerful and widespread organization. In 2005, its youth membership consisted of 3.3 million youth, ranging from Tiger Cubs to Explorers. Together with adult leaders, a total of 4.1 million were involved in Boy Scouts of America in 123,582 packs, troops, and other units, directed by a professional staff consisting of almost 4,000. In addition to its membership in the United States, Boy Scouts of America is part of a worldwide scouting movement involving more than 100 other countries. The program emphasizes mental and physical fitness, vocational and social development, and the enrichment of youth hobbies and prevocational interests, relying heavily on adventure and scouting skills and service activities.

The Boy Scouts of America has been regarded as a middle-class organization in U.S. society and as a small town or suburban rather than a big city phenomenon. As the urban environment has changed so has scouting's impact in the inner city. Heather MacDonald, reporting on scouting in inner New York City reported,

> Feeling dispirited about today's youth? Try attending a Boy Scout meeting. You will find a parallel universe to today's vulgar, sexualized youth culture, filled with gestures of sometimes unbelievable delicacy and a code of conduct as anachronistic as sixteenth-century courtiership. Take Harlem's Troop 759. Six boys, from tall to small, sit expectantly around a card table in the basement of a red brick church on Morningside Avenue. The gangly senior patrol leader, Osmond Ollennu, a tenth-grade son of Ghanaians, calls the troop to opening ceremonies ("C'mon, men, form a straight line!"), and Osmond's little brother leads it in the Pledge of Allegiance, followed by

four full-throated repetitions of the scout motto ("Be Prepared!") and one scout slogan ("Do a Good Turn Daily"). Then Osmond, who is the troop's second-in-command, announces inspection. While the boys stand quietly in line, he gently reties a neckerchief here, straightens a collar there, occasionally whispering a reminder in a boy's ear. The troop's leader, a dignified 18-year-old named Henry Lawson, inspects Ollennu in turn.

Speaking of scouting's values:

Scoutcraft teaches, among other things, persistence in the face of disappointment. When it rains and your boots are filled with mud, "you can either take a bad hand and fold, or you can keep playing it, and it will get better," explains Scott Slaton, an Eagle Scout from Atlanta, Georgia, who works with inner-city scouts.[6]

Girl Scouts of the U.S.A. The largest voluntary organization serving girls in the world, the Girl Scouts of the U.S.A. is open to girls between the ages of 5 and 17 who subscribe to its ideals as stated in the Girl Scout Promise and Law. It is part of a worldwide association of girls and adults in more than 90 countries through its membership in the World Association of Girl Guides and Girl Scouts. Its membership in 2002 consisted of 2.7 million members and 928,000 adults, including volunteers, board members, and staff specialists.

Founded in 1912, the Girl Scouts of the U.S.A. provides a sequential program of activities centered around the arts, the home, and the outdoors, with emphasis on character and citizenship development, community service, international understanding, and health and safety. Senior Girl Scouts in particular may take on responsibilities in hospitals, museums, child care, or environmental programs. Like the Boy Scouts of America, the Girl Scouts of the U.S.A. today conducts special programs for the poor; those with physical, emotional, or other disabilities; and similar populations.

In June 2004, the Girl Scouts initiated a project focusing on core business strategies. The project's outcome is to develop a strategy to ensure the future success and growth of Girl Scouts. They have chosen to emphasize five strategic priorities including development of outcomes-based leadership models, revitalizing volunteerism, branding the Girl Scout name with a new contemporary approach, increasing funding substantially, and restructuring of the organizational and governance structure to be more efficient and effective. In the early stages of development, Girl Scouts hope to revitalize and address contemporary issues and needs.[7]

Boys and Girls Clubs of America The Boys and Girls Clubs movement is the fastest-growing youth-serving organization in the United States today. Originally composed of two separate organizations, the merged club movement holds a U.S. congressional charter and is endorsed by 21 leading service, fraternal, civic, veteran, labor, and business organizations. Today, the Boys and Girls Clubs movement serves 4.4 million youth members in over 3,700 club locations, with a staff of 44,000 full-time trained professionals and over 172,000 adult volunteers. Its members come from minority families (66 percent), are 7 to 12 years old (56 percent), 13 to 18 years old (31 percent), and are closely equal gender-wise: male (55 percent) and female (45 percent). Programs include sport and games, arts and crafts, social activities, and camping, as well as remedial education, work training, and job placement and counseling. The national goals of the Boys and Girls Clubs of America include the following: citizenship education and leadership development; health, fitness, and preparation for leisure; educational vocational motivation; intergroup understanding and value development; and enrichment of both family and community life.

With the help of special funding from corporations, foundations, and government agencies, the organization has developed program curricula for several key projects in the social services area. Although each club is an independent organization with its own board and professional staff, the national headquarters and seven regional offices provide essential services to local clubs in such areas as personnel recruitment and management training, program research and development, fundraising and public relations, and building design and construction assistance.

The Boys and Girls Clubs have had success recruiting Latinos and began a three-year recruitment drive in 2004 with a $3.1 million grant. Similar success has been present in working with military youth as they have set up clubs on a number of military installations internationally. An endowment has been established to create a long-term involvement with Native Americans. The endowment totaled $7.5 million in 2004. Boys and Girls Clubs continued to work with other organizations such as the National Association of Police Athletic Leagues, United Neighborhood Centers, and the Salvation Army.

Police Athletic Leagues   In hundreds of communities today, law enforcement agencies sponsor Police Athletic Leagues (PALs). Operating in poverty areas, the league programs rely primarily on civilian staffing and voluntary contributions for support, although they sometimes receive technical assistance from officers on special assignment from cooperative municipal police departments. In a few cities, police officers provide the bulk of full-time professional leadership in PAL programs. PALs typically provide extensive recreation programming, indoor centers, and summer play streets, with strong emphasis on sport and games, creative arts, drum and bugle corps, and remedial education. Many leagues also maintain placement, counseling, and job training programs and assist youth who have dropped out of school.

The PAL is one of the few youth organizations that continues to have resisting juvenile delinquency as a primary thrust. One of its principal purposes has been to promote favorable relationships between young people and the police in urban settings, and it has been markedly successful in this effort. Like other voluntary agencies, PALs rely on varied funding sources, including the United Way, independent fundraising campaigns, contracts with government, and often partial police department sponsorship.

Camp Fire USA   Founded in 1910 under the name Camp Fire Girls, this organization has been concerned with character building through a program of outdoor recreation, community service, and educational activities. Beginning in the 1970s, the membership of the Camp Fire Girls declined sharply, from a high of more than 600,000 to approximately 325,000 in the early 1980s. The organization responded to this challenge by changing its name to Camp Fire USA and embracing a coeducational membership diverse in racial, ethnic, religious, and economic terms. With over 6,500 volunteer and paid leaders, the staff and board members work extensively in cooperation with local schools in conducting child-care programs. Many Camp Fire programs also sponsor day and resident camping programs for young people from kindergarten age to 21. In 2004–2005, they reached over 750,000 youth. Like other youth-serving groups, Camp Fire USA serves as a strong advocate for youth in such areas as juvenile justice, child abuse, AIDS, and teen suicide.

Religiously Affiliated Youth-Serving or Social Agencies

Many religious organizations sponsor youth programs with recreational components today, including activities sponsored by local churches or synagogues and activities sponsored by national federations that are affiliated with a particular denomination.

Recreation programs provided by local churches or synagogues tend to have two broad purposes: (1) to sponsor recreation for their own members or congregations in order to meet their leisure needs in ways that promote involvement with the institution, and (2) to provide leisure opportunities for the community at large or for a selected population group in ways that are compatible with their own religious beliefs. Typical activities offered by individual churches and synagogues may include the following:

- Day camps, play schools, or summer Bible schools, which include recreation along with religious instruction
- Year-round recreation activities for families, including picnics, outings, bazaars, covered dish suppers, carnivals, single-adult clubs, dances, game nights, and similar events
- Programs in the fine and performing arts, including innovative worship programs involving dance and folk music
- Fellowship programs for various age levels, including discussion groups on religious and other themes
- Varied special interest or social service programs, including day-care centers for children, senior citizens clubs or golden age groups, and recreation programs for disabled persons
- Sport activities, including bowling and basketball leagues, or other forms of instructional or competitive participation

On a broader level, such organizations as the Young Men's Christian Association (YMCA), Young Women's Christian Association (YWCA), the Catholic Youth Organization (CYO), and the Young Men's and Young Women's Hebrew Association (YM-YWHA) provide a network of facilities and programs with diversified recreation, education, and youth service activities. Although their titles include the words *young* or *youth*, they tend to serve a broad range of children, youth, adult, and aging members.

YMCA *and* YWCA   Voluntary organizations affiliated with Protestantism in general rather than with any single denomination, the Ys are devoted to the promotion of religious ideals of living and view themselves as worldwide fellowships "dedicated to the enrichment of life through the development of Christian character and a Christian society." However, the actual membership of the Ys is multireligious and multiracial. In

2004, there were 2,594 YMCAs with 20.1 million members making it one of the largest nonprofits providing recreation. There were an additional 559,000 volunteers.

In many communities, the YMCA offers the best facilities and leadership for indoor aquatics, sport and games, physical fitness, social and cultural programs, and family-centered programs. These activities are usually aggressively marketed and bring in substantial revenues. Both the YMCA and YWCA derive funding from varied sources: membership fees, corporate and private contributions through the United Way, fundraising drives, and government and foundation grants.

Nonprofit organizations, such as the YMCA, provide important services, including fitness programs, for members.

Muslim Youth Groups There is no single national organization providing leadership for Muslim youth groups, rather multiple groups are providing leadership, all with some or a total emphasis on youth. These include the Islamic Society of North America, Muslim American Society, and Young Muslims. The Islamic Society of North America (ISNA) provides information on aging, domestic violence, matrimony, leadership, and youth.

In addition to meeting recreational needs, the YWCA in particular has changed its image from a traditional, predominantly white conservative organization to one more directly concerned with social needs and problems. This new attitude is illustrated by the types of courses, clinics, workshops, and services offered on a local basis. The nature of programs is as varied as the YWCA itself and typically is responsive to local needs. The list of programs is long and diverse. Some examples include racial justice, domestic violence, women's economic advancement, self-sufficiency, relationships, chemical dependency, career development, antiviolence, transitional house, child care, and many more. The YWCA has maintained a strong national presence and focus while supporting and encouraging local diversity of programming and services.

The YWCA's brand or slogan, "Eliminating Racism, Empowering Women," reflects the change that has occurred in the organization over the last few years. Serving women for over 145 years, the YWCA has been socially active in the 300 communities it serves. It is engaged in such activities as shelter services for women and their families, child-care services, sport and fitness programs for women and girls, girls' leadership development, public leadership involvement, and more recently creating tech-based programs for girls.

■ *Ethnic background impacts the types of activities individuals participate in, but does not diminish participation.*

There are Muslim youth groups concentrated in local communities and regions. The Islamic Center of Southern California, for example, provides an educational, social, spiritual and moral environment, and physical activities to motivate young American Muslims to live by and serve Islam and to identify themselves as Muslims, creating a nurturing learning environment in which a basic core knowledge of Islam is provided. In addition, they encourage education, self-expression, the creation of a social environment to build healthy interaction, and foster an American Muslim identity.

Catholic Youth Organization   The leading Catholic organization concerned with providing spiritual, social, and recreational services for young people in the United States is the Catholic Youth Organization. CYO originated in the early 1930s, when a number of dioceses under the leadership of Bishop Sheil of Chicago began experimenting with varied forms of youth organizations. It was established as a national organization in 1951 as a component of the National Council of Catholic Youth. Today, the National CYO Federation has an office in Washington, D.C., as well as many citywide or diocesan offices. The parish, however, is the core of the Catholic Youth Organization, which depends heavily on the leadership of parish priests and the services of adult volunteers from the neighborhood for direction and assistance.

Young Men's and Young Women's Hebrew Association   Today, there are over 250 YM-YWHAs, Jewish Community Centers, and camps serving over one million members throughout the United States. Like the YMCAs and YWCAs, the Jewish Ys do not regard themselves primarily as recreation agencies, but rather as community organizations devoted to social service and having a strong Jewish cultural component. Specifically, the YM-YWHA has defined its mission in the following way:

• To meet the leisure-time social, cultural, and recreational needs of its membership, embracing both sexes and all age groups

- To stimulate individual growth and personality development by encouraging interest and capacity for group and community participation
- To teach leadership responsibility and democratic process through group participation
- To encourage citizenship education and responsibility among its members and, as a social welfare agency, to participate in community-wide programs of social betterment

Special Interest Organizations

Numerous other types of voluntary nonprofit organizations can best be classified as special interest groups, concerned with promoting a particular area of activity or social concern. Their functions may include leadership training, public relations, lobbying and legislation, establishing national standards or operational policies, or the direct sponsorship of program activities. Special interest organizations may be free of commercial involvement or may represent manufacturers of equipment, owners of facilities, schools, or other businesses that seek to stimulate public interest and support and, ultimately, to improve their own business success.

Conservation and Outdoor Recreation   Numerous nonprofit organizations seek to educate the public and influence governmental policies in the areas of conservation and outdoor recreation. In some cases, they lobby, conduct research, and sponsor conferences and publications. In others, their primary thrust is to mount projects and carry out direct action on state or local levels.

Sierra Club   Founded in 1892 and headed initially by the famous naturalist John Muir, the Sierra Club has sought to make Americans aware "of what we have lost and can lose during 200 years of continuing exploitation of our resources for commodity purposes and failure to realize their value for scenic, scientific, and aesthetic purposes." The Sierra Club has gained an international focus, emphasizing issues of global warming and the effects of recent disasters such as the tsunami in south Asia and Hurricane Katrina. Its activities are not restricted to conservation; it is also the nation's largest skiing and hiking club, operating a major network of ski lodges and "river runners," numerous wilderness outings, and ecological group projects.

Appalachian Mountain Club   This organization has a regional focus; its purpose when founded in 1876 was to "explore the mountains of New England and adjacent regions . . . for scientific and artistic purposes, and . . . to cultivate an interest in geographical studies." Since its inception, it has explored and mapped many of the wildest and most scenic areas in Massachusetts, New Hampshire, and Maine, in addition to promoting such sports as skiing, snowshoeing, mountain climbing, and canoeing.

Although practical conservation remains a primary concern of the club, it also has acquired various camp properties, published guides and maps, and maintained hundreds of miles of trails and a network of huts and shelters throughout the White Mountains for use by its members. It promotes programs of instruction and leadership training in such activities as snowshoeing, skiing, smooth and whitewater canoeing, and rock climbing.

Outdoor Leadership Programs A number of other national nonprofit organizations teach outdoor leadership skills and promote sound environmental practices in the wilderness. The National Outdoor Leadership School sponsors a variety of courses in backpacking, mountaineering, rock climbing, sea kayaking, and other outdoor adventure activities in settings throughout the western states, Alaska, and such foreign countries as Australia, Mexico, Patagonia, and Kenya. Outward Bound uses five core programs for character development and self-discovery through challenge and adventure. Initiated in the early 1960s, early programs trained the first Peace Corps volunteers. Since that time it has become a worldwide organization providing training and experiences to over 500,000 people. The Association for Experiential Education is a professional membership association focusing on experiential education for students, educators, and practitioners. It provides program resources, a national conference, and accreditation for environmental education sites.

Organizations Promoting Youth Sport and Games

There are thousands of national, regional, and local organizations promoting and regulating sport of every kind. Although many of these govern professional play or high-level intercollegiate competition, others are concerned with sports and games on a purely amateur basis. One example of such an organization is Little League.

Founded in Williamsport, Pennsylvania, in 1939, Little League is the largest youth sports program in the world today. In its various leagues, including softball, it serves more than 2.6 million players in the United States and over 3 million players in 91 countries. In 2006, there were almost 7,500 organized leagues; in the same year, 290 new programs were chartered, 135 of them outside the United States. Vietnam was one of the new nations initiating a Little League program. Prior to the Little League Baseball World Series, up to 16,000 tournament games are played in a six-week time frame. Little League operates an impressive headquarters complex and stadium in Williamsport, where camps, conferences, and the annual World Series are held. It has standardized rules of play, requirement for financial operation and fee structures, insurance coverage, approved equipment, and other arrangements for member leagues and teams. Little League also conducts research into youth sport and carries out a great variety of training programs for league officials, district administrators, umpires, managers, and coaches, as well as a series of publications.

Youth sport in general are assisted by national organizations that set standards and promote effective, values-oriented coaching approaches, such as the National Alliance for Youth Sports, the Positive Coaching Alliance, and the National Clearinghouse for Youth Sports Information. Examples of organizations that are particularly concerned with individual sport include Youth Basketball of America, the Young American Bowling Alliance, and the United States Tennis Association (USTA). The latter organization has mounted a vigorous campaign to promote tennis to children and youth through the schools and public recreation agencies. USTA has awarded over $4 million to support community park and recreation tennis programs.

Arts Councils and Cultural Organizations

Another major area of activity for voluntary agencies is the arts. In addition to nonprofit schools and art centers that offer painting, drawing, sculpture, and similar programs, there are literally thousands of civic organizations that sponsor or present performing arts. These include symphony orchestras, bands of various types, choral societies, opera or operetta companies, little theater groups, ballet and modern dance companies, and similar bodies.

In many communities, special interest organizations in the arts are coordinated or assisted by umbrella agencies that help to promote their joint efforts. The Pasadena Arts Council was the first umbrella organization chartered in California. It provides a number of services to its members and the community including a resource guide for artists, a business center for artists and new arts organizations, an information clearinghouse, networking events, financial sponsorship, an arts calendar, and a bi-monthly publication. The Pasadena Arts Council efforts are similar to those in communities across the United States.

Service and Fraternal Clubs

Another category of nonprofit organizations that provide recreation for their own membership and sponsor programs for other population groups is community service clubs and fraternal organizations.

These include service clubs such as the Kiwanis, Lions, or Rotary clubs, which represent the business and professional groups in the community and which have as their purpose the improvement of the business environment and contributing to social well-being. A number of organizations established specifically for women, such as the Association of Junior Leagues, the General Federation of Women's Clubs, and the Business and Professional Women's Club, have similar goals.

The goals of such groups may include publicizing environmental concerns or issues, promoting the arts and other cultural activities, helping disadvantaged children and youth, and providing programs for people with disabilities. For example, many Kiwanis organizations are involved in providing camping programs for special populations.

Promotional and Coordinating Bodies

A final type of nonprofit organization in the recreation, parks, and leisure-service field consists of associations that serve to promote, publicize, or coordinate activities within a given recreational field. In bowling, for example, the American Bowling Congress is composed of thousands of individuals whose careers or livelihoods depend on bowling and who therefore seek to promote and guide the sport as aggressively as possible, including setting standards and regulations and sponsoring a range of major tournaments each year.

There are hundreds of such nonprofit organizations in the fields of travel, tourism, entertainment, and hospitality, covering the range from associations of theme park or waterpark management to associations of tour directors or cruise ship operators. As an example, the Outdoor Amusement Business Association works to upgrade standards and services throughout the carnival and outdoor show industry. Its membership consists chiefly of manufacturers and distributors of trailers, tents and tarps, games supplies, and similar materials, as well as operators of many different kinds of traveling shows, concessions, and carnivals. Similarly, the International Association of Amusement Parks and Attractions conducts market studies, publishes standards and guidelines, and sponsors huge conventions and trade shows for thousands of companies worldwide in the tourism, entertainment, and amusement field. The World Waterpark Association assists water parks with trend analysis, customer satisfaction, business skills, training, publications related to the waterpark industry, and an annual trade show.

Within local communities, there are often several types of coordinating groups that serve to exchange information, conduct studies, identify priorities, develop planning reports, provide technical assistance, train leadership, and organize events related to recreation and leisure. In some cases, these include councils of social agencies, including religious, health care, youth-serving, and social work groups.

COMMERCIAL RECREATION

We now turn to the type of recreation sponsor that provides the largest variety of leisure opportunities in the United States today—commercial, profit-oriented businesses. Such organizations have proliferated in recent years, running the gamut from small "mom-and-pop" operations to franchised programs and services; large-scale networks of health and fitness clubs, theme parks, hotels, and casino businesses; manufacturers of games, toys, and hobby equipment; and various other entertainment ventures.

The Nature of Commercial Recreation

Commercial recreation is easily defined. John Bullaro and Christopher Edginton write:

> A commercial leisure service organization can be thought of as a business, the primary purpose of which is to serve people while at the same time making a profit. [It] has two basic characteristics. First, it creates and distributes leisure services; second, it has as its primary goal, profit.[8]

The profit motive distinguishes a recreation business from any other type of leisure-service sponsor. Although public or voluntary agencies may charge for their services and may seek to clear a profit on individual program elements—or at least to run them on a self-sustaining basis where possible—their overall purpose is to meet important community or social needs. However, the commercial recreation organization has as a primary thrust the need to show a profit on the overall operation. Without commercial businesses that provide a host of important and high-quality leisure experiences, our recreational opportunities would be sharply diminished.

Commercial recreation sponsors today have the following characteristics: (1) They must constantly seek to identify and capitalize on recreational interests that are on the rise in order to ensure a constant or growing level of participation; (2) they are flexible and independent in their programmatic decisions and are not subject to the policy strictures of a city or town council or an agency board of trustees; (3) they constantly seek to promote and create a climate of desirability by packaging a product that will appeal to the public, by systematic marketing research and by clever advertising and public relations; and (4) to be successful, they depend on effective entrepreneurship—a creative and aggressive approach to management that is willing to take risks in order to make gains.

■ *Amusement parks are a growth industry serving millions of people annually.*

Categories of Service

Commercial recreation services may be classified under several major headings, including the following:

- Admission to facilities, either for self-directed participation (as in the use of a rented tennis court or admission to an ice skating rink or billiard parlor) or for participation with some degree of supervision, instruction, or scheduling (as in admission to a ski center with use of a ski tow).
- Organized instruction in individual leisure activities or areas of personnel enrichment, such as classes in arts and crafts, music, dance, or other hobbies.
- Membership in a commercially operated club, such as a for-profit tennis, golf, or boat club.
- Provision of hospitality or social contacts, ranging from hotels and resorts to bars, casinos, singles clubs, or dating services, which may use computers, videotaping, telephone contacts, or other means to help clients meet each other. At the socially less acceptable end of this spectrum of services are escort services, massage parlors, and sexually oriented telephone conversation operations.
- Arranged tours or cruises, domestic or foreign, which may consist solely of travel arrangements or which may also include a full package of travel, housing accommodations, meals, special events, side trips, and guide services.
- Commercial manufacture, sale, and service of recreation-related equipment, including sport supplies, electronic products, boats, off-road vehicles, toys, games, and hobby equipment.
- Entertainment and special events, such as theater, rock concerts, circuses, rodeos, and other such activities, when they are sponsored by a for-profit business, rather than a nonprofit, tax-exempt group.

Several of these types of commercial recreation businesses are described in the concluding section of this chapter. Others, such as sport and games and travel and tourism, are presented in Chapters 10 and 11.

Outdoor Recreation

The broad field of outdoor recreation—defined as leisure pursuits that depend on the outdoor environment for their special appeal or character—represents an important area of commercially sponsored services. Although a major portion of outdoor recreation is carried on in government-managed settings, many activities are provided by for-profit enterprises.

In 2001, the U.S. Fish and Wildlife Service reported that 105.9 million Americans aged 16 and older fished, hunted, and watched wildlife each year, including 34 million anglers and 13 million hunters, a decline in each activity from the previous year. There was an increase in wildlife watchers to 61.4 million. Outdoor recreation equipment sales had grown at a steady rate for over 10 years. In 2003, fishing tackle sales totaled $2 billion, hunting and firearm sales were $5.6 billion, alpine skiing was $337 million, and camping was $1.5 billion.

Commercial recreation in the outdoors takes many forms, including hunting preserves and guide services; charter fishing and other private fishing operations; marinas and other boating services; and the provision of ski centers and schools, paintball centers, and numerous other pursuits.

In many cases, a single company, such as Pocono Whitewater Adventures in Jim Thorpe, Pennsylvania, may offer several different types of adventure activities, such as river rafting, whitewater kayaking, family biking excursions, or paintball, at different seasons of the year. Numerous hunting businesses throughout the United States offer the opportunity to shoot big game and in some cases exotic species imported from other continents. Both inland and ocean fishing represent another huge industry. Boating alone represents a major segment of the outdoor recreation market, with annual retail sales in 2002 estimated at almost $30 billion. Florida ranked first with sales of $1.48 billion, followed by California at $1.42 billion, and then Texas, Michigan, Minnesota, New York, North Carolina, Wisconsin, Washington, and New Jersey. Sport fishing sales were even greater in Florida as they hit $4 billion in 2002.

Health Spas and Fitness Clubs

Commercial fitness centers and health clubs constitute a major source of leisure spending in the United States. Although those who join such facilities may have varying kinds of motivations, ranging from actual health concerns to a cosmetic concern with appearance, the reality is that health spas often offer an attractive social setting, particularly for single men and women.

This overall field includes a variety of program emphases, such as aquatic and fitness centers with varied pool facilities, exercise equipment rooms, aerobics and Jazzercise classes, yoga or Oriental exercise groups, conditioning counseling or remedial services, and similar options with annual fees that may range up to thousands of dollars.

As a variation of such health-connected services, many nonprofit hospitals or long-term care facilities have established for-profit subsidiary companies that offer a wide range of exercise programs, physical therapy, aerobic classes, and innovative techniques that include hypnosis, pain management, acupuncture, and other alternative forms of treatment serving the public at large. They may also focus on holistic and homeopathic treatment, including meditation groups, clubs dealing with specific forms of illness, such as arthritis, "overeaters anonymous," "living with loss," and massage and reflexology methods.

Family Fun Centers

Another recently evolved for-profit recreation enterprise includes family fun centers that combine children's play activities and equipment, video games, and other computerized activities with refreshments.

These businesses developed as an outgrowth of such "kiddie exercise" programs as Gymboree, which expanded as franchised chains that were usually situated in shopping malls. Family fun centers such as Malibu Grand Prix broadened their appeal, by adding more family-slanted activities, such as miniature golf or other indoor games, and packaged them with fast food options such as pizza, hot dogs, and soft drinks for birthday party and other group visits.

Other For-Profit Ventures

Beyond the examples just cited, commercial recreation today includes a host of other kinds of social and hobby activities and amusement or entertainment ventures. Private golf or tennis clubs, bowling alleys and billiard parlors, contract bridge or chess clubs, night clubs and dance halls, and even dating services and gambling casinos are all part of this picture. In a sense, movies, television, video games, book publishing, and music CDs are all aspects of popular culture that represent forms of commercialized leisure. A growing marketplace is quilting. Long thought to be the domain of grandmothers, quilting stores are present in many communities. They sell material, quilting-related items, and specialized quilting machines, and sponsor classes, tours, cruises, exhibitions, and competitions.

In addition, both amateur sport participation and professional spectator sport and travel and tourism involve huge elements in the commercial recreation field and are discussed in detail in a later chapter.

DIFFERENCES AND SIMILARITIES AMONG AGENCIES

This chapter has described the provision of organized recreation services today by three types of organizations: public or governmental, nonprofit or voluntary, and commercial recreation businesses. Clearly, each of these types of leisure-service organization plays a different role in the overall recreational system, while at the same time interacting with and supplementing the other types.

Public recreation and park agencies, for example, have a major responsibility for maintaining and operating outdoor resources such as parks, forests, playgrounds, sport

■ *Amateur sporting events in major urban centers are frequently integrated into existing parks where activites are sharing adjoining spaces.*

and aquatic facilities, and, in many cases, indoor centers, performing arts halls, conference or convention halls, stadiums, and similar facilities. Their obligation is to serve the public at large, including individuals and families at all socioeconomic levels and without regard to ethnic, religious, or other demographic differences. However, given the intensified use of marketing-based fees and charges for many recreation programs, many government recreation and park agencies today are not reaching community groups with limited economic capability.

Nonprofit voluntary agencies are generally most concerned with social values and with achieving constructive outcomes either for the community or for specific population groups. They see recreation both as an end in itself and as a means to an end and are generally respectful of the environment and sensitive to gender- and race-related issues. Particularly in terms of serving young people and special recreation interests, they are able to offer richer programs than many public agencies.

Of the three types of sponsors, commercial recreation sponsors provide by far the greatest range of recreational services and opportunities today, and they represent a steadily growing sphere of organized leisure programming. In some ways, profit-oriented businesses are similar to public and nonprofit recreation and park agencies in terms of their offerings and the leisure needs they satisfy. What distinguishes them is their ability to commit substantial sums to developing facilities and programs that will attract the public. Huge corporations that are able to design and build theme parks, aquatic complexes, stadiums, health and fitness clubs, and other types of specialized equipment or programs obviously have a tremendous advantage in appealing to those who are able to pay the necessary fees and charges. Commercial recreation sponsors have harnessed technology and industry in creating spectacular environments for play and have used the most subtle and sophisticated public relations and advertising techniques to market their products successfully.

Social Values in Recreation Planning

It would be wrong to assume that commercial recreation businesses are entirely free to provide any sort of leisure activity without considering its social impact.

Health clubs, camps, theaters, dance halls, gambling casinos, taverns, and a host of other facilities are subject to regulation under state, county, and municipal laws. These may include provisions regarding the sale of liquor, sanitary conditions, service to minors, safety practices, hours of operation, and similar restrictions. Many enterprises that require licenses may have these withdrawn if the operators do not conform to approved practices. Similarly, trade associations often influence practices, even though they may not have the legal power to enforce their rulings. Public attitudes—as expressed in the press, through the statements of leading citizens, civic officials, or religious organizations, or through consumer pressures—often are able to influence the operators in desired directions. For example, when Time Warner was sharply criticized in the press for its promotion of violent, racist, and sexist rap music products, it divested itself of the involved recording label.

The competition of other organizations and products is another key factor in the management of commercial recreation agencies. Often, better products and services within a branch of the industry will serve to drive out inferior competitors. The entire field of recreation service and participation may be viewed as a marketing system in which the economic forces of supply and demand work so that as a new product or service appears, existing products and services are threatened. Within this framework, there is a constant pruning and reshuffling of recreation enterprises as competing sponsors seek to maintain public interest and attendance.

PARTNERSHIPS AMONG MAJOR LEISURE-SERVICE AGENCIES

Although public, nonprofit, and commercial leisure-service agencies are dealt with separately in this chapter, it is important to emphasize that in actual practice they often join together in cooperative ventures. For example, a survey of over 100 cities found that almost all municipal recreation and parks departments conducted programs with other agencies and organizations; more than half of the respondents had 10 or more synergetic programs during the year. They worked closely with voluntary agencies, schools and colleges, service clubs, and business and industry to promote sport, cultural, and other types of events and projects.

Partnering among public, nonprofit, and commercial recreation providers is commonplace. Where these agencies once jealously guarded their own areas, they have embraced the concept that partnering better serves the public and individual agencies. Public and nonprofit agencies are frequently judged on their effectiveness by the number and quality of the partnerships they establish.

Many forms of partnerships are created by park and recreation agencies working with nonprofits, commercial organizations, other government agencies, private individuals, special interest groups, and others. They can be as simple as the city parks and recreation department providing space for a model airplane club to construct a runway or as complex as multiple agencies working together to manage a unique natural resource. There is a long history of the National Park Service working with state park agencies and local park and recreation departments. The Bureau of Land Management has transferred land to public agencies, such as to the Grand Junction, Colorado, Parks and Recreation Department, to help maintain a buffer between

■ *Sponsorship of recreation programs is increasing. Sponsors frequently have their organizations depicted at the event.*

urban development and natural areas. Special recreation associations, initially unique to Illinois, are the creation of multiple park districts joining together to develop a professional organization with the primary purpose of providing services to people with disabilities. The special recreation associations operate as a separate service, yet integrate their services into existing park district programs using the resources of the association that exceed those of any individual park district.

Numerous examples may also be shown of partnerships in the areas of open space acquisition and environmental recovery. The Trust for Public Land (TPL) annually takes on numerous projects working with local public agencies, nonprofit, and neighborhood groups. Recently TPL teamed up with Saint Paul, Minnesota, to renovate an abandoned railyard that was both an eyesore and a toxic problem. Neighborhood groups, redevelopment groups, and volunteers all joined together to work on the project. TPL entered into negotiations with the railroad and over a three-year period cleaned up the contamination with $3.5 million in donations and contributions from multiple sources, including government agencies. The now-named Vento Nature Sanctuary is part of the Mississippi National River and Recreation Area.[9]

Similarly, nonprofit organizations are frequently involved in collaborative program efforts. Typically, Boy and Girl Scout troops often work closely with churches and religious organizations or with school boards. The YMCA encourages numerous partnership arrangements with local park and recreation departments, schools and colleges, public housing boards, hospitals, and even correctional institutions. In 2006, the YMCA funded 40 community collaborative projects working jointly with the Center for Disease Control to expand community ability and to identify or create programs that create positive health-related behavior change. The YMCA joined with over 20 national organizations to make the program a success. Examples of programs are Montgomery, Alabama; Rochester, New York; Tulsa, Oklahoma; and Santa Clara, California.

Differing collaborations are beginning to emerge as agencies begin serving an older American population. Lewisburg, Pennsylvania, created the first multigenerational park as a destination designed to bring together differing age groups to enjoy experiences while in close proximity. The emphasis was on the environment, families, and activity recognizing that such an approach met the needs of many different age groups. Many communities are now recognizing that older Americans use parks more frequently than other age groups and are beginning to cooperate within their communities to modify parks to fit the needs of seniors. The University of Illinois is working with a variety of groups, including park and recreation agencies to develop New Active Green Environments facilities that strive to improve the cardiovascular health, muscle, and flexibility strength of older Americans understanding that the new older generation is different from all previous aging generations.[10]

Finally, professional societies have been successful in initiating a number of partnerships, particularly in the area of youth sports. The National Recreation and Park Association (NRPA), for example, joined *Sports Illustrated* in Good Sports, an initiative with the National Recreation and Parks Association, to create a local assessment of the strength and gaps in youth sport. In addition, the NRPA developed joint ventures with the United States Tennis Association; the National Football League's Flag Football program; Major League Baseball's pitch, hit, and run program; the National Basketball Association's junior NBA and junior WNBA; and the Hershey Track and Field youth program to reach millions of children and youth through these sport. Collaborative arrangements of this type are growing in number and variety and are helping to build a climate of mutual assistance among the different elements that constitute the leisure-service system.

SUMMARY

Government's role with respect to organized leisure services is a diversified one. On the federal level, government is concerned with the management of outdoor recreation resources, either as a primary function or within a multiple-use concept, through such agencies as the National Park Service, U.S. Forest Service, Bureau of Land Management, and TVA. The federal government also assists the states and local political units through funding and technical assistance for programs serving children and youth, those with disabilities, the elderly, and similar groups.

State governments operate major park systems and play an important role in promoting environmental conservation and outdoor recreation opportunities. They also set standards and pass enabling legislation that defines the role of local governments in the area of recreation and parks. In addition, states have traditionally maintained networks of state hospitals and special schools for those with disabilities, although this function has been reduced in recent years as a result of deinstitutionalization trends toward placing many such individuals in community settings.

The chief sponsors of government recreation and park programs are on the local level—city, town, county, and special district government agencies. They operate varied facilities and generally offer a wide range of classes, leagues, or special events in sport, the arts, social activities, and other leisure areas. They also provide or assist in many programs in the human services area. Although many municipal departments have expanded their revenue source operations, departments in other larger and older cities suffer from depleted staff resources and have limited program and maintenance potential.

Voluntary agencies place their greatest emphasis on using leisure to achieve positive social goals. Several types of youth-serving organizations are described, including both sectarian and nonsectarian groups. Such agencies rarely consider themselves to be primarily recreation organizations; instead, they generally prefer to be regarded as educational, character-building, or youth-serving organizations. However, recreation usually does constitute a sector of their program activities.

A second type of nonprofit leisure-service agency consists of special interest groups, which usually promote a particular area of activity in outdoor recreation, sport, the arts, or hobbies. Such groups, although they may include many enthusiasts as members, are often formed to promote business interests within the particular leisure specialization.

Commercial recreation businesses offer an immense amount of public recreational opportunities today in such areas as travel and tourism, outdoor recreation, sport, popular entertainment, and the mass media, hobbies, and crafts and toys. Their primary goal is to make a consistent profit. In many cases, they are huge and highly diversified operations, such as the Walt Disney organization, with its theme parks, resorts, and television, movie, and popular music components. From a social perspective, although many for-profit businesses offer constructive, high-quality programs, in some cases—as in sectors of the entertainment industry—they are believed to contribute to youth violence, sexism, and racial hostility.

QUESTIONS FOR CLASS DISCUSSION OR ESSAY EXAMINATION

1. Review the major recreation and park functions of either the federal government or state governments, identifying key agencies and their leisure-related roles. Apart from managing resources for outdoor recreation, what are the other important activities of these two levels of government?
2. Municipal recreation and park departments, including city, town, or other types of local public agencies, provide a diverse range of leisure opportunities for community residents today. What are some of the major trends in municipal recreation programming in recent years, and what problems have affected such departments as a result of fiscal austerity?
3. Discuss the concept of partnership arrangements among governmental and other types of nonpublic community organizations, in terms of recreation programming. What are the values and what are several examples of such partnership arrangements?

4. What are the major differences between voluntary nonprofit agencies and government departments providing recreation facilities and programs? Compare goals and objectives, funding, individuals or groups served, and program elements.

5. Define commercial recreation agencies and indicate several of the major categories of leisure services provided by such businesses. Select one major area of commercial recreation, such as outdoor recreation or travel and tourism, and describe trends in this field, the nature of service offered, and problems or issues connected to that particular recreation area.

ENDNOTES

1. President George W. Bush, excerpt from National Park Week proclamation, 2003.

2. www.nps.gov/policy/report.htm.

3. Daniel D. McLean, *The 2006 Annual Information Exchange* (Raleigh, NC: National Association of State Park Directors, 2006).

4. Carey Goldbert, "Boston Leading a Renewal of Old Northern Cities," *New York Times* (3 November 1998).

5. www.bls.gov/news.release/volun.nro/0.htm.

6. Heather MacDonald, "Why the Boy Scouts Work," *City Journal* (Winter 2000), www.city-journal.org.

7. Girl Scouts, www.girlscouts.org.

8. J. Bullaro and C. Edginton, *Commercial Leisure Services: Managing for Profit, Service, and Personal Satisfaction* (New York: Macmillan, 1986): 17.

9. V. Monks, "Off the Tracks," *Land and People* (Vol. 18, No. 1, 2006): 20–29.

10. Geoffrey Godbey, "Providing More for Older Adults," *Parks and Recreation* (October 2005): 76–81.

CHAPTER 9

SPECIALIZED LEISURE-SERVICE AREAS

• • •

Inclusive recreation is gaining greater understanding and acceptance. Individuals with disabilities and their families are more aware of their rights to access recreation than ever before. More agencies and programs are including children, teens, and adults with disabilities in activities along with people without disabilities. Inclusion for participants with disabilities is advocated by the National Recreation and Parks Association (NRPA), the National Therapeutic Recreation Society (NTRS), and the American Therapeutic Recreation Association (ATRA). This philosophical shift toward inclusion and the many efforts to bring people with disabilities into the mainstream of recreation opportunities have changed the way public recreation agencies provide leisure services.[1]

The military morale, welfare, and recreation (MWR) specialization area has become increasingly important during the early part of the twenty-first century due to U.S. involvement in military conflicts in Afghanistan and Iraq. Boosting morale and retaining U.S. service personnel are now important priorities of the U.S. Department of Defense. MWR has aided in the progress towards these goals by offering their personnel services that include fitness centers, family recreation programs, sports, and other areas of recreation.[2]

Employee recreation services continue to be a substantial area of leisure services. As health problems associated with nutrition, fitness, smoking, and stress continue to plague U.S. society, business and industry search for ways to positively impact employee attendance, performance, recruitment, and retention. With health insurance costs spiraling upward and competition for talented employees increasing, companies are acutely aware of the need to be proactive with employee health, wellness, and job satisfaction.

Campus recreation services are intended to serve the university and college student, faculty, and staff. These programs have been challenged to *address the needs of more diverse campus communities, nontraditional recreation interests, and financial constraints. Universities are competing for quality students and view the recreation and sport components as viable recruiting and retention factors.*

Private-membership and retirement community recreation round out our look at specialized leisure service delivery areas. With a long history of restricted access, many private recreation organizations continue to cater to the wealthy and powerful members within a given community. Retirement-oriented organizations first look at age, usually a minimum of 55, and then one's ability to reside within the community and pay dues for services. Fortunately, there is a wide cost range for retirement community membership around the country.

◆ ◆ ◆

INTRODUCTION

Having examined three areas of organized leisure services that are designed for the public at large, we now turn to five categories of recreation services that meet more specialized needs and interests. These five areas are recreation for people with disabilities; armed forces morale, welfare and recreation services; employee recreation services, campus recreation; and private-membership organizations. Each of these areas serves a specific type of population or organization, with goals and program elements geared to meet its specific needs.

Throughout the analysis of these five leisure-service areas, emphasis will be placed on the dynamic changes they are going through in the transition from the traditional models that evolved in the twentieth century to more innovative forms of service in the new millennium.

THERAPEUTIC RECREATION SERVICE

The roots of today's use of recreation to improve health conditions in treatment settings can be traced back to Benjamin Rush, an American physician, and Florence Nightingale, a British nurse. Both of these figures were advocates of the therapeutic value of recreation. Over the past 50 years, the expanded use of recreation and leisure in hospitals, physical rehabilitation, mental health, and long-term care settings has demonstrated its increased value as a treatment approach and the importance of having a recreation therapist on the treatment team. During this same period, there was tremendous growth in the provision of specialized or adapted recreation services in the community for people with disabilities.

Early Development of Therapeutic Recreation

The history of past centuries provides a number of examples of the use of recreation in the treatment of psychiatric patients, in both Europe and America. The fullest impetus for therapeutic recreation, however, came in the twentieth century in three types of institutions: hospitals and rehabilitation centers for those with physical impairments, hospitals for people with mental illness, and special schools for those with developmental disabilities.

After both World War I and World War II, there was a wave of concern about the need to rehabilitate veterans who had sustained major physical injuries or psychological trauma while in service. As a consequence, Veterans Administration and military hospitals developed comprehensive programs of rehabilitative services, including physical and occupational therapy, psychotherapy, social services, vocational training, guidance, and recreation. In such settings, recreation was perceived as being one of several techniques that contributed to patient recovery.

At the same time, recreation gained recognition as a form of allied or adjunctive service within such civilian institutions as special homes or schools for individuals with mental retardation or other disabilities, nursing homes and long-term care institutions, and state or private psychiatric hospitals or mental health centers. Gradually, *therapeutic recreation,* as it came to be known, gained acceptance in the health-care field. Colleges and universities initiated major curricula or degree options in this field, and professional societies developed standards for practice and accreditation and certification procedures for practitioners.

Emerging Models of Therapeutic Recreation

With growing interest in this field of professional practice, educators and practitioners sought to clarify its identity and essential functions. In the mid-1970s, for example, Gerald O'Morrow identified five models of service that reflected different approaches in the field:

1. *Custodial model:* Recreation programs are provided in long-term care settings in which little effort is made to provide rehabilitation or meaningful educational or other needed services. Recreation is primarily employed to lighten the atmosphere and improve the morale of the institution; it may also be part of the reward-and-punishment system, or may be a useful means of creating a favorable public relations image for the outside world.

2. *Medical-clinical model:* In most treatment settings, this has been the dominant pattern. Recreation is viewed as an important element in the treatment plan, and is designed to help treat illness, under medical direction. It has been most widely found in psychiatric institutions or physical rehabilitation settings.

3. *Therapeutic milieu model:* Also found predominantly in programs for people with mental illness or who are socially deviant, this approach stresses the need to create a healthy environment, or therapeutic community, in which all staff members and patients or clients themselves act as therapeutic agents. Recreation becomes a useful medium for group living, planning and carrying out projects, and the development of daily living skills.

4. *Education and training model:* This is a goal-oriented approach, often used with people with mental retardation; it places heavy emphasis on occupational therapy, remedial education, vocational training, and similar modalities. Recreation is used to teach basic cognitive or social skills, and may also be used as part of behavior modification programs.

5. *Community model:* This describes the type of therapeutic recreation service that is provided in the community at large. Often, it has been the goal of institutional personnel to help equip their patients or clients to return to community life and function successfully; in many cases, beginning contacts and involvements have been made while they are still under care in the treatment setting.[3]

In an effort to clarify the appropriate focus and philosophy of therapeutic recreation service, in the early 1980s the National Therapeutic Recreation Society (NTRS), a branch of the National Recreation and Park Association, developed a comprehensive definition of the field. NTRS identified three services that should be offered as part of a comprehensive approach to therapeutic recreation: (1) therapy, (2) leisure education, and (3) recreation participation. In any given situation, the therapeutic recreation specialist should be ready to provide any or all of these services:

> The decision as to where and when each of these services would be provided would be based on the assessment of client need. Different individuals have a variety of different needs related to leisure utilization. For some clients, improvement of a functional behavior or problem (physical, mental, social, or emotional) is a necessary prerequisite to meaningful leisure experiences. For others, acquiring leisure skills, knowledge, and ability is a priority need. For others, special recreation participation opportunities are necessary, based on place of residence or because assistance or adapted activities are required.[4]

The NTRS statement is based on a principle known as *continuum of care*. It implies that at each stage of a patient's illness and recovery (or a client's involvement over a period of time with a service agency), program experiences are provided that are geared to achieving maximum benefit for the subject appropriate to that stage and helping the individual move along constructively to the next stage.

What came to be known as the *leisure ability model* was based on a number of assumptions about the role of leisure in every individual's lifestyle and about important characteristics and needs of persons with disability. Charles Sylvester, for example, cited a fundamental principle that extended beyond a narrow concern with helping an individual in the recovery process or contributing to his or her functional behavior. This broader view, he writes, was summed up in the NTRS's 1982 *Philosophical Position Statement:*

> All human beings, including those individuals with disabilities, illnesses, or limiting conditions, have a *right* [emphasis added] to, and need for, leisure involvement as a necessary aspect of the human experience. The purpose of therapeutic recreation service is to facilitate . . . an appropriate leisure lifestyle for individuals with limitations.[5]

It also was recognized that persons with disabilities had unique needs with respect to leisure and recreation. Although all individuals need diverse recreation outlets, those with disabilities encounter barriers that those without disabilities do not, substantially narrowing their options for participation. In part this is due to significant, and sometimes multiple disabling conditions that restrict physical, cognitive, and/or emotional functioning. Many times, however, the problems with access to recreation opportunities can be attributed to attitudinal, architectural, programmatic, and transportation barriers.

Smith et al.[6] explored the question of why persons with disabilities have been underserved by community recreation and leisure services. They suggest that in the first half of the twentieth century the way society generally treated people during this period who did not fit the norm was to separate and hide them away and this produced a similar philosophy within the evolving field of recreation. Examples include the "old folks homes" for older people who were indigent, or warehousing people with mental retardation in large institutions away from populated areas, and placing people with mental health problems in similarly remote "insane asylums." While attitudes toward vulnerable populations were shifting during the 1960s, 1970s, and early 1980s, there were other barriers for public parks and recreation to contend with, both real and perceived. These included lack of funding, inaccessible facilities, untrained staff, lack of knowledge to develop such programs, lack of accessible community transportation, continuing attitudinal barriers, and lack of awareness of the great need for recreation participation by people with disabilities.

In some cases, recreation and park departments barred people with disabilities from their programs, arguing that serving such people would impose higher risk of accident lawsuits and increased insurance costs. We now know this is not true. In other cases, parents, relatives, and schools have sheltered them excessively, or the individual's perceived lack of ability or fear of rejection by others caused him or her to limit his or her recreation participation.

Expansion of Field   Due both to the legislation cited earlier and to growing public awareness and support for such programs, institutions and organizations providing leisure services for persons with disabilities proliferated in the 1970s and 1980s. They included the following:

- Hospitals of all types, serving those with every form of illness or disability in active treatment programs
- Nursing homes and long-term or intensive care facilities, serving chiefly older adults with functional impairment but also persons in other age categories who have had major trauma (strokes or disabling injuries) and cannot live independently
- Schools or residential centers for individuals with developmental disabilities, severe learning disabilities, or emotional disabilities
- Special schools, treatment centers, correctional institutions, and other institutions for youth and adults who have committed crimes or engage in deviant behavior
- Residential centers for older adults who, while not requiring full-time nursing care, cannot safely live independently
- Centers for physical medicine and rehabilitation, which provide programs of physical, psychological, and vocational rehabilitation
- Programs provided by public recreation and park agencies
- Programs provided by voluntary agencies, including both organizations concerned with a particular disability and its varied service needs and organizations designed to provide recreation and related social services to those with different categories of disability
- Work-based and other day programs that assist persons with disability living in the community

Contrasting Emphases in the Field   Gradually it became apparent that although the NTRS leisure ability model intuitively described what therapeutic recreation sought to accomplish at the time, its limited scope does not apply to all present-day practices. Other models have emerged that attempt to meet the broad needs of the profession as it continues to provide services in both treatment and recreation settings.

An extremely important event for the field occurred in 1984. Breaking away from NTRS, a group of practitioners and educators decided it was time to establish an autonomous organization that could focus on the needs of recreation therapy being practiced in treatment or clinical settings without the oversight and financial controls levied by a parent organization. This focus included the development of treatment-oriented practice models, administrative structures, financial reimbursement, practice guidelines, and an emphasis on evidence-based practice. That new organization, the American Therapeutic Recreation Association (ATRA), is today a vibrant agent for advocacy, support, and growth in the field of recreation therapy. According to ATRA, therapeutic recreation is defined as:

> . . . the provision of Treatment Services and the provision of Recreation Services to persons with illnesses or disabling conditions. The primary purposes of Treatment Services, which are often referred to as Recreational Therapy, are to restore, remediate or rehabilitate in order to improve functioning and independence as well as reduce or eliminate the effects of illness or disability. The primary purposes of Recreational Services are to provide recreation resources and opportunities in order to improve health and well-being.[7]

Certainly the need continues to exist for recreation professionals prepared to work with participants with disabilities in a variety of community-based settings. Generally, these services have become more widely available, particularly in larger metropolitan areas. Examples of these programs include the EXPAND program for people with disabilities in Boulder, Colorado; the Cincinnati Recreation Commission Division of Therapeutic Recreation in Cincinnati, Ohio; and the Indy Parks Therapeutic Recreation Division in Indianapolis, Indiana. With laws in place that mandate facility and program accessibility across public and private sectors, expectations are greater that people with disabilities will have equitable access to a wide variety of quality recreation opportunities. While therapeutic recreation specialists have historically provided and/or supervised these services, it is not necessary that this be the case. Many community programs have moved ahead with the help of volunteers, consultants, and staff training programs to develop adapted, specialized, or inclusive recreation programs in order to meet the recreation, leisure, and sport participation needs of their citizens with disabilities.

Recreation Therapy as Treatment

The therapeutic treatment model of service is specifically designed to carry out individualized goals of rehabilitation within the overall treatment program. It is found in most therapeutic recreation textbooks and curricula today and is the basis for national and regional workshops dealing with hospital or rehabilitation-centered programs.

The practice of recreation therapy as a treatment discipline has become increasingly sophisticated. The body of research knowledge has expanded, protocols for treatment approaches have been developed, university curriculums have become broader in scope, and more populations are being served. There is also greater recognition of the discipline within health care systems and what it has to offer. Facilitating this is the reinforcement of standards by health care–accrediting bodies, such as the Commission of Accreditation of Rehabilitation Facilities and the Joint Commission on Accreditation of Healthcare Organizations. These two major accrediting organizations have specific criteria for providing qualified therapeutic recreation services, which includes a requirement that said services be provided only by a certified therapeutic recreation specialist (CTRS).

In 1981, the National Council for Therapeutic Recreation Certification (NCTRC) was established as an autonomous credentialing body to oversee the development and administration of the CTRS professional certification. A research-based therapeutic recreation job analysis was performed and used to develop the certification exam, which was administered for the first time in November 1990. This exam and the requirements set by NCTRC to sit for the exam are the primary certification standards for both clinical and recreation applications of therapeutic recreation. The primary functions of NCTRC are:

> NCTRC establishes evaluative standards for the certification and recertification of professionals; grants certification to individuals who voluntarily apply and meet established criteria, and monitors adherence to these standards by certified therapeutic recreation professionals.[8]

ATRA developed standards of practice to guide the delivery and management of therapeutic recreation services. These standards were first published in 1991 and then revised in 1994 and again in 2000. The current standards, as shown here, reflect state-of-the-art practice in this field. Given the emphasis on treatment applications in clinical settings, the standards do not reflect what is expected in a community recreation setting. The community programs are viewed instead as special or inclusive recreation.

Shift to Special Recreation in Community Settings

Although the primary thrust of the organized therapeutic recreation field continued to be on the clinical approach in formal treatment programs, there was a pronounced growth of concern about persons with disabilities in community settings. This shift was in part a response to the deinstitutionalization of hundreds of thousands of individuals with mental illness and mental retardation that took place in the 1960s and 1970s. For the first time, great numbers of such individuals were no longer in isolated custodial institutions, but lived in the community, receiving services in local mental health centers and residing in independent or semi-independent environments.

Realistically, many of the community programs and services that were planned for such individuals were not provided or were seriously underfunded. As a consequence, numerous reports in the 1990s indicated that large numbers of persons with mental illness were homeless or in prisons and jails, rather than safe residential settings.[9]

ATRA Standards of Practice

Developed by the American Therapeutic Recreation Association, the standards reflect levels of service provision for therapeutic recreation professionals to implement in a variety of settings. The standards assist the therapeutic recreation professional in assuring the systematic provision of quality therapeutic recreation services. Note that standards 1–7 address direct practice and 8–12 target the management of therapeutic recreation services; they should not be viewed as complete without full consideration of the structure, process, and outcome components found in the *ATRA Standards or Practice Manual* (2000).

Standard 1: The therapeutic recreation specialist conducts an individualized assessment to collect systematic, comprehensive, and accurate data necessary to determine a course of action and subsequent individualized treatment plan.

Standard 2: The therapeutic recreation specialist plans and develops the individualized treatment plan that identifies goals, objectives, and treatment intervention strategies.

Standard 3: The therapeutic recreation specialist implements an individualized treatment plan using appropriate intervention strategies to restore, remediate, or rehabilitate in order to improve functioning and independence as well as reduce or eliminate the effects of illness or disability. Implementation of the treatment plan by the therapeutic recreation specialist is consistent with the overall patient/client treatment program.

Standard 4: The therapeutic recreation specialist systematically evaluates and compares the client's response to the individualized treatment plan. The treatment plan is revised based upon changes in the interventions, diagnoses, and patient/client responses.

Standard 5: The therapeutic recreation specialist develops a discharge plan in collaboration with the patient/client, family, and other treatment team members in order to continue treatment, as appropriate.

Standard 6: Recreation opportunities are available to patients/clients to promote or improve their general health and well-being.

Standard 7: The therapeutic recreation specialist adheres to the ATRA Code of Ethics.

Standard 8: The therapeutic recreation department is governed by a written plan of operation that is based upon ATRA Standards of the Practice of Therapeutic Recreation and standards of other accrediting/regulatory agencies, as appropriate.

Standard 9: The therapeutic recreation department has established provisions for assuring that therapeutic recreation staff maintain appropriate credentials and have opportunities for professional development.

Standard 10: Within the therapeutic recreation department, there exists an objective and systematic quality improvement program for the purposes of monitoring and evaluating the quality and appropriateness of care, and to identify and resolve problems in order to improve therapeutic recreation services.

Standard 11: Therapeutic recreation services are provided in an effective and efficient manner that reflects the reasonable and appropriate use of resources.

Standard 12: The therapeutic recreation department engages in routine, systematic program evaluation and research for the purpose of determining appropriateness and efficacy.

Source: ATRA Standards of Practice Task Force. American Therapeutic Recreation Association, 1991.

Nonetheless, there was a great surge of interest in providing community-based leisure opportunities for persons with disabilities throughout the United States. It was recognized that far greater numbers of persons with disabilities lived in the community than in residential treatment centers, and that they had equally strong needs for recreation. Municipal recreation and park agencies began to assume a higher degree of responsibility for providing programs for people with disabilities—usually rather limited activities for groups with a particular type of impairment, such as people with visual impairments, mental retardation, or mobility impairment. Voluntary agencies also gave fuller emphasis to programming social activities, adapted sport, or camping for persons with disabilities.

Like any evolving concept or profession, terminology is an important consideration. Terminology has both philosophical and communication implications. When referring to programs that provide recreation services to people with disabilities, Smith and his co-authors, who are leaders in the field, write:

> At this point, we take the position that a polarity does exist. We believe that inclusive recreation (i.e., recreation including persons with disabilities) and therapeutic recreation (i.e., recreation as a clinical intervention directed toward treatment or rehabilitation aims) stand as two separate entities. . . . Further, we believe the time has come to embrace new wording to describe the full inclusion of persons with disabilities into the recreation mainstream. We propose *inclusive recreation* be used because it is a broader term than special recreation and it better reflects equal and joint participation of persons with and without disabilities. The term *special recreation* can continue to be employed to describe special or adapted activities, such as the Special Olympics and wheelchair sports, through which specific needs are met.[10]

Although they do not deliberately gear programs to achieving specific treatment or rehabilitative goals within a clinical framework, those providing special or inclusive recreation do have important purposes. They value recreation as an important life experience for persons with disabilities and seek to achieve positive physical, social, and emotional outcomes, making whatever adaptations in programming, facilities, equipment, or leadership methods are appropriate.

In an attempt to gain an overview of community-based special recreation programs, the Prince George's County, Maryland, Department of Parks and Recreation carried out a survey of 18 county or municipal programs serving persons with disabilities throughout the United States. It revealed a wide range of program trends and positive developments in the field of special recreation, but also uncovered problems in such areas as competition for funding, recruitment and placement of volunteers, changing community attitudes, and educating both persons with disabilities and their families as to the importance of recreation and their basic rights.

Expansion of Sport and Outdoor Recreation Participation

At every level, people of all ages with physical or mental disabilities who previously had been unable to engage in active forms of play are now taking part in varied forms of sport, camping, and outdoor recreation pursuits. Many of these activities are promoted by Wheelchair Sports, USA, a multisport organization for athletes who compete annually in regional, national, and international games. Included among the competitive events for both men and women are archery, athletics (track and field, pentathlon, road racing), basketball, quad rugby, shooting, swimming, table tennis, tennis, and weightlifting. Thousands of young athletes also participate in Special Olympics events, while many others compete in marathons, bowling leagues, and other individual or team sport.

In terms of outdoor recreation, since the 1950s, camping and outdoor adventure programs have become increasingly geared for individuals with disabilities. Michael Kelley points out that numerous research studies have confirmed the positive effects of outdoor adventure activities, such as wilderness backpacking, canoeing, mountaineering, whitewater rafting, and other Outward Bound–type programs for emotionally disturbed or chronically mentally ill individuals.[11]

Use of Technology and Assistive Devices

Sophisticated technology is being brought into play to permit persons with disabilities to participate successfully in different leisure activities. For several decades, various modified instruments or pieces of equipment have been used to help disabled individuals take part in card and table games, arts and crafts, team and individual sport, and other pursuits. For example, the kinds of equipment used for blind persons in sport and games include

> (1) guide ropes that enable blind individuals to run at top speed without fear, holding a short rope attached to a ring that slides along a wire without interference; (2) audible goal detectors (consisting of a motor-driven noisemaker that makes clicking sounds at a constant rate); (3) audible balls for modified ball games, such as kickball, that have either a battery-operated beeper or bell placed inside; and (4) a portable aluminum rail for use in bowling that is movable from lane to lane and orients the blind bowler.[12]

Aerodynamic wheelchairs are now being used by disabled racers, and carbon-fiber prosthetic feet enable amputee athletes to run almost as fast as nondisabled athletes. Research into the use of electrodes to stimulate the leg muscles of persons with spinal cord injuries is helping to maintain bone, joint, and muscle health which has positive effects on cardiovascular functioning and recreation participation, while numerous other devices are being invented each year to facilitate independent functioning for people with disabilities. Electronic devices such as "aura interactor" strap-on vests enable deaf people to dance without straining to hear the music and help blind video game players to feel laser beams "bouncing" off the screen.

Cooperative Networks of Agencies

Because many community and nonprofit organizations lacked the staff resources or special facilities required to provide comprehensive leisure-service programs for persons with disabilities, the 1980s and 1990s saw a trend toward developing cooperative networks of such agencies. In such structures, two or more public or nonprofit human-service organizations—or a combination of both types—share their funding and facilities to provide needed recreation programs in a number of locations. For example, there are over 20 independent Special Recreation Associations (SRAs) in northern Illinois, based on revenue generated from special direct property taxes. All SRAs are coordinated by boards representing the cooperating communities. They interface with municipal recreation and park departments and offer programming for persons with all types of disabling conditions in both integrated and segregated groupings.

In another example of joint cooperation, Boston Children's Hospital and the University of Massachusetts–Boston are implementing a project designed to increase communication between families and health care services, improve access to recreational opportunities, and ease the transition to adulthood for children with disabilities and special health care needs. This project is funded by the Department of Education's National Institute on Disability and Rehabilitation Research, as part of its national "Opening Doors" program. The cooperative nature of the project is critical to its success. They are involving community-based organizations like the Massachusetts Consortium for Children with Special Health Care Needs, the Parent Advocacy Coalition for Education Rights (Minnesota), and the YMCA of Greater Boston, along with a number of other organizations. While the emphasis is not exclusively on meeting the recreation needs of the participants and their families, the recreation component is seen as critical to the overall success of the program as it seeks to assist in the difficult process of children with disabilities transitioning to adulthood and self-reliance.

Throughout the country, numerous independent nonprofit organizations, such as RCH, Inc., in San Francisco, have established facilities and programs that are designed to meet varied life needs—recreational, social, educational, and vocational—of people in different categories of disability.

New Emphasis on Inclusion

In the late 1990s, instead of the term *special recreation*, professional organizations began to use the term *inclusion*, meaning simply the involvement and full acceptance of people with disabilities in a wide range of community settings. In 1998, for example, a National Recreation and Park Association survey team conducted an intensive study of the inclusion practices of 900 public recreation and park agencies. It analyzed the types of services provided and the categories of individuals served, the accommodations that were made in terms of facilities and equipment, and the problems and staff training needs in the communities that were surveyed.[13] In September 2000, a major National Institute on Recreation Inclusion (NIRI) conference was held in Deerfield, Illinois, bringing together representatives from many different kinds of agencies and highlighting the outstanding programs that were being developed in this area. Since then, NIRI has held yearly national conferences around the United States.

Impact of Health-Care Management Trends

In a sense, the broad-based shift to community programs serving persons with disabilities is a response to dramatic changes that have taken place within the nation's health-care system. First, as indicated, deinstitutionalization was responsible for closing down or cutting back many of the large state hospitals or special schools that had formerly employed thousands of therapeutic recreation professionals. Beyond this, many residents or patients who remained in such settings tended to be so ill or limited in their capabilities that it was difficult to develop meaningful programs for them.

In communities generally, the entire health-care system has been in a dramatic state of reaction and change for the past 20 years. Given reduced Medicare funding and insurance companies and managed care administrators that slash their approved services, many hospitals have been forced to merge, eliminate emergency care operations, or reduce staffs and lengths of patient stays. Similarly, nursing homes, especially commercially operated chains, have experienced economic pressures that have compelled them to reduce services, barely meeting state-imposed standards.[14] All of these factors have pressured clinically based therapeutic recreation specialists to develop new program-delivery strategies and to conduct evaluation and research studies that confirm the value of their services.

Examples of Efficacy Research

A key element in the maturing of therapeutic recreation as a field of professional service—particularly in clinical settings—has been the increased emphasis given by educators and practitioners to the evaluation of therapeutic recreation program outcomes. The most comprehensive compilation of efficacy study findings was carried out by Coyle, Kinney, Riley, and Shank as part of a study at Temple University. Supported by the National Institute on Disability and Rehabilitation Research of the federal Department of Education, this report compiled the positive findings of hundreds of research studies on therapeutic recreation's impact from a medical perspective.[15]

Beyond this, numerous articles have appeared in the *Therapeutic Recreation Journal*, the *ATRA Annual*, and the *American Journal of Recreation Therapy* documenting the positive outcomes of therapeutic recreation services, based on research and demonstration projects with patients ranging from those with spinal cord injuries to regressed geriatric patients. Still others have urged broadening the scope of therapeutic recreation to such other areas of need as HIV/AIDS patients, working with at-risk youth and in correctional settings, and working with pathological gamblers, a growing problem.

In a summary of the changes that have affected this field of service, Riley and Skalko describe demographic shifts, the dynamics of the health-care industry (including cost containment and expansion of outpatient services), and the changing nature of the workplace—all of which pose challenges for professionals. They predict that future therapeutic recreation professionals will work with a far greater range of individual and social problems:

> Therapeutic recreation specialists will market their skills and talents . . . across delivery settings . . . and will increasingly capture service-delivery roles in home

health, homeless care, domestic abuse, substance abuse, at-risk youth services, transplant units, adult day services, partial hospitalizations, retirement services, and care for the frail elderly.[16]

The efforts of researchers, ATRA, NTRS, NCTRC, agencies that deliver services, and therapeutic recreation practitioners, have combined to broaden the scope of services, improve the quality of services, and make therapeutic recreation (TR) services available to more people with illnesses and disabling conditions than ever before. Many factors are still unfolding in the areas of health care, community recreation services, efficacy-based research, university TR programs, and credentialing, which will affect the future of TR.

ARMED FORCES RECREATION

For many years it has been the official policy of the military establishment to provide a well-rounded morale, welfare, and recreational program for the physical, social, and mental well-being of its personnel. During World War I, Special Services Divisions were established to provide social and recreational programs that would sustain favorable morale, curb homesickness and boredom, minimize fatigue, and reduce AWOL (absent without leave), and venereal disease rates.

Today, each branch of the armed forces has its own pattern of recreation sponsorship, although they are all under the same morale, welfare, and recreation (MWR) program, which is administratively responsible to the Office of the Assistant Secretary of Defense for Manpower, Reserve Affairs, and Logistics. They serve several million individuals, including active duty, reserve, and retired military personnel and their dependents; civilian employees; and surviving spouses of military personnel who died in active duty. In addition, MWR services are also provided to Coast Guard personnel, who are not part of the Department of Defense.

Goals and Scope of Armed Forces Recreation Today

The mission statement of the U.S. Army Morale, Welfare, and Recreation program provides an important reminder of the importance of looking at the military as a family and not just soldiers, sailors, and airmen:

> Army MWR is a comprehensive network of support and leisure services designed to enhance the lives of soldiers (active, Reserve, and Guard), their families, civilian employees, military retirees and other eligible participants. . . . Their mission is to serve the needs, interests and responsibilities of each individual in the Army community for as long as they are associated with the Army, no matter where they are.
>
> MWR contributes to the Army's strength and readiness by offering services that reduce stress, build skills and self-confidence and foster strong esprit de corps. MWR services also help the Army attract and retain talented people. MWR is proof of the Army's commitment to caring for the people who serve and stand ready to defend the nation.[17]

The scope of the work of MWR is quite large. In 2005, Army MWR served 4.8 million patrons with an operating budget of $1.5 billion and over 37,000 employees.

Since 2001, MWR has provided recreation, fitness, and social programs for soldiers deployed in support of Operation Iraqi Freedom, Operation Enduring Freedom, and operations in the Balkans. MWR facilities are located at 47 sites in Iraq, 9 sites in Afghanistan, and 6 sites in Kuwait. With the United States engaged in these ongoing conflicts throughout the world, MWR has taken on greater importance.

Program Elements

MWR programs include an extensive range of sport, fitness, social, creative, outdoor recreation, travel, entertainment, and hobby leisure pursuits. In the Air Force, for example, an extensive program of sports activities has typically included six major elements: (1) instruction in basic sport skills; (2) a self-directed phase of informal participation in sport under minimum supervision or direction; (3) an intramural program, in which personnel assigned to a particular base compete with others at the same base; (4) an extramural program, which includes competition with teams from different Air Force bases or with teams from neighboring communities; (5) a varsity program, which involves high-level competition with players selected for their advanced skills who compete on a broader national or international scale; and (6) a program for women in the Air Force.

In addition to such programs attached to individual services, the armed forces promote an extensive range of competitive sport programs. Through interservice competition in such sport as basketball, boxing, wrestling, track and field, and softball, all-service teams are selected; armed forces teams then are chosen to represent the United States in international competition.

Hundreds of Army, Air Force, Navy, and Marine bases have adopted the popular Start Smart Sports Development Program, which helps children as young as age three learn basic motor skills that progress to organized sport involvement, and in which parents become heavily involved in leadership roles.[18]

Fitness Programs   Health and wellness have become a major focus of armed forces recreation. To improve fitness levels of personnel, the Air Force installed health and wellness centers (HAWC) on each base; these centers are well equipped and are staffed with leaders qualified to provide the following services: fitness and health risk assessments, exercise programming and weight counseling, stress management and smoking cessation assistance, and similar activities.

On some military bases, fitness is promoted through well-publicized and challenging special events. At the Marine Corps Base at Camp Lejeune, North Carolina, the Lejeune Grand Prix Series features a number of competitive events that involve hundreds of service personnel in a European Cross Country race over natural terrain; a Tour d'Pain, a grueling endurance cycling race; a Masters Swim Meet; a Davy Jones Open Ocean Swim; a Toughman Triathlon; and other types of races.

Outdoor Recreation   Often, outdoor program activities are keyed to the location of a base. For example, Fort Carson, Colorado, sponsors an extensive ski program that features an annual Ski Expo, with over 150 vendors and representatives of ski areas and average attendance of more than 5,000 skiing enthusiasts. Responding to widespread interest in mountain climbing and rock climbing, this Army base constructed a 17,400-

square-foot outdoor recreation center that features a 32-foot-high indoor climbing wall, with the look and feel of natural rock, and climbing routes geared to different skill levels. Other bases offer instruction, equipment, and facilities for such water-based activities as fishing, wind-surfing, jet skiing, scuba diving, and similar pastimes.

Family Recreation   The Department of Defense has become increasingly aware of the need to provide varied family-focused programs to counter the special problems that may affect the spouses and children of military personnel. Particular emphasis is given to the need to serve military youth. Steven Waller and Asuncion Suren write:

> Adolescents residing in military installations are confronted with the same range of social problems that occur within society as a whole. Crime, violence, substance abuse, the social environment, and the unproductive use of leisure time are critical issues that confront military youth.[19]

As one response to this challenge, MWR planners have developed a Drug Demand Reduction Task Force, a program designed to combat substance abuse affecting at-risk youth on military bases and in communities where the bases are located. This program employs structured recreation activities, including athletics and high-risk outdoor pursuits, day and residential camps, and other counseling and educational programs designed to build self-esteem, self-discipline, and leadership among youth—particularly in Marine and Navy base settings.

The Defense Department focused during the 1990s on improving child-care services in the military, in the effort to remake a program known as the "ghetto" of child care—marked by long waiting lists, uneven leadership, and high costs. After creating an expanded network of child-care centers, after-school programs, and referral services, the military tripled the number of children being served and was hailed by the National Women's Law Center, a nonprofit research and advocacy group, as "a model for childcare reform nationwide" in May 2000.[20]

For older youth, the Defense Department's concern led to the development of a Strategic Youth Action Plan by the Office of Family Policy. Special emphasis was placed in this plan on strengthening family relationships.

Community Relations   Many military bases in the United States and overseas place a high priority on establishing positive relationships between armed forces personnel and nearby communities. Civilian MWR personnel working around the globe in such settings as Europe, Korea, and Central America, and even Saudi Arabia, Turkey, and Africa, seek to provide a wealth of outdoor recreational experiences and positive intercultural experiences with local residents:

> Activities for family members [overseas] may include living aboard a tall ship for a few days and learning how to work together and sail the coast of Holland or backpacking in the Swiss Alps. Soldiers and airmen learn teamwork, leadership, communication skills, and technical skills . . . from a ropes course, playing paintball, rock climbing, kayaking, or rafting down an Austrian river. . . . [Our mission is also to] bridge the cultural gap and introduce the Americans to their new—albeit temporary—homeland by integrating activities and resources with those of the host nation.[21]

On just one such distant base, on the island of Sasebo, Japan, Navy MWR specialists provide a huge range of leisure services, including travel tours to scenic locations and festivals in the region, fitness and outdoor recreation activities, hobby shops, professional entertainment, holiday events, extensive youth programs, library services, varied sport tournaments, and even such unusual services as a "pet-holding" facility for military families going on vacation. Although such varied programs are not typical of all military installations, the Sasebo MWR operations offer leisure opportunities that far excel those in many stateside civilian communities.

Resorts   The Army maintains a full range of resorts for all military members. Armed Forces Recreation Centers (AFRC) are affordable Joint Service facilities operated by the U.S. Army Community and Family Support Center and located in different areas, including Germany, Florida, and Hawaii. They offer a full range of resort hotel opportunities for members of all branches of the military service, their families, and other members of the Total Defense Force. The resorts are self-supporting, funded by revenues generated internally from operations.

Fiscal Support of Armed Forces Recreation

Military recreation has traditionally depended on two types of funding: *appropriated funds*, which are tax funds approved by Congress, and *nonappropriated funds*, which are generated on the military base through a combination of post exchange profits and revenue from fees, rentals, and other recreation charges. The Navy Personnel Command in the Department of Defense defines the different types of recreation funds generated by Navy personnel and their dependents to help provide financial support for their recreation activities. Specifically, these are

> monies received from Navy exchange profits, fees and charges placed on the use of recreation facilities and services or other authorized sources for the support of Navy recreation programs. Unit Recreation Funds are those which serve the recreation needs of individual ships, shore stations and other Navy activities. Composite Recreation Funds are those which serve two or more activities which share the same recreation facilities. Consolidated Recreation Funds are those which serve the recreation needs of several separate installations within a geographical area.[22]

In the late 1980s, the Department of Defense classified all MWR activities as either mission-sustaining activities (such as overseas entertainment, physical fitness centers, or temporary lodging facilities) or business activities (such as amusement machine centers, bingo, golf courses, marinas, and rod-and-gun clubs). Guidelines suggested that there be higher levels of fiscal support for more critical services and lower support levels for purely recreational activities that have the potential for being self-sustaining.

Since that time, with growing budget cutbacks and the need to maximize revenues from clubs, messes, post exchanges, and varied forms of commercial sponsorship or partnerships, MWR planners have initiated a range of new fiscal strategies. The effort has been to reduce the costs of operations, standardize procedures, and eliminate redundant programs or personnel. The Navy, for example, established 10 major regions to simplify the planning and supervision of programs, increasingly encouraged hrough much of its ongoing operations, morale, welfare, and recreation stresses that it serves several million individuals in the world's "largest leisure-delivery system." In promotion for a major trade show for suppliers and other commercial concerns doing business with the military—the 2006 MWR EXPO—it itemized dozens of different kinds of equipment and services used by the armed forces, stating:

> The MWR EXPO is the single largest gathering of MWR professionals and brings together the many components of the Morale, Welfare and Recreation industry. The event features products and services that are sold to thousands of military and government agencies for use in community support activities on military installations throughout the world. If a company manufactures, distributes, sells or represents products or services in one or more of the following categories, it may exhibit at the 2006 MWR EXPO: Clubs & Lodging, Fitness & Health, Food Service & Hospitality, and Parks & Recreation.[23]

public/private projects, and established new planning processes to "reinvent" facility development and other projects.

Through the 1990s, as base closures and budget cuts continued, military recreation professionals sought to develop an even more business-oriented approach to their services. Pat Harden, past director of Navy recreation training at Patuxent River, Maryland, pointed out that two prevailing orientations generally guided armed forces recreation: (1) the quality-of-life approach, which sees MWR recreation and club services essentially as an amenity, although deserving of Department of Defense support; and (2) the businesslike marketing approach, which urges that all recreation services be viewed primarily as a commodity to be merchandised, with a minimum of social and mission support goals or constraints.

Instead, Harden argues, it is essential to define the important mission of MWR programs within the overall Department of Defense structure and to work effectively to achieve the goals related to this mission. He quotes a defense department official as follows:

> Readiness is the cornerstone of this administration. A ready-to-fight force is linked intrinsically to the morale, sense of well-being, commitment, and pride in the mission of each Service and family member. Our Morale, Welfare, and Recreation programs play a direct role in developing and maintaining these characteristics within our force and are more important than ever during this time of transition, when profound changes are taking place that are having a powerful impact on Service members and their families.[24]

EMPLOYEE SERVICES AND RECREATION PROGRAMS

A third important area of specialized recreation programs involves the role of business and industry in providing recreation and related personnel services to employees and in some cases their families or other community residents.

Background of Company-Sponsored Programs

Employee recreation (formerly called "industrial recreation") began in the nineteenth century, but did not expand rapidly until after World War II. In 1975, the *New York Times* reported that 50,000 companies were spending $2 billion a year on recreation-related programs. A 1995 report from the National Employee Services and Recreation Association (NESRA) indicated that its members represented a $196.8 million market and were serving an average of 3,760 people, including employees, retirees, and their families.

While the providers of employee services and recreation originally were manufacturing companies and other industrial concerns, today many different types of organizations also sponsor employee activities. They include such diverse groups as food market chains, airline companies, insurance concerns, hospitals, and government agencies.

Goals of Employee Recreation

The major goals of the institutions providing employee programs and services include the following.

Improvement of Employer–Employee Relations Earlier in this country's industrial development, there was considerable friction between management and labor that often resulted in extended and violent strikes. A major purpose of industrial recreation programs at this time was to create favorable employer–employee relationships and instill a sense of loyalty among workers. Today, with relative peace in most industries, this remains a significant goal of employee recreation. It is believed that such programs tend to create a feeling of belonging and identification among employees, and that group participation by workers at various job levels contributes to improved worker morale, increased harmony, and an attitude of mutual cooperation.

In the intense competition that characterized many businesses in the early and mid-1990s in a period of company downsizing and mergers, these goals became particularly important as a way of strengthening employee work morale and performance. Jerry Junkins, chairman and chief executive officer of Texas Instruments in Dallas, Texas, expressed this view:

> We see employee services and recreation as one part of a total package that includes competitive salaries, benefits, and health promotion services and activities. All of these are designed to let our people know we value them, and we view them as the key contributors to our company's success. . . . We've tried to design our ES & R programs to address the total well-being of our employees and their families by providing them with programs that can enhance their physical, mental, and emotional health.[25]

Directly Promoting Employee Fitness and Efficiency Corporations large and small today have become concerned about maintaining the health of their employees. One reason may be the skyrocketing costs of health insurance. Since 2001, health insurance premiums of U.S. employers have increased an average of 68.2 percent. A major factor in this increase is the nation's obesity epidemic. Obesity accounts for more annual health care costs than drinking and smoking. The state of Texas estimated in 2006 that obesity costs Texas businesses $3.3 billion due to health care, absenteeism, decreased productivity, and disability.

Numerous reports from varied company sources document the effectiveness of recreation and fitness programs in achieving health- and productivity-related goals:

> At General Electric in Cincinnati, exercisers [in company-sponsored fitness programs] were absent from work 45 percent fewer days than nonparticipants.
>
> General Mills found that participants in its employee fitness program had a 19 percent reduction in absenteeism compared to a 69 percent increase in nonparticipants.
>
> Toronto Life Assurance found that employee turnover during a 10-month period was substantially lower for program participants than for nonparticipants—1.5 percent versus 15 percent.[26]

Such justifications for expanded programs of employee services and recreation became increasingly important in the last years of the 1990s and the beginning of the twenty-first century. National prosperity and a record-breaking rate of employment meant that many companies had to use new strategies to recruit new employees and to retain their present workers.

Recruitment and Retention Appeal

An attractive program of recreation and related personnel services that can meet the needs of both the employee and his or her family is a persuasive recruitment weapon. Crompton, Love, and More documented the role of recreation, parks, and open space in many companies' decision-making process with respect to relocation.[27] Outlining a number of strategies for effective personnel recruitment, Amy Berger writes:

> As you promote your department and its offerings, you send a message to current and future employees that your department is what makes your company a great place to work. Promotional campaigns are most successful when all of your company's departments join forces to educate employees on the services available and encourage their involvement on an individual basis.[28]

In terms of retention, many companies find that successful employee programs help reduce job turnover. Litton Laser Systems in Apopka, Florida, now owned by Northrop Grumman, for example, credits its low employee turnover and high morale to its social activities committee (SAC), a group of employees who manage social, recreational, and sports events and other services for all company members and their families.

Company Image and Community Role

An important part of the recreation and services function involves external relations—the company's external, community-based role. Barbara Altman comments that in the mid-1990s, many companies sought to redefine the idea of corporate citizenship. Research showed that

> pressures in the business and social environment were prompting issues in community relations practice. Executives were struggling with how to operationalize community

responsibility, how to respond to their multiple communities, and how to explain the linkage between community involvement and business strategy.[29]

At Litton Laser Systems, one expression of this concern was found in the organized employee giving program, which resulted in large sums being raised each year for United Way, the American Heart Association, American Red Cross, and a special "Loaves and Fishes" Charity program.

In many cases, company recreation programs and facilities serve community groups, and, in others, the director of the employee services and recreation program also is given responsibility for numerous community-relations activities of the company. The employee services coordinator for the M. D. Anderson Cancer Center at the University of Texas in Houston, Texas, recruits

employees for community events such as the Houston/Tenneco Marathon and the University of Texas Health Science Center Sportathon. We sponsor health fairs and guest lectures during the Texas Medical Center Wellness Week. We promote cultural events in Houston throughout the workplace with the Council for the Visual and Performing Arts.

We maintain seasonal special events, such as our Employee Christmas Dinner, Christmas decorating contest, National Hospital Week, Savings Bond drive, United Way, etc. . . . We handle discount programs for employees dealing with sporting and cultural events and various coupon books. We maintain our institutional bulletin board which publicizes our programs and those from other departments. We are also in charge of the monthly Outstanding Employee Award program.[30]

■ *Many large companies offer recreation programs for their current employees, retirees, and their families. These programs are one means of increasing employee moral.*

In other settings, the employee services program provides a means through which company executives can move purposefully to transform the business's internal and external image. As a vivid example, the Coors Brewing Company in Colorado, which long had a reputation for conservative policies and funding right-wing political groups, sought deliberately to change its image, encouraging sensitivity training for its diverse workforce and shifts in its national identity as well. It sponsors 10 "resource councils" representing gays, women, and Native Americans, among others, and supports programs ranging from a marathon gay dance party in Miami to the first large-scale corporate mammography program in the country.

Program Activities and Services

Many companies established extensive and well-equipped recreation and fitness centers and staffed them with qualified personnel. The Texins Activity Center in Dallas, serving employees of Texas Instruments, contains a multi-use gymnasium; strength and cardiovascular exercise areas; conference rooms; child-care rooms; club rooms; a natatorium with a six-lane, 25-lap pool; two aerobic studios; an indoor running track; and varied outdoor facilities.

Wellness Programs and Fitness Centers   The largest single thrust in employee service and recreation programs is toward providing health and wellness activities. Beyond simply offering exercise equipment or classes, wellness programs may include activities that promote physical, emotional, social, environmental, and even spiritual health. Kondrasuk and Carl listed the varied components that typically are found in many company-sponsored wellness programs today:

> *Screenings, health risk appraisals (HRA):* Blood pressure, weight, body fat, pulse, diabetes, AIDS, cardiovascular diseases, cancer and mammography, lifestyle and environmental questionnaires.
>
> *Exercise programs:* Endurance/cardiovascular/aerobics, strength training, flexibility.
>
> *Education/awareness and possible interventions:* Stress reduction, smoking cessation, obesity/weight control, lipid control, back pain, blood pressure/hypertension reduction, retirement and pre-retirement counseling, pre- and post-natal education, employee/family counseling on emotional issues, relaxation programs/meditation, producing healthier environments (like health food in vending machines).
>
> *Developing healthful skills, behaviors:* First aid, CPR use, back injury prevention, increasing seat belt use.[31]

Administrative Arrangements

Various approaches to the management of employee service and recreation programs exist. In some, the company itself provides the facilities and leadership and maintains complete control of the operation. In other organizations, the company provides the facilities, but an employee recreation association takes actual responsibility for running the program. Other companies use combinations of these approaches. Frequently, profits from canteens or plant vending machines provide financial support for the program, as does revenue from moderate fees for participation or membership. Many activities—such as charter vacation flights—are completely self-supporting; others are fully or partly subsidized by the company.

Some companies restrict participation in recreation programs to employees and their families, while others make them available to the surrounding community. For example, the Flick-Reedy Corporation designed its main building for the recreational use of the entire community, with thousands of children and adults using its gymnasium, auditorium, and dining room for special banquets and events each year.

Scheduling Flexibility: Off-Shift Programming

Employee service and recreation managers must adapt to the special circumstances of their organizations and the changing needs of the employees they serve. Often this may involve providing a wide range of special courses designed for vocational or career development, cultural interest, or personal enrichment.

Some large corporations seek to meet the needs of their employees who work second and third shifts by scheduling facilities such as health clubs or weight rooms to be available at odd hours of the day and night. For example, Phillips Petroleum and

Pratt and Whitney schedule morning and midnight softball and bowling leagues for off-shift workers and make gyms, tennis courts, and other facilities, as well as discount ticket operations, available to them at convenient times.

Innovation and Entrepreneurship

Just as in other sectors of the leisure-service field, employee service and recreation practitioners have experienced the need to become more fiscally independent by generating a fuller level of revenues through their offerings and by demonstrating their value in convincing terms.

The purposes of adopting businesslike values and strategies are (1) to enable employee programs to become less dependent on company financial support and (2) to ensure that funds allocated to them by management yield significant, quantifiable benefits. A number of employee service and recreation directors in major corporations have been quite innovative in developing revenue sources based on businesslike ventures. Hauglie cites an example of such ventures:

> At Control Data Corporation in Minneapolis, Minnesota, a business plan was developed for an employee store, including a needs assessment, marketing strategy, profit-and-loss projections, and start-up funding requirements. Following approval, which included a business loan from the company, the project was set in motion. By the early 1990s, three employee stores were operating successfully, and Control Data's initial investment was paid back within the first year of the program's operation.[32]

Changes in Professional Association

Over the past two decades, the primary professional organization in this field, the National Employee Services and Recreation Association, has seen a steady broadening of the responsibilities of its member companies. Today, although recreation continues to be a major function in human resource departments, there are 10 important elements within their overall operations. As defined in January 2000, when the organization changed its title to the Employee Services Management (ESM) Association, they include the following: (1) employee stores, (2) community services, (3) convenience services, (4) recreation programs, (5) special events, (6) voluntary benefits, (7) dependent care assistance, (8) recognition and awards programs, (9) travel services, and (10) wellness/fitness programs.[33]

In promoting these services, the ESM association publishes a magazine and buyer's guide; maintains an e-mail service and membership directory; holds an annual conference and exhibit; sponsors an awards of excellence program and a certification program; and conducts varied continuing education, information, and research projects. In promoting high standards of performance in the employee services and recreation field, it maintains two kinds of memberships: (1) *organizational members,* who are actually employed in companies with management or leadership responsibilities; and (2) *associate members,* who provide services, equipment, or supplies to company employee programs.

CAMPUS RECREATION

The nation's colleges and universities provide a major setting for organized programs of leisure services involving millions of participants each year in a wide range of recreational activities. Although their primary purpose is to serve students, faculty and staff members also may be involved in such programs on many campuses.

All institutions of higher education today sponsor some forms of leisure activity for their resident and commuter populations. Many of the larger colleges and universities have campus unions, departments of student affairs, or student centers that house a wide range of such activities. Frequently, a dean of student life is responsible for overseeing these programs, although intramural and recreational sports often may be administratively attached to a department or college of physical education and recreation or to a department of intercollegiate athletics.

The diversified leisure-service function may include operating performing arts centers (sometimes in cooperation with academic departments or schools in these fields), planning arts series, film programs, and forums with guest speakers, and similar cultural events. Student union buildings may include such specialized facilities as bowling alleys, coffee houses, game rooms, restaurants, bookstores, and other activity areas.

Rationale for Campus Programs

Several logical reasons for sponsoring college and university recreation programs may be cited. Discussion of some of these follows.

Leisure as Cocurricular Enrichment   Not all of the learning that takes place in higher education is provided in the classroom or laboratory. Many special interests of students can be explored to the fullest only by *cocurricular* (nonclass) experiences, ranging from the journalism major who works on the staff of the campus newspaper or literary magazine to the botany major who becomes involved in wilderness backpacking or camping. Often such programs are carried on with the express cooperation of the campus department most directly involved with the leisure interest.

Maintaining Campus Control and Morale   Historically, U.S. colleges acted *in loco parentis*; that is, they were obligated to maintain a degree of control over the private lives of their students in areas such as drinking, gambling, sexual behavior, or the general domain of health and safety. For centuries, they therefore maintained codes of behavior, rules for on-campus living, curfews, and numerous other restrictions that controlled various forms of leisure behavior.

If anything, these problems became more acute during the 1990s, with continuing reports of binge drinking in colleges, dangerous hazing practices, and even an ugly rise in racial tensions and incidents on a number of campuses.[34] As a consequence, the *New York Times* reported in March 1999 that many campuses turned full circle in a revolution of new rules for college students. Ethan Bronner writes:

> Reflecting a range of societal changes—consumerism, litigiousness, a shift in intergenerational relations, and increased fears about campus drinking—colleges are offering and students are often demanding greater supervision of their lives.[35]

At this time, many colleges began to take concrete steps to change the culture of drinking on their campuses—some by banning alcohol entirely, others by cracking down on underage drinking or limiting the use of liquor in sorority and fraternity houses.[36]

In general, it is now believed by many that colleges must play a larger role in guiding the lives of students outside of the classroom. Although few administrators are seeking a return to the days of single-sex dormitories, dress codes, curfews, and other rigid rules, a consensus has grown that many of today's college students lack the responsibility to handle their new-found freedom sensibly and that it is necessary to establish and enforce some guidelines for students' social behavior.

Beyond being part of the effort to control negative kinds of behavior, campus recreation promotes positive student growth throughout the college experience. At a number of Eastern colleges, students are drawn into outdoor recreation or community service projects, beginning with their freshman orientation period. At Lehigh University and Lafayette College, for example, new students are drawn into overnight canoe and backpacking trips and begin to make new friends immediately. Similarly, entering students at Bryn Mawr College are assigned one-day service projects with the Philadelphia Zoo, the Children's Hospital of Philadelphia, and Habitat for Humanity.

Enhancing the University's Image   Particularly in an era in which colleges and universities must compete for the enrollment of high-quality students, maintaining an appealing and impressive institutional image is critical. Probably the best-known vehicle for doing this is by fielding teams that play glamorous schedules in such popular sport as football or basketball. However, there are many other ways of building a positive image: through academic distinction, by winning prizes and awards, by having outstanding orchestras or theater companies, by having a distinguished university press, and through the accomplishments of alumni.

Certainly, having attractive recreational facilities and campus leisure programs also helps to build a positive image—particularly for potential students who visit a campus and are considering whether they want to live there for the next four years. Higher education appeals to a number of values and needs—not the least of these is the student's desire for an exciting and interesting social life.

Contributing to Student Development   Beyond enriching a student's formal academic experience, involvement in noncurricular experiences contributes significantly to his or her overall personal growth. In an article on academic productivity, Judith Bryant and James Bradley cite a Harvard University report, *Teaching, Learning, and Student Life*, which stresses that out-of-classroom activities relate directly to higher grades and to social integration. Furthermore, a study of recent alumni of the University of Tennessee found that participation in intramural sports was an important factor in several areas of personal growth.[37]

Range of Campus Recreation Experiences

Campus recreation programs today are becoming more diversified, including a wide range of recreational sport, outdoor activities, entertainment and social events, cultural programs, activities for persons with disabilities, and various other services.

■ *Campus recreation activities typically include intramural sports, special events, clubs, and fitness.*

Recreational Sport   During the 1970s and 1980s, both intramural leagues and sport clubs expanded rapidly in many institutions, with a growing emphasis on lifetime sport and on coeducational participation. Due in part to changed sex-role expectations and the effect of Title IX, many more girls and women are involved in sport today than in the past. More and more colleges and universities are providing varied facilities for sport and games, including aquatic facilities, boxing/martial arts and exercise rooms, saunas and locker rooms, extensive outdoor areas with night lighting for evening play, and other special facilities for outdoor hobbies and instruction.

An outstanding example of college sport programming is found at Virginia Commonwealth University in Richmond, Virginia, which sponsors a host of recreational sport activities and events and fitness programs in six impressive campus facilities. Programs include a huge range of instructional, club, and intramural activities in such areas as individual, dual, and team sport; aerobics; dancing; yoga; martial arts; aquatics; and social programs. Participation in all programs and facilities is free for students through the general student fee. Spouses, staff, and faculty members pay modest annual fees. Similar sport programs are offered throughout the United States.

Outdoor Recreation   Outdoor recreation, which includes clinics, clubs, and outings, may involve hiking, backpacking, camping, mountain climbing, scuba diving, sailing, skiing, and numerous other nature-based programs. These are often sponsored by campus outing clubs, which may in turn be affiliated with national organizations or federations. Gary Nussbaum points out that a well-developed outdoor recreation program may yield positive benefits in student achievement and satisfaction, and suggests that such programs should be used to enrich the intramural programs at many colleges and universities.

In addition to actual sponsorship of such activities, campus recreation directors may provide varied support and information services. Examples might include

> the inexpensive rental of backpacking and camping gear . . . the provision of information including resource data, the location of clothing/equipment outfitters, and a directory of other clubs, organizations, and commercial enterprises offering outdoor recreation services. . . . [and] Outdoor literature (e.g., "how-to" books, periodical works) may be a joint provision of the intramural office and the university library.[38]

Southern Illinois University, for example, offers a diversified range of appealing trips and outings, clinics, and classes, including rock climbing and backpacking, spelunking (cave exploration), canoeing, biking, and Earth Day events.

Special Events: Entertainment and Cultural Programs   Many campuses sponsor large-scale entertainment events and cultural series. Typically, singers, rock bands, and comedians are booked to entertain students in stadiums, field houses, and campus centers. The college or university's own departments of music, theater, and dance may provide performing companies that present concerts or other stage presentations, along with other kinds of specialized programs.

Large-scale special events that students plan and carry out themselves—such as sports carnivals or other major competitions—are highlights of campus social programs. They involve both intimacy of interaction among leaders and participants and an intense outpouring of energy as people share fun in a crowded school or college setting. Similar excitement may be noted at major musical events such as rock concerts, although such programs often require supervision to assure adherence to campus policies regarding alcohol and drugs.

Services for Special Populations   Students with disabilities are being encouraged and assisted to participate in general campus recreation programs whenever possible. However, for those students whose disabilities are too severe to permit this or who have not yet developed the needed degree of confidence and independence, it has been necessary to design special programs using modified facilities and adapted instructional techniques or rules.

Outstanding examples of such programs are those offered by the University of Illinois, which provides special teams in the areas of football, softball, basketball, swimming, and track and field for physically disabled students. Other activities, such as archery, judo, swimming, bowling, and softball, have been adapted for such special groups as the visually impaired.

Community Service Projects   Many students also become involved in volunteer community projects such as repairing facilities, working with the elderly, or providing "big brother" or tax assistance services. Such efforts are important for two reasons: (1) They illustrate how student-life activities may include a broad range of involvements beyond those that are clearly recognizable as recreational "fun" events; and (2) they serve to blend academic and extracurricular student experiences, increasing the individual's exposure to life and enhancing his or her leadership capability.

Findings of the Cooperative Institutional Research Program at the University of California at Los Angeles show that the more students are involved in their education, the more likely they are to remain at an institution: "The most successful students . . . are those who live and work on their campuses, participate in college activities and academic programs outside of their classes, and interact with faculty and staff members."

Overview of Campus Recreation

Campus recreation provides students with practical experience within a wide range of functions that supplement and enrich their academic programs. For example, many students may gain administrative or business skills, often on an advanced level. The Associated Students' Organization of San Diego State University in California provides a setting for such learning experiences. This multimillion-dollar corporation, funded by student fees, operates the Aztec Center, the college's student union building. Among its services are a successful travel agency, intramurals and sport clubs, special events, leisure classes, lectures, movies, concerts, an open-air theater, an aquatics center, campus radio station, child-care center, general store, campus information booth, and other programs. The bulk of its recreational activities is operated directly by the Recreation Activities Board, a unit within the overall Associated Students' Organization.

Such experiences illustrate the important contributions made by campus recreation programs, along with other student noncurricular activities, to the college or university experience. They involve the whole student in meaningful and creative ways and thus provide a meaningful transition to adult life and potential career opportunities.

Although the term *campus recreation* is usually applied only to higher education settings, recreation also is closely linked to other levels of educational experience. Many elementary and secondary school systems also provide recreation facilities and programs that meet significant leisure needs.

School District Programs

Throughout the twentieth century, many school districts established extensive programs of extra- and cocurricular activities for students, including clubs, sport, music and drama groups, and similar types of leisure involvement. Although the budget restraints of the 1980s and 1990s compelled many districts to reduce such offerings, they still provide an opportunity for school-centered recreation in many communities. Beyond this, a growing number of school systems now provide impressive adult education classes on a fee basis; these may include both remedial or diploma-oriented options and offerings relating to varied hobby interests, such as languages, arts and crafts, sport skills, literary and musical topics, investment planning, fitness, and other similar self-enrichment subjects.

In other settings, this cooperation may take the form of shared responsibility for constructing and maintaining facilities that are used jointly by schools and municipal authorities. Frequently, such facilities become multiservice community centers that blend educational, recreational, and social services. For example, in New Brighton, Minnesota, the Mounds View School District owns 12,500 square feet of the parks and recreation department's 70,000-square-foot Family Service Center, which the district uses for its early childhood and family education program. The park department also is renting an additional 1,000 square feet to the school district for the adult education component of its program and 1,000 square feet to the nonprofit Northwest Youth and Family Service, a teen counseling group.[39]

Similarly, in Sunnyvale, California, the city of Sunnyvale, in cooperation with the elementary school district, constructed a $3.5 million addition to its Columbia Middle School in the mid-1990s. The AMD Sports and Service Center (named after Advanced Micro Devices, a local company that contributed $1 million to the project) includes a gymnasium, counseling rooms, and a health center. The gymnasium is used by the school during the day and by the city during nonschool hours.

PRIVATE-MEMBERSHIP RECREATION ORGANIZATIONS

A significant portion of recreational opportunities today is provided by private-membership organizations. As distinguished from commercial recreation businesses—in which any individual may simply pay an admission fee to a theme park, for example—private-membership bodies usually restrict use of their facilities or programs to individual members and their families and guests.

Within the broad field of sport and outdoor recreation, many organizations offer facilities, instruction, or other services for activities such as skiing, tennis, golf, boating, and hunting or fishing. While some private-membership organizations are commercially owned and operated, others exist as independent, incorporated clubs of members who own their own facilities, with policy being set by elected officers and boards and with the actual work of maintenance, instruction, and supervision being carried out by paid employees.

An important characteristic of many private-membership organizations has been their social exclusiveness. Membership policies often screened out certain prospective members for reasons of religion, ethnicity, or other demographic factors.

It is important to recognize that although the ostensible function of such private organizations is to provide sociability as well as specific forms of leisure activity, the clubs also provide a setting in which the most powerful members of U.S. communities meet regularly to discuss business or political matters and often reach informal decisions or plans for action. Those who are barred from membership in such clubs are thus also excluded from this behind-the-scenes, establishment-based process of influence and power.

In the late 1970s and early 1980s, such organizations received more public scrutiny, as the U.S. Senate Banking Committee initiated an investigation of the payment of employee membership dues to private clubs and social organizations by financial institutions. It was found that women as well as African Americans and other ethnic minorities were frequently excluded from private clubs.

In a number of cases, national membership organizations have been compelled to open their membership rolls to minority group members because of lawsuits that have threatened them with withdrawal of tax-exempt status. However, as recently as the early 1990s, some organizations, such as Rotary International, continued to do battle in the courts to maintain their sexually discriminatory policies and expelled member clubs that have yielded on the issue. In 1987, at a time when women made up 44 percent of the workforce and 37 percent of managers and executives, *U.S. News & World Report* commented that to exclude them from an organization designed for business promotion no longer seemed justifiable—yet, only in the late 1990s did many private golf clubs begin to admit more than token numbers of members of racial or religious minority background, or to grant full membership privileges to women as a result of costly lawsuits penalizing them for gender discrimination.

Continuing Efforts to Discriminate

Despite such changes, many private-membership organizations continue to represent exclusive enclaves of the rich and powerful. Country clubs, as indicated, are generally of two types: (1) nonprofit "equity clubs," owned and operated by members; and (2) commercially owned, for-profit clubs. Over 70 such clubs are owned by Club Corporation International; surprisingly, this organization has frequently been sued by its members for not being exclusive enough, and for permitting too many nonmembers to use its facilities as paying guests. Private, they argue, should mean private.[40]

Residence-Connected Clubs

Other types of private-membership recreation organizations continue to flourish—particularly in connection with new forms of home building and marketing. Many real estate developers have recognized that one of the key selling points in home development projects is the provision of attractive recreational facilities. Thus, tennis courts, golf courses, swimming pools, health spas, and similar recreation facilities are frequently provided for the residents of apartment buildings, condominiums, or one-family home developments, whether the residents are families, singles, or retired persons.

An important trend in U.S. society has been the rapid growth of housing developments in the suburbs, with community associations that carry out such functions as street cleaning, grounds maintenance, security, and the provision of leisure facilities such as tennis courts, golf courses, and swimming pools. Once found chiefly in the Southwest, such developments and community associations now have spread throughout the United States. In 1970, there were 10,000 such associations. In 1990, they numbered 130,000. By 2006, the number had grown to 286,000 with 57 million residents governed by associations.

Although such real estate developments tend to be expensive and thus intended chiefly for affluent tenants or homebuyers, there are exceptions. For example, a giant apartment development in Brooklyn, New York, known as Starrett City, was constructed in the mid-1970s to serve middle-income tenants drawn from varied ethnic populations—approximately half were of African American, Hispanic, and Asian origin. Its thousands of residents enjoy a huge clubhouse with meeting rooms, hobby, craft, and dance classes, and an extensive pool program and tennis complex, as well as numerous classes, teams, and special events through the year.

In some cases, large condominium-structured apartment buildings also have extensive leisure facilities and programs. For example, in Philadelphia, one such building with 776 residential units has a bank, restaurant, 10 stores, doctors' and dentists' offices, garages, and two swimming pools, all under one roof. It also has a library, card room, fitness center, and numerous clubs and committees, including a welcoming committee, Weight Watchers, a writers' club, book club, and computer club.

Vacation Homes

A specialized form of residence-connected recreation is often found in vacation home developments. During the 1960s and 1970s, direct ownership and time-sharing arrangements for such homes became more popular, often in large-scale developments situated close to a lake or other major recreational attraction.

The baby boom, with millions of couples reaching the age and financial status at which they are able to afford vacation homes, has led to a rapid rise in the number of such developments. According to the National Association of Realtors, over 12 percent of home purchases in 2005 were vacation homes. The total number of households owning vacation homes was 6.6 million. The average vacation home buyer was 52 years old with annual earnings of $82,800. The largest percentage of homes (47 percent) was less than 100 miles away from the primary residence with the second greatest percentage (43 percent) over 500 miles or more.

Typically, time-sharing apartments or condominiums in attractive vacation areas today cost as much as $15,000 to $20,000 for the right to use the facility one week each year. Although this may seem expensive, it is minimal compared with the cost in vacation areas where the "jet set"—the wealthy elite of U.S. society—enjoy their vacations. Illustrating the tendency to seek privacy in exclusive surroundings, a number of millionaires and billionaires who formerly enjoyed their vacations in Aspen, Colorado, left that area when it became too well known and popular. Today they fly their own jets to a stunningly beautiful mountain hamlet in Wyoming known as Saratoga. Members of the Old Baldy Club live in "cottages" that would be considered mansions anywhere else. When asked how much it cost to join the Old Baldy Club, a local resident received the reply, "If you have to ask, you can't afford it."

Retirement Communities

Similarly, large retirement villages offer recreation and social programs for their residents; often they are actually called *leisure villages*. A vivid example may be found in Sun City, Arizona. Established in 1960, this community has about 45,000 residents. Marla Dial writes:

> At the Sundial—one of seven multimillion-dollar recreation centers here—residents can participate in everything from swimming and weight training to sewing, ceramics, or art classes. The building also houses a mineral museum, photo lab, and shuffleboard facilities. Eleven golf courses have been built over the years, and designers are making each one tougher, as they find that retirees are better golfers than they first thought.
>
> "You can do as little as you want to, you can do as much as you want to," said [one long-term resident]. "That's the life here. It keeps us moving, keeps us young."[41]

FACILITIES OPEN TO SUN CITY WEST RESIDENTS

Recreation Centers	4	Tennis Courts	27
Golf Courses	9	Tennis Platforms	8
Mini Golf Courses	2	Swimming Pools	6
Bowling Lanes	30	Shuffleboard Courts	5
Table Tennis Tables	7	Racquet/Handball Courts	2
Billiard/Pool Tables	30	Fitness & Dance Rooms	5
Softball Field	1	Lawn Bowling Rinks	32
Walking Tracks	3	Bocce Ball Courts	14

* 7,000 seat Sundome Center for the Performing Arts
* 300 seat Kuentz Theater
* West Valley Art Museum
* Sun Cities Symphony Orchestra & Chorus
* City park at Beardsley with bandstand and ramadas
* Nearby shopping mall with 14 movie theater complex
* 3,300 RV Storage Compound
* 40,000 volume R.H. Johnson Library

<u>Physical Activities</u> Outdoor/indoor walking tracks and swimming pools, regulation and platform tennis, regulation and mini golf, lawn bowling, Bocce, volley ball, fitness rooms, therapy pools, shuffleboard, table tennis, racquet ball, handball, bowling, softball, horseshoes, ballroom dancing, square dancing, and line dancing.

<u>Crafts, Hobbies, and Games</u> Almost 100 chartered clubs, many state clubs, professional woodshop and metalshop facilities, card rooms and space allotted for hobbies and crafts such as lapidary, silk flower creations, sewing, ceramics, silversmithing, pottery, leather tooling, stained glass, painting, calligraphy, model railroading, and others.

Retirement Community Recreation

Many retirement communities offer extensive recreation facilities and programs and encourage residents to attend cultural events in the surrounding area. Others, as in Sarasota, Florida's, Pelican Cove, have uniquely beautiful natural surroundings, including a marina with easy access to open bay waters.

Many retirement communities offer extensive recreation facilities and programs for their residents.

So successful has the Sun City formula been that in the 1980s and 1990s, two additional communities were developed in the area—Sun City West and Sun City Grand. With many younger, earlier retirees, these communities not only feature the traditional pastimes of the elderly, but also such newer or more demanding activities as weight training, rollerblading, and rock climbing. Growing numbers of semiretired residents continue to volunteer, do part-time work, or even start their own businesses—and in some cases accept such challenges as training for triathlons or helicopter hiking in the remote Canadian Rockies.[42] In numerous other retirement communities, such as Leisure World in Laguna Hills, California, such recreational facilities as pools, tennis courts, and riding stables often are found.

Significantly, the time-shares section of the vacation homes market has grown dramatically, vaulting the industry from a modest $300 million business in 1978 to an estimated $7.7 billion operation in 2004.[43]

COMPARISONS AMONG SPECIAL-FOCUS AGENCIES

There are both differences and similarities among the five different types of leisure-service organizations meeting special needs that are described in this chapter.

Therapeutic recreation is obviously concerned chiefly with meeting the needs of persons with disabilities in U.S. society, as well as using recreation as a purposeful tool to achieve goals of habilitation or rehabilitation. Although its major emphasis is on providing both clinical and community-based recreation programs, the strong thrust today is toward mainstreaming and integration of individuals with disabilities within the larger population. As such, it shares many common program elements and facilities with the overall community recreation system.

Armed forces recreation involves a huge, sprawling, worldwide operation. It is essentially made up of hundreds of smaller individual programs on both domestic and foreign bases or on ships. Uniquely, it is governed by a bureaucratic structure and specific policies that originate within the defense department, while at the same time responding to the special needs and resources of different branches of the military services and to local capabilities and interests. Its services and programs range from businesslike and commercialized approaches to entertainment or hospitality to purposeful, social service activities meeting the needs of children and youth or dependent families.

Employee recreation service differs from other special branches of the leisure-service system in that it has become just one of 10 important functions designed to improve the quality of life in the work environment and to contribute to the effective operation of its sponsoring companies. Within this spectrum of service, recreation has the unique responsibility of upgrading company morale and human relationships, as well as promoting the positive image of the overall enterprise. As in both therapeutic and armed forces recreation, employee programs must be concerned with achieving important agency goals and with documenting their worth in concrete, measurable terms.

Campus recreation, whether primarily concerned with sport programming or with broader cultural and curriculum-connected activities, today is seen as an integral element in the overall higher education structure. Particularly in colleges and universities in which older adolescents and those just entering adulthood are faced with the challenge of their first real social independence, it is critical that campus recreation help students develop positive lifestyle values and patterns of leisure choices. As part of this purpose, campus activities should serve as an attractive counterbalance to less-desirable leisure involvements.

Finally, private-membership leisure-service organizations are heavily influenced by socioeconomic factors, in that they tend to be provided for individuals and families who are relatively elite in financial and demographic terms. Although they have been undergoing a gradual process of democratization, many such groups continue to be exclusive and focus on a narrow range of recreational interests. One exception is found in the growing number of retirement communities, which often sponsor a considerable variety of recreational programs, particularly for younger individuals and couples who are entering such communities.

SUMMARY

Five specialized areas of leisure-service delivery described in this chapter illustrate the diversity of agencies that provide organized recreation opportunities today. In each case, they have their own goals and objectives, populations served, and program emphases—yet they are important elements within the overall leisure-service system and represent attractive fields of career opportunity for recreation, park, and leisure-service students today.

Therapeutic recreation service, in its two areas of professional emphasis—clinical or treatment service and community-based special recreation—is probably the most highly professionalized of all the separate disciplines in the leisure-service field. It has a long history of professional development, with separate sections of state and national societies, early emphasis on registration and certification (as Chapter 11 will show more fully), numerous specialized curricula, and a rich literature and background of research. With the possibility of lessened support being given to clinical therapeutic recreation in an era of cost cutting, hospital retrenchment, managed patient care, and deinstitutionalization, it is probable that community-based special recreation, with its emphasis on mainstreaming, will constitute an increasingly important element in therapeutic recreation.

Armed forces recreation professionals serve a distinct population composed both of large numbers of relatively young service men and women—often single and away from home—and of families and dependents with special needs prompted by the military setting. Morale, fitness, and mission accomplishment are important armed forces recreation goals, which are reflected in an increasingly businesslike approach to planning, marketing, and evaluating programs. With reduced budgets caused by downsizing and a greater emphasis on fiscal self-sufficiency, military recreation has undergone major transformations in recent years, yet it continues to offer a wide range of attractive program opportunities and often has excellent facilities, both stateside and abroad.

Employee recreation and services today have gone far beyond their original emphasis on providing a narrow range of social and sports activities designed to promote company worker relationships. They are carried on in many different kinds of organizations and include varied health- and fitness-related program elements, as well as such other personnel services as discount programs, company stores, community relationships, and other benefits-driven functions—all necessarily provided within a business-oriented framework that demands productivity and demonstrated outcomes.

Campus recreation is carried on within an educational setting with relatively little interaction with the overall recreation and parks field. At the same time, it has important responsibilities in terms of promoting the overall well-being of students, helping to reduce negative or destructive forms of play, extending and enriching academic learnings, and contributing to other college and university goals.

The last type of organization described in this chapter, the private-membership association, includes a wide range of country clubs, golf clubs, yacht clubs, and other social or business membership groups that often tend to be socially exclusive. They represent a growing trend in the United States today, with millions of families now living in residential developments that have their own community associations to provide services, including recreation. This tends to limit their interest in or dependence on public, tax-supported recreation services.

QUESTIONS FOR CLASS DISCUSSION OR ESSAY EXAMINATION

1. What are the major goals of recreation in the armed forces? Describe some of the key programming areas and indicate how military recreation planners have adapted to problems posed by cutbacks in military bases and personnel and fiscal restraints.
2. One of the chief emphases in employee services and recreation programs involves health and fitness. Using examples taken from the chapter, what forms of services are provided and what documented evidence is there to support their value?
3. Campus recreation has a number of important values for colleges and universities today. Identify and describe these and then focus in detail on the *in loco parentis* function of institutions of higher education. What does this principle involve, and why is it particularly important today? Applied to your own institution, how does the administration provide a degree of control over students' lives, and what part does campus recreation play in this effort?

4. Describe the two major thrusts in therapeutic recreation service today. In terms of special recreation, explain the current thinking with respect to mainstreaming individuals with disabilities.

5. What is the unique role of private-membership organizations and what are some examples of this type of leisure-service sponsor? How do they differ from governmental, voluntary nonprofit, and commercial recreation agencies? Indicate some of the social issues regarding such private organizations.

ENDNOTES

1. National Institute on Recreation Inclusion brochure (Deerfield, IL, September 2000).

2. U.S. Army Community and Family Support Center, United States Army MWR: Fiscal Year 2005 Report.

3. Adapted from Gerald O'Morrow, *Therapeutic Recreation: A Helping Profession* (Reston, VA: Reston Publishing, 1976): Chapter 7.

4. *Statement of Philosophy of Therapeutic Recreation* (Arlington, VA: National Therapeutic Recreation Society, 1982).

5. Charles Sylvester, "Therapeutic Recreation and the Right to Leisure," *Therapeutic Recreation Journal* (2nd Quarter 1992): 10.

6. R. Smith et al., *Inclusive and Special Recreation: Opportunities for Persons with Disabilities*, 5th ed. (McGraw Hill Higher Education, 2001).

7. American Therapeutic Recreation Association, www.atra-tr.org/about.htm.

8. National Council for Therapeutic Recreation Certification, www.nctrc.org/aboutnctrc.htm.

9. Michael Winerip, "Bedlam in the Streets," *New York Times Magazine* (23 May 1999): 42.

10. R. Smith et al., *Inclusive and Special Recreation: Opportunities for Persons with Disabilities*, 5th ed. (McGraw Hill Higher Education, 2001): 12

11. Michael Kelley, "The Therapeutic Potential of Outdoor Adventure: A Review with Focus on Adults with Mental Illness," *Therapeutic Recreation Journal* (2nd Quarter 1993): 110–121.

12. Ladd Colston, "The Expanding Role of Assistive Technology in Therapeutic Recreation," *Journal of Physical Education, Recreation, and Dance* (April 1991): 15.

13. *NTRS Report* (Vol. 23, No. 3, May–June 1998): 8–9.

14. Harold Brubaker, "Nursing Homes' Era of Profits Dashed by Debt," *Philadelphia Inquirer* (9 July 2000): E1.

15. C. Coyle et al., *Benefits of Therapeutic Recreation: A Consensus View* (Philadelphia: Temple University and National Institute on Disability and Rehabilitation Research, 1994).

16. B. Riley and T. Skalko, "The Evolution of Therapeutic Recreation," *Parks and Recreation* (May 1998): 69.

17. U.S. Army Community and Family Support Center, "About MWR," www.armymwr.com/portal/about.

18. "Start Smart Popular on Military Bases Worldwide," *Parks and Recreation* (December 1998): 27.

19. S. Waller and A. Suren, "Recreation and Military Youth," *Journal of Physical Education, Recreation, and Dance—Leisure Today* (April 1995): 22.

20. Elizabeth Becker, "Child Care in Military Is Praised as a Model," *New York Times* (17 May 2000): A19.

21. Gail Howerton, "American Armed Forces Overseas: The Few, the Proud, the Creative," *Parks and Recreation* (December 1994): 57.

22. R. Kraus and J. Curtis, *Creative Management in Recreation and Parks* (St. Louis, MO: Mosby, 1982): 206–207.

23. MWR Expo brochure (Kentucky International Convention Center: MWR, 2006).

24. Carolyn Becraft, quoted in Pat Harden, "Armed Forces Recreation Services: Our Hallowed Ground Raison D'Etre," *Parks and Recreation* (December 1994): 24.

25. "NESRA's Employer of the Year," *Employee Services Management* (May/June 1991): 17.

26. Steven Blair, "Worksite Health Promotion 'Bottom-Line' Facts and Figures," *Employee Services Management* (May/June 1995): 31–33.

27. J. L. Crompton, L. L. Love, and T. A. More, "An Empirical State of the Role of Recreation, Park and in Companies' (Re)Location Decisions," *Journal of Park and Recreation Administration* (Vol. 15, No. 1, Spring 1997): 37–58.

28. Amy Berger, "Advertise Your Company as an Employer of Choice by Promoting Your Employee Services Department," *Employee Services Management* (October 1999): 24–25.

29. Barbara Altman, "Corporate Community Relations in the 1990s: A Study in Transformation," *Business and Society* (June 1998): 221.

30. "Member Success Profile," *Employee Services Management* (September 1991): 13.

31. J. Kondrasuk and C. Carl, "Wellness Programs: Present and Future," *Employee Services Management* (December/January 1991–1992): 9.

32. Joe Hauglie, "Adopting an Entrepreneurial Attitude," *Employee Services Management* (May/June 1991): 14.

33. Employee Services Management brochure (Oakbrook, IL: ESM Association, Spring 2000).

34. "New Hampshire Campuses Address Rise in Racial Tensions," Associated Press (29 November 1998).

35. Ethan Bronner, "In a Revolution of Rules, Campuses Go Full Circle," *New York Times* (3 March 1999): A1.

36. Carolyn Kleiner, "Schools Turn Off the Tap," *U.S. News and World Report* (30 August 1999).

37. J. Bryant and J. Bradley, "Enhancing Academic Productivity: Student Development and Employment Potential," *NIRSA Journal* (Fall 1993): 42.

38. Gary Nussbaum, "Adventures in Intramural Outdoor Recreation Programming," *Journal of Physical Education, Recreation, and Dance* (February 1987): 58.

39. "Family Service," *Athletic Business* (October 1995): 32.

40. Diana Henriques, "Bickering in the Clubhouse," *New York Times* (14 June 1998): B1.

41. Marla Dial, "At 35, a Model Retirement Community Finds Life Still Golden," Associated Press (8 January 1995).

42. Joseph Shapiro, "No Sunset for Sun City," *U.S. News and World Report* (28 June 1999): 78.

43. Edwin McDowell, "A Few Weeks to Call Your Own," *New York Times* (29 January 2000): C1.

CHAPTER 10

TRAVEL AND TOURISM

◆ ◆ ◆

Tourism has become the world's largest industry and touches every corner of the United States. Many communities and counties have tourism bureaus, states have state tourism offices, and advertising for tourism has grown at a prodigious rate. Employment in the tourism industry is significant in every state. Almost every American annually travels as a tourist.

Tourism, as an industry, is as simple as a rural community's fall apple festival or as complex as the hosting of the Super Bowl or some other major event. There are tens of thousands of tourism-based events across the United States annually. Tourism has become interwoven with the fabric of our society and is an essential component of recreation and leisure.

◆ ◆ ◆

INTRODUCTION

Travel and tourism is a major area of diversified recreational involvement that is facilitated or sponsored by every type of leisure-service agency. The terms travel and tourism are easily defined.

Travel simply refers to movement from one location to another. It may be carried out by plane, ship, railroad, bicycle, or other means of transportation. In some definitions, travel is considered to involve trips taken over a minimum distance or from one region or country to another.

Tourism is described by McIntosh, Goeldner, and Ritchie as the activities of persons traveling to and staying in places outside their usual environment for not more than one consecutive year for leisure, business, or other purposes. They continue:

[Tourism is] a vast conglomerate of transportation systems, service providers, recreational facilities, accommodations, consumer products, and specialized services—

273

among many others. Practically everything that you see, touch, hear, and taste has something to do with tourism. You visit national parks, you touch animals at the zoo, you hear a symphony, you eat at a restaurant—all are related to tourism.[1]

Tourism involves transportation in many forms and international tourism frequently involves air travel.

The World Tourism Organization (WTO), a United Nations–sponsored body, defines tourism as "the activities of persons traveling to and staying in places outside their usual environment for not more than one consecutive year for leisure, business and other purposes not related to the exercise of an activity remunerated from within the place visited."[2]

A related term, *hospitality industry* or *visitor industry*, refers to the vast system of accommodations—such as hotels, restaurants, entertainment and shopping facilities, and other services—that are part of the overall travel and tourism system.

SCOPE OF TOURISM

Overall, the travel and tourism industry has been described as one of the world's largest businesses. Close to 7 percent of the gross national product in the United States is generated by travel and tourism, according to the U.S. Chamber of Commerce. It is the nation's second-largest employer, second only to health services. Worldwide, its impact is immense.

According to the WTO, in 1990 there were 455.9 million international tourist arrivals, and by 2005 the number had risen to 808 million. In 2005, the top five internationally visited destinations, based on international tourist arrivals, were France (76 million), Spain, (56 million), the United States (49 million), China (47 million), and Italy (37 million). The United States was the world's top tourism earner with $82 billion in international tourism receipts. The top three tourism generating regions of the world in 2004 were Europe (431 million tourists), Asia and the Pacific (151 million), and the Americas (128 million).[3] The terrorist attack on the World Trade Center in New York City on September 11, 2001, had a significant impact on world travel and particularly on the

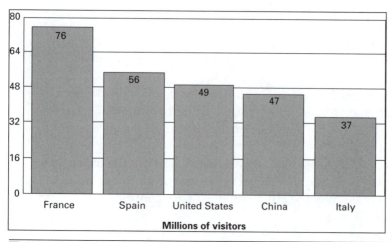

Five Most Popular International Destinations

United States. Within the first 20 months after September 11, the U.S. economy was negatively affected by over $74 billion dollars.

The U. S. Census Bureau reported that 60.89 million Americans traveled to a foreign country (outbound tourists) in 2000, spending $57.5 million.[4] According to the U.S. Office of Travel and Tourism Industries, the number of outbound tourists in 2004 increased to 61.7 million.[5] International tourism receipts combined with passenger transportation make tourism the world's number one export earner, ahead of automotive products, chemicals, petroleum, and food.

Many different kinds of organizations provide tourism opportunities. Thousands of commercial sponsors of tourist attractions and transportation services, theme parks and water parks, cruise ships, charter airline operators, group tour managers, hotel chains, sport arenas, entertainment venues, casinos, zoos, aquariums, wild animal parks, and numerous other businesses satisfy the tourism market. Many government agencies manage parks, historical sites, oceanfront areas, and other kinds of events that attract millions of recreational visitors.

Similarly, many nonprofit organizations sponsor sport events, cultural programs, educational tours, religious pilgrimages, and other special travel programs that serve millions of tourists each year. Armed forces morale, welfare, and recreation units offer travel services to men and women in uniform, and industrial and other business concerns frequently schedule charter flights for their employees. Local convention and visitors bureaus facilitate vacation travel and promote regional tourist attractions.

Within this overall structure, the basic tourism industry consists of five key elements: (1) the tourist, who is motivated by a variety of motivations and needs, ranging from the search for novelty or excitement to aesthetic or cultural involvement; (2) the businesses that provide the bulk of transportation services, as well as the attractions that entertain visitors, along with other nonprofit cultural and environmental groups that maintain zoos, aquariums, botanical gardens, and events; (3) governments of host communities that encourage and facilitate tourism programs and attractions, often sponsoring them jointly with other agencies; (4) accommodations, consisting of lodging, food and beverage services, camping sites, and other amenities that facilitate tourist visits; and (5) locals of host communities, who provide cultural identity to the destination through their lifestyles, customs, and traditions.

Role of the Internet

An important development in the late 1990s involved the rapidly growing number of websites developed by different elements in the travel industry to facilitate the overall tourism marketing system. Lori Krebs reported on the role of the Internet in tourism, suggesting that it was "different than any other promotional medium" in that it functions from within the system and is a form of social activity for the Internet user. In addition, she argued, the Internet is an image formation agent and an information source. Finally, Krebs stated that the Internet is a competitive comparison tool for individuals seeking travel-related information, tickets, lodging, and the like.[6]

Although many long-time travel buyers still look to brochures and travel agencies to provide information and arrange reservations, most new customers now buy travel services via the Web. Robert Schley writes:

> Key benefits of researching travel options through the Internet include: the sheer quantity of up-to-date information available, the convenience of accessing it from your desktop or laptop computer, and the ability to interact with other travelers interested in the same destinations. If you are interested in visiting a particular city, you might find listings of hotels and restaurants and important sights to visit, just like a guidebook . . . complete with colorful photos, current price listings, and menus, as well as a guide to current or upcoming events in that city.[7]

In the United States, the number of Internet users exceeded 150 million for the first time in September 2003. Internationally, by mid-2006 there were 694 million Internet users, up from 13 million in 1996, with global websites making it easier for travelers from abroad to make tourism arrangements. According to forecasts, it is expected that by the year 2010 almost every adult under 55 in the developed world will have access to the Internet, with travel and tourism representing a key area of consumer online involvement. In today's competitive Internet travel market, the once–market leader, Travelocity.com, has watched its 95 percent share of all airline seats steadily erode to Expedia.com and Orbitz.com. In 2002, the three companies spent a combined total of $224 million on marketing. The U.S. online tourism market is expected to grow to $113.5 billion.

In addition to serving as a medium for the purchase of travel products and services, the Internet also is being widely used by organizations to disseminate travel-related information. Websites such as TripAdvisor.com, with 3.5 million registered users,[8] and zoomandgo.com allow tourists to post ratings of tourism businesses and discuss travel experiences with others.[9] In addition, travelers are also using travel blog sites, such as bootsnall.com, travelblog.org, and quietamerican.com/vacation.html, to send notes, photos, and sound recordings to others during the course of their trip.[10] Websites that predict airline ticket prices (e.g., Farecast.com, FareCompare.com) and track flight performance[11] (i.e., flight on-time ratings, delay statistics, and cancellation history) are also becoming increasingly popular among travelers.

The Internet also has contributed to the phenomenal growth of e-tourism, a technological strategy that combines electronic commerce (e-commerce) and innovative tourism business models to broaden the distribution networks of destinations and tourism organizations.[12] E-tourism provides opportunities for tourism businesses to increase their interactions via the Internet with a cross-section of tourism stakeholders, such as tourists/customers, government agencies, community groups, and other related organizations. In fact, e-tourism is being increasingly utilized by developing countries and poorer nations as a cost-effective way to reach international tourists and markets.[13]

MAJOR AREAS OF TOURISM SERVICES

Several major elements in the overall travel and tourism enterprise are now examined, beginning with theme parks, water parks, and marine and wildlife parks.

Theme Parks, Water Parks, and Marine and Wildlife Parks

Closely linked to the growth of tourism as a form of recreation has been the expansion of theme parks such as California's famous Disneyland. This major entertainment complex was built at a cost of over $50 million in the 1950s and covers 65 acres in Anaheim, California. Its success led to the construction of a second major Disney complex, Walt Disney World, at Lake Buena Vista, Florida.

Amusement parks are present in almost every major community and provide locally available thrill experiences for participants.

Crompton and Van Doren point out that Disney effectively resurrected a dying industry. The outdoor amusement park, once an important form of popular entertainment, had become a cultural anachronism. Disney's contribution, they note, was to emphasize cleanliness, courtesy, and safety, in marked contrast to the traditional amusement park. Furthermore, they write:

> The theology of pleasure is reinforced by promotional messages. The theme park creates an atmosphere in which the visitor is likely to experience fantasy, glamour, escapism, prestige, and excitement. . . . Once inside the gate, the visitor is completely shut off from the outside world and immersed in an enjoyable recreational experience. . . . The theme park's primary market is the family; theme parks keep a family involved and entertained for a whole day.[14]

New Kinds of Theme Parks Other entertainment entrepreneurs soon followed the Disney example, and by 1976 at least three dozen parks of similar scale had been built around the United States. Some parks concentrate on a single theme, such as Opryland, U.S.A. in Nashville, Tennessee, and Holiday World and Splashing Safari in Indiana. Others incorporate moving rides through settings based on literary, historical, or international themes; entertainment; and typical amusement park "thrill" rides such as roller coasters and parachute jumps. By 2005 theme parks were reporting 335 million annual visits and $11.2 billion in revenues.

Another unusual facility, opened in the early 1980s by Busch Gardens, was Adventure Island in Tampa, Florida. This 30-acre water park provides vistas of white sand beaches, glistening waters, palm trees, and tropical plants. Built on varied levels with complex waterfalls, slides, pools, cliffs, and rocks, Adventure Island provides an all-inclusive water experience in which visitors slide down twisting water chutes, ride the waves in the Endless Surf pool, dive from cliffs, and enjoy other forms of aquatic play.

Expansion of Disney Entertainment Empire   None of the other chains of theme parks or outdoor play centers could match the diversity and inventiveness of the Disney planners. In 1982, Disney opened EPCOT (an acronym for Experimental Prototype Community of Tomorrow), an $800 million, 260-acre (105.2 hectares) development that was conceived as being more than a theme park. Instead, EPCOT was intended to be a place that would offer an environment where people of many nations might meet and exchange ideas. It consists of two sections: Future World, which contains corporate pavilions primarily concerned with technology; and World Showcase, which has international pavilions designed to show the tourist attractions of various nations around the world.

■ *Mickey Mouse has world-wide recognition as the ambassador for Disney and the Disney resorts and amusement parks.*

Since then, Disney World has added a number of other spectacular and imaginative attractions, including Typhoon Lagoon, the Disney MGM Studios, and, in 1995, Blizzard Beach, Florida's first "snow-capped" water park; it is patterned after an alpine ski resort, with mountain slopes covered with toboggan slides, ski jumps, and slalom runs. In 1983, a Disneyland opened in Japan on 202 acres (81.7 hectares) of landfill in Tokyo Bay. It featured the traditional Disney characters and popular rides and attractions. Although the attraction was owned by a Japanese corporation, Disney provided technology and guidance during the construction and operation of Tokyo Disneyland for a share of the gross ticket take. Then, with the opening of Disneyland Paris, otherwise known as Euro Disney, the company created the largest theme park in Europe. Although the park initially was resisted and had to revise its approach to suit French and European patrons, by 1995 Disneyland Paris began to return its first sizable profits.

Throughout the 1990s, Disney continued to add new attractions and program features. In 1997, Disney's 200-acre (80.9 hectares) Wide World of Sports offered a 7,500-seat stadium and other facilities as a venue for the Atlanta Braves, the Harlem Globetrotters, and the Indiana Pacers as well as thousands of other competitors on every age level in several different sports. Through a cooperative arrangement with the Amateur Athletic Union, national youth tournaments in baseball, basketball, softball, and tennis, among others, are held at this facility. In 1998, Disney's spectacular Animal Kingdom offered an $800-million "African plain," populated by hundreds of wild animals of every description, with 10 million visitors expected in the first year.

Other Parks   There are literally hundreds of theme parks in the United States today. The resurrection of parks might be considered complete. Orlando, Florida, can be considered the theme park capital of the United States. Universal's Orlando Islands of Adventure is typical of many of today's large theme parks. The park has five distinctive themes, similar to what Disneyland introduced. The themes are linked to Universal Studios films, cartoons, or specific activities. For example, Toon Lagoon, a water park, has rides named for different cartoon characters, such as Dudley Do-Right's Rip Saw Falls. ThemeParkInsider.com readers rate this park as the number one theme park in the country.

Cedar Point, located in Sandusky, Ohio, is an example of a regional theme park that provides multiple experiences on a single site. Its website provides links to four types of rides: roller coaster, thrill rides, water rides, and kids rides. Typical of a growth industry in theme parks is the roller coaster. Cedar Point boasts 17 different roller coaster rides, ranging from the Wicked Twister, a 215-foot-tall (65.5 meters), 72-mph (115.9 kph) steel stunner, to the Woodstock Express, a roller coaster with a top speed of 25 mph (40.2 kph) that is targeted toward young riders.

However, not all theme parks rely on such forms of entertainment. Dollywood, for example, a complex of shops, rides, shows, craft centers, restaurants, and other theatrical features based on folk themes, is an outstanding tourist attraction in the Great Smoky Mountain National Park Region. Linked to the image of Dolly Parton, the popular movie actress and country music star, Dollywood offers gospel music performances, harvest celebrations, a "showcase" series of well-known performers, and other programs attuned to its traditional Appalachian Mountain environment.

Water Parks   A specialized type of theme park today consists of water parks—tourist destinations that feature wave pools, slides, chutes, shows, and other forms of water-based play and entertainment. There are about 1,000 water parks today that provide such outdoor play in the United States, mainly in southern states with warmer climates. They are not restricted to warmer areas, however. The Wisconsin Dells for example, is famous for the number of indoor and outdoor water parks in the region. One of the largest water parks is located inside the west Edmonton Mall in Canada.

Often, water attractions are part of larger theme park operations. In Universal's Islands of Adventure, for example, the Jurassic Park River Adventure, Bilge Rat Barges, and Poseidon's Fury offer either whirling and steep whitewater rides and sluice falls or swirling vortexes that spray riders thoroughly. Each year, dozens of new water parks open, with the latest technology, marketing, and management skills taught to their operators at conventions held by the American Water Park Association.

Zoos, Marine Parks, and Wildlife Parks   The addition of rides and other entertainment features to animal attractions is making marine and wild animal parks increasingly popular among tourists. Annually, members of the American Zoo and Aquarium Association in the United States receive approximately 143 million visitors. For example, Sea World San Diego which attracted 4 million visitors in 2003[15] claims to provide guests with "both adventure and a personal connection with marine life,"[16] by offering thrill rides combined with entertainment activities involving sea mammals such as Commerson's dolphins and Orca whales.[17] The popularity of wild animal parks has also seen steady growth in recent years. Per year, approximately 1.5 million tourists visit San Diego's Wild Animal Park, where visitors of all ages are offered the opportunity to view big game and exotic animals in natural (or semiwild) settings.[18]

Other Fun Centers

In heavily populated metropolitan areas throughout the United States, other entrepreneurs have developed a variety of indoor fun centers, ranging from children's play, gymnastics, and exercise chains to family party centers, video game arcades, and huge restaurants with game areas. Typifying the latter, Dave and Buster's, an immensely successful chain of adult "fun and food" offerings in Dallas, Houston, Atlanta, Chicago, Philadelphia, and expanding into 20 states, Canada, and Mexico offers a host of simulated fun experiences: golf, motorcycling, race car driving, space combat, and virtual reality, among others.

Similarly, the children's and family play centers that have been established in thousands of suburban neighborhoods and shopping malls around the United States offer a combination of computer and video games, billiards and other table games, miniature golf, entertainment by clowns and magicians, music, and popular fast-food refreshments. Offering packaged birthday parties and other family play services, they illustrate commercial recreation's success in providing attractive play activities that have supplanted more traditional home-based and "do it yourself" kinds of recreation.

Cruise Ships

Over the past three decades, the growing prosperity of many Americans has made it possible for greater numbers of vacationers to indulge themselves with more varied forms of travel. Luxury cruise ships are no longer simply a vehicle for getting from one place to another or for extended, leisurely ocean voyages. Instead, they have evolved into floating amusement parks, health spas, classrooms, and nightclubs. The major cruise companies have developed huge new vessels and are catering to younger and less-affluent individuals by offering relatively inexpensive short-term trips.

Today, more than 80 cruise ship lines offer a remarkable variety of vacation options afloat, ranging from small sail-propelled schooners to giant, luxurious ocean liners. In many cases, their attractions include gourmet meals, early morning workouts, nightlife and gambling, language classes and charm clinics, deck games, and visits to exotic ports. In North America, the cruise industry recorded 9.5 million passengers in 2003. There are over 250 different cruise liners currently in operation, visiting more than 2,000 ports of call. The number of passengers actually fell following the terrorist attacks on New York City's World Trade Center and for the next several years the industry struggled to return to pre–9-11 passenger levels.

According to a recent report from the International Council of Cruise Lines, the total economic impact in the United States of the cruise lines, their passengers, and crew members reached $30 billion in 2004, increasing by 18 percent from 2003. This spending, in 2004, generated 315,830 jobs and $12.4 million in total wages to U.S. employees.[19]

Variety of Cruise Experiences   As in the overall tourism field, cruise passengers' motivations and interests take many different forms. While some travelers prefer luxurious, pampered, and relatively inactive trips, others enjoy excursions and activities that are demanding or that provide unusual leisure experiences. For example, Windjammer Cruises, which schedules sailing vacations to over 60 ports, chiefly throughout the Caribbean region, offers its passengers such optional possibilities as

■ *Many cruise ships have become floating entertainment palaces such as this three-tiered dining room.*

kayaking and parasailing, deep sea fishing and scuba diving, nature walks and mountain biking, and cultural and historic tours on a host of island visits.

Other specially designed cruises offer such formats or themes as nudism (BareNecessities sponsors "clothing-optional" trips for "naturists"); sobriety cruises (sponsored by Sober Vacations International in California); or golf, combining shipboard lessons and lectures with visits to notable links (offered by Wide World of Golf); as well as many other unique travel tours with sea and land adventures.

OTHER TOURISM THEMES

Apart from traveling to theme parks and similar attractions or embarking on vacation cruises, tourists today seek to satisfy a remarkable range of personal interests and motivations.

Cultural and Historical Interests

The term *cultural* may have two possible meanings when applied to tourism motivations. It may suggest interest in attending major performing arts festivals, visiting famous art museums, or having other kinds of aesthetic experiences. Another meaning involves interest in being exposed to new and different cultures.

Cultural tourism is based on the mosaic of places, traditions, art forms, celebrations, and experiences that portray this nation and its people, reflecting the diversity and character of the United States. Garrison Keillor, in an address to the 1995

White House Conference on Travel & Tourism, best described cultural tourism by saying,

> We need to think about cultural tourism because really there is no other kind of tourism. It's what tourism is. . . . People don't come to America for our airports, people don't come to America for our hotels, or the recreation facilities. . . . They come for our culture: high culture, low culture, middle culture, right, left, real or imagined—they come here to see America.[20]

■ *Cultural tourism often involves experiencing the culture, whether it be indigenous or historical.*

A 1998 study by the Travel Industry Association (TIA) found 92.4 million representing 46 percent of all U.S. adult travelers included a cultural, arts, heritage, or historic activity while on a one-way trip of 50 miles or more during the previous year. Of these travelers, visiting an historic site such as an historic community or building was the most popular cultural activity (31 percent), followed by visiting a museum (24 percent), visiting an art gallery (15 percent), and seeing live theater (14 percent).

In a broader sense, cultural tourism may include exposure to such regional or ethnically different locations as the Amish countryside in Pennsylvania, smaller communities throughout French Canada where the culture is determinedly Gallic, or visits to Native American reservations throughout the West—destinations that have special appeal for many Europeans. It may also involve what Canadian authorities term "heritage tourism," with trips to see old mines, factories, or prisons that have been redesigned to provide today's visitors with a fuller understanding of the past.

Increasingly, festivals or holiday events commemorate famous battles of the past, scenes of the Civil War, or other historic events. Even rodeos, which illustrate the real-life work of cowboys in the American West, or lumberjack contests and similar competitions at state fairs, serve as experiences that make this kind of tourism meaningful. Confer and Kerstetter sum up the meaning of heritage tourism:

> It is about the cultural traditions, places, and values that groups throughout the world are proud to conserve. Cultural traditions such as family patterns, religious practices, folklore traditions, and social customs attract individuals interested in heritage tourism, as do monuments, museums, battlefields, historic structures, and landmarks. [It also includes] natural heritage sites—gardens, wilderness areas of scenic beauty, and valued cultural landscapes.[21]

Ancestral tourism focuses on people who are trying to find the family roots and is frequently called in the industry, "trading on the family roots." Americans are particularly interested in their family history and spend millions of dollars annually on ancestral tourism. Ancestral tourism involves such experiences as traveling to historical sites, visiting international destinations where ancestors were known or suspected to originate, attending conferences and workshops on genealogy, and so forth. The industry has continued to grow as Americans turn inward toward an understanding of their roots.

Linked to this type of cultural and historic exploration, such organizations as American Youth Hostels or the Elderhostel movement, which serves older travelers, combine educational and cultural exposures with what are usually short-term stays in foreign lands or distant locations.

Sport Tourism

Sport tourism has become a major force in the tourism marketplace beginning in the mid-1980s. There have always been major sporting events that drew tens of thousands and even millions of people, but more recently sport has "become regarded as the world's largest social phenomenon"[22] while tourism became the world's biggest industry. Sport tourism traditionally is defined as two separate functions: (1) travel to participate in sporting events and (2) travel to be a spectator. There are several models describing sport tourism, with the majority separating participation from observation. Building on participation and observation the discussion begins to focus on settings for sport tourism. Gammon and Robinson provide a model suggesting *sport tourism* for individuals who travel specifically for sport while *tourism sport* involves individuals traveling and participating in sport as a secondary activity. The latter is typically seen as ancillary to the primary purpose of travel and not considered in discussions of sport tourism.[23]

It is estimated that Americans took 60 million trips in 1998 to attend or take part in a sports event, spending $27 billion and accounting for nearly 6 percent of the 1.2 billion trips that year. The vast majority of these events were for regional or local events. The Friday night high school sport has a strong following in certain parts of the United States. On any fall Saturday afternoon, college football stadiums across the country are full of eager fans and parking lots are reminiscent of social gatherings as tailgate parties become more important than the game itself. Following a team to a football bowl game becomes an excuse for an extended holiday vacation. In 2003, over 46 million people attended college football games and another 21.6 million attended professional football games. Data is not available for high school football game, basketball game, or other sport attendance, but with over 16,000 high school athletic administrators, it can be suggested that attendance is high.[24]

Sporting events and sport places both serve as destination events. The 1896 Olympic stadium sits in downtown Athens and receives more visitors than the now closed Athens 2006 Olympic site. The College Football Hall of Fame, Professional

■ *National and international sporting events brand their events with logos promoting recognition among visitors, advertisers, and participants.*

Baseball Hall of Fame, and the NCAA Hall of Champions all draw many visitors. Visitations to sport facilities when teams are out of town or out of season is now commonplace. The Indianapolis Pacers and Conseco Fieldhouse charge an admission when visiting the fieldhouse, which goes to local charities. Yankee Stadium is probably the most visited baseball stadium in the United States, because it holds a rich heritage of baseball greatness.

Major sporting events draw large numbers of tourists and have significant impacts on the local, regional, and national economies. The Indianapolis Motor Speedway, home of the Indianapolis 500, is the site of the oldest auto race in the world. The Indianapolis Motor Speedway operated a single race from 1911 to 1993. In 1994, the Brickyard 400, a major new NASCAR race, was initiated and is now called the "Allstate 400 at the Brickyard." Six years later a Formula One race was added, making Indianapolis the race capital of the world. Indianapolis reported the first Formula One race resulted in the single busiest day at the Indianapolis International Airport for private jets, while the owners of limousines and hotels reported similar results. These events pale by comparison to mega sport events such as the Olympic Games or the Soccer World Cup. Indianapolis draws over 185,000 spectators to the Indianapolis 500, the largest one-day sporting event in the world. The 2000 Sydney Olympics, a multiple-day event with many venues, by comparison, drew 6.7 million people and the 2006 World Cup drew 3.4 million spectators.

Religion-Based Tourism

Centuries ago, one of the motivations spurring international travel was pilgrimages. Today, religion-oriented travel is one of the industry's fastest-growing segments. Tours highlight Christian, Jewish, Muslim, and even Buddhist places of importance. Describing a visit to the Mount of the Beatitudes in Israel, part of a two-week Holy Land church group trip arranged with the help of the Israel Government Tourist Office, one tourist commented:

This is the most joyful day of my life. To think I am standing where Christ preached the Sermon on the Mount, saying his words in this sacred place, is really a fantasy come true.[25]

Although Jerusalem represents the best-known and most popular such destination, other religion-based tours involve trips to Pamplona in Spain, which has appeal for all three major religions, and to ancient synagogues, churches, and cemeteries throughout Europe, the Middle and Far East, and the Americas:

> The dream of spiritual pilgrimage is one travelers are fulfilling in rapidly increasing numbers, making religious tourism a $1 billion a year business worldwide and creating a boom for tour companies specializing in religious themes. . . . Trips range from deeply religious programs with prayer services conducted by accompanying clergymen to cultural heritage journeys that bring spiritual connection [by exploring a people's past] through historical documentation rather than religious rituals.[26]

Nauvoo, Illinois, has become an American religion-based tourism site. Home to the Latter-day Saints (Mormons) from 1839 to 1842, and has received increased tourism focus over the last 25 years as the Latter-day Saint Church and nonprofit groups have restored much of the original area and in 2002 replaced the 1846 temple. Tourism visits soared from 200,000 in 1999 to 1.5 million in 2002. The impact on the economy of this community of 1,100 was $22 million.

■ *Religious-based tourism can take place in many settings such as this monastery near Sparta, Greece.*

Often, such trips are not narrowly denominational but bring members of various faiths together to explore their linked heritages and contrast their present beliefs and practices.

Health-Related Tourism

Recognizing that religious travel is for many persons a means of obtaining spiritual well-being and emotional health, it should be stressed that for many other individuals health needs represent a primary motivation for travel. In Europe, particularly, visits to traditional health spas that are based on natural mineral springs are being gradually replaced by stays at more modern health and fitness centers. These destinations often combine varied forms of exercise, nutritional care, massage, yoga, and other holistic approaches to health care to provide a fuller range of services to visitors. Whereas weight reduction or recovery from alcohol or drug addiction is the primary focus of many such centers, others involve a much broader approach to achieving "wellness."

A recent trend related to health-motivated travel is medical tourism. In response to rising health care and insurance costs in their home countries, citizens from the United States and United Kingdom are increasingly seeking cheaper medical and surgical care in developing countries such as India, Thailand, and Mexico.[27] Medical tourism packages usually include luxury room accommodations in hospitals and are often combined with flights, transportation, and resort hotel bookings, interpreters, and airport concierge services.[28]

Ecotourism and Adventure Travel

With the growth of environmental concerns and programs over the past few decades, a form of leisure travel has emerged that is deeply concerned with the preservation and protection of the natural environment. Generally referred to as *ecotourism*, but sometimes as *nature tourism*, this approach is closely linked to environmentally sensitive outdoor recreation, in that it implies a strong degree of respect for the environment—both ecological and human. Nora Haenn writes that it is not just a new mode of traveling. Instead, ecotourism is

> a new way for travelers to relate to the places they visit. Any kind of travel adventure can take the tourist to a new place. Ecotourism's distinction is to inspire in the traveler a special kind of connection with the environment. By encouraging respect and appreciation for the environment and people of foreign lands, ecotourism promises the tourist will gain an emotional closeness to [the places visited].[29]

Ecotourism has grown an average of 20 to 34 percent a year since 1990 and in 2004 was growing globally three times faster than the traditional tourism industry. About 2.4 million Americans annually are ecotourists. One organization has suggested ecotourism is a $77 billion market, representing 5 percent of the overall U.S. travel market.

Ecotourism may be carried on at various levels of personal challenge and comfort. In one type of planned journey, travelers were scheduled to stay overnight at a camp deep in the rain forest of Brazil, with other stays on the Amazon River and in a remote jungle hotel, learning about the lives of indigenous people in this region. Later, one of the members of the group commented that "shimmying catwalks, cold showers, pushy monkeys, and killer bees were quite enough for this reluctant ecotourist."

The concept of ecotourism is entrenched in the principles of sustainable tourism, also termed *geotourism*. Sustainable tourism advocates tourism activities which are compatible with the ecological processes, sociocultural characteristics, and economic structure of the destination and that enhance the geographical character of a place.[30]

As a variant of this approach, some tourist companies offer "action vacations" that provide the traveler the chance to visit foreign lands not simply to lie on a beach but to take part in an archaeological dig, study wildlife or the local environment systematically, teach English to children, or be involved in health-care projects. As a result of heightened interest among tourists to make voluntary contributions to the communities they visit, a new form of tourism, *volunteer tourism*, is gaining popularity across the globe. Tours catering to "volun-tourists" provide cultural immersion along with opportunities for self-fulfillment through volunteer work. For example, the Cultural Restoration Tourism Project, a San Francisco–based nonprofit group, offers tours focusing on the renovation of Buddhist temples in Nepal and Mongolia starting at

$1,080 per person and I-to-I, a for-profit United Kingdom–based company offers tour packages starting at $996 for conservation and humanitarian relief (including post-tsunami recovery) work in India, Sri Lanka, China, Nepal, Vietnam, Mongolia, Costa Rica, and South Africa.[31, 32] With less of a social service orientation and more of a recreational focus, such vacations may involve high-risk adventure pastimes such as trail rides through wild country, cave diving, hang gliding, mountain climbing, or whitewater rafting on turbulent streams.

Extreme versions of adventure tourism may involve the opportunity to track down tornadoes, offered as a package deal by a number of companies in the Midwest or Southwest regions of the United States during the tornado seasons of the year.[33] Most extreme was the tour designed by a Nashua, New Hampshire, company in the mid-1990s, which offered to take thrill-seeking tourists to combat zones in parts of the former Soviet Union and spots on the Indian Ocean.

Other well-heeled adventurers today embark on expeditions to climb the Matterhorn, fly to the North Pole, break the sound barrier in a Russian MIG-25 fighter jet, or pay deposits to take suborbital rides into space (defined as 62 miles up) scheduled to be offered by commercial rocket builders.

Space Tourism Recognized as the world's newest form of tourism, it has been talked about for decades, but not until Dennis Tito of the United States blasted off into space from the Russian Space Center in April 2001 was it that the world had its first true space tourist. Since that time three additional space tourists have flown to the International Space Station on a Soyuz spacecraft. The Russian rationale for allowing individuals to become space tourists was to raise badly needed revenue for the Russian space program. Since the collapse of communism, and even before, Russia has been hard pressed to maintain its space program.

Space has been dominated by governments since the earliest days of the space programs with either Russia or the United States dominating the world's space programs. Until 2003 when China entered the staffed space flight fraternity, only the United States and Russia had put individuals into space. Government involvement changed, however, when in October 2004, a Burt Rutan–designed suborbital aircraft flew over 328,000 feet (99,974.4 meters) in altitude and was not a government-sponsored enterprise.[34] Less than 10 months later, Burt Rutan's Scaled Composites aircraft design firm joined with Virgin Atlantic's Richard Branson to create Virgin Galactic, the world's second space-based tourism firm and the first not dependent on a government for spacecraft. Estimates suggest that by 2030 space-based tourism will be the equivalent of an airline ticket in 1939. Virgin Galactic is proposing its first scheduled flight for 2007 at a price of $50,000 a customer. Futurists envision commercial space stations, flights to the moon, lunar tourism sites, and more. Today, space tourism is a unique form of meeting the demand for new experiences so frequently demanded by tourists.[35]

Hedonistic Forms of Tourism

Still other forms of tourism are designed to provide hedonistic forms of pleasure to participants. Gambling clearly represents the most popular such activity, with millions of individuals traveling each year to major casinos throughout the world or enjoying gaming as a convenient amenity on ocean cruises or major airline flights.

Gambling is a growth industry in the United States and a recognized form of personal recreation, even if it is not perceived as psychologically and socially beneficial.

At another level, thousands of young people each year roam through the Far East, including unscheduled, free-wheeling trips through Thailand, Cambodia, and Nepal, partly to experience their exotic environments, but also to take part in the drug culture that is readily available and inexpensive in these regions. Too often, many of these free spirits end as heavily substance-addicted individuals or simply disappear from sight and are not heard of again.

Finally, a form of pleasure-seeking tourism that has emerged throughout the world involves the search for sex. With the breakup of the Soviet Union, many young women from Russia, Ukraine, and other former Iron Curtain countries have been recruited as prostitutes in regions of Southern Europe and North Africa. President George Bush, speaking to the United Nations General Assembly in 2003 said:

> Each year an estimated 800,000 to 900,000 human beings are bought, sold, or forced across the world's borders [2003 U.S. State Department estimate]. Among them are hundreds of thousands of teenage girls, and others as young as 5, who fall victim to the sex trade.[36]

As an aspect of the overall tourist industry, Sheila Jeffreys points out that the sex industry has become extremely profitable, providing substantial revenues not only to individuals and the networks involved in trafficking women but to some nations that have come to depend on sex industry profits. Given the increasingly loose standards or expectations of public morality, Jeffreys points out that a growing number of "normalizers" today take the position that sex tourism and other forms of prostitution should come to be seen as a legitimate leisure industry, one in which women and children are literally "men's leisure."[37] Obviously, such issues raise serious questions about the meaning and purpose of leisure within national life, as well as the specific kinds of controls that should be exerted over various forms of play.

MARKETING ADVANCES IN TRAVEL AND TOURISM

Perhaps more than in any other form of recreation, travel and tourism illustrate the increasing sophistication that is used to market leisure experiences today. Within this highly competitive but immensely lucrative field, as M. Uysal has pointed out, it is no longer possible to think of tourists as a large, homogeneous market. Instead, the planning and marketing of travel and tourist destinations must take into account the highly specialized interests of vacationers, their tastes in comfort and service, and their growing awareness of values and costs.[38]

Marketing segmentation studies, Uysal notes, must assess the socioeconomic and demographic variables of potential tourists, as well as product-related variables (having to do with transportation, length of stay, recreation activity, and similar factors); psychographic variables such as personal lifestyle and personality traits; geographical variables; and cultural factors such as religion, ethnic origin, and national customs.

New Links Between Public and Commercial Sponsors

It is becoming apparent that both public and commercial agencies have an important stake in promoting successful tourist programs today. In the past, tourism has been regarded as a commercial economic phenomenon rooted in the private business sector. Today, with cities, states, and entire nations competing to attract large numbers of tourists because of their contribution to the overall economy, both government agencies and private entrepreneurs have joined forces in planning and promoting tourist attractions.

At another level, as this chapter has shown, many states and local governments have moved vigorously into cooperative ventures to sponsor and promote varied forms of tourist attractions, both to heighten their positive image and to draw needed revenues and bolster local employment.

SUMMARY

Tourism involves huge sections of the leisure-service field, is provided by many different kinds of organizations, and has developed into a complex discipline in terms of job specialization, academic preparation, professional societies, and career opportunity.

Travel and tourism represent diverse forms of leisure activity, with immense economic revenues. This chapter describes some of the most popular forms of tourism, such as visits to theme parks and water parks, cruises, and tours of various types—adventure, religious, cultural, or hedonism directed. Tourism appears to be running the risk of being overbuilt in a number of areas, with the supply of costly attractions exceeding the demand in the decades ahead.

QUESTIONS FOR CLASS DISCUSSION OR ESSAY EXAMINATION

1. Tourism may be carried on for many purposes: exploration of different environments, cultural or educational purposes, adventure and risk, or hedonism. Give examples of such forms of tourism, based on class members' experiences.
2. Select either theme parks or cruise ship lines and describe their role today in the tourism industry, including current trends and new formulas for appealing to the public.

ENDNOTES

1. R. McIntosh, C. Goeldner, and J. R. Brent Ritchie, *Tourism: Principles, Practices, Philosophies* (New York: John Wiley and Sons, 1995): 2.

2. World Trade Organization, "Basic References on Tourism Statistics," 2000, www.world-tourism.org.statistics.tsa_project/basic_references/index-en.htm.

3. ITA: Office of Travel and Tourism Industries, "Travel and Tourism Research Programs," www.tinet.ita.gov/research/index.html.

4. U.S. Census Bureau, "Statistical Abstract of the United States," 2007. www.census.gov.

5. ITA: Office of Travel and Tourism Industries, "Travel and Tourism Research Programs," www.tinet.ita.gov/research/index.html.

6. Lorri K. Krebs, "The Internet and Tourism: Changing Travel Patterns and Behaviour," abstract for the 2003 Annual Meeting of the American Association of Geographers. Available at http://convention.allacademic.com/aag2003/session_info.html?c_session_id=987&dtr_id=1163.

7. Robert Schley, "Travel Planning Online," *The Futurist* (November/December 1997): 12.

8. Snapshots International Ltd., "US Online Tourism 2003," http://dx.doi.org/10.1337/us173203, 2003.

9. Gregory M. Lamb, "Next Wave of Travel Websites Feels like MySpace," *The Christian Science Monitor* (21 June 2006).

10. Gene Sloan, "Strings Can Be Pulled on Hotel-Review Sites; Travelers Tend to Be Fair, but Bogus Postings Exist," *USA Today* (17 March 2006).

11. Judith Burns, "Trip Talk: A Look at Some of the Best Blogs for Talking and Learning About Travel," *Wall Street Journal* (26 June 2006).

12. L. Berger and J. Engle, "News, Tips and Bargains; Travel Log; On-Time Ratings Tracked," *Los Angeles Times* (27 November 2005): L3.

13. D. Buhalis and O. Deimezi, "E-Tourism Developments in Greece: Information Communication Technologies Adoption for the Strategic Management of the Greek Tourism Industry," *Tourism Hospitality Research* (August 2004): 103–130.

14. J. Crompton and C. Van Doren, "Amusement Parks, Theme Parks, and Municipal Leisure Services: Contrasts in Adaptation to Cultural Change," *Journal of Physical Education, Recreation, and Dance—Leisure Today* (October 1976): 45.

15. Andy Riga, "Why We're Still Wild About Zoos," *The Gazette* (8 April 2006): B3.

16. Debora Vrana, "New Thrills, and Risk, for Theme Parks: Local Attractions Are Betting Millions on Faster, Scarier Rides to Draw Guests," *Los Angeles Times* (21 March 2004): C1.

17. Andy Newman, "Higher! Faster! Wetter! Racing to be Summer's Hot Ride; Making Summer Happen/The Thrill Merchants," *New York Times* (4 June 2004): F1.

18. Robert M. Thorson, "Where Elephants Roam? American High Plains Preserve Would Protect Species," *Hartford Courant* (16 March 2006): A9.

19. International Council of Cruise Lines, "The Cruise Industry: 2004 Economic Summary," www.icl.org/resources/2004_econ_summary.pdf, 2004.

20. National Assembly of State Arts Agencies, "Cultural Tourism Defined," www.nasaa-arts.org/artworks/cultour.shtml.

21. J. C. Confer and D. L. Kerstetter, "Past Perfect: Exploration of Heritage Tourism," *Parks and Recreation* (February 2000): 28.

22. Joseph Kurtzman and John Zauhr, "A Wave in Time—The Sports Tourism Phenomena," *Journal of Sport Tourism* (Vol. 8, No. 1): 35–47.

23. Sean Gammon and Tom Robinson, "Sport and Tourism: A Conceptual Framework," *Journal of Sport Tourism* (Vol. 8, No. 1): 21–26.

24. U.S. Census Bureau, "Statistical Abstract of the United States," 2007. www.census.gov.

25. Judi Dash, "Journeys of Faith," *New York Times* (4 April 1999): T6.

26. Ibid.

27. "VOA News: U.S. Senate Weighs Risks, Attractions of Medical Tourism," *US Federal News Service* (29 June 2006).

28. "The Global Health Service: Whether You Agree with It or Not, Medical Tourism Is Booming," *The Guardian* (18 May 2006): 26.

29. Nora Haenn, "A New Tourist, a New Environment: Can Ecotourism Deliver?" *Trends* (Vol. 3, No. 2, 1994): 28.

30. "Geotourism, the Future of Tourism: National Geographic," *AAP General Newswire* (28 November 2005).

31. Kris Petcharawises, "Vacation Volunteers, Travelers Who Want to Give Back, Donate Time and Money to Relief Efforts Around the World," *Newsday* (29 May 2005): D6.

32. Kevin Voict, "Volunteer Tourism: More Travelers Are Lending a Hand," *Asian Wall Street Journal* (23 December 2005): W4.

33. Dan McGraw, "Whirlwind Tourism," *U.S. News and World Report* (8 June 1998): 58.

34. Scaled Composites, www.scaled.com.

35. Virgin Galactic, www.virgingalactic.com.

36. "President Bush Addresses United Nations General Assembly," Office of the Press Secretary (23 September 2003), www.whitehouse.gov.

37. Sheila Jeffreys, "Globalizing Sexual Exploitation: Sex Tourism and the Traffic in Women," *Leisure Studies* (Vol. 18, 1999): 179.

38. M. Uysal, "Marketing for Tourism: A Growing Field," *Parks and Recreation* (October 1986): 61.

CHAPTER 11

SPORT AS LEISURE

◆ ◆ ◆

People desire spectator sport opportunities, and professional and amateur sports organizations have created substantial sporting events to fulfill that niche. [Many others] seek more active participation, and leisure professionals have attempted to create recreation sport opportunities for them, [in] public and private, nonprofit and for profit, college and university, and employee service recreation settings.[1]

◆ ◆ ◆

INTRODUCTION

Sport, on its various levels, represents a major area of recreational programming today and constitutes a powerful economic force through the attraction for people of every age and background. This chapter presents an overview of sport, emphasizing its role within the leisure spectrum, the rapid expansion of sport over the past several decades, and the prospects for the years that lie ahead.

SPORT AS POPULAR RECREATION

Although some athletes or social commentators may demean their importance, the reality is that sport represent far more than trivial amusement or childish play in U.S. society. Any industry that involves more than $200 billion in equipment and facilities, personnel costs, admissions charges, television fees, and other forms of expenditure must be based on more than superficial appeal.[2] Of all types of leisure involvement, it seems likely that sport command the highest degree of personal interest and emotional involvement both for those who participate actively in them and those who are part of a vast army of fans of school, college, and professional teams.

Sport are generally defined as physical activities demanding exertion and skill, involving competition, and carried on with both formal rules and general standards of etiquette and fair play. Some authorities describe them more concisely as activities with clear performance standards involving competition through physical exertion, governed by norms defining role relationships, typically performed by members of organized groups with the goal of achieving a reward through the defeat of other participants.

Clearly, sport activities, in terms of both participation and spectator involvement, represent key leisure interests for most youth and adults today. Apart from amateur, school, and college play, there are professional sport, which have clearly become a form of big business. They are moneymakers, sponsored by powerful commercial interests and promoted by advertising, public relations, television, radio, magazines, and newspapers and bolstered by the loyalty of millions of fans who identify closely with their favorite teams and star athletes.

The *2002 Abstract of the United States*, published by the U.S. Census Bureau, reported that in 2000 Americans spent $74.4 billion for sporting goods. Included in this figure were $13.6 billion for shoes, $13.5 billon for pleasure boats, $5.1 billion for bicycles and supplies, $3.9 billion for golf (excluding greens fees), and $3.8 billion for exercise equipment.

In early 2006, the National Sporting Goods Association reported that Americans spent $89.9 billion for sporting goods purchases (Table 11.1). Included in this figure were $36.9 billion for recreational transport (bicycles, pleasure boats, RVs, and snowmobiles), $16.3 billion for footwear, and $12.3 billion for clothing. From the $23.9 billions spent for sport activity–related equipment the same year, exercise equipment purchases totaled $5.2 billion in sales. Consumers also spent $3.5 billion for golf (excluding greens fees), $3.4 billion for hunting and firearms, $2.6 billion for team goods, $442 million for downhill skiing, and $397 million for tennis equipment (Table 11.2).

Beyond these figures, gate receipts for amateur, college, and professional sport significantly contributed to the impact the sport industry has on the U.S. economy.[3] In 2006, the National Basketball Association (NBA) reported for a second consecutive season the highest average attendance in its history, 17,558 spectators per game, and the highest total attendance, with a new record of 21.6 million spectators. Basketball arenas were in average filled to 91.4 percent of their total capacity.[4] Major League Baseball (MLB) experienced similar success. The league recorded the second-best record for average game attendance in the sport's history with 31,381 spectators, and broke its season attendance record—for a second year in a row—with 75.5 million

TABLE 11.1

2005 SPORTING GOODS PURCHASES BY CATEGORY (IN MILLIONS)

	2003	2004	2005	2006**	% Change 2005 vs. 2004
Equipment	22,394	23,328	23,981	24,450	3
Footwear	14,446	14,752	15,711	16,268	7
Clothing	10,543	11,201	11,650	12,292	4
Recreational Transportation*	32,396	36,560	38,493	36,856	5
Total	**79,778**	**85,811**	**89,936**	**89,886**	**5**

*Bicycles, pleasure boats, RVs, and snowmobiles; projections provided by other associations.
**Projected.
Source: National Sporting Goods Association (2006). www.nsga.org/public/pages/index.cfm?pageid=161.

TABLE 11.2

2005 SPORTING GOODS PURCHASES BY SPORT (SELECTED SPORTS) (IN MILLIONS)

Sport Activity	2004	2005	2006 (forecast)
Exercise	$5,074	$5,207	$5,363
Golf	$3,198	$3,474	$3,509
Hunting & Firearms	$3,175	$3,351	$3,418
Team Goods Sales	$2,517	$2,568	$2,619
Fishing Tackle	$2,026	$2,139	$2,182
Camping	$1,531	$1,442	$1,456
Billiards and Indoor Games	$622	$572	$567
Skiing, Downhill	$452	$442	$457
Baseball/Softball	$352	$372	$384
Tennis	$362	$397	$405
Basketball	$309	$309	$312
Skiing, Snowboards	$269	$280	$292

Source: National Sporting Goods Association (2006). www.nsga.org/public/pages/index.cfm?pageid=162.

tickets sold.[5] The most popular league in the United States, the National Football League (NFL) set its attendance record for the third straight year, with a game average of 66,453 spectators in its regular season, and a record-high total attendance with 17 million tickets sold. The tickets sold during the 2005–2006 season surpassed 90 percent of stadium capacity.[6] In accordance with gate receipts, increases were also experienced in television viewership, website traffic, merchandise sales, and

■ *Participation in public park and recreation programs allows individuals to continue to participate in sport regardless of age.*

marketing partnerships in the form of corporate sponsorship for all professional leagues.

In 2005, sports remained the dominant driver for corporate sponsorship. The World Sponsorship Monitor (TWSM) review, which observes and documents corporate sponsorship agreements (deals) from all over the world, revealed that the volume of recorded deals increased 18 percent compared to the volume of deals documented in 2004. Such deals involve sports, arts and culture, broadcast, and other. The monetary value recorded for all deals increased to $10 billion, with sport sponsorship accounting for 91 percent of this money.[7]

All these figures, from sporting goods purchases and gate receipts to the increase of sport-related corporate sponsorship deals, attest to the tremendous popularity of sport, both as a form of active recreation for all ages and as spectator entertainment.

The sport field has continued to grow, with the expansion of professional sport leagues, the emphasis on youth sport programs, and the spread of typically American sport such as baseball, football, and basketball to many other nations of the world.

However, as sport have become more commercialized and expensive for the average American family to attend, with professional players receiving astronomical salaries and team franchises skipping from city to city, many fans have become disillusioned with the changing nature of sport.

PATTERNS OF SPORT INVOLVEMENT

Participation in Sport Activities

Although sport is obviously an important form of free-time activity, in many ways it does not conform to the traditional view of leisure. Rather than relaxed activity carried on within a context of casual free choice, sport is often highly structured, purposeful, and disciplined, with elaborate rules and rich rewards.

Sport is also engaged in at several levels of competitive skills and intensity, ranging from informal neighborhood play to youth sport leagues or school and college play and extending to professional competition and even international play in the Olympics and other large-scale events.

In addition to school, college, and professional leagues, millions of sport participants are served by municipal, county, or special district recreation and park departments, nonprofit youth organizations (many of which focus on a single sport, such as Little League or Pop Warner football leagues), country clubs, and military recreation services. In general, the management of sport events, the setting of standards and rules for play, and similar functions are carried out by national organizations that govern competition and promote instructional programs for youth.

Some forms of sport are primarily masculine in participation and interest: among them are snowboarding with 74.2 percent male participation, baseball (77.7 percent), golf (79 percent), ice hockey (82.5 percent), and football (87.6 percent). Others are mainly geared toward feminine interests (exercise walking, 60.3 percent; aerobic exercising, 70.4 percent; and cheerleading, 94 percent) and still others are gender neutral (skiing with female participation at 49.4 percent; softball, 50.6 percent; swimming, 50.7 percent; and volleyball, 52.1 percent).[8] In terms of age levels, many active sport are most popular during the teenage or young adult years, although some games and active outdoor pursuits actually increase in participation among those in older age brackets. With respect to income level, participation is usually highest for those in the $50,000 to $74,999 income brackets, although sport such as golf, soccer, downhill skiing, and tennis have their highest rate of involvement in the over-$50,000 bracket. These generalizations only tell part of the story. Males were the dominant purchasers of sporting goods and admission tickets. Women, however, were the dominant purchasers of aerobic shoes and walking shoes. Age also has an impact, as the 45-year to 64-year age group was the dominant purchaser of walking shoes, exercise equipment, fishing tackle, and hunting gear.

The most popular sport activities, in terms of participation, are identified in Table 11.3. As indicated earlier, a number of the pastimes listed might better be described as outdoor recreation pursuits, such as exercise walking or camping. Others, such as skiing, swimming, or even fishing, are usually engaged in as noncompetitive recreation, although they may represent part of school or college competition or large-scale tournaments.

TEAM SPORT PARTICIPATION

The *2005 U.S. Trends in Team Sports Report* by the Sporting Goods Manufacturers Association (SGMA) reveals several key findings regarding team-sport participation. These findings provide a realistic assessment of participation patterns in sport activities, and are a useful tool for sport and recreation management professionals in developing successful strategies to serve the needs, desires, and interests of leisure-product consumers, recreational organizations, sporting goods companies, and local, state and federal governments.

An alarming situation is the millions of casual sport participants who have dropped out of team-sport activities every year since 1984. The overall number of children age six and older, who participated in team sport at least once within each calendar year since 1984, has declined. A similar trend is observed for participants who play team sport more frequently (that is 25 or more days per year). Since 1995, more that three

TABLE 11.3

2005 PARTICIPATION IN SPORT ACTIVITIES (IN MILLIONS)—RANKED BY TOTAL PARTICIPATION*

Activity	ALL PERSONS		SEX	
	Number	Percent Change**	Male	Female
Exercise Walking	86.0	1.5	34.2	51.8
Swimming	58.0	8.5	28.6	29.4
Exercising with Equipment	54.2	4.0	25.5	28.7
Camping	46.0	−16.8	25.4	20.6
Bowling	45.4	3.5	23.9	21.5
Fishing	43.3	5.2	30.3	13.0
Bicycle Riding	43.1	7.0	24.2	18.9
Billiards/Pool	37.3	8.9	23.6	13.7
Weight Lifting	35.5	35.4	22.8	12.7
Workout at Club	34.7	9.2	14.6	20.1
Aerobic Exercising	33.7	14.4	10.0	23.7
Basketball	29.9	7.3	20.5	9.4
Hiking	29.8	5.0	16.4	13.4
Running/Jogging	29.2	9.5	16.3	12.9
Boating, Motor/Power	27.5	20.9	16.0	11.5
Golf	24.7	0.8	19.5	5.2
Target Shooting	21.9	14.2	16.9	5.0
Hunting with Firearms	19.4	9.7	17.0	2.4
Baseball	14.6	−7.7	11.3	3.3
Soccer	14.1	6.4	8.3	5.8
Softball	14.1	12.7	7.0	7.1
Backpack/Wilderness	13.3	−13.3	8.5	4.8
Volleyball	13.2	11.9	6.3	6.9
In-Line Roller Skating	13.1	12.3	6.9	6.2
Skateboarding	12.0	16.5	9.0	3.0
Tennis	11.1	15.6	5.8	5.3
Scooter Riding	10.4	−19.4	6.4	4.0
Football (tackle)	9.9	15.5	8.7	1.2
Mountain Bike (off road)	9.2	14.9	5.7	3.5
Paintball Games	8.0	−15.1	7.0	1.0
Kayaking/Rafting	7.6	n.a.	4.2	3.4
Skiing (alpine)	6.9	9.5	3.5	3.4
Archery (target)	6.8	28.5	5.4	1.4
Water Skiing	6.7	26.9	3.9	2.8
Target Shooting (Airgun)	6.7	30.6		
Hunting w/Bow & Arrow	6.6	13.8	5.8	0.8
Snowboarding	6.0	−8.9	4.5	1.5
Muzzleloading	4.1	7.6	3.8	0.3
Cheerleading	3.3	−13.2	0.2	3.1
Hockey (ice)	2.4	0.4	2.0	0.4
Skiing (cross country)	1.9	−20.4	1.0	0.9

*Participated more than once (in millions); Seven years of age and older.
**Percent change is from 2004.
Source: National Sporting Goods Association (2006). www.nsga.org/public/pages/index.cfm?pageid=152.

million sport participants have quit participating and migrated to other leisure activities.

Several factors contribute to this emerging problem. In inner-city environments, the availability of free space for recreational sport is extremely limited. Empty fields where children can gather after school and play a pick-up game are not the norm. At the same time, the lack of time for parental supervision and increased concerns for child safety have led a great number of parents to search for alternative ways (recreation centers, playgrounds, private or sectarian leagues) to introduce sport to their children. This is evident for single-parent families or families where both parents support full-time jobs.[9]

Demographic changes also affect team-sport participation rates. Today, research shows that team-sport participation is as high as 70 percent for young children reaching age 11 and declines to 50 percent as youngsters reach age 18. It is evident

■ *Youth sports continues to grow as a major segment of the sport industry.*

that a combination of factors like adolescence and school workload may play a decisive role in this decline. Projections for the next 10 years are not encouraging for the same segment of the population. It is expected that participation for youth between 5–19 years old will grow only 3.6 percent, which translates to a greater decline in team-sport participation.[10]

Although unorganized team-sport participation is declining, a reversed trend is experienced in organized team activities. There, participation rates have grown steadily since 1990 for all major sport activities found in high school and college athletics, as well as recreational league play. Participation in activities organized by not-for-profit recreation and sport organizations is steadily growing, and has replaced the traditional pick-up games and neighborhood after-school play. This growth is attributed to a greater number of females participating in organized activities as a result of the attitude changes in society regarding girls participating in organized team sports, and increasing opportunities for athletic scholarships through intercollegiate sports because of Title IX. This legislation is probably the single major factor that has driven team-sport participation numbers up since 1990. According to data provided by the National Federation of State High School Associations (NFHS), approximately three million females played interscholastic sports in 2005, an increase of 54 percent since 1990.

The largest sport activity in interscholastic athletics for males is football. Participation rates have grown 14 percent since 1990. Although not the most popular sport, soccer has experienced a phenomenal growth of 55 percent and more than 350,000 participants during the same period of time. Basketball is the preferred sport for females. Participation rates have grown 18 percent since 1990. Soccer is also among the fastest growing sport choice for females. Since 1990, the sport has experienced growth that exceeds 160 percent, with a total of 300,000 girls playing the game. Fast-pitch softball, volleyball, and outdoor track and field follow soccer as the fastest-growing sport with 66 percent, 33 percent, and 28 percent, respectively.[11]

In intercollegiate athletics, the picture is slightly different. It is not a surprise that football remains the largest sport in terms of participation number with a 21 percent growth since 1990. However, the fastest growing sport for males is now baseball with a total of 27,000 athletes playing the game; this is a 33 percent increase in participation since 1990. Conversely, female athletes in college prefer soccer over basketball. The sport has experienced a growth of 201 percent since 1990 with more than 20,000 student athletes playing the game.

Beyond interscholastic and intercollegiate sports, participation in recreational league play also portrays tremendous growth. A vivid example is Amateur Athletic Union basketball, where between 1990 and 2004, the number of girls playing the game increased 346 percent; similarly, the number of boys playing the game increased by 171 percent. Similar participation growth patterns are experienced in most recreational league sports.[12]

Spectator Aspect of Sport

The importance people attribute to spectator sports is evident in a series of business-related actions: (a) television ratings and broadcasting fees, (b) player salaries, (c) franchise values, (d) public subsidy of sport facilities, and (e) cost associated with attending a sporting event.

Ratings and Broadcasting Fees

The spectator aspect of sport is vividly shown in the immense sums paid by television networks for the right to broadcast college and professional contests. The driver behind the multibillion dollar contracts networks sign with major league sport are the television ratings and audiences these sport are able to attract. Each rating point represents 1.1 million households in the United States, or 1 percent of the nation's 110.2 million houses with a television set in place. High ratings mean great audiences, and great audiences are very appealing to sponsors and advertisers.

In summer 2006, the Soccer World Cup final in Berlin attracted 17 million viewers in the United States, 150 percent over the 2002 final. More than a third of these spectators chose the Spanish-language broadcast on the UNIVISION channel.[13] During the 2006 NFL season, NBC's first regular-season broadcast in eight years had a 12.6 household rating (13.9 million households) and a 21 percent share (percentage of in-use televisions tuned to a given show). A record 19.3 million viewers tuned in to watch a Thursday night opener between the Super Bowl champion Pittsburgh Steelers and the Miami Dolphins.[14] Earlier that year, the Super Bowl mega event attracted 90 million viewers.

Similar success in securing high television ratings exists for both the NBA and MLB. Both leagues have a strong ratings record that spans several years back in time. However, MLB's 2006 World Series reported the lowest rating ever (10.1 rating), which was a 9 percent drop from the previous year's series.[15] Network officials attributed this decrease to factors related to the game starting time, the small market size of the rivals, and competition from other professional sport.[16]

High television ratings lead to fierce negotiations between league officials and network executives when television contracts are about to expire, or new media packages (Internet broadcasting, pay per view, and so forth) are available for bid.

The NFL is "unquestionably the most successful and popular sports league in America, fueled by record attendance in 2005, off-the-chart television ratings and a television contract worth nearly $25 billion over the next six years."[17] In 2006, the NBC network agreed to pay $3.6 billion for a six-year agreement with the NFL to acquire the broadcasting rights for a new prime-time package, called Football Night in America. The new Sunday night package "has become overnight the NFL's pre-eminent prime-time package, relegating to sweep-up duty Monday Night Football," which relocated from ABC to ESPN the same season.[18] ESPN has an eight-year agreement with NFL, for $8.8 billion, to broadcast Monday Night Football, a very popular programming option for ABC the previous years. Furthermore, the NFL signed separate agreements with additional networks for different programming options: CBS agreed to a six-year, $3.74 billion contract for Sunday Afternoon AFC Football, and FOX followed with a six-year, $4.28 billion contract for Sunday Afternoon NFC Football. The NFL also retained the right to broadcast selected football footage through its own television channel. For the season 2007, the NFL is expected to raise more than $3.5 billion from its television contracts.[19]

Major League Baseball, America's national pastime sport, also scored big in television broadcasting fees. In 2006, the league announced a seven-year television contract that extends deals with ESPN and FOX Sports, and added TBS into its television partners.[20, 21] Broadcasting fees for both FOX and TBS contracts are worth more than $3 billion;[22] the ESPN extension contract values around $2.5 billion.[23]

In 2006, the Big Ten Conference announced the creation of a new channel, with a national outreach, that will give the 11-school conference a showcase not only for their intercollegiate programs, but also other accomplishments at the member institutions. The new channel, scheduled to launch in August of 2007, is a joint venture with the FOX network, which as the minority owner agreed to operate the channel for the next 20 years from offices located in Chicago. This new national cable and satellite channel, along with a new 10-year agreement signed with ABC Sports and ESPN, will dramatically increase the visibility of the Big Ten Conference on television and the Internet. Conference officials said this venture will help the conference enhance its brand recognition and transform it in one of the leading academic and athletic conferences in the United States. Although the financial terms of the agreement were not disclosed to the general public, it is anticipated that minority owner FOX invested a great amount of monetary and other resources toward the realization of this venture.[24]

Franchise Values and Player Salaries

The importance and magnitude of spectator sport are also evident in skyrocketing franchise values and player salaries.[25] Franchises in most major leagues have seen their values appreciating significantly in the last 5 to 10 years, with price tags reaching as high as $700 million. An example of this phenomenon is NFL's New England Patriots. When Boston businessman Robert Kraft bought the Patriots in 1994, the team's $172 million price was the league record at that time. The value of the franchise now is believed to be above $1 billion.[26]

Money Draws European Players

European players have been drawn to the United States in increasing numbers to play in the NBA and Major League Soccer (MLS), but until recently the most prominent European soccer players have not made the move. All that changed when David Beckham, one of the world's most popular athletes and the poster boy in Europe for soccer, signed with the Los Angeles Galaxy. Beckham signed in early 2007 for a five-year deal totaling a reported $250 million. The amount includes salary, endorsements, and incentives. Beckham has been defined as a brand all by himself and according to one author he is where fashion, celebrity and soccer meet. Where the NBA brought players in to augment an already popular sport, Beckham is expected to improve the image of MLS.

To help determine the fair market value of sport franchises, *Forbes* magazine conducts an annual survey evaluating factors such as the team's annual operating income, the size of the market the team operates in, stadium value, roster value, and so forth. The 2006 *Forbes* survey revealed that five NFL teams exceeded $1 billion in worth. These teams are the Washington Redskins ($1.423 billion), the New England Patriots ($1.176 billion), the Dallas Cowboys ($1.173 billion), the Houston Texans ($1.043 billion), and the Philadelphia Eagles ($1.024 billion). The New York Yankees, valued at $1.026 billion, is the only MLB franchise that exceeds the billion-dollar price tag.[27]

Players' values also have exceeded industry analysts' projections. It has been estimated that Tiger Woods will, if he continues at his present pace, earn as much as one billion dollars in golf tournament winnings and advertising commercials over his competitive lifetime. In 2005 Tiger Woods had earnings higher than any other athlete in the world. The bulk of those earnings was endorsements. Actual winnings ranked him only in the top 25 athletes and near the bottom of that list. Woods is one of the new breed of international athletes. Others included Michael Jordan, Muhammad Ali, and now include David Beckham and other athletes who cross international boundaries.

Recently, Alex Rodriguez of the New York Yankees (MLB) signed a $252 million, 10-year agreement that makes him the most expensive MLB contract in the history of the game. Players like Kobe Bryant and Lebron James, both playing in the NBA, make $136.4 million and $80 million, respectively, just from salaries.

Public Subsidy of Sport Facilities

Another sign of the significance of spectator sports is the growing number of cities entering the race to build expensive new sport stadiums in order to prevent their professional sport teams from going elsewhere or to recruit sport franchises. In 2000 it was estimated that some $24 billion worth of already, approved sport facilities would be built in the United States by 2005, with 70 percent to 80 percent of the funds to come from public money, much of this financed by tax-free bonds.

Public financed sports arenas and facilities are common among large American cities with a significant portion of the cost placed upon tax payers.

From academic and economic perspectives, critics have suggested the spiraling costs are making the entire big league sport structure unworkable and question the assumption that publicly supported sport stadiums justify themselves financially.

Attendance Costs of Spectator Sports

The increasing cost of attending a sport event is one of the factors that creates discomfort for sport fans and their families. Attending a sporting event for any one of the major leagues today can be a personal account–draining proposition.

The Fan Cost Index (FCI), a survey conducted annually by Chicago-based Team Marketing Report, a sport marketing company, provides a comparable measure of how much a family of four likely will spend attending a professional sporting event. The survey comprises the costs of two average-price adult tickets, two average-price children's tickets, four small soft drinks, two small beers, four hot dogs, two programs, parking, and two adult-size caps.

According to the 2005 FCI, the most expensive place to attend an NFL game is the Patriots' Gillette Stadium. The average ticket price was $90.89; the FCI was $477.47, 15 percent more expensive than the year before. At the same time, the league average ticket was priced at $58.95, while the average FCI was $329.82.[28] In 2006, the league average FCI for the NBA was $267.37, for the NHL $247.32, and for the MLB $171.19 (Table 11.4). Similar data is also available for minor league baseball.[29, 30, 31]

Although the FCI provides a clear idea of the attendance costs associated with professional sport, there was still no accurate measure of value in attending sporting events. In August 2005, SportsIllustrated.com developed a new method, the Fan Value Index (FVI), to test "if baseball fans at Wrigley Field are getting the same return on their investment as the fans at PETCO Park." This comprehensive survey of the experiences at each major league ballpark considered seven criteria to assess value: average ticket price, average costs of concessions/souvenirs, accessibility, various amenities, the overall atmosphere, entertainment or dining options at the vicinity of

TABLE 11.4

FAN COST INDEX FOR MAJOR LEAGUE BASEBALL, NATIONAL BASKETBALL ASSOCIATION, AND THE NATIONAL FOOTBALL LEAGUE

Major League Baseball FCI—2006

TEAM	Avg. Ticket	Beer	(oz.)	Soda	(oz.)	Hot Dog	Parking	Program	Cap	FCI	% Change
Boston	46.46	$6.00	12	$2.75	14	$4.00	$23.00	$5.00	$15.00	287.84	4.20
Chicago Cubs	34.3	$5.00	16	$2.50	15	$2.75	$17.00	$5.00	$12.00	219.21	4.38
N.Y. Yankees	28.27	$6.00	16	$3.50	16	$3.00	$12.00	$7.75	$15.00	208.57	7.59
League Avg.	22.21	$5.42	16.7	$3.07	16.9	$3.31	$11.41	$3.89	$13.62	171.19	4.13
Tampa Bay	17.09	$5.00	16	$3.75	16	$3.25	$0.00	$0.00	$15.00	129.87	-9.69
Kansas City	13.71	$3.75	12	$2.00	14	$2.50	$6.00	$5.00	$12.00	120.35	0.0

National Basketball Association FCI—2005/2006

TEAM	Avg. Ticket	Beer	(oz.)	Soda	(oz.)	Hot Dog	Parking	Program	Cap	FCI	% Change
L.A. Lakers	$79	$7.50	18	$3.00	16	$4.00	$13.00	$5.00	$10	$402.84	1.70%
New York	$71	$6.00	20	$3.25	24	$4.30	$20.00	$10.00	$12	$388.04	0.0%
Houston	$56	$5.50	16	$3.75	22	$4.00	$20.00	$0.00	$18	$321.34	2.9%
League Avg.	$46	$5.44	16.5	$2.95	17.6	$3.40	$11.67	$3.68	$14	$267.37	2.5%
New Orleans	$29	$5.00	12	$4.00	12	$4.00	$10.00	$0.00	$20	$206.44	-4.4%
Golden State	$24	$4.50	14	$2.00	14	$3.00	$12.00	$3.00	$16	$174.27	-8.2%

National Football League FCI—2005

TEAM	Avg. Ticket	Beer	(oz.)	Soda	(oz.)	Hot Dog	Parking	Program	Cap	FCI	% Change
New England	$90.89	$5.50	16	$3.50	22	$3.50	$35.00	$5.00	$14.95	$477.47	14.99%
Washington	$67.53	$7.00	20	$5.00	22	$5.00	$25.00	$5.00	$14.95	$389.01	1.70%
N.Y. Giants	$71.59	$6.25	16	$3.50	20	$3.75	$15.00	$5.00	$17.99	$388.85	5.34%
League Avg.	$58.95	$5.52	17.5	$3.22	19.6	$3.53	$16.31	$4.53	$15.30	$329.82	5.64%
Jacksonville	$40.16	$5.00	18	$3.00	24	$3.00	$10.00	$5.00	$9.95	$234.55	-2.71%
Buffalo	$39.37	$5.50	16	$3.00	20	$3.00	$15.00	n/a	$11.00	$229.49	0.42%

The average ticket price represents a weighted average of season ticket prices for general seating categories, determined by factoring the tickets in each price range as a percentage of the total number of seats in each ballpark. Luxury suites are excluded from the survey. Season-ticket pricing is used for any team that offers some or all tickets at lower prices for customers who buy season tickets.

Source: Team Marketing Report (2006).

the stadium, and the club's overall performance in the field. In an era of escalating attendance costs and numerous entertainment options, both the FCI and the FVI can be useful to sport spectators when they choose the venue and type of sport activity they want or can afford to attend.

The public outcry at the increasing costs of attendance at professional sporting events has attracted the interest of many; among them are politicians, consumer rights activists, academicians, and various recreation associations, who see this development as a direct threat to the societal fabric by driving off low-income spectators.

The League of Fans, an organization founded by consumer activist Ralph Nader, argues that Major League Baseball, with its monopoly status, has become elitist and cares less about the average baseball fan. "Major League Baseball now caters to a different class of people, and average fans and families are not as important to them for revenue generation," says Mr. Shawn McCarthy, the organization's director. "There aren't as many children at games (and) it has transformed from an affordable form of entertainment for average fans and their families to a once-a-year treat for most."[32]

Governmental statistics seem to support this notion. According to the Bureau of Labor Statistics, the average weekly earnings of production or nonsupervisory workers on private payrolls in September 2005 were $548. Census Bureau data also is discouraging for a great number of states: the median household income, for example, in Illinois, was approximately $880 a week. It is evident that if a family in Illinois received annual income around the state median, they would have to spend about a quarter, or even a larger portion, of their weekly paycheck to go to a Chicago Bulls (NBA) game.[33]

Another alarming situation has been detected in minor league professional sports. A growing number of minor league franchises are following the example the major league sets when it comes to pricing their entertainment product. As professional clubs in most major leagues become increasingly elitist, that is pricing the general public out of stadiums built through public subsidies, there is evidence that the minor league teams are beginning to adopt a similar behavior. Owners of minor league teams publicly express threats to move their franchise to other cities (and many times materialize these threats) anytime they decide they want another new stadium, without the obligation to pay for it themselves. As a result of this situation, minor league sports are

TABLE 11.5

SELECTED SPECTATOR SPORT ATTENDANCE: 1995 TO 2004

Sport Category	Unit	1995	2000	2001	2002	2003	2004
Baseball, major league attendance	1,000	51,288	74,339	73,881	69,428	69,501	74,822
Basketball							
NCAA men's colleges							
Teams	Number	868	932	937	936	967	981
Attendance	1,000	28,548	29,025	28,949	29,395	30,124	30,761
NCAA women's colleges							
Teams	Number	864	956	958	975	1,009	1,008
Attendance	1,000	4,962	8,698	8,825	9,533	10,164	10,016
Professional							
Teams	Number	27	29	29	29	29	30
Attendance, total	1,000	19,883	21,503	21,436	21,571	21,760	22,953
National Hockey League attendance	1,000	9,234	18,800	20,373	20,615	20,409	22,065

Source: Statistical Abstract of the United States, 2006. Washington D.C.: U.S. Censusus Bureau (www.census.gov).

Note: 7,000 represents 7,000,000.

in danger of becoming less about pleasing the fan and more about maximizing revenue and generating new revenue streams, even if this course of action increases fan dissatisfaction, decreases commitment levels and fan identification with the team, and prohibits low-income families to attend professional sporting events.

To illustrate the popularity of spectator sport, attendance at major college and professional league games rose during most of the 1980s and 1990s (see Table 11.5), and between 1995 and 2004 the numbers rose at a higher rate than in previous reported years.

RELIGIOUS IMPLICATIONS OF SPORT

So fervent is the public interest in college and professional sport that many scholars have concluded that they have become America's newest folk religion. One such observer, Professor Charles Prebish of the Pennsylvania State University's religious studies program, states:

> For growing numbers of Americans, sport religion has become a more appropriate expression of personal religiosity than Christianity, Judaism, or any of the traditional religions. [Consider the] terms that athletes and sportswriters regularly use: *faith, ritual, ultimate, dedicated, sacrifice, peace, commitment, spirit.*[34]

Russell Chandler points out that football often is used as a metaphor for religious faith. He describes how a young Texas Baptist, Jarrell McCracken, wrote and recorded a script that equated football with the game of life. In the recording, which led to a multimillion dollar music and publishing business:

> Jesus was the head coach, and "Average Christian" was the quarterback. The bottom line of the sermonizing allegory was that if Christians followed their heavenly blockers and skirted the evil defenders, they made it safely to the big end zone in the sky. . . . More recently, a country singer recorded a hit song that pleaded: "Drop kick me, Jesus, through the goal posts of life."[35]

Numerous athletes have attested their religious faith through membership in the Fellowship of Christian Athletes. Often players hold prayer circles on the field, and many teams in varied sport are accompanied by chaplains who counsel and inspire them. For example, in a stirring pregame sermon before Florida State University's football team played an important game, the team's chaplain preached as follows:

> I want to talk to you today about Jesus Christ when he spoke to his team at the Last Supper. He told them he was proud of them but they'd have to play the game without him. . . . This is like Coach Bowden telling you what you have to do on offense and defense. Now remember, your coaches love you. The greatest thing you can do for them is to play the best you can and then say: "God made that tackle, not me . . . and give glory to God."[36]

At another level, the importance of sport in modern society has been illustrated by the immense support given by nations—particularly Iron Curtain countries during the Soviet era—to their athletes in international competition. So fervent has such support been that it once caused an armed conflict—the so-called Soccer War—between two

Central American nations. During the 1980s and 1990s, international competition led to a number of deadly riots, several of them instigated by Great Britain's "soccer thugs."

HISTORICAL EVOLUTION OF SPORT

Although sports have had a long history of acceptance in earlier civilizations, during much of the Renaissance and early industrial period, they tended to be disapproved by moral authorities throughout Europe and the North American continent. Often, they had an unsavory reputation because of their linkage with drinking and gambling. Rader describes the metropolitan "sporting fraternity" of the late nineteenth century:

> The saloon keepers especially courted those interested in politics, sport, and gambling. There, the two extremes of society—young "dissolute" men of some means and the workingmen—could meet to review the latest sport gossip, schedule sporting events, and take bets. . . . Without ties to wives or traditional homes, many [bachelors] sought friendship and excitement at the brothels, gambling halls, billiard rooms, cockpits, boxing rings, or the race tracks.[37]

In time, team sports gained respectability in England and the United States as the concept of "muscular Christianity" entered the literature and began to be heard in religious sermons. Churches, YMCAs, and educators all encouraged sports as a means of achieving physical fitness and self-discipline and as an alternative to other forms of dissipation in play. Gradually, sport became dominated by commercial interests, and the manufacture of sporting goods evolved into a successful industry.

Sport as a Source of Moral Values

It was widely believed that sport had several important values: (1) contributing to health and physical fitness as a form of rigorous training, conditioning, and exercise; (2) building personal traits such as courage and perseverance, self-discipline, and sportsmanship; (3) encouraging social values linked to obeying rules and dedication to team goals, as well as providing a channel for social mobility, especially for individuals from disadvantaged backgrounds; and (4) serving as a force to build group loyalty, cohesiveness, and positive morale in schools and colleges and in communities throughout the nation.

Beyond these values, sport obviously has immense appeal, both for participants and for the vastly large audience of fans who often attach themselves to their favorite teams, wearing their colors or uniforms, cheering them enthusiastically, traveling to spring practice or "away" games, and contributing as loyal alumni to the recruitment or support of star athletes. This very fervor and degree of commitment to sport has led inevitably to a number of major abuses or problems affecting sport on all levels.

Abuses and Problems of Sport Competition

Sports for children too often have been influenced by adult pressures to win at all costs. As a result, youngsters often feel excessive pressure to compete and to win, and the experience is no longer fun for them. Studies show that many children about to enter their teen years quit organized sport at this point or shift to a much more relaxed, recreational approach to games.

Linked to such pressures, adults frequently encourage overaggressive and violent play, as well as tactics that ignore sportsmanship and condone rule breaking. In extreme cases, parents may verbally or physically abuse players, parents, or coaches of rival teams and even attack officials who have made decisions ruling against them.[38]

On secondary school levels, the influence of high-pressure college sport begins to make itself felt as promising young players attend special camps financed by manufacturers of sport equipment or clothing. In many cases, parents and college coaches are no longer the primary influences in helping young players make decisions about their future. Instead, Bollinger and Goss write:

> [A] network of summer basketball camps bankrolled by shoe companies has taken over the recruiting process. Hoping to attract the loyalties of players with star potential, the companies spend more than $5 million a year on these summer programs. The young men in this system sometimes play 80 to 100 games outside of the high school season.[39]

It used to be that as early as high school, players might be wooed by agents, given free merchandise, and treated to other benefits that are prohibited at the college level. This has been pushed down to much younger youth. The *New York Times* reported one 4-year-old receiving free equipment and clothes. Nike signed a 13-year-old to a $1 million deal. Reebok built a commercial campaign around a 3-year-old.[40]

Such abuses become more extreme in college competition, in which, especially in high-visibility sport such as basketball and football, there has been a long history of academic violations. Players too often are recruited with faked course records or doctored school transcripts and are academically coddled as long as they remain eligible to compete—to the point that they accomplish little real college work and leave without degrees.

Again and again, there have been scandals and investigations involving gambling on college sport—often with players themselves betting on games—or having to do with the criminal behavior of athletes. In professional sport, conflicts between players and owners, the sudden departures of favorite athletes, or the transfer of sports franchises all have strengthened the public perception of sport as "just a business" and have eroded fan loyalty and attendance in many cities.

Other problems surrounding sport on all levels have involved physically dangerous and even life-threatening conditioning practices and hazing in sport such as ice hockey or football, which has included physical, emotional, and even sexual abuse.[41]

Finally, the practices of building expensive new stadiums with costly skyboxes and adding charges for the right to buy season tickets have dramatically escalated the financial costs for fans. In many cases, the middle-class or blue-collar audience who has traditionally supported professional sport, particularly in large, older cities, is no longer able to do so. As a result, there is disturbing evidence that the fan base for professional sports is declining and that many members of the public are instead transferring their loyalties to local, minor league teams, in part because of nostalgic affection for sport "as it used to be."

On the international scene, sports corruption has been even worse. In late 2002, the British Broadcasting System (BBC) reported a meeting of European sport ministers who were attempting to combat child exploitation in sport. In a number of documented cases, African youth were lured into contracts with professional soccer teams, but when they didn't make the team they were sometimes abandoned and became illegal immigrants without language skills or the ability to make a living. Belgium, France, and Holland have been cited as the countries most likely to see preteens and young teens brought in on tourist visas and then abandoned.

Even the Olympics Games, traditionally viewed idealistically as amateur sport at its best, were revealed in 1999 as having involved widespread bribery in the awarding of the 2000 Summer Olympics to Sydney, Australia, and the 2002 Winter Olympics to Salt Lake City.[42]

Beyond corruption at this level, the constant disclosure of prohibited performance-enhancing drugs and "blood doping" being used in international sport has helped to destroy public confidence in such events as the major bicycling event, the Tour de France, and other competitions.[43] Championship boxing matches have been shown to be under the control of criminal elements, and fixed soccer games have threatened the integrity of international competition at the highest level.[44]

FUTURE TRENDS IN SPORT

Whether such negative trends accelerate, sport managers and participants on all levels need to deal with the problems that have been presented in this chapter. Clearly, the continuing expansion of professional sport has reached a point of diminishing returns. If team owners and league policy makers are to retain or regain fan loyalty, it will be necessary to curb the growing costs of sport attendance, which are clearly tied to the astronomical salaries being paid to star players and the greediness of team owners.

Improving Youth Sport

In general, sport as a recreational pursuit appears to be on a healthier footing. Some critics complain that children and youth are excessively scheduled in athletics as well as other free-time activities and that organized play has driven out the kinds of spontaneous neighborhood games that children used to play. However, the reality is that the major national organizations in baseball, softball, basketball, football, and soccer, as well as many others in individual and team sports, have been successful in providing opportunities for play for many millions of young participants.

In terms of the need to control overemphasis on winning, excessive parental pressures, or the kinds of physical, emotional, and even sexual abuse of participants by coaches that have received publicity in recent years, a number of leading national organizations have mobilized to improve youth sport. Such private, nonprofit organizations as the Sports Coaches Association in West Palm Beach, Florida, and Parents and Coaches in Sports in Park City, Utah, have developed ongoing campaigns to enlighten parents and promote positive coaching approaches.

Organizations representing individual sport, such as Little League Baseball, the American Youth Soccer Organization, or the United States Tennis Association, have not only developed guidelines and regulations for the same purposes but have also initiated campaigns to prevent drug use among youth and to encourage fuller participation by minority group children and in inner-city areas.

Declining Support in Physical Education Programs

All of these efforts are particularly important given the marked decline in the support of physical education—including sport instruction and sponsorship—in many elementary and secondary schools throughout the United States. As a result of shifting educational priorities and economic pressures, many school physical education programs have been sharply cut back. Deborah Tannehill writes:

> Generally, the trend has progressed from daily required physical education for all children to our current status of a limited number of hours per week or credits per year in physical education. In some states, physical education is being eliminated entirely from the required school curriculum.[45]

Recognizing that one aspect of physical education that is taught almost universally across all levels is sport and games, this trend represents a severe threat to the overall health of many young people—an area of concern that is illustrated in recent findings about their lack of fitness generally.

Shifts in Sport Interests

A number of reports on leisure and recreation choice confirm a growing trend toward "alternative" and often extreme forms of physical recreation, to the point they constitute a direct threat to what team sport used to be a decade ago. Karl Greenfield points out that television has helped promote this trend, with a new band of athletes helping to drive the

> fast-growing world of nontraditional sports to an ever-increasing share of the TV ad dollar. Emerging sports such as surfing, skateboarding, snowboarding, mountain biking, rock climbing, NASCAR racing, and even bass fishing are gaining increasing TV exposure, providing greater choice for sports fans and advertisers.[46]

How Young for Sport Sponsorship

Dylan Oliver secured his first sport sponsorship at age six, a skateboarder who has unique skills and parents who are encouraging him. Beyond that he has secured a number of sponsors, from small T-shirt vendors to drink vendors like Jones Soda. He even has his own Web presence at dylanoliver.com.

The question for parents, park and recreation professionals, and sport addicts is: How soon is too soon to push your children into high-involvement sport? What price does childhood pay when children are not allowed to experience opportunities for play, socialization, and growth? The data suggests that children pushed into highly competitive sport at too young an age do not remain active in sport as they grow into their teens.

As a result, the popularity of extreme sports such as skateboarding and snowboarding for youth age seven and older has skyrocketed. Skateboarding experienced an increase in participation that reached 111 percent between 1994 and 2004, while snowboarding recorded a similarly phenomenal growth of 219 percent for the same time period.[47]

The X Games are an example of how the media have capitalized on and benefited from the move toward extreme sport. The list of events for the most recent winter X Games included snowboarder X, skier X, moto X, snowboard superpipe, and other variations of skiing and snowboarding. The success of the X Games has breathed new life into a ski industry suffering from a lack of young participants. So successful has been the resurgence of snow sports that the 2002 Winter Olympics introduced several of the X Games events into their regular schedule.

Computers and Video Gaming

Team sport today compete and will continue to compete against alternative forms of entertainment as TV, Internet socializing (Facebook, MySpace, YouTube, and so forth), and video gaming. The latest craze for video consoles such as Playstation 3, Nintendo Wii, and Xbox 360 fully supports this prediction. Nintendo recently exploited advances in motion-

■ *Extreme sports, once an outlaw form of sport, has become mainline and broadly accepted.*

sensing technology by developing a multifunctional remote control, which gamers use to simulate the movement of a tennis racket, a golf club, or a baseball bat, and play the sport within the virtual reality environment this third-generation Nintendo console creates for the user. Unfortunately, a growing number of children and adolescents prefer to get involved in virtual-reality activities than spending time playing sport. The results of this fad are evident in various research reports and scholarly studies about obesity around the nation. The National Health and Nutrition Examination Survey from 1999 to 2002 revealed that an estimated 16 percent of children between 6- to 19-year-olds are overweight. These results were up 45 percent from a similar study that took place from 1994 to 1998.[48]

Changes in Demographic Trends

As a population segment, the number of youth age 5 to 19 increased by 21 percent between the years 2000 and 2005. During this same period, the Sporting Goods Manufacturing Association (SGMA) reported that participation in team sport declined. Unfortunately, population estimates for the next 10 years are not so optimistic. This segment of the population is expected to grow only 3.6 percent, creating a very unfavorable situation for future team-sport participation. Reduced participation of youth in team sport will have a number of consequences, including a considerable drop in the sales of sport equipment.

Declining Sales of Sport Equipment

Other evidence indicates that sales of sporting equipment have declined in the last several years, reflecting lower rates of involvement by many U.S. youth and adults. Bob Fernandez sums up industry reports:

> Over the last decade, about 30 million people in the United States quit participating in traditional sports such as tennis, racquetball, baseball, volleyball, and softball, according to periodic studies of households. . . . Only soccer, basketball, and ice hockey among team sports—in addition to new sports such as in-line skating—have held their own, according to American Sports Data and other industry sources.[49]

Sectarian and Community-Based Sport Programs

Community-based sport programs and sectarian leagues also provide another alternative for participating in organized sport team activities. T-Ball USA claims that more than 2 million children participated in its programs in 2006. Upward Unlimited, a sport ministry for children, estimates that more that 500,000 children, age 4 to 12, participated in its programs during the 2004–2005 school year. Researchers and industry analysts need to pay attention to these figures because they are not accounted for in the annual SGMA report that measures participation in sport.

Participation in Organized Team Sport

As previously mentioned, there is a shift in sport participation, from casual play to organized team-sport activities. This trend is expected to grow significantly in the next few years, as societal changes and grassroots efforts from a variety of sport organizations take place.

SUMMARY

Throughout this chapter, it is clear that the major team, the small team, and the individual sport are still a dominant force in U.S. leisure. Strikingly, recent psychological research confirms the degree to which sport fans are influenced by the outcomes of games. Not only do spectators experience excitement and a sense of community through shared rooting for their teams, but their self-esteem and emotional state rise or fall markedly depending on their teams' victories or losses.

This chapter examines sport on various levels, ranging from familiar games for children and youth to high-level college and professional competition. It outlines the personal and social values that are commonly ascribed to sport involvement and describes a number of the abuses that undermine these values. Finally, the impact of professional sport on the economy, individual expenditure decisions, the growth of this marketplace, local communities through the public cost of securing and keeping a team, is altering financing decisions for communities and budgetary decisions for individuals. Finally, it suggests that overcommercialization and rapidly climbing costs threaten the fan base of professional sport and notes the trend away from some of the most familiar, traditional games in the direction of "extreme" or "alternative" physical recreation activities.

QUESTIONS FOR CLASS DISCUSSION OR ESSAY EXAMINATION

1. As class members have observed it, describe the transition from childhood interest and involvement in sport, through adolescence to adult participation or spectator experiences.
2. The chapter points out that sport are often seen as a religion. At the same time, they are widely recognized as a business. How can these two points of view be reconciled?
3. Many cities recently have built or are building expensive new arenas or stadiums to house professional teams, often with substantial subsidies. What is the rationale for using tax funds for this purpose? Argue the pros and cons of this practice.
4. The discussion related to participation in school athletics suggests that this continues to be a growth area. Based on your own experience, how would you characterize the growth of high school athletics? Does it conform to what the chapter suggests, or was your experience different? Why?
5. Extreme sport seem to have grown dramatically over the last 15 years. Identify an extreme sport and chart its growth over a 10-year period identifying key events in the development of the sport, such as new technology, television contracts, big-name athletes, the sport becoming accepted in traditional sport competition, and so forth.

ENDNOTES

1. J. B. Lewis, T. R. Jones, G. Lamke, and L. M. Dunn, "Recreational Sport: Making the Grade on College Campuses," *Parks and Recreation* (December 1998): 73.
2. Statistical Abstract of the United States. 2007. Washington D.C. U.S. Census Bureau (www.censusbureau.gov).
3. D. Broughton, J. Lee, and R. Nethery, "The Question: How Big Is the Sports Industry?" *Sport Business Journal* (20 December 1999): 39.
4. "NBA Sets All-Time Attendance Records; Regular Season Draws Highest Average Attendance and Highest Total Attendance," *Business Wire* (20 April 2006).
5. R. Blum, "MLB Breaks Season Attendance Record," Associated Press (1 October 2006).
6. "NFL Sets Attendance Record Again," Associated Press (5 January 2006).
7. "Sport Remains Dominant Driver of Sponsorship," *Sport Business International* (March 2006).
8. National Sporting Goods Association, "Female Sports Participation: 2005 vs. 2000," www.nsga.org, November 2006.
9. "Team Sports: State of the Industry," *Sporting Goods Dealer* (1 January 2006).
10. Ibid.
11. National Federation of State High School Associations, "NFHS Participation Figures Search," www.nfhs.org/custom/participation_figures/default.aspx. Accessed 1 May 2007.
12. Ibid.

13. "World Cup Edges NBA Finals in U.S. TV Ratings," *Agence France Presse* (11 July 2006).

14. "NFL Opener Attracts Record TV Audience," Associated Press (8 September 2006).

15. D. Nye, "Poor TV Ratings Reflect MLB's Popularity Slide," *The State* (3 November 2006).

16. J. Hart, "Series Ratings Weren't a Primetime Success," *Morning Call* (31 October 2006): C2.

17. R. Covitz, "NFL, Media Battle in the Trenches over Access Issues," *The Kansas City Star* (2 October 2006).

18. B. Horn, "NBC Returns as an NFL Player," *The Dallas Morning News* (5 September 2006).

19. B. Molinaro, "Even in the Preseason, the NFL Rules the Waves," *The Virginian-Pilot*, Hampton Roads, VA (11 August 2006).

20. "MLB Extends Deals with ESPN, FOX," *Pittsburg Tribune–Review* (12 July 2006).

21. "Turner, MLB Reach 7-Year TV Deal for LCS Coverage," Associated Press (17 October 2006).

22. N. Armour, "MLB Club Owners Approve New TV Contracts, Discuss Games in China," Associated Press (17 November 2006).

23. B. Jackson, "TBS Joins MLB TV Deal," *The Miami Herald* (12 July 2006).

24. J. Paul, "Big Ten Announces New TV Contract with ABC/ESPN and Creation of New Cable Channel," Associated Press (22 June 2006).

25. D. Naylor, "Investing in a Team a Losing Proposition; Franchise Values Have Not Gone Up like They Have in Other Sports," *The Globe & Mail* [Toronto, Canada] (11 June 2005): S1.

26. J. Weinbach, "Team Owners Behaving Badly," *Wall Street Journal* (5 May 2006).

27. "Five Teams Worth Over $1 Billion, According to *Forbes*," Associated Press (1 September 2006).

28. Team Marketing Report, "Fan Cost Index (FCI)," www.teammarketing.com/fci.cfm.

29. D. Barron, "Texans Still a Good Value for NFL Fans," *The Houston Chronicle* (17 September 2005): SPORTS.

30. D. Perry, "Red Sox, Patriots in a League of Their Own When It Comes to the High Price of Attending a Game," *Lowell Sun*, Massachusetts (2 June 2006).

31. Team Marketing, "TMR Fan Cost Survey," www.teammarketing.com.

32. A. Zagoria, "Comfort Zone; Low Cost, Fan-Friendliness Make Minors an Attractive Option," *Herald News*, Philadelphia, PA (21 August 2005).

33. K. Kaufman, "The Cost of Being a Fan: Not Necessarily as High as an Annual Report Says, but Awfully High," www.salon.com/news/sports/col/kaufman, 2005.

34. Charles Prebish, cited in R. Chandler, "Are Sports Becoming America's New Folk Religion?" *Philadelphia Inquirer* (3 January 1987): 1C.

35. J. Mathiesen, in Chandler, *op. cit.*, p. 5C.

36. Pat Jordan, "Belittled Big Men," *New York Times Magazine* (10 December 1995): 75.

37. B. Rader, *American Sports from the Age of Folk Games to the Age of Spectators* (Englewood Cliffs, NJ: Prentice Hall, 1983): 32.

38. James Kozlowski, "Sport League Held Liable for Brutal Attack on Coach," *Parks and Recreation* (November 1999): 45–52.

39. J. C. Bollinger and T. Goss, "Cleaning Up College Basketball," *New York Times* (5 September 1998): A11.

40. Margaret Talbot, "Why, Isn't He Just the Cutest Brand-Image Enhancer You've Ever Seen?" *New York Times Magazine* (21 September 2003).

41. Joe La Points, "A Hard Winter in Vermont: Hockey Season Canceled Over Hazing," *New York Times* (3 February 2000): D1.

42. Robert Sullivan, "How the Olympics Were Bought," *Time* (25 January 1999): 38.

43. Michael Lemonick, "Le Tour des Drugs," *Time* (10 August 1998): 76.

44. Jere Longman, "Fixed Matches Are Darkening Soccer's Image," *New York Times* (7 June 1998): 1.

45. Deborah Tannehill, "Sport Education," *Journal of Physical Education, Recreation, and Dance* (April 1998): 16.

46. Karl Greenfield, "A Wider World of Sport," *Time* (9 November 1998): 80.

47. "Extreme Sports Have National Appeal," *Parks and Recreation* (2004): 39(10): 23.

48. "Overweight Among U.S. Children and Adolescent," *National Health and Nutrition Survey,* (Washington, D.C.: Department of Health and Human Services): 1.

49. Bob Fernandez, "Seeking a Sporting Chance," *Philadelphia Inquirer* (18 June 2000): E1.

CHAPTER 12

CAREER OPPORTUNITIES AND PROFESSIONALISM

◆ ◆ ◆

Organized recreation services have been often thought of as fun-and-games operations, concerned chiefly with providing programs of sport, games, and hobbies. On the contrary, recreation administration involves major responsibility for planning and administering recreation and park programs to meet the needs and interests of the area served.[1]

Now, more than ever, the field of recreation and leisure services offers a wide variety of rewarding and fulfilling careers to candidates who possess a strong academic background, practical experience, and a passion, commitment, and dedication to the profession. From event planners to park rangers to recreational sport programmers, there are numerous career opportunities and literally thousands of jobs worldwide.[2]

◆ ◆ ◆

INTRODUCTION

Recreation, parks, and leisure services have expanded greatly over the past several decades as a diversified area of employment. Today, several million people work in different sectors of this field, including amateur and professional sport, entertainment and amusement services, travel and tourism, recreation-related businesses, and government and nonprofit community organizations.

As a distinct part of this larger group, several hundred thousand men and women are directly involved as recreation leaders, supervisors, managers, therapists, planners, and consultants in public, voluntary, commercial, therapeutic, and other types of agencies. These individuals with a primary concern for the provision of recreation services are generally regarded as professionals on the basis of their job responsibilities, specialized training, and affiliations with professional associations.

The prevailing image of leisure-service professionals has been that of public, governmental, recreation, and park employees. The leading professional associations, as well as most textbooks and college curricula, reinforced this narrowly defined identity. However, the reality is that vast sectors of employment in recreation and leisure services are not government related but, instead, have to do with nonprofit community agencies; company-sponsored, commercial, and therapeutic recreation services; sport management; and travel and tourism programs. As such, they have their own professional associations, as well as goals, job functions, and strategies that differ from those of public recreation and park specialists.

RECREATION AS A CAREER

People have worked in recreation for many centuries in the sense that there have been professional athletes and entertainers throughout history. Musicians, tumblers, dancers, huntsmen, park designers, and gardeners were all recreation specialists attending to the leisure needs first of royalty and, ultimately, of the public at large. However, the idea of recreation itself as a career field did not surface until the late 1800s, when public parks and playgrounds, along with voluntary social service and youth-serving organizations, were established.

After the beginning of the twentieth century, courses in play leadership were developed by the Playground Association of America and were taken by many teachers. In the middle 1920s, the National Recreation Association provided a graduate training program for professional recreation and park administrators, and leisure as a distinct area of public service came to be recognized. This recognition increased during the Great Depression of the 1930s as many thousands of individuals were assigned by the federal government to emergency posts providing community recreation programs and developing new parks and other facilities. However, it was not until the development of separate degree programs in a handful of colleges that higher education in recreation and parks as a distinct career field came into being.

By the second half of the twentieth century, careers in recreation and parks were seen as a growth area. A nationwide study of workforce requirements in the 1960s concluded that there would be a need for hundreds of thousands of new recreation and park professionals in the years ahead. The U.S. Department of Labor reported widespread shortages of leisure-service personnel in local government, hospitals, and youth-serving organizations. Several factors, such as the federal government's expanded activity in outdoor recreation and open space and the establishment of the National Recreation and Park Association, stimulated interest in this field. In the 1970s, as employment grew, curricula in recreation and leisure service gained increased acceptance in higher education.

Scope of Employment Today

People spend free time participating in sport, arts, and nature activities; visiting museums, zoos, and aquariums; and attending special events, shows, and performances; as well as traveling to tourism destinations. With all of this recreation going on, people are needed to work in these and many other jobs.

Jay Brown, National Park Service, Park and U.S. Ranger at Voyageurs National Park, Graduated August 2005

The U.S. Park Ranger of today wears many hats. First, and most evident, I am a federal law enforcement officer capable of investigating a full spectrum of crimes including minor resource violations (for example, seashell collection) to the most major violent crimes such as rape or murder. Second, in most national parks, my fellow rangers and I are the primary emergency medical response force. With most rangers trained, at minimum, as emergency medical technicians, rangers are the initial response for all emergency medical situations occurring within the park. Third, I am relied on for the implementation of all levels of search and rescue. These search-and-rescue incidents often include the utilization of technical (ropes) rescue, swift water rescue, fixed-wing aircraft, park helicopters, and unfortunately, body recovery operations. Fourth, I am certified in wildland fire suppression. Given that many of our National Parks contain vast acreage of forested land, it is practical and necessary that park rangers harbor fire-suppression skills and in many areas the use of these skills is imminent. Finally, in addition to these duties, I am expected to know the natural, cultural, and historical aspects of the park in which I work. A good ranger is able to convey his or her knowledge of flora, fauna, and other assets of our national parks to visitors in a way that is not only educational but instills a passion to preserve and protect these unique places, leaving them unimpaired for future generations.

Several factors contribute to the satisfaction I have for my job. First, as a lover of the outdoors, I am afforded the opportunity to live and work in the nation's most beautiful natural areas. Second, I have the opportunity to meet visitors who many have waited a month, year, or sometimes even a lifetime to visit these magnificent places. Third, given the fact that the park ranger wears so many hats, every day is new, different, and interesting.

Employment opportunities in parks and recreation are highly diversified. Recreation workers are found in local parks and recreation agencies, on cruise ships, planning major festivals such as the Sundance Film Festival, planning promotional events for the Phoenix International Raceway, and working with people with disabilities in a therapeutic recreation setting. They can be found in all of our national parks from Acadia to Zion. They serve as park rangers, interpreters, guides, and activity planners.

The educational backgrounds of people working in recreation vary. A plethora of summer and part-time positions require a high school diploma—or less as is the case with many lifeguards and camp counselors. However, these positions are not considered professional positions, but a means to gather experience in order to obtain a professional position in the recreation field. As responsibilities increase in recreation-related jobs, so do degree requirements. Entry-level positions in the field such as after-school program supervisors, special-event planners, and facility supervisors may require a bachelor's degree, and middle- and upper-level management positions may require a master's degree.

Although data on the total number of jobs in recreation is limited, we do know that the tourism industry is one of the nation's largest employers with 7.3 million people working in this industry.[3] The 2004 Bureau of Labor Statistics estimated that over 1.2 million people were employed in recreation and entertainment.[4] Furthermore, the National Park Service employs 20,000 people to take care of its 84-million acres of land; state parks employ 54,884 people full and part time.[5]

The Bureau of Labor Statistics expects the demand for most recreation jobs to grow as fast as the average through 2014 which means they expect a growth of 9–17 percent through this time. Part of what is driving this growth is the rate of retirement of baby boomers previously discussed in other chapters. They also predict that therapeutic recreation will see a growth that is faster than average with an increase of 18–26 percent over the next several years.[6]

RECREATION CAREER AREAS

Kraus, Barber, and Shapiro divided the profession into 10 different areas ranging from campus recreation to tourism.[7] Although there are several similarities in each of the different areas, there are also differences that make each career area worthy of discussion. The areas have been discussed in previous chapters, and a review of the 10 areas will be accompanied by sample jobs in each.

Public Agencies

Public and governmental organizations serve users at the local, state, and federal levels. These organizations are often fully or partially funded by taxes and are direct service providers of such things as local, state, and national parks; adult sport leagues; and youth day camps. People working in this sector of the profession may be employed by the Ohio Department of Natural Resources, the National Park Service, or the City of Aurora (Colorado) Library, Recreation and Cultural Services Department. They may have job titles such as park ranger, facility coordinator, or naturalist.

■ *Boulder (CO) Parks and Recreation Department holds special events for all ages throughout the year.*

Nonprofit Organizations

Nonprofit agencies may offer recreation as a predominant function of the agency such as the Boys & Girls Clubs or as a secondary function with agencies like the YWCA. Funding for nonprofit agencies most likely will come from membership fees, program user fees, fundraising efforts, grants, and government contracts to provide services to people in need. Professionals hired in the nonprofit sector could work at such places as the Girl Scouts, the YMCA, or a Jewish community center. About 11 percent of all recreation jobs are in the nonprofit sector.[8]

Commercial Recreation

Commercial recreation has been referred to as the for-profit and market sectors. Although travel and tourism may be the most commonly considered recreation-related businesses, there are several others. Travel and tourism are broad and far-reaching terms that deserve their own discussion later in this section. The commercial sector is quite encompassing and includes such businesses as bowling alleys, billiards centers, miniature golf courses, and outdoor outfitters that offer whitewater rafting or canoe trips. Because these organizations are expected to make a profit, funding comes from the sales of goods and services. Within the commercial sector as well as nonprofit and public sectors, event management is a widely sought-after career path. The International Festival and Events Association reports that its members alone plan events that infuse $25 billion into communities across the country as well as serve 405 million people

■ *Commercial agencies can be involved in special events such as ones that feature pumpkin picking, hayrides, and a haunted trail.*

annually.[9] Job titles for event planners include event coordinator, tourism director, and marketing director. Events such as the Alamo Bowl, Canadian Tulip Festival, Milwaukee Summerfest, and the Kentucky Derby Festival all have a special-event planning staff.

Armed Forces Recreation

The armed forces has the moral, welfare, and recreation (MWR) department providing services for enlisted men and women and their civilian family members. Funded by the Department of Defense, programs are provided by both military personnel and civilian recreation staff. Outdoor programming, health and fitness centers, and youth activities are just a few examples of programs designed to increase the morale and overall health and wellness of the service-men and -women and their families. MWR employees can be found on most military bases around the world. For example, the U.S. Navy offers MWR programs in 24 states and 13 countries.[10]

Employee Recreation

Employee recreation became popular in the 1970s as the labor movement was growing. Large companies began to offer programs, events, and sport leagues for their employees. It was thought that employees who were active would have lower absenteeism illness and on-the-job injuries. Employee recreation runs the gamut in offerings.[11] Some companies such as Hewlett Packard offer fitness, healthy cooking, and other wellness activities in addition to special interest clubs like wine tasting, theatre, and cricket.[12] Others may offer trips and tours for employees while the more elaborate employee recreation programs, such as State Farm Insurance, may own a park with a pool, picnic facilities, and programs just for employees and their guests.

Campus Recreation

Campus recreation services are offered on many college and university campuses. Program offerings are as diverse as the student body. Program areas encompass such things as sport leagues, club sport (i.e., figure skating, archery, and water polo), fitness programs, special events, outdoor adventure programming, and drop-in recreation. Services are provided for students, staff, and faculty. Job titles within campus recreation may include membership services director, intramurals supervisor, and special-events manager.

Private-Membership Organizations

Private-membership organizations predominantly serve middle- and upper-income users. Many country clubs, tennis clubs, and yacht clubs provide services to those who pay annual fees to join. On the increase are gated communities, many which are retirement communities, where a portion of the homeowner's association fee helps pay for programs and facilities offered to community residents. For example, in Walnut Creek, California, the Rossmoor Retirement Community offers its residents over 200 clubs and programs, a fitness center with a personal trainer, two private golf courses, a library, miles of walking trails, swimming pools, and tennis courts, among other services for members.[13] Recreation programmers are needed to plan and implement all of these activities.

Therapeutic Recreation

Therapeutic recreation (TR) can be offered through public, nonprofit, or commercial sector agencies by providing programs for people with disabilities. TR uses functional intervention, leisure education, and recreation services to help people with disabilities enhance the quality of their lives. TR services may be offered through hospitals, rehabilitation centers, nursing homes, community mental health centers, prisons and detention centers, local parks and recreation departments, and outpatient facilities. As with the rest of the career areas discussed, TR comes in many forms. Programs are available in the areas of fitness, health, hobbies, and culture among others. These professionals may provide music therapy, art therapy, and even pet therapy. People working in therapeutic recreation may have jobs such as therapeutic recreation specialist, recreation therapist, or director of therapeutic recreation services.

Sport Management

Sport management, like TR, is not restricted to a particular sector, but is found in a multitude of areas. People working in sport management may work in college athletics programs, sport marketing, semiprofessional and professional sports, amateur sport such as the Olympics, or they may work in arenas, coliseums, or stadiums. Working in this area may mean having job titles such as media director, sport tourism manager, event coordinator, or group sales representative.

Tourism and Hospitality

This area is a large industry ranging from hotels, motels, and restaurants to casinos, amusement parks, and museums. Travel and tourism generate $1.3 trillion in economic activity in the United States every year.[14] *Tourism industry* is an umbrella term encompassing the businesses and other organizations associated with travel, whether it is for pleasure or business. This subsection may include transportation such as airlines or rail, meeting and convention services, meeting planning, and attractions. *Hospitality* is a component of tourism and includes the accommodations, and food and beverage associated with hotels and other hospitality entities. Jobs in this industry include sales manager, meeting planner, hotel manager, or catering director.[15]

Cruises are just one example of commercial recreation job opportunities.

PROFESSIONAL IDENTIFICATION IN RECREATION

What does being a professional mean? At the simplest level, it indicates that one is paid for one's work—as opposed to an amateur, who is not paid for it. Thus, an athlete who receives pay for playing for a team is classified as a professional.

However, this obviously is not a sufficient definition of the term in that many forms of paid work are not considered to be professional. A more complete definition of the term would suggest that a professional is one who has a high degree of status and specialized training and provides a significant form of public or social service.

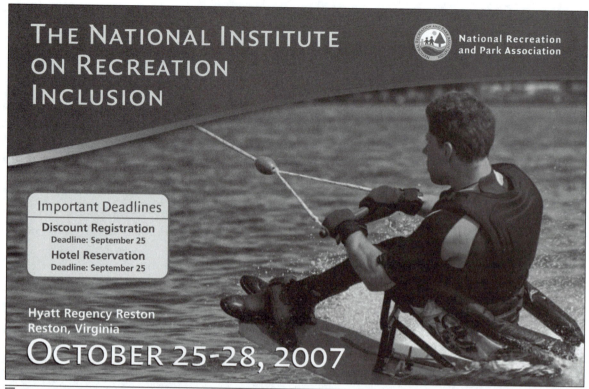

THE NATIONAL INSTITUTE
ON RECREATION
INCLUSION

National Recreation
and Park Association

Important Deadlines

Discount Registration
Deadline: September 25

Hotel Reservation
Deadline: September 25

Hyatt Regency Reston
Reston, Virginia
OCTOBER 25-28, 2007

Training for parks and recreation positions does not stop with a degree. The National Institute on Recreation Inclusion features sessions focusing on how to include people with and without disabilities, just to name a few.

Within a number of specialized leisure-service areas today, such as company-sponsored employee programs, therapeutic recreation, or fitness and health spas, professionalism might be narrowly defined as the possession of a required certification based on a combination of education, experience, and examination. In other situations,

Abby Schoolman, Youth Counselor for Norwegian Cruise Line, Graduated August 2005

As a youth counselor I have two kinds of days: Sea Days, when guests never leave the ship, and Port Days, when guests are able to go ashore. On Sea Days, we have three different three-hour themed programs such as Spy Night, Survivor Challenge, and The Great Big Egg Drop. On Port Days, Norwegian Cruise Lines only has the three-hour evening program, so we get time off to explore these beautiful ports as well. One of the things I love the most about my job is that I get to travel and see the world. I have stayed in recreation because it gives me the opportunity to try so many different things. One day I am planning activities for children, and the next I am the Easter Bunny for a photo opportunity. I have had the chance to show guests to their tour bus, and I had the opportunity to be on a stage looking out at one thousand people while performing in a crew talent show. There is so much variety in my work. I never get bored! That is why I love the recreation field!

membership in a designated professional association or society may be recognized as a hallmark of professionalism. However, the following seven criteria have generally been accepted as key elements of professionalism.

Criterion 1: Social Value and Purpose

The goals of organized community leisure-service agencies are described in Chapter 7. In general, they deal with such elements as improving the quality of life, contributing to personal development and social cohesion, helping to prevent socially destructive leisure pursuits, and protecting the environment.

People are willing to pay for their own personal leisure and more reluctant to pay taxes to support leisure for the public good such as parks and trails.

In the nonprofit field, the YWCA is dedicated to the empowerment of women and girls and the elimination of racism. The oldest U.S. organization owned and managed by women, its member organizations provide safety; shelter; day care; physical fitness and recreation programs; counseling; and other social, health, educational, and job-related services to millions of women and girls and their communities each year.

Other youth-serving organizations tend to have similar goals. Although many of their services may not be specifically concerned with recreation, they provide rich programs in sport, social activities, the arts, outdoor recreation, and other pastimes. In essence, leisure programs are used both as an end in themselves and as a means of achieving other agency goals of personal development and community improvement.

Criterion 2: Public Recognition

The rapid expansion of the leisure-service field over the past several decades does not necessarily mean that the public at large understands and respects it fully or that they regard it as a distinct area of professional service. To illustrate, most individuals today know what recreation is, and many regard it as an important part of their lives. Most are prepared to pay substantial portions of their income for recreational goods or services, such as memberships in health clubs, vacations, sport equipment, television sets, and other leisure-related fees and charges. However, they are often less willing to pay taxes in support of public recreation and park facilities and programs than they are to spend privately for their own leisure needs.

A time-use study done by the Bureau of Labor Statistics found that 96 percent of people over the age of 15 reported having some sort of leisure whether it be socializing, sport, or exercising.[16] In 2001, there were over 735 million visitors to state parks, and in 2004, there were 67.5 campers and another 6.2 million lodge and cabin guests.[17] The

National Park Service reported another 423 million users in 2005.[18] Although these are just a minute portion of the leisure-service opportunities available, it demonstrates that a large portion of the population use recreation services.

Even though the value of organized recreation service may be acknowledged, how aware is the public at large of the leisure-service field as a profession? The likelihood is that most individuals recognize the roles of recreation professionals within specific areas of service. For example, they are likely to be familiar with the function of a recreation therapist in a mental hospital or nursing home or the function of a community center director, a park ranger, or a sport specialist in an armed forces recreation program. What they tend not to understand is that recreation represents a field of practice that requires special expertise and educational preparation in a college or university. At issue is the image of the recreation professional.

Dylana Carlson, Sandestin Program Manager, American Hospitality Academy, Graduated Summer 2004

During my senior internship doing resort activities, I realized how much of an impact my internship supervisor had on my experience. I too wanted to be able to mentor and supervise other interns to realize their full potential. After completing my internship, I was able to fulfill this interest in being an intern supervisor for recreation and hospitality majors completing their senior internships.

My job consists of supervising, leading, and guiding hospitality interns on a day-to-day basis. After an intern is interviewed and selected, I correspond with him or her with arrival and housing information. I act as the liaison between the resort and the intern to ensure that the intern experiences a well-rounded internship. I coordinate with managers and the human resources department at the resort, along with home country contacts or professors at the interns' university. Our goal for each intern is to provide practical training, education, and cultural exchange for a well-rounded experience. This consists of planning and implementing weekly educational classes, monthly cultural events, and social events along with volunteer projects within the community.

My favorite experience with my job is being able to visit other countries. My employer listens to my personal and professional goals and offers me learning experiences within this range. For example, I had the opportunity to travel overseas to promote our internship program. Through this, I have experienced Jamaica, Slovakia, Bulgaria, Czech Republic, Romania, and Mexico.

Another aspect of my job that I love is the chance to teach weekly seminars that prepare the students for management-type roles after graduating. This experience is invaluable to me for my future in the field, because I have a long-term goal to teach at the university level in recreation.

I love that the recreation field is open to creativity within the workplace. There are so many people in the workforce who are limited by their positions on what experiences they have on a daily basis. People within the recreation field celebrate diversity and creativity, which are personal values I hold. This is why I have continued in this field.

Image of the Professional   The public's perception of those working in the recreation field tends to be unclear. Often, the recreation professional is confused with the physical educator because of the perceived strong emphasis on sport in many recreation programs and the close connection between the two fields in early professional preparation.

Recreation professionals themselves have assumed such a wide variety of roles that no single image stands out. Sessoms commented a number of years ago that "we would like to be all things to all people: entertainers, promoters, counselors, psychiatric aides, and social analysts," concluding:

> I am afraid the public sees us either as ex-athletes, or gregarious, fun-and-game leaders wearing short pants, knee socks, and an Alpine hat, calling for all to join in.[19]

He later suggested that one of the problems was that recreation was not perceived as an occupational field that required special preparation and long-term training. It would seem clear that if recreation and leisure-service employees are to sharpen their identity and support, they must enrich their own competence through specialized professional study and by joining organizations that strengthen their field.

Criterion 3: Specialized Professional Preparation

A measure of the professional authority of any given field is the degree of specialized preparation that people must have to function in it. Typically, the most highly regarded professions in modern society, such as medicine or law, have rigorous requirements with respect to professional education. These evolved through the years and involve higher education curricula on the graduate level, supported in some cases by required internships or periods of professional practice and by comprehensive examinations prepared or administered by professional societies.

Professional Preparation in Recreation and Parks   The early period of the development of higher education in recreation, parks, and leisure services was described earlier in this text. Over the past five decades, college and university curricula in recreation and parks have been developed on three levels: two-year, four-year, and graduate (master's degree and doctorate) programs.

Two-Year Curricula   During the late 1960s and early 1970s, many community colleges began to offer associate degree programs in recreation and parks. Typically, these sought to prepare individuals on para- or subprofessional levels, rather than for supervisory or administrative roles. Most community colleges offered recreation majors a choice of two types of programs: terminal and transfer. *Terminal programs* were intended to equip students immediately for employment and gave heavy emphasis to developing basic, useful recreation leadership skills, often within a specific field of practice. *Transfer programs* were intended for students who hoped to transfer to four-year degree programs.

Four-Year Programs   The most widely found degree program in recreation and parks has been the four-year bachelor's degree curriculum. Initially, most such programs consisted of specialized degree options in college departments of health, physical education, and recreation, although some were located in departments or schools of landscape architecture, agriculture, forestry, or social work. Today, although many departments still are situated administratively in schools or colleges of health, physical education, and recreation, they have achieved a high level of curricular independence, with their own objectives, courses, degree requirements, and faculty.

Four-year programs typically have established degree options in areas such as recreation programming, recreation and park management, resource management, outdoor recreation, therapeutic recreation, sport management, and commercial recreation. The normal pattern has been to require all department majors to take certain core courses representing the generic needs of all preprofessionals, including basic courses in recreation history and philosophy, programming, management, and evaluation and/or research, and then to have a separate cluster of specialized courses for each option.

What once started as a training ground for public parks and recreation professionals has grown to meet the changing demands of the field. There was growing academic awareness of the job opportunities in other recreation areas. As a result, a number of college and university programs changed their titles and departmental affiliations to reflect the new interest in commercial recreation, travel and tourism, sport management, hotel and resort management, and similar specializations. Typically, a considerable number of departments added the term *tourism* to their titles and established enriched programs in this area—in some cases in collaboration with schools of business in their institutions. In other cases, therapeutic recreation majors were transferred administratively to departments or schools of public health or health-care services. As the most striking example of proliferation in this field, as of 2006 there were over 200 independent departments of sport management designed to meet personnel needs in this growing field.[20]

In many cases, curriculum revision was based on the requirements or recommendations of professional societies, such as the Resort and Commercial Recreation Association (RCRA), the North American Society for Sport Management (NASSM), the National Association for Sport and Physical Education (NASPE), and the National Employee Services and Recreation Association (NESRA).

Master's Degree and Doctoral Programs   Although it is generally agreed that the four-year curriculum should provide a broad base of general or liberal arts education along with the core of essential knowledge underlying recreation service, the specific function of graduate education in this field is not as clearly defined. Some authorities have suggested that graduate curricula should accept only those students who already have a degree in recreation and should focus on providing advanced professional education within a specialized area of service. However, there tends to be little support for this position, and many graduate programs accept students from other undergraduate disciplines as well as those holding undergraduate degrees in recreation.

In general, authorities agree that master's degree work should involve advanced study in recreation and park administration or in some other specialized area of service, such as therapeutic recreation. The assumption is that individuals on this level are preparing for supervisory or managerial positions or, in some cases, roles as researchers or chief executive officers.

Specialized Body of Knowledge   At the outset, many recreation and park degree programs were established as "minor" specializations in other areas of study, such as physical education. As such, they tended to lack theoretically based courses within the field of study. Over the past four decades, this deficiency has been largely corrected.

The knowledge and skills components of higher education in recreation, parks, and leisure studies are formulated in terms that are specifically applicable to the recreation field, although they may involve content taken from other scholarly disciplines or fields of practice.

Given the recent impressive growth in both research studies and publication of findings, it seems clear that the field has a legitimate body of knowledge that must be possessed by professionals. Indeed, within some areas of practice, there has been systematic study of the competencies and knowledge that entry-level practitioners should possess. These skills, knowledge, and abilities guide curricula so students are equipped with the skills needed to get their first job.[21]

Increasingly, undergraduate curricula have been redesigned to include specific areas of knowledge and job performance based on standards of practice or certification examinations that have been developed by professional societies.

On undergraduate levels, a major element in the process of imparting practical knowledge and skills to students consists of required field work and internship experiences. Although these vary from institution to institution, in general they require at least a semester of full-time commitment to work in an agency of high quality within the student's expressed field of professional interest. Such placements should extend far beyond an agency's using field work or internship students in routine or mechanical roles as a source of cheap labor. Instead, they are meant to involve a full range of realistic job assignments and exposures, as well as conscientious counseling and supervision by professional staff members.

Accreditation in Higher Education   The most significant effort that has been made to upgrade curricular standards and practices in recreation, parks, and leisure studies has come in the accreditation process. *Accreditation* of a degree program involves meeting standards set by a larger governing body. These standards ensure students are being exposed to standards of practices within the field.

■ *NRPA publishes an accreditation and certification brochure outlining the benefits of agency and university accreditation and the certification program.*

Why Professional Involvement....
Jim Donahue, CPRP
Past President, National Recreation and Park Association
Director of Parks, Recreation and Information Processing, Perinton, New York

I have been involved with the National Recreation and Park Association (NRPA) for the past several decades. The experiences I have had in this 20,000 member organization are extremely positive and second to none. So, what makes involvement in NRPA so special?

I have been a member of NRPA for more than 20 years, serving on a regional council, a professional branch, the policy-making board of trustees, and serve as president-elect, president, and past-president for the association. I was able to travel the country and speak about the positive impacts recreation and parks have on people's lives. I met with senators, congressional delegates, city mayors, town council people, and citizen support groups to discuss the importance of recreation and parks. I never dreamed as I entered the profession in the mid 1970s that I would eventually travel and speak to groups in 38 states, including Alaska and Hawaii, and move forward the message of recreation and parks.

Involvement in the NRPA provides opportunities to meet other recreation and park professionals and dedicated citizens who are working to make a difference in people's lives. I have had the opportunity to meet with large city and small community parks and recreation directors and their staff to see the challenges faced by these professionals as well as all the good they are doing for their communities.

One of the most gratifying experiences I have had to date with NRPA is the opportunity to meet with the top management of *Sports Illustrated* magazine in New York City and promote the idea of a national celebration of sports towns. The resulting Sports Town, USA program provided more than five million dollars in advertising to NRPA and national visibility to local community recreation and parks departments. There are many partnerships NRPA has with National Sports Associations, Center for Disease Control, and the like that help build visibility and viability for the profession.

The mission of the National Recreation and Parks Association is "To advance parks, recreation and environmental conservation efforts that enhance the quality of life for all people." Everyone has a part to play in accomplishing this mission. I was fortunate in my career to have the support from my family and workplace to afford me the opportunity to be involved with such an important association. The professionals and citizen supporters I have met have an incredible spirit and passion for recreation and parks. We teach and learn from one another. We share successes and failures in hopes of making things better for our citizenry.

The park and recreation accreditation program is administered by the Council on Accreditation. This group of academic faculty and practitioners in the field represent the National Recreation and Park Association and the American Association for Physical Activity and Recreation.

Academic programs become accredited for a number of reasons. First, and usually most importantly, is to ensure program quality and uncover areas needed for improvement. A secondary reason is that students graduating from an accredited university may take the Certified Park and Recreation Professional examination upon completion of their degree (certification discussed later).

Undergraduate baccalaureate programs in parks and recreation are eligible for accreditation. At this time two-year programs and graduate programs cannot go through the accreditation process. In this process, there are set accreditation standards that programs must meet in the areas of organization and operation standards, program content, and professional competencies. After completing a self study of these areas, an outside review team visits the campus to judge how well standards are met. Suggestions

Each year, thousands of recreation and park professionals, civic officials, board members, educators, and students attend the National Recreation and Park Congress. Varied workshops, general sessions, exhibitor displays, and continuing education events provide inspiration and expertise, along with exposure to outstanding programs in different regions of the country.

for improving weaknesses are made with the understanding that these things are for the betterment of the degree program.

Accreditation began in the early 1980s with about 50 programs being accredited. There has been a steady increase in the number of programs being accredited and this number has risen to 96 in 2006.

Criterion 4: Existence of Related Professional Associations

Another important characteristic of professions in modern society is that they have strong organizations, shared values, and traditions. How does the recreation and park field measure up to this criterion?

In the United States, professional recreation associations have been in existence for a number of years. Like their counterparts in other professions, recreation and park associations have the following functions: They (1) regulate and set standards for professional development; (2) promote legislation for the advancement of the field; (3) develop programs of public information to improve understanding and support of the field; (4) sponsor conferences, publications, and field services to

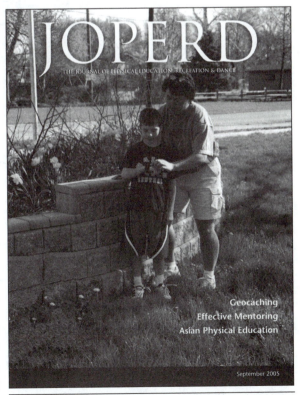

■ *The Journal of Physical Education, Recreation, and Dance is a monthly publication of AAHPERD focusing on educating professionals in the field.*

improve practices; and (5) press for higher standards of training, accreditation, and certification. There are a number of professional associations available for park and recreation professionals, that provide those and other services.

National Recreation and Park Association   Because of the varied nature of professional service in recreation and parks and the strong role played by citizens' groups and nonprofessional organizations, many different associations were established through the years to serve the field. Five of these (the National Recreation Association, the American Institute of Park Executives, the National Conference on State Parks, the American Association of Zoological Parks and Aquariums, and the American Recreation Society) merged into a single body in 1965, with Laurance S. Rockefeller as president. Within a year or two, other groups, such as the National Association of Recreation Therapists and the Armed Forces Section of the American Recreation Society, merged their interests with the newly formed organization.

This national body, the National Recreation and Park Association, is an independent, nonprofit organization intended to advance parks, recreation, and environmental conservation efforts that enhance the quality of life for all people.[22] This organization is arguably the broadest in scope for the recreation profession by embracing most of the professional categories listed earlier in the chapter. NRPA is directed by a board of trustees, which meets several times each year to guide its major policies. Several separate branches and sections carry out the work and serve to coalesce the special interests of members; these include the American Park and Recreation Society, National Society for Park Resources, Ethnic Minority Society, Armed Forces Recreation Society, National Therapeutic Recreation Society, Society of Park and Recreation Educators, Citizen Board Member Branch, National Aquatics Branch, Commercial Recreation and Tourism Section, Leisure and Aging Section, and the Student Branch.

Throughout the 1980s and 1990s, and into the 2000s, NRPA played a vigorous role in helping to bring about a fuller national consciousness of the value of recreation and leisure through various public information campaigns, publications, research efforts, and legislative presentations. The organization responds to thousands of inquires and requests for technical assistance from practitioners, establishes national partnerships for local departments, oversees conferences and training opportunities, and provides numerous publications for members. In addition, NRPA representatives regularly testify before congressional subcommittees in support of legislation and funding proposals dealing with the environment, social needs, and similar national problems.

Other Professional Organizations   Many other organizations sponsor programs supporting the recreation and park field or one of its specialized components. For example, the American Alliance for Health, Physical Education, Recreation, and Dance (AAHPERD) has several thousand members who have a specialized interest in education for leisure, school-sponsored recreation, the promotion of school camping and outdoor education, and adapted physical education and recreation programs for people with disabilities.

The branch of AAHPERD that has been most directly concerned with these functions has been the newly formed American Association for Physical Activity and Recreation, which worked closely on the accreditation process with NRPA through the National Council on Accreditation. It plays a key role in promoting community isit some of these associations on the Web:

National Recreation and Park Association	www.nrpa.org/
American Alliance for Health, Physical Education, Recreation, and Dance	www.aahperd.org/
American Camping Association	www.acacamps.org/
National Intramural-Recreational Sports Association	www.nirsa.org/
American Therapeutic Recreation Association	www.atra-tr.org/
North American Society for Sport Management	www.nassm.org/
Resort and Commercial Recreation Association	http://r-c-r-a.org/
World Leisure and Recreation Association	www.worldleisure.org/
Association of Outdoor Recreation and Education	www.aore.org/
International Special Events Society	www.ises.com/
Professional Convention Management Association	www.pcma.org/

education and leisure education projects; publishes an outstanding series of special-theme inserts in the *Journal of Physical Education, Recreation, and Dance*; and assists in job placement of recreation personnel.

Other organizations that have made important contributions to this field include the following:

- American Camping Association, the national professional organization of the organized camping movement
- National Intramural Recreational Sports Association, which promotes intramural sport in colleges and universities
- American Therapeutic Recreation Association, which represents the interests and needs of recreational therapists
- North American Society for Sport Management, which focuses on sport management
- Resort and Commercial Recreation Association, which was established for the resort and commercial recreation industries
- World Leisure and Recreation Association, which deals with the international recreation and leisure movement
- Association of Outdoor Recreation and Education, an outdoor association focused on serving the needs of not-for-profit outdoor recreation and education entities
- International Special Events Society, an organization for special-event planners, suppliers, and affiliated companies
- Professional Convention Management Association, whose members work in the meeting and convention planning industry

It is clear that no one organization can possibly speak for or represent the entire leisure-service field today. As each specialized area of recreation has become more active and successful, it has tended to form its own professional society to deal with its unique needs and interests.

Criterion 5: Credentialing, Certification, and Agency Accreditation

Credentials are qualifications that must be satisfied through a formal review process before an individual is permitted to engage in professional practice in a given field. Obviously, this is a very important criterion of professionalism. If anyone can call him- or herself a qualified practitioner in a given field—without appropriate training or experience—that field has very low standards and is not likely to gain or hold the public's respect.

Because the recreation and park field has been so diversified, no single standard or selection process has been devised for those who seek employment in it. However, within the field of recreation and parks, certification programs have been developed to increase the professionalism of the field as well as set some standards that all certified professionals should possess.

Certification in a profession indicates that a certain level of skill and knowledge has been attained. Certification in parks and recreation is no exception. Although there are several different certifications available for different specialties in the field, the most recognized are the Certified Park and Recreation Professional (CPRP) and the Certified Therapeutic Recreation Specialist (CTRS).

Certified Park and Recreation Professional   In the early 1980s, the NRPA Board of Trustees set in motion a two- to five-year plan that sought to link the three elements of certification, accreditation, and continuing education in a certification procedure that would apply broadly to the overall recreation, parks, and leisure-service field.

The new Model Certification Plan for Recreation, Park Resources, and Leisure Services Personnel was designed to provide a national means of attesting to the educational and experiential qualifications of people receiving compensation in the recreation field. Its purpose was to establish standards for certification in the recreation, park resources, and leisure-services professions; provide recognition of individuals who have qualified; and afford a guarantee to employers that certified personnel have attained stated education and experience qualifications.

Among the unique elements of the plan was the stipulation that everyone seeking certification after November 1, 1986, would be required to hold a degree from a college or university with a curriculum accredited by NRPA. Other stipulations were that recertification would be mandatory every two years, beginning in 1983, and that individuals would be required to earn a minimum of two continuing education units (CEUs) or equivalent college course work within each 24-month period from the date of certification. The test was revised in 1989, 1999, and again in 2006. The most recent version covers three broad content areas including (a) management (i.e., budget and staff supervision), (b) programming (i.e., planning, assessment, and implementation), and (c) operations (i.e., facility operation and resource management).

Three levels of certification are available: Certified Park and Recreation Professional (CPRP), Provisional Park and Recreation Professional (PPRP), and Associate Park and Recreation Professional (APRP). The CPRP status indicates that the individual has met the education/experience requirements and has passed the CPRP examination. To obtain CPRP status, the individual must have a minimum of a bachelor's degree and pass the certification exam. The PPRP is a temporary certification used if the educational requirements have been met and remains until the exam is passed. The APRP is for individuals who have less than a four-year degree.

In scanning the latest job search announcements, it is clear that more and more public parks and recreation departments are requesting applicants be certified. These employers see the value in obtaining a certain level of education and a commitment to staying current by continually attending workshops and conferences.

Certified Therapeutic Recreation Specialist Therapeutic recreation was one of the first professional specializations in recreation to initiate a strong national certification plan. In order to obtain a CTRS certification, professionals may follow either an academic path or an equivalency path. The academic path is for people who have completed a bachelor's degree or higher with a major or a recreation degree option in therapeutic recreation. The equivalency option is for people without a degree specifically in therapeutic recreation, but a bachelor's degree in another area as well as full-time work experience in therapeutic recreation. Regardless of the path chosen, both require successfully passing the CTRS exam.[23]

Standards in Nonpublic Leisure-Service Agencies Both the National Recreation and Park Association and the American Association for Physical Activity and Recreation, which have been the prime movers in the attempt to strengthen professionalism in leisure-service agencies, have had as their main targets either public recreation and park departments or schools and colleges. In general, the employees in nonprofit and commercial agencies have not been identified as key players in the recreation certification movement. Hiring in such agencies therefore has not been influenced by the NRPA/AAPAR accreditation efforts or the certification plan just described.

However, national organizations such as the Ys, Scouts, and Boys' and Girls' Clubs are obviously concerned with helping their local councils, branches, or other direct-service units maintain a high level of staff competence. They do that through specialized training. For example, the YMCA has its own professional organization

Joe Derrig, Corporate Meeting Planner, Walgreens, Graduated August 2005

As a meeting planner, it is my responsibility to work on the event logistics for our three large annual meetings. On any given day, I could be working on all three events in one day. Some of the responsibilities that I have are going to onsite visits, allocating the meeting rooms for each meeting, estimating the number of attendees, reviewing food and beverage needs, coordinating presenters and their presentations, updating our meeting database, or talking on the phone with an outside vendor for ground transportation or language translation services. In the beginning of our planning, you can find me searching numerous meeting websites trying to find the "perfect" location for our next meeting. What I like best about my job is being able to be a part of planning a large event from concept ideas through to the finished project. It takes a lot of time, blood, sweat, and tears to pull everything together. When it is completed, it is a very bittersweet moment.

dedicated to providing training to all levels of staff. The Association of YMCA professionals provides chapter, regional, and national training opportunities for YMCA staff, career and human resources manuals, and financial support for training needs.[24]

Other Certifications   Because not all jobs in the leisure-service profession are best associated with the CPRP or CRRS certification, a number of others available may better reflect job responsibilities.

> *Certified meeting professional*   For people who plan meetings, conventions, and exhibitions.[25]
>
> *Certified playground inspector*   This certification is offered by the National Playground Safety Institute.
>
> *Aquatics facility operator (AFO)*   An AFO is trained in managing and operating aquatics facilities.
>
> *Wilderness Education Association National Standard Program*   This 21–35 day program is for people wishing to be certified as outdoor leaders and work in outdoor education, outdoor leadership, and wilderness therapy.[26]
>
> *Certified special-events professional (CSEP)*   Awarded by the International Special Events Society certification is earned through education, experience, and service to the industry. Professionals are required to earn 35 points through education attainment, professional association leadership, and special-event industry experience, then they must pass an examination that includes objective questions, solving a case study, and the review of a professional portfolio.[27]

National Association for Interpretation   offers certifications in a number of outdoor-related areas including Certified Interpretive Guide, Certified Interpretive Host, and Certified Interpretive Planner.[28]

Agency Accreditation Process   Another example of the thrust toward fuller professionalism in the organized recreation, park, and leisure-service field is found in the accreditation process for local public departments initiated in the mid-1990s. For an agency to become accredited, it must examine all aspects of its operations, from maintenance to marketing, and adhere to carefully developed standards of excellence. An outside team of park and recreation practitioners visit the agency to see how well it is meeting the set standards and to offer suggestions for improvements to the agency. Currently, there are 59 accredited agencies.[29] Many of the directors of the accredited agencies have used accreditation as a benchmark for improving services offered to the community and to show the public their tax-supported agency is using its resources wisely.[30]

Agency accreditation is also done in the camping industry. The American Camping Association accredits camps that meet specific safety, health, and program quality standards. An onsite visitation team examines such areas as facilities, transportation, human resources, programs, and health and wellness.[31]

Criterion 6: Code of Ethical Practice

A final important measure of any profession is that it typically outlines the public responsibilities of practitioners and establishes a code of ethical behavior. In fields such as medicine or law, where the possibility of malpractice is great and the stakes are high, strict codes of ethics prevail.

In the field of leisure services, it might appear that any issues related to ethical practice are not as critical as in these other professions. However, in specialized areas

Angelyn Hyland, Recreation Supervisor, Belvidere Park District, Graduated August 2005

My specific responsibilities include aquatics, teen programs, and special events. In the summer, my main focus is the pool. I supervise and train the lifeguards and concession/cashier/guest services staff. I have six managers who are at the pool each day to ensure that everything runs without a hitch. I help with in-service training throughout the summer, conduct staff meetings, schedule rentals and birthday parties, supervise special events, and serve as a resource for staff and patrons to our facility. Teen programs are new to our park district. I just recently started them from scratch. We offer such programs as an after-school program called "The Zone," a Limo Scavenger Hunt, and a Battle of the Bands Event. It was neat being able to interact with the teens and participate in activities with them. One particular special event I worked with was the Daddy-Daughter Sweetheart Dance. What a fun evening for the girls and their dads! What makes it more special for me is remembering when I was their age and going with my dad... to the very same dance! What I love most about my job is the passion I have for it and being able to share that passion with my staff and participants.

such as therapeutic recreation, where patients or clients are likely to be physically, emotionally, or economically vulnerable, the opportunities for harmful, negligent, or unprofessional behavior are great. In other areas of leisure service as well, professionals should have a strong sense of obligation to those they serve, to their communities, and to the profession itself.

NRPA's Professional Code of Ethics stresses integrity, honesty, public confidence, professional excellence, fiscal responsibility, and support of equal employment opportunities, while the American Camping Association stresses integrity, truthfulness, fairness to all people, and an agreement to comply with relevant laws of the community.[32, 33]

International Special Events Society (ISES) Principles of Professional Conduct and Ethics Your special event is important—the last thing you want to worry about is the integrity of your special-events professional. That's why all ISES members subscribe to the ISES Principles of Professional Conduct and ethics, listed here.

Each member of ISES shall agree to adhere to the following:

- Promote and encourage the highest level of ethics within the profession of the special events industry while maintaining the highest standards of professional conduct.
- Strive for excellence in all aspects of our profession by performing consistently at or above acceptable industry standards.
- Use only legal and ethical means in all industry negotiations and activities.
- Protect the public against fraud and unfair practices, and promote all practices which bring respect and credit to the profession.
- Provide truthful and accurate information with respect to the performance of duties. Use a written contract clearly stating all charges, services, products, performance expectations and other essential information.
- Maintain industry accepted standards of safety and sanitation.
- Maintain adequate and appropriate insurance coverage for all business activities.
- Commit to increase professional growth and knowledge, to attend educational programs and to personally contribute expertise to meetings and journals.
- Strive to cooperate with colleagues, suppliers, employees, employers and all persons supervised, in order to provide the highest quality service at every level.
- Subscribe to the ISES Principles of Professional Conduct and Ethics, and abide by the ISES Bylaws and policies.[34]

[Used with permission from the International Special Events Society. © 2007. All rights reserved.]

Criterion 7: Existence of Extensive Professional Development Opportunities

A true profession will have many avenues for professionals to develop their skills, knowledge, and abilities in their chosen career after their degrees are completed. Conferences, workshops, seminars, and institutes are held at the state, regional, and national levels, focusing on training opportunities in all areas of the profession. For example, the American Camping Association has an annual national conference and several regional conferences such as the Tri-State Camp Conference and the New

England Conference. The National Intramural Recreational Sports Association offers workshops and institutes throughout the year such as National Fitness Institute, Outdoor Recreation Symposium, and the National School of Recreational Sports Management. Recreation is a changing profession and it is necessary to continually educate its practitioners in order for them to continue to provide quality services.

In addition to workshops and trainings, most professional associations have monthly, quarterly, or annual publications with articles focusing on issues in the field. The American Alliance of Health, Physical Education, Recreation and Dance has the *Journal of Physical Education, Recreation and Dance*; the North American Society of Sport Management has the *Journal of Sport Management* and the Resort and Commercial Recreation Association has *Resort+Recreation*.

CURRENT LEVEL OF PROFESSIONAL STATUS

When the seven accepted criteria of professionalism reviewed here are used as the basis for judgment, it is apparent that the recreation, parks, and leisure-service field has made considerable progress toward becoming a recognized profession.

Some elements are already securely in place, such as the development of a unique body of knowledge and the establishment of a network of college and university programs of professional preparation. As for the professional organization element, the National Recreation and Park Association and other national associations or societies do represent a significant force for upgrading and monitoring performance in the recreation field, but their attempts to serve the interests of a wide variety of leisure-service agencies also illustrate the field's continuing fragmentation. Realistically, many practitioners in such specialized disciplines as special-event planning, employee recreation, and varied aspects of commercial recreation tend to identify more closely with their separate fields than they do with the overall leisure-service field. Even in the more difficult areas of certification and the development of ethical codes, some considerable progress has been made, although the concept of enforcement continues to be a problem in both areas.

Professionalism in recreation, parks, and leisure services has increased greatly over the past five decades, along with the growing recognition of the field's value in modern society. Because of the immense scope of the diversified recreation field in terms of employment, it has the potential for becoming even more influential in contributing to community well-being in the years ahead.

SUMMARY

Recreation, parks, and leisure services have grown immensely as a career field, with several million people now employed in the 10 different areas of organized recreation. Of this overall group, it is estimated that several hundred thousand individuals should be regarded as professionals due to their academic training, job functions, and organizational affiliations.

This chapter describes several important criteria of professionalism, including the following:

1. Having a significant degree of social value, in terms of providing benefits to individual participants and/or to community life
2. Being recognized by the public as a meaningful area of social service or as a legitimate occupational field
3. Requiring specialized professional preparation on the college or university level, based on a distinct body of theoretical and practical knowledge
4. Having profession-related associations that involve national and regional organizations that sponsor conferences, research, publications, and other efforts to upgrade practice and that promote collegiality and a sense of commitment among the practitioners
5. Having a credentialing system to ensure that only qualified individuals—usually identified through a system of certification—are permitted to undertake professional-level tasks
6. Having a code of ethics to ensure that responsible and effective service is provided to the public
7. Having extensive professional development opportunities

Although the recreation, parks, and leisure-services field has not as yet met all of these criteria of professionalism fully, it has made substantial progress on most of them. As recreation and leisure become increasingly important aspects of life in the years ahead, the challenge to the leisure-service field will be to become even more highly professionalized by building on the foundation that has already been laid.

QUESTIONS FOR CLASS DISCUSSION OR ESSAY EXAMINATION

1. Before reading this chapter, what was your understanding of the meaning of the term *profession*? Since reading the chapter, has your understanding of this word changed? How important do you believe it is for any occupational field to be regarded as a profession?
2. Several criteria are generally accepted as hallmarks of professionalism, such as having a social mandate or set of important social values or having a body of specialized knowledge. Select any four of these, and discuss the extent to which you believe the recreation, park, and leisure-service field meets these criteria of professionalism.
3. Some educators believe that the field of professional preparation in recreation and parks has two contrasting sets of priorities: (1) the need to provide practical skills in personnel management, budgeting, marketing, programming, and similar functions; and (2) the need to focus on the theoretical (philosophical, historical, etc.) study of recreation and leisure. Do you believe this is a significant concern? Present an argument for either of these two positions.
4. The leisure-service field has developed into 10 different specialized areas, such as public, nonprofit, commercial, and therapeutic recreation, with some of these having a number of distinct subspecializations. Do you believe that it is possible for this fragmented field to develop and maintain a single, common identity in order to gain fuller public support and understanding? How could this be done?

ENDNOTES

1. www.nrpa.org/content/default.aspx?documentId=757. Accessed 15 April 2007.

2. C. M. Ross et al., *Mastering the Job Search Process in Recreation and Leisure Services* (Boston: Jones and Bartlett Publishers, 2006).

3. Travel Industry Association of America, www.tia.org. Accessed 15 April 2007.

4. Bureau of Labor Statistics, U.S. Department of Labor, *Occupational Outlook Handbook, 2006–07 Edition*, Recreation Workers, www.bls.gov/oco/ocos058.htm. Accessed 15 April 2007.

5. D. D. McLean, *2005 Annual Information Exchange* (Terre Haute, IN: The Center for State Park Research Indiana State University, 2006).

6. C. M. Ross et al., *Mastering the Job Search Process in Recreation and Leisure Services* (Boston: Jones and Bartlett Publishers, 2006).

7. R. Kraus et al., *Introduction to Leisure Services: Career Perspectives* (Champaign, IL: Sagamore Publishing Inc., 2001).

8. C. M. Ross et al., *Mastering the Job Search Process in Recreation and Leisure Services* (Boston: Jones and Bartlett Publishers, 2006).

9. International Festivals and Events Association, www.ifea.com/about/. Accessed 13 April 2007.

10. Navy MWR Intern Program, www.mwr.navy.mil/mwrprgms/intern.html. Accessed 15 April 2007.

11. R. Kraus et al., *Introduction to Leisure Services: Career Perspectives* (Champaign, IL: Sagamore Publishing Inc., 2001).

12. Hewlett Packard Employee Recreation program, www.hprecreation.com/clubs.htm. Accessed 15 April 2007.

13. Rossmoor Retirement Community Clubs and Activities, www.rossmoor.net. Accessed 15 April 2007.

14. www.nrpa.org/content/default.aspx?documentId=757. Accessed 15 April 2007.

15. J. C. Crossley et al., *Introduction to Commercial Recreation and Tourism: An Entrepreneurial Approach*, 4th ed. (Champaign, IL: Sagamore Publishing Inc.)

16. Bureau of Labor Statistics, U.S. Department of Labor, "American Time Use Survey—2004 Results Announced by BLS," www.bls.gov/news.release/pdf/atus.pdf.

17. Travel Industry Association of America, www.tia.org. Accessed 15 April 2007.

18. National Park Service Public Use Statistics Office, www2.nature.nps.gov/stats/. Accessed 15 April 2007.

19. H. Douglas Sessoms, "A Critical Look at the Recreation Movement," *Recreation for the Ill and Handicapped* (Washington, D.C.: National Association of Recreation Therapies, 1965): 11, 14.

20. North American Society for Sports Management, "Sports Management Programs: United States," www.nassm.com/InfoAbout/SportMgmtPrograms/United_States.

21. A. R. Hurd and B. E. Schlatter (in press), "Establishing Cooperative Competency Based Internships for Parks and Recreation Students," *Journal of Health, Physical Education, Recreation & Dance*.

22. National Recreation and Park Association, "Mission, Values, and Goals," www.nrpa.org/content/default.aspx?documentId=490. Accessed 15 April 2007.

23. "Certification Standards Part 1: Information for New Applicants," New York, NY: NCTRC.

24. Association of YMCA Professionals, www.aypymca.org/. Accessed 15 April 2007.

25. Convention Industry Council, Certified Meeting Professional (CMP) Program, www.conventionindustry.org/cmp. Accessed 15 April 2007.

26. Wilderness Education Association, www.weainfo.org/courses.html. Accessed 15 April 2007.

27. International Special Events Society, Certified Special Events Professional, www.ises.com/CSEP/. Accessed 15 April 2007.

28. National Association for Interpretation Certification Program, www.interpnet.com/certification/index.shtml. Accessed 15 April 2007.

29. National Recreation and Park Association CAPRA Accredited Programs, http://www.nrpa.org/content/default.aspx?documentId=1040. Accessed 15 April 2007.

30. National Recreation and Park Association, "CAPRA Testimonials," http://www.nrpa.org/content/default.aspx?documentId=3521. Accessed 15 April 2007.

31. American Camping Association, "About Accreditation," http://www.acacamps.org/accreditation/hnolearn.php. Accessed 15 April 2007.

32. National Recreation and Park Association, "Professional Code of Ethics," www.nrpa.org/content/default.aspx?documentId=493. Accessed 16 April 2007.

33. American Camping Association, "Code of Ethics," www.acacamps.org/membership/ethics.php. Accessed 16 April 2007.

34. International Special Events Society, "Principles of Professional Conduct and Ethics," www.ises.com/about/principles.cfm. Accessed 16 April 2007.

CHAPTER 13

FUTURE PERSPECTIVES OF RECREATION AND LEISURE

◆ ◆ ◆

Definition of Future

The future has always had a very special place in philosophy and, in general, in the human mind. This is true largely because human beings often want a forecast of events that will occur. It is perhaps possible to argue that the evolution of the human brain is in great part an evolution in cognitive abilities necessary to forecast the future, i.e., abstract imagination, logic, and induction. Imagination permits us to "see" (i.e., predict) a plausible model of a given situation without observing it, therefore mitigating risks. Logical reasoning allows one to predict inevitable consequences of actions and situations and therefore gives useful information about future events. Induction permits the association of a cause with consequences, a fundamental notion for every forecast of future time.[1]

◆ ◆ ◆

INTRODUCTION

The remarkable growth of organized recreation, park, and leisure services has been documented throughout this text. Despite the impressive recent history of this social movement and field of professional activity, a number of serious questions still exist in regard to the appropriate role of recreation in community and national life.

For example, how can recreation contribute more effectively to the battle against such social ills as poverty, racial or ethnic hostility, crime and delinquency, and economic deprivation? What solutions can be found for the overcrowding and vandalism that affect many urban, state, and federal parks and recreation facilities? How do we provide effective recreation services in an era of "pay-as-you-go" recreation? What is the appropriate role and responsibility of urban, suburban, rural recreation agencies, and nonprofit organizations?

How should the major priorities of organized recreation service in the United States be determined? In what ways can or should government provide more effective and efficient services in this field? What are the special responsibilities of organized recreation toward people with physical and mental disabilities, toward the new aging, or toward those who may have had inadequate opportunities in the past because of their gender or other demographic factors?

How have technological developments—especially the Internet, blogging, iTunes, social networking, online gaming, Blackberrys, and cell phones—affected both leisure patterns and the management of recreation programs? How will leisure-service professionals respond to such changes in the years ahead?

Should recreation sponsors simply seek to meet the expressed wishes of the public for enjoyable play, or do they have a moral responsibility to also present socially constructive and desirable leisure programs? Are we moving toward an experience-based society as exhibited by "thrill junkies" or do there remain those focused on learning, caring, and giving? With regard to violence, overemphasis on winning in sport, and policies governing drinking, drugs, gambling, or sexually oriented play, what should the role of recreation professionals be?

How will the changing social and economic conditions in the decades ahead affect the public's leisure values and patterns of participation, and how can recreation, park, and leisure-service professionals and organizations respond effectively to the challenges of the future?

NEED FOR A SOUND PHILOSOPHICAL BASIS

Obviously, such issues should be resolved within the context of a coherent set of values, moral beliefs, and social priorities. What is needed is a sound philosophy of recreation and leisure that can serve the leisure-service field in ongoing policy formulation and program development.

Meaning of Philosophy

The term *philosophy* often conveys an image of ivory tower abstraction, divorced from practical or realistic concerns. Understandably, many practitioners are likely to be suspicious of any approach that appears to be overly theoretical, rather than pragmatic and action based. The nature of the manager/practitioner is to be in the here and now. They look for answers that will assist them today and tomorrow, not six months or three years in the future. Philosophy, more often than not, provides more questions than answers. In far too many instances, it is easier to deal with the present than to anticipate the future and one's appropriate role in shaping that future.

How, then, is *philosophy* to be defined? Of the possible examples presented in previous chapters, the definition, stating that philosophy consists of the body of principles underlying a major discipline or human activity, as expressed in guidelines for conduct, is the most useful for our purpose.

This chapter will not present a single approach of recreation and leisure and argues that it represents the only acceptable system of goals and values. Instead, it will (1) identify seven prevailing approaches to providing organized recreation services in the present; (2) discuss various changes that are occurring today in terms of work and leisure availability, demographic influences on leisure, and prevailing social values as they affect recreational participation; (3) present a number of forecasts of future trends; and (4) suggest some guiding principles for the organization of community recreation services in the years ahead.

OPERATIONAL PHILOSOPHIES OF RECREATION AND LEISURE

It is possible to identify several approaches or orientations found in leisure-service agencies today that may be called *operational philosophies*. These include the following: (1) the quality-of-life approach, (2) the marketing or entrepreneurial approach, (3) the human services approach, (4) the prescriptive approach, (5) the resource manager/aesthetic/preservationist approach, (6) the hedonist/individualist approach, and (7) the benefits-based approach.

Quality-of-Life Approach

The *quality-of-life approach* has been the dominant one in the field of organized recreation service for several decades. It sees recreation as an experience that contributes to human development and to community well-being in various ways: improving physical and mental health, enriching cultural life, reducing antisocial uses of leisure, and strengthening community ties.

The quality-of-life orientation stresses the unique nature of recreation as a vital form of human experience—one that is engaged in for its own sake rather than for any extrinsic purpose or conscious social goal. Generally, proponents of this view have agreed that recreation satisfies a universal human need that has been made even more pressing by the tensions of modern urban society, the changed nature of work, and other social conditions. In an early text, Meyer, Brightbill, and Sessoms commented that community recreation led to the development of democratic citizenship and sound moral character and to the reduction of social pathology.

Those holding this view argue that the pleasure, freedom, and self-choice inherent in recreation and leisure are their most vital contributions to the lives of participants. Quality-of-life advocates have tended to assume that public recreation should be supported for its own sake as an important area of civic responsibility, and that adequate tax funds should be provided for this purpose. In today's era of intense competition for limited tax dollars, the quality-of-life issue remains important, yet the concept of full tax support for parks and recreation is recognized as no longer viable.

Marketing or Entrepreneurial Approach

The *marketing* or *entrepreneurial approach*, a business-oriented approach to providing organized recreation and park programs and services, evolved rapidly during the latter part of the twentieth century as a direct response to the fiscal pressures placed on public and voluntary leisure-service agencies. As noted in earlier chapters, steadily mounting operational costs and a declining tax base during that time forced many recreation and park departments to adopt what has come to be known as the marketing approach to agency management. This approach is based on the idea that public, voluntary, or other leisure-service providers will flourish best if they adopt the methods used by commercial enterprises. It argues that they must become more aggressive and efficient in developing and promoting recreation facilities and programs that will reach the broadest possible audience and gain the maximum possible income.

Proponents of the marketing approach take the position that recreation and park professionals should not have to plead for tax-based support solely on the basis of the social value of their programs, but should seek to become relatively independent as a viable, self-sufficient form of community service.

It should be recognized that the marketing trend has influenced far more than public recreation and park agencies alone. Many large nonprofit youth-serving organizations, such as the YMCA, YWCA, and YM-YWHA, have been forced to increase their reliance on self-generated revenues and to move into more aggressive marketing of a wide range of leisure programs, including their fitness services.

Although the marketing approach has been enthusiastically received by many recreation and park managers, it raises a number of issues with respect to the essential purpose of public and voluntary leisure-service agencies. The argument has been made that increased fees and charges—whether imposed by the agencies themselves or by concessionaires or contractors working under privatization plans—tend to exclude the people in greatest need of inexpensive public recreation opportunities, such as children, persons with disabilities, and people who are economically disadvantaged.

Human Services Approach

In direct contrast to the marketing approach is the *human services approach* to organized recreation service. This approach regards recreation as an important form of social service that must be provided in a way that contributes directly to a wide range of desired social values and goals. The human services approach received a strong impetus during the 1960s, when recreation programs were generously funded by the federal government as part of the war on poverty, and recreation was used to offer job training and employment opportunities for economically disadvantaged youth and adults in America's ghettos.

The human services approach is similar to the quality-of-life approach in its recognition of the social value of recreation service. However, it does not subscribe to the latter's idealization of recreation as an inherently ennobling kind of experience, carried on for its own sake. Instead, within the human services framework, recreation must be designed to achieve significant community change and to use a variety of appropriate modalities.

This does not mean that recreation personnel should seek to be health educators, employment counselors, nutritionists, correctional officers, legal advisors, or housing experts. Rather, it implies that they must recognize the holistic nature of the human condition, provide such services when able to do so effectively, and cooperate fully with other practitioners in the various human services fields when appropriate.

Operating under this approach, many public recreation departments have sponsored youth or adult classes in a wide range of educational, vocational, or self-improvement areas and also have provided day-care programs, special services for persons with disabilities, roving leader programs for juvenile gangs, environmental projects, and numerous other functions of this type.

In its forceful emphasis on the need to meet social problems head on and achieve beneficial human goals, the human services approach to recreation and park programming may at times be at odds with the marketing approach to service. In the marketing approach, efficient management and maximum revenue are often the primary aims. In the human services orientation, social values and human benefits are emphasized.

Prescriptive Approach

Of the orientations described here, the *prescriptive approach* is the most purposeful in the way it defines the goals and functions of the recreational experience. The idea that recreation should bring about constructive change in participants has been stressed in a number of textbooks on programming. For example, Ruth Russell describes "programmed recreation" chiefly as a form of organized and purposeful activity designed in an orderly and deliberate way to achieve desirable individual and group results.[2]

The clearest cases of prescriptive recreation programs are found in therapeutic recreation. For example, Paul Wehman and Stuart Schleien describe the curriculum design sequence in therapeutic recreation as it is used to develop either an individualized education program or an individualized habilitation plan. In order to help patients or clients master important motor skills, improve social behavior, or achieve other goals of treatment, members of the treatment team review the individual's level of illness or disability, past recreation, education, other experiences and skills, and current level of functioning. On the basis of this review, a curriculum is devised to include the following program components: (1) a program goal, (2) an instructional objective (short term), (3) a task analysis of each skill, (4) the verbal cue required for instruction in the skill, (5) materials that are required for instruction, and (6) teaching procedures and special adaptations for each skill.[3]

Although it is similar to the human services approach in its emphasis on deliberately achieving significant social goals, the prescriptive approach differs in its reliance on the practitioner's expertise and authority. In contrast, a recreation professional working within a human services framework would be much more likely to value the input of community residents and to involve them in decision making.

Resource Manager/Aesthetic/Preservationist Approach

The unwieldy title *resource manager/aesthetic/preservationist approach* is used as a catch-all model to lump together three elements that are not synonymous but that exhibit a high degree of similarity. The *resource manager* obviously is concerned with managing, using, and protecting the outdoor environment. The balance between use, preservation, and protection is a difficult issue that is hotly contested by planners and stakeholders. The *aesthetic* position is one that values the appearance of the environment, both natural and artificial, and stresses the inclusion of cultural arts and other creative experiences within a recreation program. The *preservationist* seeks to maintain the physical environment not simply out of a respect for nature, but to preserve evidence of a historical past and a cultural tradition.

This approach to recreation planning is more likely to be evident in agencies that operate extensive parks, forests, waterfront areas, or other natural or scenic resources. Thus, one might assume that it would chiefly be found in such government agencies as federal and state park departments that administer major parks and outdoor recreation facilities. However, this is not the full picture. Many urban recreation and park planners are responsible for large parks. Recent years have seen a growth of new large urban parks in areas that are experiencing growing populations with economically advantaged residents. Often they may help to rehabilitate or redesign rundown waterfront areas, industrial sites, or gutted slum areas. In many cases, their purpose is to preserve or rebuild historic areas of cultural interest that will maintain or increase the appeal of cities for tourism and cultural programming. Preservation and restoration are the primary focus for older parks while new development with revenue producing facilities are becoming more common in newer or newly developed park and recreation agencies and communities.

Environmental Awareness   A key element in this approach is the deep reverence that many individuals have today for nature in its various forms. Daniel Dustin described the experience of being interconnected with the natural world and the spiritual value that human beings derive from their varied experiences with wilderness.[4] Douglas Knudson points out that love for nature and acceptance of responsibility for it is

> more than watching birds with binoculars or identifying spring wildflowers. It is the perceiving—the understanding—of the ways in which nature operates. The relatedness of all elements of the environment provides the key to perception. The rhythm of natural changes provides the beat. When man perceives the processes, he understands better the Creation and feels the refreshment of recreation in its deepest sense.[5]

Interest in environmental and cultural sites remains high and management of such areas is an important national issue.

However, environmental programming approaches cannot be carried out simply through a poetic evocation of the beauty of nature. Political and economic realities also come into play when environmental decisions must be made. The George W. Bush presidency has been particularly challenged both in the media and the courts for its environmental record. Between 2001 and 2005, the National Resources Defense Council (NRDC) documented issues relating to parks, wilderness areas, forest recreation, air pollution, water quality, public health, endangered species, and nuclear insecurity. "Knight Ridder" compiled 14 pollution-oriented indicators from government and university statistics. Eight of the 14 indicators showed a worsening trend, two showed improvements and three others zigzagged.

Statistics that have worsened include:

- Superfund cleanups of toxic waste fell by 52 percent.
- Fish-consumption warnings for rivers doubled.
- Fish-consumption advisories for lakes increased 39 percent.
- The number of beach closings rose 26 percent.
- Civil citations issued to polluters fell 57 percent.
- Criminal pollution prosecutions dropped 17 percent.
- Asthma attacks increased by 6 percent.
- There were small increases in global temperatures and unhealthy air days.[6]

Addressing outdoor recreation experiences, a 2005 California State Parks report suggests, "The market for outdoor recreation experiences appears to be changing. If we do not change our way of managing outdoor recreation, we risk irrelevance and erosion of public support."[7] Society is becoming so diverse that traditional management methods are not keeping pace with expectations of users. The environmental awareness approach must change to adapt to the expectations of the new user.

Hedonist/Individualist Approach

The *hedonist/individualist approach* to recreational programming is concerned chiefly with providing fun and pleasure. It regards recreation as a highly individualistic activity that should be free of social constraints or moral purposes. The term *hedonist* is used to mean one who seeks personal pleasure, often with the implication that it is of a sensual, bodily nature. The term *individualist* is attached because this philosophical approach stresses the idea that each individual should be free to seek his or her own fulfillment and pleasure untrammeled by group pressures or social expectations.

Obviously, certain forms of leisure activity that have gained increased popularity in U.S. life fit this description. The accelerated use and generally freer acceptance of drugs, alcohol, gambling, and sex as a commercialized recreational pursuit, and other forms of sensation-seeking entertainment and play illustrate the hedonist approach to leisure. These forms of play may best be described as morally marginal, in the sense that they are legal in some contexts or localities and illegal in others, regarded as acceptable leisure experiences by some population groups and condemned by others.

Drug and Alcohol Abuse The use of mind-altering or mood-changing substances as a form of pleasure-seeking or socializing experience has been found in many cultures and human societies, both past and present. Alcohol may be legally sold and consumed by adults throughout most of the United States and is generally considered to be a useful social lubricant consumed at weddings and family parties, business luncheons, neighborhood taverns, and a host of other kinds of recreation settings. In contrast, the use of narcotic drugs is illegal unless medically prescribed, and provides the basis for an immense underworld industry.

Drugs are generally regarded as a far greater threat to health and safety than alcohol—yet, each year, while cocaine, crack, and heroin take about 7,000 American lives, alcohol claims about 100,000. Someone is killed by a drunk driver every 24 minutes, and over 500,000 people are injured in alcohol-related traffic accidents each year.

Organized Gaming   Over the past three decades, organized legal gaming in the form of casinos, lotteries, racetrack betting, and numerous other commercially sponsored games has proliferated at breakneck speed in the United States. In 1988, casinos were present in only two states—Nevada and New Jersey. Today they are present in 11 states. Casinos operated by Indian tribes are present in 28 states. More pervasive are lotteries, present in 41 states, plus the District of Columbia. In 1995, casinos netted $61.0 billion and in 2004 they netted $28.9 billion. Total gaming, including off-track betting, Internet gaming, and the like netted $45.1 billion in 1995 and $72.9 billion in 2006. These numbers are huge when placed in the context of the U.S. economy. Internet gambling, much of it illegal, accounted for $11.9 billion in 2005 and involved 23 million people worldwide, including an estimated 8 million Americans.

Throughout the United States, city after city has fallen for the economic lure of legalizing varied forms of gambling, authorizing riverboat casinos that never leave the shore (except when they travel to a more attractive setting financially), and approving off-track betting parlors and varied slot machine gaming operations. While the

◼ *Gambling continues as an immensely profitable industry in the United States in casinos; on riverboats, cruise lines, and airplanes; through the Internet; and via racetrack simulcasts.*

argument is made that tax revenues, gaming-related jobs, and visitor spending help to sustain local economies, there is growing evidence that the social costs of gambling make it an unprofitable enterprise for most localities.

What is most significant about the tremendous growth of the gaming industry is that it illustrates a basic transformation in America's prevailing value system. Although some still reject legalized gambling as not only destructive of the lives of millions of compulsive bettors but also as a cynical exploitation of the public trust, the majority of citizens today tend to accept it as an appropriate kind of leisure experience—and state and local governments look to gambling as a savior to replace lost taxes.

Commercialized Sex   A third form of morally marginal leisure that is a key component of the hedonist approach to recreation and leisure is the use of sex as a form of play or entertainment. Commercialized sex expanded dramatically over the three decades following the counterculture movement of the 1960s. It takes many forms, including legalized houses of prostitution in Nevada, call girl rings, and the escort services and massage parlors that represent thinly disguised forms of prostitution in many cities; sex films, books, and magazines that may now be legally purchased; the widespread rental of X-rated videocassettes for home viewing; and the increased showing of explicit sexual images and themes on network television programs and of "hard porn" on cable television.

A recent manifestation of commercialized sex as an element in popular culture involves its broader exploitation within the mass media of entertainment and communication. Increasingly, the phenomenon of *cyberporn*—the transmission of varied types of erotica on the Internet—has prompted national concern. Awareness that children have easy access to such materials and that the Internet is being used for recruitment of sexual partners led to continuing efforts to curb such abuses.

Although public, nonprofit, and other types of community-based leisure-service organizations generally do not sponsor substance abuse, gambling, or sex-oriented types of entertainment, such activities are widely available through commercial sponsorship and, in many cases, have governmental approval or tacit acceptance.

Benefits-Based Management Approach

The final philosophical approach to the design and implementation of recreation, park, and leisure-service programs—the *benefits-based approach*—is relatively new. It was the subject of a number of presentations at NRPA congresses in the 1990s and has been discussed in numerous publications. Essentially, this approach holds that it is not enough to verbalize a set of desirable goals or mission statements or to carry out head counts of participation and tally the number of events sponsored by a leisure-service agency. Instead, governmental, nonprofit, therapeutic, armed forces, and other types of managed recreation agencies should more clearly define their roles and purposes in terms of community and participant benefits.

In practice, the benefits-based approach is based on a three-step implementation process:

1. *Benefits and opportunity identification:* Determine a core group of benefits that users seek and agencies can realistically provide, along with the management changes needed for benefits achievement.

2. *Program implementation:* Make facility or staff modifications needed to achieve desired benefits, and carry out systematic monitoring procedures during programs.
3. *Evaluation and documentation:* Analyze data, determine if program benefits were achieved, develop reports, and disseminate findings to appropriate audiences.[8]

Within this process, it is essential that target goals be defined in terms of concrete and measurable benefits. A benefits-based approach focuses its measures on *outcomes* that measure long-term change or effect, rather than *outputs* that simply describe a program.

Benefits-based management is grounded in the understanding of outcomes of participation in recreation programs, whether they be organized or unorganized and whether they be group, family, or individual. An understanding of the benefits derived from participation in various recreation activities is essential to the success of benefits-based management programs. A variety of "benefits" reports have been published. Most recently California State Parks reported on the health and social benefits of recreation. The report focused on benefits related to (1) physical health, (2) mental health, (3) social benefits related to strengthening communities, (4) promoting social bonds, (5) and youth development.[9] The Trust for Public Lands focused its report on the need for more city parks and open space. Its 2006 report addressed (1) economic benefits, (2) public health benefits, (3) environmental benefits, and (4) social benefits.[10]

Philosophical Approaches: No Pure Models

It should be stressed that although these seven approaches to the definition and management of organized leisure services are separate and distinct philosophical positions, it is unlikely that any single agency or government department would follow one approach exclusively.

The changing nature of the political, economic, and social environment has forced park and recreation agencies to reevaluate traditional approaches to delivering public parks and recreation. No single approach has been discarded, but some have fallen out of favor with politicians and professionals. Especially impacted has been the human services approach. As mentioned elsewhere, the availability of funding for parks and recreation has not kept up with inflation and in many cases has been significantly reduced. The influence of the war on terrorism and the ongoing conflict in Iraq has had a negative influence on funding for public parks and recreation—yet agencies are expected to provide more programs and services and to maintain existing and new facilities, constituencies, and markets. The business marketing approach, the fastest growing approach to delivery, has been embraced at all levels of government. Services remain available, utilizing the human services approach, especially in major urban areas. In suburban areas, with higher family incomes, super-sized recreation centers are replacing older neighborhood centers or are being created in the place of smaller centers. In growing urban fringe areas where recreation services or centers have never been present, or present as only a small operation, the supercenter is an attractive amenity for their growing population. Supercenters typically charge membership fees, higher prices for programs, cater to an upscale economic population, and are located in areas of the community where disadvantaged individuals may not have ready access. In addition, the supercenters have more of a club ambience than traditional recreation centers representing a move away from the human services approach.

KEY RATIONALE GUIDING LEISURE-SERVICE DELIVERY TODAY

For recreation, parks, and leisure-service practitioners, it is possible to identify a number of key principles that should be used to guide their professional operations today. First, it is assumed that such individuals—no matter what their fields of specialization—regard recreation and leisure as important to human growth and community development. A contemporary philosophy of organized recreation service therefore should deal with such important issues as the place of recreation and leisure in modern life, the role of government, the development of programming based on significant social needs, and the place of leisure education.

Place of Recreation in the Modern Community

In U.S. society, our view of recreation as a social phenomenon and area of community involvement is influenced by our governmental systems. In our Constitution and in court decisions that have influenced government policy and practice through the years, we have accepted the view that, on various levels, government has the responsibility for providing certain major services to citizens. These include functions related to safety and protection, education, health, and other services that contribute to maintaining the quality of life of all citizens.

Linked to this system of governmental responsibility is our general acceptance of the Judeo-Christian concepts of the worth and dignity of all human beings and the need to help each person become the most fully realized individual that he or she is capable of being. Through government and through many voluntary community associations, we have accepted the responsibility for providing needed services and opportunities for people at each stage of life and for those who because of disability have been deprived in significant ways.

Needs of Individual Citizens

Recreation and leisure are important aspects of personal experience in modern life for the physical, social, emotional, intellectual, and spiritual benefits they provide. Positive leisure experiences enhance the quality of a person's life and help each person develop to the fullest potential. To make this possible, government and other responsible social agencies should provide recreation resources, programs, and, where appropriate, leisure education to help people understand the value of free time when constructively and creatively used.

Government's Responsibility

In addition to providing these personal benefits, recreation helps a community to meet health needs, gain economic benefits, and maintain community morale. On each level (local, state, and federal), appropriate government agencies should therefore be assigned the responsibility for maintaining a network of physical resources for leisure participation, including parks, playgrounds, centers, sport facilities, and other special recreation facilities. Government should be responsible for planning, organizing, and carrying out programs, under proper leadership, for all age levels.

Government cannot and should not seek to meet all of the leisure needs of the community. It must recognize that other types of community organizations—including voluntary, private, commercial, therapeutic, industrial, and educational groups—sponsor effective recreation programs, which are often designed to meet specialized needs or more advanced interests. Therefore, its unique role should be to provide a basic floor of recreational opportunity, to fill the gaps that are not covered by other organizations, and to provide coordination and overall direction to community leisure-service programs.

There has been a growing body of opinion that local government recreation and park agencies should take less responsibility for the direct provision of program activities, particularly when limited by fiscal constraints, and should move instead into the role of serving as an advocate for recreation and leisure in community life and providing coordinating or facilitating assistance to other agencies.

A major concern should be to ensure an equitable distribution of recreational opportunities for the public at large. This would not guarantee that all residents have totally equal programs and services, but would represent a pledge that, within the realities of community needs and economic capabilities, facilities and programs will be distributed so as to bring about a reasonable balance of such opportunities for different neighborhoods and community groups.

Influence of the Nonprofit Sector

The nonprofit sector has accepted an increasingly larger role in the provision of recreation and leisure-based social services. An important part of the effort has focused on youth-serving agencies in at-risk neighborhoods. There are several reasons why nonprofits have taken an increasing role. First, this is not a new model for nonprofits to assume, but rather a continuation and expansion of services when local members of the community realize that the government cannot provide needed services. Secondly, more individuals are willing to give to nonprofits, are able to give substantial sums of money, and are willing to give to their community. Nonprofits are frequently seen as a more desirable and effective organization to address social ills than is government. Finally, government has recognized its inability to meet all of the needs of a community and either encourages nonprofits and/or works jointly with them.

OTHER GUIDELINES

In addition to these general guidelines, there are a number of others that are of particular relevance to the role of leisure-service professionals.

Coordination and Partnering

U.S. society today has many organizations of various types that provide leisure services, but they often do so with marked duplication and in wasteful competition with each other. At the same time, there are continuing gaps in service that result in unmet needs.

It is therefore essential that public, private, voluntary, commercial, and other types of leisure-service organizations cooperate fully in determining community needs and accepting appropriate functions and roles for themselves in providing recreational opportunities. This helps to prevent unnecessary competition among agencies and to identify and fill gaps in community leisure services. Similarly, the various types of sponsors could share resources and know-how and even develop partnerships that would be more effective than the work of any single agency could be.

Participant Input

A sound contemporary philosophy of recreation dictates that participants themselves should be as fully involved as possible in the determination of program emphases and needs. This can be accomplished through the use of neighborhood committees or advisory councils, recreation and park boards, task forces, or volunteers. Most planning mandates community involvement. Such participation has a dual benefit: (1) Community residents are able to provide leadership, advice, assistance, and other resources to the program; and (2) they are engaged supporters of the

■ *Participant input has resulted in new and more creative neighborhood and regional park designs and play features.*

program and represent an active constituency for it in political and other strategic terms.

Although this principle is most obviously of use in government-sponsored recreation and park programs, it also applies to other types of membership organizations or specialized services. Particularly in such fields as campus, employee, and voluntary agency recreation, volunteer participation in planning groups and in the actual operation of programs is essential.

Balance of Marketing and Human Services Approaches

The marketing and human services approaches to leisure-service management appear to represent sharply opposed philosophical orientations. Can they be reconciled? As earlier chapters have shown, economic and other factors have compelled a much more aggressive and fiscally oriented thrust in the marketing of leisure services, among nonprofit as well as profit-oriented agencies. Entrepreneurship is encouraged and rewarded in some agencies—yet, a number of authors have emphasized that although organizations in the public sector may adopt an entrepreneurial approach, they must also be concerned with social and economic priorities that benefit the overall community.

From a pragmatic point of view, it is necessary to link the marketing and human services approaches through appropriate objectives, policies, and management techniques. This means that while every effort should be made to plan and market recreation programs and services as efficiently and economically as possible—with the intention of maximizing revenues for support of the department—it is also necessary to establish certain social priorities and to meet these critical needs despite their costs or the inability of recipients of special services to pay their way.

Within this context, the benefits-based management approach described earlier in this chapter provides a potentially useful means of reconciling the marketing and human services models. Agency targets may incorporate both fiscal and social elements and, when achieved, should result in a higher level of financial support overall for recreation and park budgets.

A useful approach that is followed in armed forces recreation involves classifying varied program elements based on their contribution to the mission of the MWR operation. Those with the highest value with respect to MWR's goals receive fuller financial support, without fees being imposed for participation. Other program elements must charge fees that support their operational costs and make them self-sustaining.

Need for Effective Leisure Ethic

Finally, there is a need to promote effective leisure education among the various sectors of the public and among professionals in other areas of community service or in special disciplines. The heritage of our Puritan forebears and our centuries-long dependence on the Protestant work ethic have combined to make many Americans suspicious of recreation and to keep them unaware of its potential value in human society and in the day-to-day lives of individuals and families.

The effort to encourage a fuller understanding and appreciation of creative and constructive forms of leisure involvement is particularly critical today in light of the changes that have occurred over the past two decades. As described in earlier chapters, many of the most popular forms of entertainment in sport, the mass media, tourism, and similar leisure domains are now dominated by a few huge conglomerates—multibillion dollar businesses that determine the kinds of free-time attractions to be presented to the public. Their primary concern is profitability, and often their products and services include negative or self-destructive forms of play that are designed and marketed in highly sophisticated and efficient ways.

In the mid-1990s, it became clear that the nation was greatly concerned about the breakdown of traditional family values and social structures and that the mass media of entertainment were increasingly being seen as a leading cause of major social problems. This development provides an important opportunity for recreation, park, and leisure-service professionals to make their voices heard and to promote a positive and constructive set of leisure values among Americans of all ages.

FACING THE CHALLENGE OF THE FUTURE

The principles and guidelines that have been presented here deal essentially with the present. However, those who read this book—primarily college and university students in recreation, park, tourism, sport, and leisure-studies curricula—are looking ahead to careers in the future. What will the rest of the twenty-first century bring us in terms of demographic, social, and economic changes that can radically affect our uses of leisure?

Traditional forms of leisure are growing, but at a slower rate than the population. New diverse forms of leisure, often individual or Internet based, are growing outside of traditional program areas. Academic programs and curricula based on a twentieth century model will not prepare students and professionals for the challenges of the twenty-first century. Recognition of a social responsibility ethic grounded in community engagement structured in the context of a do-more-with-less government reality is what students and professionals must be prepared to address. The awareness of environmental and social justice in society and how public park and recreation will address these issues are paramount to the profession's future.

Many contemporary authorities in the leisure-service field emphasize that bringing about needed changes will require a new wave of entrepreneurship. Recreation and park professionals in all spheres of service need to think more imaginatively and innovatively, need to be more goal-oriented and flexible, and need to be more willing to take risks in order to achieve outstanding results. They need to cultivate an organizational and professional climate that is interactive, with everyone sharing common purposes and working to achieve them.

EFFORTS TO PREDICT THE FUTURE

In the mid- to late-1990s, there was much interest and discussion about how the twenty-first century would impact parks and recreation. This discussion appears to have been lost with the arrival of the twenty-first century. The end of a century builds a momentum of hope for change, of a better tomorrow, of new opportunities, of choice, evoking concerns and anticipations. When people came back to work on January 2nd, 2000, they found their computers still worked, the bills were still due, the people in leadership positions had not changed, and their lack of ideas for the future had not changed. It was a business-as-usual model; that is the pessimistic model of the twenty-first century. It also represents reality for many people. For others, a different reality is present. Individuals who embrace change—willingly, hesitantly, or wish they didn't have to—are impacting parks and recreation in the twenty-first century. Much continues to be written about the new century and more appropriately the great changes to occur in this century. The remainder of this chapter looks at key issues facing the future of the parks and recreation profession and some of the implications.

Agendas in the Twenty-First Century

There has been no single national effort by park and recreation organizations to address the twenty-first century's impact on parks and recreation; individual organizations have focused on trends that impact themselves. The broader societal impact has been left for others to deal with. The U.S. Forest Service operates a trends center; states generate five-year state comprehensive outdoor recreation plans that are of varying quality with some to significant trend analysis. Many municipalities have master plans for development and some have strategic plans. In both instances, trend analysis may be a small or significant part of the plan. Some state park and recreation associations, especially California, make efforts to keep their members abreast of trends. The problem facing trend analysis in parks and recreation is the diversity of the profession itself. Some trends cross boundaries between urban recreation, outdoor recreation, city parks and recreation departments, state park systems, national parks, and nonprofits, but there are many other trends that do not. National trends paint a broad picture for individuals to look at while regional and local trends may be significantly different. Making assumptions that trends will occur as predicted is equally dangerous. In 1999, the economy looked as if it would continue to be positive. First the economy began to falter, then on September 11, 2001, the economy, society, and trends were thoroughly disrupted by the great tragedy of that day.

How then do park and recreation organizations focus on trends that have some basis of validity? There are those who are considered as futurists and have a track record of success. Trends, at their best, are educated guesses about the future. They are influenced by those who are suggesting them—their knowledge, biases, and creative ability to anticipate change.

The trends have led to conclusions about the future of parks and recreation, and especially about public and nonprofit agencies that requires a response. Some of these trends emerged at conferences and workshops held in the mid- to late-1990s and remain current. Others were gleaned from a variety of sources including futurist literature. Key conclusions include:

- Park and recreation professionals must embrace societal change as it is the only way to serve the public and ensure the future of their organization.
- The trend toward greater public participation in decision making is a reality and public agencies must ensure that employees are trained to facilitate and respond to public input.
- Wellness will continue to be a major issue. Obesity is the most immediate issue facing public park and recreation agencies. Major efforts are required involving partnerships to address this growing issue.
- Public agencies will continue to receive less of the public dollar for operations, maintenance, and repairs. The public will continue to support and fund land acquisitions through bond referenda and other sources, but the agencies will have to learn entrepreneurship to maintain operations.
- Success will continue to depend on an organization's ability to build cooperative relationships and establish networks and coalitions with other organizations.
- Federal leadership in the recreation and parks movement will wane as the challenges of an aging society, globalization, international commitments, and other unforeseen challenges reduce the ability to support traditional services.
- Park and recreation agencies need to embrace the new generations and use their technological competence to introduce them to the outdoors, fitness, and expanded leisure opportunities.

- Demographic complexity, expressed as age complexity, income complexity, gender complexity, and lifestage complexity are indications of social shifts in society that require park and recreation agencies to rethink for who, what, and how they offer programs.
- An understanding of current users, nonusers, potential users, and their motivations is the foundation for creating change and meeting the needs of the current and future generations.
- Public agencies must provide environmental leadership on a local and global perspective. For too long, the parks and recreation profession has been quiet on this front.
- There is a mandate to embrace tourism, the world's largest economy, on a local, regional, and national level in ways that have not been done before. Partnerships are only a part of the role to be taken; there is a need to think like a tourist destination.
- Agencies must rethink the recreation experience in light of increased technology impacting leisure activities, segmentation and specialization of participation, individualized personal recreation, time deepening, time shifting, and activity stacking.

CHALLENGES AND STRATEGIES FOR THE FUTURE

Challenges Linked to Population Diversity

Age Diversity   That portion of the population called baby boomers (those born between 1946 and 1964)—or boomers as they are known—is staggering. In addition, the population distribution as whole has changed dramatically over the last 50-plus years and the impact on society and government will be significant. In 1967, the median age in the United States was 29.5. In 2006, the median age had grown to 36.2. That may not seem significant until you view Figure 13.1 and see how the boomers impact the age span of Americans. The senior (boomer) population will continue to grow. The first boomers were born in 1946 and are now beginning to retire. The later boomers were born in 1960 to 1964, and for the most part, are past their child-bearing years and have made their contributions to society's population growth. The white line represents the size of each age group in the 1990s with the gray area representing the results of the 2000 census. The 36- to 54-year-old age groups (43 to 61 in 2007) represent the boomers. They are 28 percent of the total U.S. population. Note their size in relation to other portions of the population and how the bulge is shifting upwards to older age groups.

Society is changing in more ways than just aging. In 1915, the population reached 100 million people. Fifty-two years later in 1967, it reached 200 million people and 39 years later, it reached 300 million. Foreign-born residents represented 15 percent of the U.S. population in 1915, 8 percent in 1967, and 12 percent of the population in 2006. In 1915 and 1967, the largest percent of the foreign-born population came from Europe; today it is Mexico.[11]

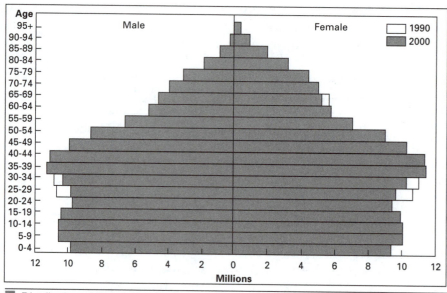

■ *Distribution of Population by Age and Sex; U.S. Census Bureau*

Aging Society   As demonstrated previously, the United States is an aging society. For the first time in history, Americans are reaping the benefits of advances in science,

■ *More and more adults are celebrating "the new old". . . a new generation of seniors, aging on their own terms.*

technology, health care, nutrition, and affluence as never before. The life expectancy of Americans has nearly doubled in the past century; in 1900, the life expectancy was 47 years and in 2000, it had risen to 77. Individuals living into their late 80s and mid-90s is no longer uncommon. Concern has risen about how the new generation of elderly will be cared for. Some have suggested as much as 20 percent of the workforce will focus on the aging boomers. In some states, particularly the midwest and northeast, health care is already the largest industry.

Yet, can we expect the boomers, as they enter retirement, to do the same as earlier seniors? The answer appears to be no. They will make their own mark on society and do it their way, which is a continuation of their lifelong contributions to change in society. The early assumption was made that boomers would go into full retirement as so many others have. Changes in the economy, retirement benefits, concerns about Social Security and Medicare, health care costs, longevity, and overall health have changed perceptions about retirement. In a report by Merrill Lynch, they found only 17 percent of boomers surveyed said they would never work again, and this 17 percent was the least financially prepared for retirement.[12] By contrast, 76 percent of those surveyed plan to work during stages of retirement. When asked why they will continue to work, 34 percent said it was important to earn money and 67 percent wanted the continuing mental stimulation and challenge to motivate them. The end of mandatory retirement in 1986 allowed many seniors to continue to work and contribute to the workforce. Simultaneous with the end of mandatory retirement, the Social Security system retirement ages were raised to 66 and 67. Between 1994 and 2005, there was a 17 percent increase in the number of men working between ages 62 to 64, a traditional retirement period. Overall, the workforce of men and women age 60 to 64 grew from 52.8 million to 58 million.[13] Boomers do not see retirement as a period of relaxation and reduced lifestyle, but rather a continuation of challenges and personal growth— but on their own terms. The decision to retire is based more on the ability to do what they want and having the resources to do it, than on the need to retire in a more traditional sense.

This picture is incomplete without a better understanding of the composition and well-being of the over-65 population. Eighty-two percent of this group are white, 8 percent black, 3 percent Asian, 6 percent Hispanic, and 1 percent mixed race. The percentage of white will decline by 2050 with Hispanics becoming the largest over-65 minority, followed by African Americans. This age group is overwhelmingly married (79 percent for the 65–74 age group). As an example, only 19 percent of men live alone while 40 percent of women do. Poverty is an issue among the over-65 group with 9.8 percent reported living at the poverty level or below in 2004. Although this is a continuing concern, the numbers have declined steadily from 1959 when the poverty rate was 35.2 percent.[14]

What does all of this mean? First, the 72-and-out rule is gone. It has been assumed for generations that most people would die by the age of 72. That has not been true for decades, but never more so than with boomers. There are 75 million over-50s in the United States and they hold approximately 90 percent of America's $44 trillion in liquid assets. The wealth is not evenly spread across this population. An amazing 42 percent of all boomers plan to move in retirement. Boomers are moving south and west to warmer climates. Boomer men are planning to work less, spending more time with their spouses, and relaxing more. Women see retirement as an opportunity for career development, community involvement, and continued personal growth. Demands for recreation and leisure will increase, but not necessarily for traditional services. The boomers will be better able to pay for services and activities and will be more demanding of creative and nontraditional services.

Park and recreation professionals will be challenged to determine how to serve boomers. The days of senior centers, bingo, cards, Friday afternoon movies, and bus tours will not be over, but will not attract the large number of seniors who see themselves as independent. Cities are establishing separate senior service departments or integrating them into existing departments. There will be a need to continue to provide traditional services to those who desire them, but for many, they will seek new experiences and greater challenges. Recent research holds promise for improving recreation programming for boomers and other seniors. Some research suggests that older adults will focus on more meaningful relationships at the expense of less-important relationships. Healthy older adults may benefit from activities that focus on

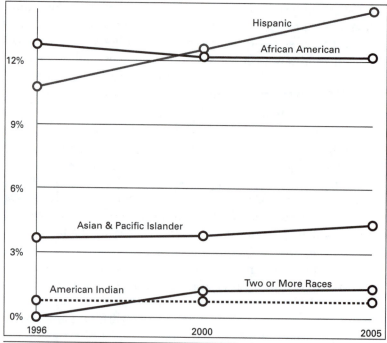

■ *Changes in Minority Population as a percent of the total U.S. population 1996–2005*

goal selection and optimization. Older adults with more limited health should benefit from adapted and facilitated activities.[15] Regardless of the approach taken, public park and recreation agencies need to understand that older adults are more diverse and have higher expectations than any previous generation.

Ethnic and Racial Diversity   As we have already seen, the United States is becoming more diverse. The immigration of Europeans has lessened dramatically, replaced by rapid integration of Hispanics, and lesser so of Asian, Middle Eastern, and African populations. The 2000 census showed the diversity. Hispanics were the fastest growing minority in the United States as depicted in Figure 13.2. The decline in the African American percentage is almost wholly explained by the declaration of two or more races by individuals, which was first initiated with the 2000 Census.

Research into the influence of race and ethnicity has been slow in developing. Some early research set the stage for a better understanding of why there are differences. More recently, Hibbler and Shinew identified four factors that explain the differences in leisure patterns. The four reasons are

> (1) the limited socio-economic resources of many African Americans; (2) a historical pattern of oppression and racial discrimination towards African Americans; (3) distinct cultural differences between African Americans and European Americans; and (4) feelings of discomfort and constraint by African Americans in public leisure settings.[16]

There is a growing realization that assimilation of immigrants is a complex issue. They are more ethnically diverse, may have complex intergenerational changes, and are growing rapidly in number. For example, Mexican immigrant women have seen it as their responsibility to maintain their culture. Beyond immigrant and generational issues, different ethnic groups view leisure at once similarly and differently. African Americans prefer shopping, going to church, and open spaces that serve active recreation-related function. Caucasians show a greater preference for open space for land; wildlife;

■ *New immigrants bring with them their own culture and customs. Integration into American society is often difficult.*

passive-, individual-, or family-based recreation; and conservation. Hispanics and Asians tend to come to outdoor areas in larger family groups for social purposes. African Americans, Caucasians, and Hispanics all shared similar views toward social-setting attributes such as sharing experiences, being by oneself, and so forth. Research has made progress in explaining differences in race and ethnic decisions and preferences for leisure, but the field is still not well understood.[17, 18]

Children   Americans are experiencing the most sustained economic growth of any time in history. For the most part, U.S. children are growing up in relative luxury compared to their grandparents, who grew up in relative luxury compared to their grandparents. There are also greater challenges facing today's youth than at any time in history. The list of challenges facing youth is debilitating, but at the same time, youth have a resilience not found in many adults. Public park and recreation agencies, nonprofit youth-serving organizations, and government social service agencies all have made strides to work with disadvantaged and at-risk youth. This is especially true in urban and inner-city areas.

Globalization is contributing to a period of major society change and has particular impact on children. This era of globalization is evidenced by advances in investment, technology, manufacturing, mobility, and investment coinciding with dramatically increased prosperity. Although corporate decision making may be influenced by globalization, it is the social frameworks that are frequently being negatively impacted. It has created a scale of migration from Mexico and Central America previously unseen. As previously discussed, the migration of Hispanic populations represents the fastest growing immigrant group over the last 20 years. Youth from developing countries are less likely to be academically, socially, economically, physically, and emotionally prepared to enter the U.S. social fabric and lead full and productive lives. Already the Hispanic population has the highest high school dropout rate in the United States.

The youth population has been declining as a percent of the total population, from 26 percent in 2000 to a projected 24 percent in 2010 where it is expected to stabilize for a decade. The good news is that couple households represent 75 percent of all the children and 25 percent represents single-parent households.[19]

The shift to an urban society continued to increase until in 2000, 83 percent of all children lived in urban areas, including the suburbs and exurbs. Generations of contact and grounding with a rural environment have been replaced by city parks, community recreation centers, YMCAs, YWCAs, Boy Scouts, Girl Scouts, Camp Fire USA, and other organizations. In many cases, these organizations changed their orientation from a strong rural to a strong urban perspective. Today's camps are less likely to be overnights away from home than they are to be day camps in parks or on nonprofit-owned properties usually in or near the neighborhood where the children live.

A major area of concern for U.S. youth is their well-being. Many different reports and groups study well-being besides the U.S. government. The Annie E. Casey Foundation sponsors the *Kids Count* report on the well-being of America's youth which

TABLE 13.1

AMERICA'S CHILDREN AT A GLANCE

Characteristic	2004 Data
Children 0–17 in total population	73.3 million
Children as a proportion of the population	25%
Racial and ethnic composition (age 0–17)	
White	76.5%
White, non-Hispanic	58.9%
African American	15.5%
Asian	3.9%
All other races	4.1%
Hispanic (of any race)	19.2%
Children 0–17 living with 2 married parents	67%
Children 0–6, not in kindergarten who received some form of nonparental child care	61%
Children 0–4 with employed mothers whose primary child care is with a relative	48%
Related children ages 0–17 in poverty	17%
Children 0–17 in households classified by USDA as "food insecure"	19%
Children 0–17 covered by health insurance	89%
Children 5–17 with activity limitations due to chronic health conditions	8%
Children 6–17 who are overweight	18%
Regular cigarette smokers—12th graders	14%
12th graders reporting having 5 or more alcoholic beverages, in a row, in last 2 weeks	28%
12th graders reported using illicit drugs in the previous 30 days	23%
Youth offenders ages 12–17 involved in serious violent crimes	14 per 1,000
Young adults 18–24 who have completed high school	87%
Adults ages 25–29 who have completed a bachelor's or more advanced degree	29%

Source: Federal Interagency Forum on Child and Family Statistics, "America's Children in Brief: Key National Indicators of Well-Being," http://childstats.gov, 2006, 14–16.

is updated every other year. They measure items such as children's availability to health care and environmental conditions, economic growth of families, education, and the education conditions of young children. Childstats.gov is another government organization focused on well-being. This group looks at similar statistics to *Kids Count* and publishes an annual report on well-being. Table 13.1 depicts data focusing on youth well-being. This snapshot captures some of multiple areas of concern. A review of the table suggests areas of social concern, such as tobacco use, lack of child care services, illicit drug use, violent crime, and the like. The United States is better able today to quantify social issues and the status of youth than at any time in history. Conversely, it creates greater demands on public agencies, including nonprofits and parks and recreation programs, to address these areas of concern.

Leisure professionals have a direct concern with these issues. The public parks and recreation movement was grounded as a social services movement that needs to frequently reinvest itself. Poverty is the most pervasive and abusing condition impacting children in America. UNICEF, in a 2005 report said,

> Children living in poverty experience deprivation of the material, spiritual, and emotional resources needed to survive, develop and thrive, leaving them unable to enjoy their rights, to achieve their full potential or to participate as full and equal members of society.[20]

The child poverty rate declined during the 1990s, but was still at 17 percent for children between 0 and 17 years of age and 6 percent for children under 6. This occurred in spite of 78 percent of children's parents in the workforce. The problem rises from disparity in the workforce. Skilled and professional laborers have seen continued growth in income while those without skills have seen a rise in less-secure forms of employment that frequently provides minimal or no health care. Lack of health care impacts 11 percent of children and 16 percent of children were not immunized in 2004 despite efforts at the state and local level.[21, 22, 23]

Leisure is a commodity in the lives of children that is essential and developmental. Government and nonprofit agencies are joining to serve urban at-risk youth to provide services and opportunities. The challenges are significant and agencies are balancing meeting needs and simultaneously serving other populations of taxpayers who demand services and are frequently willing to pay for them.

Changing Teens and Family Lifestyles   The discussion of children is incomplete without a discussion of teens and of changing family lifestyles. The Harris Poll regularly tracks trends among teens and has become an important source for information about this age group. Many other organizations watch trends in teens for various reasons including market forces, college directions, family issues, social stresses, and so forth. The Partnership for a Drug-Free America identified five teen trends: (1) they are stressed; (2) they are hypersexualized; (3) friends are the new family; (4) the traditional family has been redefined; and (5) diversity isn't something they are taught—they live with it.[24]

Today's researchers have discovered that any study of teens must also include tweens, that age group from 8 to 12 years of age. Tweens are between being children and teens and the five-year timeframe represents a period of dramatic physical, emotional, and social growth. For example, 61 percent of tweens said their mother understands them best, but only 20 percent of teens said the same thing.[25] These groups are different and create sometimes challenging dynamics in family lifestyles. Activities families do most often together include eating dinner at home, watching television, going out to eat together, food and grocery shopping, watching rented movies, and visiting relatives.[26]

Teens interaction patterns change between 12 and 18. They begin to rely more heavily on their peers, are trend conscious, and react to peer pressure. The Harris Poll and Pew Internet Initiative found teens to be major users of the Internet and have become the innovators in social networking. MySpace.com is a prime example of how teens connect on the Internet. Twenty-five percent of teens instant message, 12 percent use cell phones, and only 5 percent still use email—what they call an arcane technology. This generation and its immediate elders, born between 1978 and 1997, are called *millennials*.

Environmental Challenges

Americans have and continue to struggle to think beyond their borders. As a group, they, for the most part, fail to see a global picture as it relates to the environment. Americans are not alone in this narrow view of the world, yet they seem to epitomize a lack of concern for the environment. Whether it be a loss of open space, the continued purchasing of gas-guzzling vehicles, or a super-size approach to living and buying, it seems our indifference amid our wealth is considered by some of the world community as selfish and inexcusable.

Environment and Population   The United States represents just 5 percent of the world's population and consumes almost 25 percent of every natural resource—more than any other nation in the world.[27] Americans have the largest "ecological footprint" of any country in the world.[28] Beyond this, the United States is the only industrial country still experiencing rapid growth and projections are that this will not end soon. A list of how Americans lead the world in consumption of natural resources includes the loss of 3,000 acres (1,214 hectares) of farmland daily. Land converted for development occurs at twice the rate of population growth. We have become a nation of sprawl represented by low-density development in the suburbs and exurbs. The exurbs are growing at a rate almost three times that of urban areas. The United States accounts for almost half (46 percent) of the annual carbon dioxide emitted into the environment and represents the primary cause of global warming. Americans produce five pounds of garbage per day; five times the average amount in developing countries.[29]

The Center for Environment and Population suggests that the United States is now a metro nation, a "lifestyle [that] differs from urban-centered lifestyles in that it requires extensive use of motor vehicles and rapid, extensive land development."[30] The McDonalds influence on U.S. culture to super-size everything has moved from french fries to houses, shopping centers, recreation centers, and land and resource consumption. The center goes on to report, "the 'super-sized' lifestyles of so many people affect the quality of everyday life causing, among other things, more frequent, worse traffic jams, and expenditure of more money and effort to heat and keep-up more and/or larger homes."[31] The impact on recreation is not lost. Demand for recreation

Wal-Mart Challenges the Way Americans Light Their Homes
In late 2006, Wal-Mart made a decision to change American's buying habits for lightbulbs. For over 100 years, Americans have purchased the traditional lightbulbs even though for over 10 years CFL or energy-saver fluorescent bulbs have been available. A CFL uses 75 percent less electricity, lasts 10 times longer, produces 450 pounds fewer greenhouse gases from power plants, and saves consumers $30 over the life of each bulb, but they don't produce the same level of light or as strong a light as traditional lightbulbs. Wal-Mart took it upon itself to sell 100 million bulbs by 2008. Efforts such as this by major retailers can help to overcome some of the negative aspects of global warming. Success of the venture would save Americans $3 billion in electricity costs and avoid the need to build additional power plants for 450,000 new homes.

facilities, park areas, and access to these is growing in metropolitan and adjacent areas. Congestion in this country's key natural resources has been well documented by the National Park Service and it is now being impacted at the state and community level.

Environmental and Open Space Loss   The environment is coming under increasingly difficult challenges, both as a part of national policy, and among Americans as a whole. In Iowa, the state government gives new homeowners a five-year tax relief if they purchase a new home on previous open space or farmland. Between 1992 and 1997, the United States paved over more than six million acres of farmland, an area approximately the size of Maryland. The United States developed (took out of active farm production) twice as much farmland in the 1990s as in the 1980s and the 2000s show no letup.

■ *Urban sprawl consumes 6,000 acres of land daily.*

Youth prefer computers to the out-of-doors. Parents are afraid to send their children outdoors because they too have lost their outdoor ethic. As a society, Americans have almost fully transitioned from a generation raised on or near farms to a generation raised in an urban environment. Like a zoo or museum, the outdoors is a place to visit and see, but not to partake of. Scares such as polluted beaches, Lyme disease, wasting disease in elk, and others have encouraged parents already unfamiliar with the outdoors to keep their children home. Attendance at national parks, national forests, state parks, and other rural recreation and preservation areas has been on decline at a time when the population is increasing. The influx of immigrants without an outdoor ethic has impacted the response to wilderness, outdoors, and preservation. This has been reflected in Congress as it has become more difficult to secure funds for park and recreation lands. For example, the Arctic National Wildlife Refuge is continuously under attack by politicians and oil interests in an effort to open the area to increased oil production.

Former Vice President Al Gore has become a leading spokesperson for the environment and climate change. His comments have helped focus much debate and most importantly have, for the moment, recharged some of America's concern about the environment. While Al Gore is the most visible person to address environmental concerns, he is not alone. Many national associations focusing on the environment are encouraging individuals to express concern and demand action. Oftentimes this action is local and even bounded by the property owned. The National Wildlife Federation encourages individuals to certify their backyards for wildlife. The Audubon Society encourages individuals to take the healthy yard pledge by reducing pesticides, conserving water, planting native species, protecting water quality, and supporting birds and other wildlife.

Many of the same organizations that are promoting local environmental awareness and action are also active at the national and international level.

Loss of Environmental Ethic   Discussed elsewhere in this book, the loss of the environmental ethic by Americans is very real. A 2005 Harris Poll indicates that 74 percent of Americans agreed that "protecting the environment is so important that requirements and standards cannot be too high, and continuing environmental improvements must be made regardless of cost."[32] At the same time, Americans appear to be participating at a lower rate in traditional visits to state and national parks. Table 13.2 shows a mixed picture of attendance with a decline between 2000 and 2004 for state and national parks. Just looking at attendance numbers would suggest that every American visits a state or national park several times a year. The reality is different. As the right hand columns demonstrate, when comparing attendance to the actual U.S. population, the percentage of Americans visiting state and national parks is in decline. It would appear that visiting these areas is becoming either less important or out of the reach of Americans.

The issue is less clear than it might at first appear. Attendance may be down for state and national parks, yet the willingness of Americans to vote funding for parks and open space remains high. From 2000 through 2005, Americans voted $53.7 billion in 840 local and state elections providing funding for parks and open space acquisition, maintenance, and operation. These are state, county, and local endeavors where voters choose to tax themselves to provide open spaces and parks. The vast majority of the

TABLE 13.2

CHANGES IN ATTENDANCE AT STATE AND NATIONAL PARKS WHEN COMPARED TO TOTAL POPULATION GROWTH

Year	State Parks	National Parks	Population	% Change in Relation to Total Population	
				% State Park	% National
2004	697,445,710	276,900,000	293,907,000	–12.91%	–5.27%
2000	766,842,123	279,900,000	281,424,602	–3.45%	–1.66%
1995	752,266,297	269,600,000	266,557,000	–5.76%	–2.76%
1990	744,812,234	258,700,000	248,718,302	13.04%	–5.83%
1985	631,746,699	263,400,000	238,466,000		

funds were for acquisition of lands. The money has not been equally distributed across the United States. The northeast, the largest center of population in the United States, has voted for considerably more measures than any other region. Five midwestern states did not pass a single measure as did two western states and three southern states. The other 40 states passed at least one measure to support parks and open space. Does this mean local spaces are more important than national or state places? Probably not, but there are clearly shifts in preferences and only part of those shifts can be attributed to ethnic and cultural influences.[33]

In addition to federal, state, and local agencies providing recreation and park opportunities and places, there are many watchdogs of government agencies. The federal government's handling of environmental issues impacting national parks and wilderness areas has been a particular area of criticism. The National Environmental Trust has pointed to air quality significantly diminishing the quality of individual experiences of visitors (see Figure 13.3). They point to a 27-year-old requirement administered by the Environmental Protection Agency that has not been enforced. The Natural Resources Defense Council points to the impact of climate change on western U.S. national parks stating,

> Many scientists think the American West will experience the effects of climate change sooner and more intensely than most other regions. The West is warming faster than the East, and that warming is already profoundly affecting the scarce snow and water of the West. In the arid and semi-arid West, the changes that have already occurred and the greater changes projected for the future would fundamentally disrupt ecosystems. The region's national parks, representing the best examples of the West's spectacular resources, are among the places where the changes in the natural environment will be most evident. As a result, a disrupted climate is the single greatest threat to ever face western national parks.[34]

Global Warming as an Archetype of Global Environmental Issues   Humans have impacted the environment as never before. The 1997 Kyoto Protocol named after an international conference convened in Kyoto, Japan, is often credited as the most

Glaciers vanish from Glacier National Park.

Yellowstone's grizzlies face a food shortage.

Scenic meadows disappear in the Rockies.

Crowds and pollution increase in Yosemite.

Beaches flood in Coastal California parks.

Colorado Plateau parks become too hot to handle.

Mountain landscapes fade in Cascadia parks.

Endangered national parks in the western United States.
Source: Environmental News Service, "Human Impact Triggers Massive Extinctions," www.ens-newswire.com/ens/aug1999/1999-08-02-06.asp, 1999.

significant environmentally based international agreement of the twentieth century. The essence of the agreement was for developed nations to reduce their greenhouse gases (CO_2 emissions) to 5 percent below their 1990 levels and for less-developed countries to be allowed to make a lesser contribution to reductions. Of the 166 countries that signed the protocol, only the United States and Australia refused to ratify it. Other countries including India and China and other smaller developing countries were exempt from the protocols because most greenhouse gases are coming from developed countries.

There are various agreements and discussions occurring regarding the environment on an international scale. The Kyoto Protocol and global warming are an archetype of issues facing the world today and into the twenty-first and twenty-second centuries. A longer list of environmental issues includes loss of diversity (biodiversity), ocean and fresh water pollution, clean air issues, the impact of urban environments, the loss of forests and most especially tropical rainforests, and the impact of megadisasters such as the tsunami impacting the coasts of Indonesia, India, and other countries in 2004, or Hurricane Katrina's devastation along the gulf coast of the United States.

Diversity relates to the frequency of plant and animal life in the world. In 1999, the International Botanical Congress reported, "the 'human footprint on Earth' is increasingly impairing the planet's ability to maintain the quality of human life, and may lead to the loss of up to two-thirds of all plant and animal species during the second half of the 21st century."[35] Water quality issues range from closing of polluted beaches, now a common problem along the U.S. coastline, to depletion of major portions of the world's fisheries by mid-century. The world's fresh water supply is improving, but almost half of world's population does not have running water in their homes or access to sanitation systems. Clean air, long an issue in the United States, has taken on global dimensions with automobile and industrial emissions creating major health problems in both developing and developed countries and is linked to global warming.

The problems appear to be massive and in some cases governments seem to be oblivious. Public park and recreation organizations, environmental- and outdoor-based nonprofits, and federal land management and protection agencies traditionally have been proponents of protection and rationality. The organizations sometimes have been at odds, especially at the national level when the executive branch of government has been perceived as unfriendly to the environment. Local government has a mixed response to environmental issues and city, county, and state agencies have not provided the level of leadership that once was common. Park and recreation agencies can provide leadership by example in their communities into the twenty-first century.

Influence of Technology on Leisure

Technology impacts the way people live and the way they experience leisure. For example, California State Parks in 2005 issued a trend report including a discussion about technology. Some of its conclusions are provided here:

- Americans *love* their toys and baby boomers expect "amenity-rich" experiences.
- Technology will continue to affect how we work and how we play.
- Each generation [is] better educated, more adept with, and more dependent on, technology than the previous generations.
- Technological advances affect the affordability, accessibility, and required skill level of many recreation activities.
- Technology allows "mass customization."
- New activities will be developed around innovative devices and products.
- Technology creates entirely new recreation uses.
- People tend to self-define and organize around their chosen form of recreation.
- Each group tends to want (demand) their own exclusive allocation of resources.[36]

These findings only tell part of the story. The current younger generation is the first generation to grow up with computers; hence they are called *digital natives*. The Pew Internet and American Life project defines digital natives as having been born in 1985 or later, and have been one of exposure to computers and the Internet. Table 13.3 depicts key events in their lives connected to the Internet. Parents and other individuals born before 1985 are considered to be *digital immigrants* or those who have had to adapt to technology rather than having grown up with it. It is a little like being an immigrant and having to learn a whole new language and culture.

Technology has changed the way we communicate. As little as 30 years ago, mail was the most common communications method. There was only one long-distance telephone company nationwide. Long-distance telephone calls were expensive and usually reserved for special occasions or for business enterprises. Most families subscribed to a morning newspaper and watched the network news on one of three

TABLE 13.3

KEY EVENTS IN THE LIVES OF THE FIRST GENERATION OF DIGITAL NATIVES

Date/Age	Technology Event
Birth—1985	Personal computers 10 years old
Kindergarten—1990	World Wide Web program written
Middle School—1996	PalmPilot goes on market
High School—1999	Sean Fanning creates Napster
Graduate High School—1999	iPod
Late Teens–Early 20s—1997	Blogs
Late Teens–Early 20s—2001	Wikipedia
Late Teens–Early 20s—2003	Del.icio.us
Late Teens–Early 20s—2003	Skype
Late Teens–Early 20s—2004	Podcasts
Late Teens–Early 20s—2005	YouTube, Facebook

Source: Lee Raine. "Digital Natives: How Today's Youth Are Different from Their 'Digital Immigrant' Elders and What That Means for Libraries," Metro–New York Library Council, Brooklyn Museum of Art. (Presentation). Washington, D.C.: Pew Internet and American Life Project, 2006: 1.

commercial channels. They listened to one or two local stations and only in larger markets was there a variety of music available on the radio.

Today Americans, on average, spend more waking time communicating and using media devices such as the television, radio, MP3 devices, and cell phones, than any other activity. The cell phone is an example of how technology has impacted individuals, families, work, and communities. Even the elderly use their cell phones to make contact while traveling, even if most of the time the phone sits turned off while at home. For younger adults (over 30), it is still primarily a telephone, but its use is expanding among this digital immigrant generation. The under-30 sector of the population uses their cell telephone to surf the Web, IM (instant message), take photos and create short videos, play games, get mobile maps, watch television or videos, listen to music, and more. The cell phone has become the digital Swiss army knife.[37]

It is more than just cell phones that impact our lives. A recent credit card commercial aired on national television depicts a marathon runner stopping at a convenience store during the race to purchase some water. The purchase is made by scanning a chip in his credit card almost instantaneously and allowing the runner to return to the race and maintain his lead. Automobiles regularly drive through toll booths without stopping as the toll is automatically recorded and deducted from a fund established by the driver with the toll agency. The fund is replenished automatically by computers for the toll agency and the bank. Purchasing on the Internet can be done by credit card or a variety of other means. A number of companies, such as Amazon.com and eBay, have flourished providing this type of service.

Citizens can attend town meetings, business meetings, and the like without leaving their home or office. Skype became the first free or low-cost Internet-based international telephone service and it has had a major impact on the developing world. Many bloggers share their email and Skype addresses simultaneously. The Internet has

■ *Technology impacts every aspect of our leisure.*

even had a significant influence on how people deal with illness. One study reported 54 percent of the adults responding saying the Internet played a major role as they helped another person cope with a major illness. The number who said the Internet played a role as they coped with a major illness increased 40 percent over a two-year period.[38] Nina Tote, cofounder of TypePad, reported at the 2006 TED conference on a woman who shared the last months of her life through a blog talking about life and the progress of her cancer. Everyone knew she had died when the final blog was written by her sister who reported the personal power the blog provided her sister of being able to share with others during the final months of her life. Forty-five percent of Internet users (60 million Americans) report the Internet played a major role in a decision made in the previous two years.[39] The top areas where the Internet assisted in decision making included additional training for a job; helping another person with a major illness or medical condition; choosing a college or school; purchasing a car; making a major investment or financial decision; finding a new place to live; changing jobs; or dealing with one's own major illness or other health condition.[40]

Technology is influencing recreation and leisure in ways that were never imagined even 10 years ago. As park and recreation professionals come to grips with technology's influence, it is from multiple perspectives: (1) professionals need to ask, "How can technology help me?"; (2) "How can I use technology to help our community, residents, and program participants?"; (3) "How do I reach those who we are not reaching or those who chose not to take advantage of our services?"; and (4) "How do we position ourselves to make the most of technology today and in the future?"

A number of implications result from technology that park and recreation professionals need to consider. They include, but are not limited to:

- Teens are less engaged in traditional recreation activities than their predecessors. They are more engaged in technology-based activities such as creating Web pages, posting photos and videos on social network sites, modifying music, sharing music, and being involved with their peers through the Internet and IM.
- There is greater competition for an individual's time. The notion of "free time" is almost a lost term. Technology has made this generation the most connected in history.
- Community members want active involvement, even if it is through the Internet. They do not want to be talked to, but talked with. The same is true for participating in programs offered by public and nonprofit agencies.
- Communicating images, program information, and building brands is far more difficult because of the plurality of communications alternatives. Sending home flyers through the public schools, sending brochures out in the mail, and advertising on traditional television stations will no longer reach the desired public. Knowledge about how different groups communicate, where they get their information, and how that information is determined to be important becomes essential for public agencies attempting to reach community members.
- Understanding the old "word-of-mouth" model is magnified a hundred- or even thousandfold is essential. Administrators used to believe that one person could influence five to eight people he or she came in contact with. Today that one person can influence thousands and even hundreds of thousands without ever making physical contact with people. Images of organizations and their public goodwill can be positively or negatively influenced by minor as well as major events.
- Public park and recreation agencies must learn to think and act in a digital age. Members must embrace technology as an important part of their operation, but more importantly, they must understand how their community members have embraced technology, whether they be 92 or 2. This suggests professionals need to be flexible and able to transition between digital natives, digital immigrants, and digital refusers.

Globalization of Leisure Globalization of leisure cannot be discussed without a short conversation on globalization. Globalization has been equally called a blessing and a curse, and sometimes by the same person. In the context of change, globalization is a relative newcomer. Economists first used the term in the early 1980s. Globalization is frequently referred to as the Americanization of the world. Another view sees globalization as the integration of economic, political, cultural, and environmental systems and structures worldwide. All of these areas are worthy of study, but from a leisure perspective, cultural and environmental influences have the greatest potential for current and future impacts.

Environmental globalization viewed from a protected-areas perspective provides a good example of globalization impacts. In the United States, we call protected areas parks, wilderness areas, national parks, state parks, national forests, and the like. Internationally, they are called protected areas. The World Conservation Union defines a *protected area* as "an area of land and/or sea especially dedicated to the protection and maintenance of biological diversity, and of natural and associated cultural resources, and managed through legal or other effective means."[41] The impetus for protected areas originated from the United States National Park Service, who early on were, and continue to be, leading proponents of creating protected areas. Early models into the 1970s tended to follow a U.S. format. Environmentalism, however, is not independent of its social context and is linked with other social and economic issues, politics, and competitions. The globalization of protected areas was initially Americanization based, but the movement matured and the American model is but a single model that has been shared globally. In some instances, protected areas have been created and indigenous populations continued to live on and utilize the lands as they have done for generations. In other instances, transnational boundaries have been crossed where two or more countries joined together to create a larger protected area. The globalization of environmentalism as related to protected areas has benefited from the ability to share models, lessons learned, adaptation to local settings, and the greater awareness a global perspective brings to resource managers.

TABLE 13.4

TOURISM AND GLOBALIZATION : EXAMPLES OF CONNECTIONS

Tourism	Globalization
Movement of people (tourists, workers in tourism industry)	Movement of people (immigrants and their cultures)
Movement of ideas (new cultural values with tourists; ways of doing business in tourism industry)	Movement of ideas (new technologies across the globe)
Movement of capital (tourism industry investment; foreign exchange earnings through tourism)	Movement of capital (instant movement of capital across borderlines)
Needs new technology to expand (wide-bodied jets)	Spread of new technology around the globe
Started at the latest in ancient Greece (limited to particular groups in society)	Started with first movement of humans (from Africa to Indonesia in 17,000 years using some of their original tools, maybe domesticated animals, etc.)
Enormous growth in the last 100 years	Time-spaced compression, in particular in the last 30 years
Toward traveling as a right for everyone; development of a world tourism culture?	World tourism culture?
Tourism needs local culture, or at least the image of it (differentation between destinations)	Toward a world culture

Source: Daniel L. Williams. "Leisure Identities, Globalization, and the Politics of Place," *Journal of Leisure Research* (Vol. 34, No. 4, 2002): 311.

Tourism provides the most easily identifiable impact of globalization. Some have even suggested that globalization is replacing sustainability as an organizing concept for tourism. According to Reiser, tourism and globalization have numerous examples of connections (see Table 13.4) and include, "the movement of people, the movement of ideas and the movement of capital across borderlines."[42] Tourists, or visitors, come with a set of expectations and are frequently challenged by the experiences. Visitors to Guatemala's Mayan cultural sites are often surprised by the tourist maps overlaid with transnational corporation logos. It moves the perception of a colonial site to a transnational site potentially impacting the visitor's experience. In heritage tourism, the plazas and barrios of Central America are the traditional gathering spots of local residents. Historic sites are residential areas, or as one described these areas, the communal urban "front porches" that globalization is changing. The impact of globalization on culture is significant and challenges long-held traditions, mores, and customs. It has been suggested that globalization is a time-space compression, emphasizing the way modernity restructures time-space relations and uproots social meanings and identities.[43] Globalization is changing the way we view, interact, and respond to the world. It has forced individuals and organizations to rethink their role in the homes, communities, and society. Williams argues that, "by recognizing modernity's fragmenting and disorienting qualities we can begin to focus on the strategies people have available and draw onto assemble a coherent narrative of self."[44]

SUMMARY

This chapter identifies seven distinct operational philosophies that influence the provision of organized recreation services today. These range from the quality-of-life and marketing orientations to a more recent model of service, the benefits-based management approach. While the chapter notes that most leisure-service organizations employ a blend of two or more orientations in their policy making and program planning, it suggests that the benefits-based model and the marketing or entrepreneurial model appear to be particularly favored in an era of dramatic social and economic change.

The concluding section of the chapter discusses a number of contemporary changes affecting parks and recreation. The changes relate to areas of direct concern to park and recreation professionals and include futures conclusions; population diversity; an aging society; ethnic and racial diversity; children, teens, and families, the environment and population; open-space loss; loss of an environmental ethic; global warming as an archetype of global issues; the influence of technology on leisure; and the globalization of leisure. Several examples of studies that predict future trends in American society are summarized, with an emphasis on the need to anticipate and deal with change in a proactive way rather than through passive or reluctant responses. Ultimately, this chapter serves to illustrate the blending of theoretical and practical concerns that must characterize all fields of public service if they are to be successful.

QUESTIONS FOR CLASS DISCUSSION OR ESSAY EXAMINATION

1. This chapter presents seven different approaches to recreation, park, and leisure-service management today (for example, the quality-of-life and the marketing or entrepreneurial models of service). Select any three of these orientations and show how their influence is reflected in the practices of recreation agencies with which you are familiar. Which of the seven approaches do you find most compatible with your own views?

2. Key conclusions of the future of parks and recreation can be viewed as challenges. Select two of these challenges and prepare a report that discusses how society and government have changed and impacted parks and recreation. Further, discuss viable alternatives that parks and recreation might utilize to respond to the change.

3. This chapter presents issues related to environmental change, challenges to the environment, and an American loss of an individual environmental ethic. Select one of these and do additional library research validating or refuting the claims in this chapter.

4. The Internet has had a tremendous impact on U.S. society and on leisure lifestyles in particular. What are some of its major effects, both positive and negative?

5. The chapter presents a number of predictions for the future with respect to demographic, social, economic, and other changes. Which of these do you believe present the most important challenge for the recreation, park, and leisure-service field? In what ways should leisure-service professionals seek to meet them constructively in the twenty-first century?

ENDNOTES

1. http://en.wikipedia.org/wiki/Future.

2. Ruth Russell, *Planning Programs in Recreation* (St. Louis: C. V. Mosby, 1982): Chapter 2.

3. P. Wehman and S. Schleien, *Leisure Programs for Handicapped Persons* (Baltimore: University Park Press, 1981): 89.

4. Daniel Dustin, "Managing Public Lands for the Human Spirit," *Parks and Recreation* (September 1994): 92–96.

5. Douglas Knudson, *Outdoor Recreation* (New York: Macmillan, 1980): 31.

6. CommonDreams.Org NewsCenter, www.commondreams.org/headlines04/1013-12.htm, January 2007.

7. California State Parks, *Park and Recreation Trends in California*. 16.

8. Lawrence Allen, "Time to Measure Outcomes," presentation at 1994 NRPA Congress.

9. California State Parks, *The Health and Social Benefits of Recreation* (Sacramento: California State Parks, 2005).

10. Paul M. Sherer, *The Benefits of Parks: Why America Needs More City Parks and Open Space* (San Francisco: The Trust for Public Lands, 2006).

11. U.S. Department of Commerce, "300 Million," *Facts for Features* (9 August 2006).

12. Stephen Mitchell, "Retirement Evolution: Reexamining the Retirement Model," *LIMRA's Market Facts Quarterly* (Vol. 25, No. 1, 2006): 82–85.

13. Murray Gendell, "Full-Time Work Rises Among U.S. Elderly," *Population Reference Bureau.* U.S. Census Bureau April, 2006.

14. U.S. Census Bureau, www.census.gov.

15. Sarah Burnett-Wolle and Geoffrey Godbey, "Active Aging 101," *Parks and Recreation* (2005): 30–40.

16. Dan K. Hibler and Kimberly J. Shinew, "Moving Beyond Our Comfort Zone: The Role of Leisure Service Providers in Enhancing Multiracial Families' Leisure Experiences," *Parks and Recreation* (Vol. 37, No. 2, 2002): 26.

17. Ching-hua Ho et al., "Gender and Ethnic Variations in Urban Park Preferences, Visitations, and Perceived Benefits," *Journal of Leisure Research* (Vol. 37, No. 3, 2005): 281–306.

18. Kimberly J. Shinew, Myron F. Floyd, and Diana Parry, "Understanding the Relationship Between Race and Leisure Activities and Constraints: Exploring an Alternative Framework," *Leisure Sciences* (Vol. 26, 2004): 188–191.

19. U.S. Census Bureau, www.census.gov.

20. UNICEF, *The State of the World's Children Report* (New York: United Nations, 2004).

21. Annie E. Casey Foundation, *Growing Up in North America: Child Well-Being in Canada, the United States, and Mexico* (Baltimore, MD: 2006).

22. Annie E. Casey Foundation, *2006 Kids Count Data Book: State Profiles of Child Well-Being* (Baltimore, MD: 2005).

23. Federal Interagency Forum on Child and Family Statistics, *America's Children in Brief: Key National Indicators of Well-Being* (Washington, D.C.: U.S. Government Printing Office, 2006).

24. Partnership for a Drug-Free America, www.drugfree.org/Parent/Knowing/Teen_Trends, 2005.

25. HarrisInteractive, "Parents Changing Roles in Tweens' and Teens' Lives," *Trends & Tudes* (Vol. 2, No. 5, 2003): 2.

26. Ibid, 2.

27. Center for Environment and Population, *U.S. National Report on Population and the Environment* (New Canaan, CT: 2006): 4.

28. Jonathan Loh et al., ed., *WWF Living Planet Report* (WWF International, New Economics Foundation, World Conservation Monitoring Centre, Switzerland, 2004).

29. U.S. Environmental Protection Agency, "Basic Facts: Municipal Solid Waste," www.epa.gov/epaoswer/non-hw/muncpl/facts.htm.

30. Center for Environment and Population, 55.

31. Ibid, 55.

32. The Harris Poll 77, www.harrisinteractive.com/harris_poll/index.asp?PID=607, October 2005.

33. The Trust for Public Land, www.tpl.org.

34. Stephen Saunders and Tom Easley, *Losing Ground: Western National Parks Endangered by Climate Change*, The Rocky Mountain Climate Organization and the Natural Resources Defense Council, 2006.

35. Environmental News Service, "Human Impact Triggers Massive Extinctions," www.ens-newswire.com/ens/aug1999/1999-08-02-06.asp, 1999.

36. Paul Romero, Stuart Hong, and Laura Westrup, "Trends Worth Talking About," California and Pacific Southwest Recreation and Park Training Conference, Sacramento: March 2005.

37. Lee Rainie, "Digital Natives: How Today's Youth Are Different from Their 'Digital Immigrant' Elders and What That Means for Libraries," Metro–New York Library Council, Brooklyn Museum of Art. (Presentation). Washington, D.C.: Pew Internet and American Life Project, 2006, 5.

38. John Horrigan and Lee Rainie, *The Internet's Growing Role in Life's Major Decisions* (Washington, D.C.: Pew Internet and American Life Project, April, 2006): 1.

39. TED Blog, www.tedblog.typepad.com.

40. Ibid, 2.

41. World Commission on Protected Areas, *National System Planning for Protected Areas* (Cambridge, UK: 1998).

42. Dirk Reiser. "Globalisation: An Old Phenomenon that Needs to Be Rediscovered for Tourism," *Tourism and Hospitality Research* (Vol. 4, No. 4, 2003): 310.

43. Daniel L. Williams, "Leisure Identities, Globalization, and the Politics of Place," *Journal of Leisure Research* (Vol. 34, No. 4, 2002): 355.

44. Ibid, 362.

PHOTO CREDITS

INDEX